ISLAMIC FINANCIAL MARKETS AND INSTITUTIONS

The rapid pace of progress in the Islamic financial market and investment space, coupled with the COVID-19 pandemic and its aftermath and recovery, has provided the necessary challenges to build a strong case for Islamic investment. This timely and unique book focuses on the foundations of Islamic financial markets and institutions in the context of various products, their market application, Islamic asset management, and regulation.

The authors provide a thorough overview of Islamic financing instruments and markets, such as Islamic debt and equity markets, through shares and the stock market, mutual funds, private equity, lease financing, *Sukuk*, green *Sukuk*, money market instruments, exchange-traded funds, cryptocurrencies, derivatives and so forth, which have emerged as alternative sources of financing. They offer insight into the numerous infrastructure institutions which have sprung up since the first decade of the new century, such as the Accounting and Auditing Organizations for Islamic Financial Institutions, Islamic Financial Services Board, Islamic International Rating Agency, and International Islamic Liquidity Management Corporation, as well as those being established, to satisfy different industry needs.

With its uniquely competitive approach to the mainstream financial market, this book facilitates a greater understanding of the concept of Islamic investment. Through a discussion of the current state and future prospects of Islamic financial markets, the book's theoretical and practical approach offers academics, practitioners, researchers, students, and general readers a well-balanced overview of Islamic financial markets, its ethics, *Shari'ah* foundation, the instruments and operational mechanism used by Islamic capital, money, and debt markets.

Abul Hassan is a Research Scientist II/Associate Professor in Finance at the KFUPM Business School, King Fahad University of Petroleum and Minerals, Dhahran, Saudi Arabia.

Aktham Issa AlMaghaireh is a Professor of Finance at United Arab Emirates University, Abu Dhabi, UAE.

Muhammad Shahidul Islam is a faculty member in the Department of Accounting and Finance, at the KFUPM Business School, King Fahad University of Petroleum and Minerals, Dhahran, Saudi Arabia.

ISLAMIC FINANCIAL MARKETS AND INSTITUTIONS

Abul Hassan, Aktham Issa AlMaghaireh and Muhammad Shahidul Islam

Routledge
Taylor & Francis Group
LONDON AND NEW YORK

Cover image: ipopba (Getty Images)

First published 2023
by Routledge
4 Park Square, Milton Park, Abingdon, Oxon OX14 4RN

and by Routledge
605 Third Avenue, New York, NY 10158

Routledge is an imprint of the Taylor & Francis Group, an informa business

British Library Cataloguing-in-Publication Data
A catalogue record for this book is available from the British Library

Library of Congress Cataloging-in-Publication Data
Names: Hassan, Abul, 1973- author. | AlMaghaireh, Aktham Issa, author. | Islam, Muhammad Shahidul, author.
Title: Islamic financial markets and institutions/Abul Hassan, Aktham Issa AlMaghaireh and Muhammad Shahidul Islam.
Description: 1 Edition. | New York, NY: Routledge, 2023. | Includes bibliographical references and index.
Identifiers: LCCN 2022008430 (print) | LCCN 2022008431 (ebook) | ISBN 9780367336738 (hardback) | ISBN 9780367336721 (paperback) | ISBN 9780429321207 (ebook)
Subjects: LCSH: Banks and banking – Islamic countries. | Banks and banking – Religious aspects – Islam. | Finance – Islamic countries. | Financial services industry – Islamic countries.
Classification: LCC HG3368.A6 H3847 2023 (print) | LCC HG3368.A6 (ebook) | DDC 332.10917/67 – dc23/eng/20220225
LC record available at https://lccn.loc.gov/2022008430
LC ebook record available at https://lccn.loc.gov/2022008431

ISBN: 978-0-367-33673-8 (hbk)
ISBN: 978-0-367-33672-1 (pbk)
ISBN: 978-0-429-32120-7 (ebk)

DOI: 10.4324/9780429321207

Typeset in Bembo
by Apex CoVantage, LLC

CONTENTS

ABOUT THE AUTHORS

Dr. Abul Hassan has more than 15 years' of teaching and research experience at the undergraduate and postgraduate levels. Currently, he is working as a Research Scientist II/Associate Professor in Finance at the KFUPM Business School, King Fahad University of Petroleum and Minerals, Dhahran, Saudi Arabia. Earlier he taught at Durham University, Staffordshire University, UK; University of Brunei Darussalam, Brunei and Gloucestershire University, UK; and held academic positions in different capacities from teaching Assistant to Senior Lecturer / Associate Professor. He has a first-class MA in economics (India) and MSc in international banking (Loughborough University, UK) and a Ph.D. in investment from the University of Durham, UK. He is a Fellow of the Higher Education Academy, UK. As of December 2021, he has published 41 research papers in international peer-reviewed academic journals and presented 21 research papers at international conferences around the world. He is a principal author of two books (published by Palgrave Macmillan and Routledge). He has been invited as a guest speaker to different universities across the globe. He has been visiting faculty at Trisakti University, Jakarta, since 2007 for supervision and training of its doctoral candidates.

As a part of his scholarly interests, Dr. Hassan regularly reviews books in the *Muslim World Book Review* published in the UK and has refereed research papers for high-ranking academic journals and conferences/seminars. In 2010 he was awarded Best Outstanding Reviewer by the Emerald Group, UK, for its journal *Humanomics* (now renamed *International Journal of Ethics and Systems*). One of his papers, 'Towards Understanding A Sharia Compliant Firm', was awarded as the best paper in the International Conference on Accounting, Finance, Economics and Management organised by the University of Glasgow, UK, from 7–9 April 2015.

Aktham Issa AlMaghaireh is a Professor of Finance at United Arab Emirates University (UAEU). He has over 22 years of experience in financial economic research and teaching in Jordan, the United Kingdom, and the United Arab Emirates. He obtained his Ph.D. and MSc in Finance from the Department of Economics and Finance at Durham University, and holds a Master degree in Economics from Yarmouk University (Jordan). He earned his BA in Economics from the same university. His research interests include emerging financial markets, risk management, corporate finance, bank efficiency and distress, capital market microstructure, and Islamic finance. He has held many research grants individually and in collaboration with other researchers. Over the years, Prof AlMaghaireh has published more than 100 papers in peer-reviewed journals, including the *International Review of Financial Analysis, Journal of International Financial Markets, Institutions and Money, Emerging Markets Review, Finance Research Letters, Energy, Journal of Commodity Markets, Energy Economics, Research in International Business and Finance, Empirical Economics, Resources Policy, International Finance, International Economics, Applied Economics, Quarterly Review of Economics and Finance, Journal of Asset Management, International Journal of Theoretical and Applied Finance* etc. He has also published three chapters in edited books. He has received numerous awards and recognition for his research and teaching, including the Abdul Hameed Shoman Arab Researchers Award, the Ministry of Higher Education & Scientific Research National Medal, and the UAEU Faculty Research Recognition Award for outstanding achievement in research (2017, 2018, 2019, 2020, 2021).

Muhammad Shahidul Islam is a faculty member in the Department of Accounting and Finance, at KFUPM Business School, where he teaches accounting-related subjects. He earned a master of science degree in computer information systems from Boston University in 1985. He has been an active member of the KBS-Aramco Finance Team for development initiatives as one of the project leaders for professional certification endeavors. He has also worked on numerous research/consultancy projects and co-authored journal publications in business and accounting.

Mr. Islam supervised a considerable number of students doing their accounting/MIS cooperative work in organisations like Saudi Aramco and the global accounting firms PWC, DTT, E&Y, and KPMG. He also has an MBA degree from the University of Dhaka, Bangladesh (1978). He has won the KFUPM award for Excellence in Teaching/Advising several times.

FIGURES

TABLES

PREFACE

The rapid expansion of global Islamic finance has significantly contributed to the expanding role of the Islamic financial markets, particularly secondary markets, for investments and securities, as we enter the fourth decade of transition and innovation in contemporary Islamic finance. Islamic finance can be perceived as the practice of conducting commercial and financial transactions which are in harmony with *Shari'ah* principles. As an amalgamation of religion, theology and the law, the *Shari'ah* refers to the religious Islamic legal framework which forms the crux of conducting business and finance. *Shari'ah* as a term literally translates to 'the way' or 'the right path'. Thus, *Shari'ah* acts as a guiding pillar for believers on how they should live their lives. As per the revelations of the Qur'an and the Sunnah, *Shari'ah* is considered to be perfect, unchangeable and the most divinely guided law.

The role of the *Fiqh* is crucial in the context of Islamic financial transactions. *Fiqh* literally translates into 'understanding', and thus refers to the totality of human understanding of the divine law or the *Shari'ah* principles as defined by *Shari'ah* experts. *Ijtihad* (effort), or legal reasoning based on the 'roots of the law', is the basic methodology used in this determinative and interpretive effort (*usul al-fiqh*). Islamic jurisprudence has been founded on the following roots (*usul*):

1. The Qur'an: This is Islam's Divine book and Allah's revealed word (it must be noted that the legal nature of this holy book is only about 3%).
2. The Prophet Mohammed's (peace be upon him) Sunnah: This is the binding authority of his dicta and decisions.
3. The *Ijma*: This is the consensus of the community of scholars.
4. The *qiyas*: These are the analogical deductions and reasoning.

The *Shari'ah* constitutes certain perceptions and principles. There are several Islamic schools of jurisprudence include four major Sunni schools (Hanafi, Hanbali, Maliki, and Shafi) and the Shia Jafari school. The *Shari'ah* can be understood as a comprehensive body of law as explained by *Shari'ah* scholars over the last 1,400 years, particularly in the context of Islamic finance. It encompasses almost all aspects of trade and finance that are addressed by a well-developed corpus of secular law. Contracts, legal capacity, mutuality, sales, consideration, leases, construction activities, joint ventures, guarantees, different types of partnerships, estates, equity and trust, litigation, and many other activities are all covered.

Investors wanting to purchase *Shari'ah*-compliant investments are often hesitant in going ahead, as they are not sure whether their investments are actually *Shari'ah* compliant. This happens mostly because a considerable number lack the knowledge to make that decision for themselves. The *Shari'ah* supervisory board (SSB) is a structure that has evolved over the last few decades to bring comfort to *Shari'ah*-compliant individuals. Most Islamic financial institutions and banks, as well as many elevated families and individuals in society, have at least one *Shari'ah* scholar on their *Shari'ah* board. The SSB is responsible for overseeing the entity's or individual's entire range of *Shari'ah*-compliant investment practices, as well as the entity's or individual's principles, methodology, and operational operations. The SSB is made up of a diverse collection of individual scholars who are responsible for making confidential decisions about structures and undertakings subjected to the proprietorship of the business that retains the board, leading with *Shari'ah* explication occurring in isolated pockets rather than in a coordinated manner across markets or even schools of Islamic law.

Since the inception of Islamic finance in 1975, there have been a number of innovations that have had a significant impact on the field of Islamic banking and financial services. In order to remain consistent with *Shari'ah* principles and governed by Islamic ethical norms, the Islamic financial system restricts a number of actions, some of which are not necessarily criminal in secular nations:

1. Paying or charging interest: 'All types of interest are *riba* and hence, forbidden' (Hadith). Islamic regulations on transactions (known as *Fiqh al-Muamalat*) were designed to restrict the use of interest.
2. Investing in businesses that engage in illegal activities: Selling alcoholic beverages or pork, generating vulgarity in the media, and pornography are examples of activities that are prohibited.
3. *Maisir: Maisir* is commonly interpreted as 'gaming', but in Islamic finance, it refers to 'speculation'. In Islamic finance, participation in contracts in which the ownership of a good is contingent on the occurrence of a predefined, unpredictable event in the future is considered as *maisir* and is absolutely banned.
4. *Gharar: Gharar* is commonly interpreted as 'ambiguity' or 'uncertainty'. According to most proponents of Islamic finance, *Gharar* entails excessive risk and may generate uncertainty and fraudulent behaviour similar to that found in mainstream banking's derivative products.

This ban encompasses both direct and indirect benefits. It has an impact on every facet of a *Shari'ah*-compliant company's funding and structure. We can take the example of the impact of these ideas on equities and private equity investing. Investors complying with *Shari'ah* norms would have very few opportunities in making investments in limited companies around the world if these principles were strictly adhered to. In the present day and world, most companies pay interest or have interest-bearing investments of some sort or form. *Shari'ah*-compliant investors can potentially be wiped out of the global equity and private financial markets. However, under the *Shari'ah* screening process, a certain amount of interest income and expenditure is permissible.

Several factors govern the distribution of work, revenues and losses among partners in partnerships and joint ventures. An example in this regard would be how all profit and loss distributions must be pro rata, and some preferred stocks are not authorised. This happens to contradict *Shari'ah* rules. One person offers services, and another person contributes capital in certain partnership forms and joint ventures (*mudarabah* agreements). Only the capital supplier may be fined financially if the arrangement fails. Work and capital contributions may be distributed among all partners or venturers in different types of partnerships or joint ventures (*sharika* and *musharaka* arrangements). This has to be inclusive of sharing losses. These laws are evidently seen to have a significant impact on the structure of capital market goods and players along with that of the entire Islamic financial services industry.

The implementation of transactions complying with *Shari'ah* norms is found to often involve the practice of leasing. *Shari'ah* principles subjected to leasing are quite important. An example of an applicable leasing idea is the obligation of the lessor of property to maintain the integrity of the property being leased. This implies that the lessor cannot transfer structural maintenance or related liabilities to a lessee, for example, the maintenance of casualty insurance. This is why triple net leases are prohibited irrespective of them being widely employed in conventional finances. These concepts are likely to have a major impact on a number of financial and operational procedures used by entities in the capital markets, including funds as well as major investments and capital market goods used by these companies.

Principles of *Shari'ah* which are applied to several kinds of sales are exceptionally well-defined and developed as per one's expectations, owing to the fact that the formation of the *Shari'ah* in Middle Eastern countries was largely focused on trading operations. Leasing is recognised as a sort of sale – the sale of a property's usufruct. The sale is restricted to only tangible assets with a few exceptions. Debt and other financial instruments which are not indicative of ownership interest in intangible assets are not eligible for sale. Furthermore, a property that is not owned and possessed cannot be sold. These principles act as the main stumbling blocks to the creation of *Shari'ah*-compliant short sells, options trading, and derivatives transactions. These principals equally form the foundation in structuring *Sukuk* (Islamic bond and securitisation) transactions and products. Certain specific standards governing delivery, reception, ownership, risk allocation, down payments and nearly all other aspects of sales transactions are also included. The capacity to construct secondary markets, tradable equities and the complete spectrum of transactions done by *Shari'ah*-compliant financial goods and organisations are all affected by these restrictions.

Marks of Islamic Finance Development

Islamic finance has evolved into a global economy starting from a nascent industry, over all these years where Muslims as well as non-Muslim groups collaborate and learn from one another to develop products and services that are related. It has achieved major objectives. Islamic finance as an established form of financial operation is now being well recognised by global financial regulatory authorities and federal reserves. In the recent years, it has equally come up to be able to provide sophisticated and lucrative financial services at competitive prices without having to disassociate from *Shari'ah* norms. All of this was accomplished in under 37 years. Once a distant intellectual dream that only educated Muslims and a smaller part of the population was aware of, Islamic banking and finance has progressed from the 1970s and is a well-known, practical reality today. Despite having an unfriendly environment and zero support from the auxiliary or shared institutions essential for its efficient operation, it has achieved development as a novel system of financial intermediation in 1985. It has attained worldwide attention through its usability and viability.

A great number of international financial institutions and regulators have all expressed interest in Islamic finance. This includes the Federal Reserve Board, the Financial Conduct Authority of the United Kingdom, the Prudential Regulatory Authority (formerly the Financial Services Authority) of the United Kingdom, the International Monetary Fund and the World Bank, as well as leading academic institutions such as Johns Hopkins University, Harvard University, and MIT in the United States; Durham University, London School of Economics, Aston University, Cardiff University, Bangor University, Newman University and Oxford University in the UK; and most institutes in the Middle East and Southeast Asia. It is being practiced in more than 90 countries globally; the number of Islamic financial institutions (IFIs) operating in the sector has crossed 500. Some international organisations and regional financial centers are helping to standardise Islamic banking products, thereby increasing its credibility.

Islamic windows or full-fledged affiliates are used by most of these multinational conventional financial institutions as well as their subsidiaries in offering Islamic financial products. This is symbolic of a strong sign of ethically responsible business in the future. This, in turn, is more likely to elevate the harmony and security of the individual who previously might have avoided the traditional banking and financial system or felt guilty because of the association of interest (*riba*) in their transactions. The three monolithic religions – Judaism, Christianity and Islam – have strictly prohibited them. The resulting outcome has taken the shape of a paradigm change for financial services in terms of a moral compass being developed for banking and financial systems based on the ethical values of Islam without compromising the relevance and relatability of these services with that of the real economy.

The global facilitators and standardised bodies for Islamic finance, such as the Islamic Financial Services Board (IFSB), the Accounting and Auditing Organization for Islamic Financial Institutions (AAOIFI), the Islamic International Rating Agency (IIRA), and the International Liquidity Management Centre (ILMC), are responsibly demonstrating reorganisation and increasing the trust of Islamic finance amidst customers and authorities. Middle Eastern countries (Bahrain, Kuwait, Saudi Arabia, United Arab Emirates, and Qatar) and Southeast Asian countries (Malaysia, Brunei, and Indonesia) have served as hubs for Islamic finance for almost three decades. Interestingly, in recent times, cities such as London, Luxembourg, New York, and Singapore are attempting to act as Islamic finance hubs.

The discipline of Islamic finance has been founded on Islamic ethical precepts. Demand for Islamic finance is increasing not only in majority-Muslim countries but also in Muslim communities located in non-majority-Muslim countries. We can take the example of Britain, where there are 18 conventional banks which offer Islamic products and six full-fledged Islamic banks. Non-Muslims account for more than 10% of Islamic financial services customers in the United Kingdom. Non-Muslims account for around 38% of Islamic bank customers in Malaysia. A considerable number of institutions in North America provide Islamic financial services, primarily to Muslims. Undoubtedly, future Islamic finance projections will be better, especially if the volatility of the global financial system continues to persist and highlights issues such as the occasional credit crunch/financial crisis, leading to fears that they cannot be resolved by making minor tweaks to the global banking system but rather by injecting into it.

Rationale for the Book

Undeniably, there is a desperate need to educate stakeholders about asset management in the Islamic financial market. The list of stakeholders is inclusive of but not limited to students, professors, the public, financial institution professionals, regulators and piemakers. Business and finance students who want to pursue their academics and/or work in the burgeoning Islamic banking and finance industry also seem to be highly interested, as well as all stakeholders in this expanding business in the form of asset management of the Islamic financial market and institutions as well as their goods and services. They all should be familiar with the basic principles of Islamic financial markets and institutions, through its Islamic capital and money market and their products, market applications, and its infrastructure in the perspectives of Islamic asset management. Further, this book provides a comprehensive overview of the Islamic financial market segments within the Islamic financial services industry.

Learners should be equally aware of the ethics and morality on which Islamic finance has been founded and the practical application of *Shari'ah* principles to

Islamic financial instruments, markets and products. Simultaneously, learners should be well aware of its salient features, legal positions, functions, risk management, and the Basel accords, all of which are applicable to the Islamic finance industry. It is quite unfortunate that irrespective of the importance of these aspects of Islamic asset management, which is popular among most stakeholders, there is a limited number of reference works available to familiarise them with the theoretical and practical implications of Islamic finances. This book is about one aspect of the aforementioned: examining Islamic ethical principles, products, markets and organisations in the context of Islamic asset management. It has to be notably mentioned that understanding and interpretation of the *Shari'ah* results in the issuing of *Shari'ah* principles and performance criteria are based on standard-setting organisations such as the AAOIFI, the IFSB, and others.

Everyone, including policymakers, bankers, business executives, industrialists, *Shari'ah* scholars, university students, and the public in general needs to know about the Islamic financial market in depth, its operational procedures, and the philosophy and features which it is based upon. The ultimate goal of this book is to simplify these topics and explain them in plain English with proper clarity. Islamic asset management's products developers, who are responsible for implementation, and financial specialists must be conversant with the basic criteria of Islamic ethical principles in products, services, performance evaluation, assets, and risk management.

Organisation of the Book

In order to establish the groundwork for further examination of the Islamic financial system, the nature, scope, objectives and key moral elements of Islamic finance are briefly reviewed in this book. The primary focus throughout the book is the descriptions of the moral foundations of Islamic financial products, markets, institutions and Islamic asset management, as well as their operational modules. Issues regarding supervision and regulation of the Islamic financial industry have been projected with the utmost attention. The book consists of 21 chapters.

The concepts of Islamic finance are discussed in Chapter 1, which explains that Islamic finance is a sort of financing that must adhere to *Shari'ah* law (Islamic law). This also extends to investments that are permitted by *Shari'ah* law. Islamic finance as we know it arose in tandem with the establishment of Islam. However, it was not until the 1990s that a proper Islamic financial market was established. As of December 2019, the Islamic finance sector has been observed to be increasing at a rate of 15%–20% per year, with Islamic financial institutions managing approximately US$2.5 trillion and is expected to grow to US$3.7 trillion by 2024.

Primary and secondary markets have been categorised in the conventional financial system. Chapter 2 discusses the functions of these two markets and argues that in most cases, Islamic markets are not characterised by a separate primary market and hence rely on structures of the conventional primary market system for issuing common stocks and *Sukuk*. However, the role of 'liquidity' is imperative in maintaining the functional efficiency of an Islamic secondary market through methodical and effective distribution of economic resources in allocating capital and risk productively, generating accuracy and disseminating issuer-specific information and effectiveness of the Islamic secondary market.

Chapter 3 discusses the Islamic capital market, which is, at its core, a place where *Shari'ah*-compliant financial assets are traded. This system works similarly to a traditional capital market in the sense that it encourages and enables investors to seek *Shari'ah*-compliant investment possibilities, whereas a traditional capital market just allows investors to make investments and borrowers to locate funds to borrow. The fundamental point of the debate is that individuals who merely want to invest and transact in the Islamic capital market can choose from a variety of products (both stock and debt). Financial activity is separated from non-financial activities using Islamic capital instruments and products. This chapter also discusses Islamic screening criteria.

The Islamic equity markets are discussed in Chapter 4, which covers the components of an Islamic equity market and explains alternative *Shari'ah* screening techniques. Equity financing, which is similar to *mudarabah* and *musharaka* financing, complies with the *Shari'ah* requirement of risk and reward sharing. *Shari'ah* screening techniques were developed in response to the necessity to discover *Shari'ah*-compliant stocks. This chapter also illustrates the distinctive characteristics of various Islamic capital market products and examines liquidity issues in Islamic capital markets.

Islamic mutual funds serve to help small investors who do not have access to the capital market. Extra funds from the general public are directed to the Islamic capital market through Islamic mutual funds. Chapter 5 focuses on the main feature of these funds, which is that they offer limitless diversification opportunities to modest investors who might not have been otherwise able to do so, primarily because of their lack of financial expertise.

From the perspective of Islamic asset management, private equity provides an appealing channel for *musharaka*-based investments in institutional Islamic funds, leading to a rising trend of Islamic banks getting involved in private equity deals through the formation of their own private equity funds. Chapter 6 discusses the emerging market for private equity in the Muslim world in general and the Middle East in particular. Private equity steadily gaining traction in the region has been possible because major investors in most Middle Eastern countries and Islamic financial institutions have had excess money in recent years.

Chapter 7 develops an asset pricing model replicating value-based pricing (based on total assets), mechanisms underlying financial operations in the Islamic economic system, and the system's assumed Islamic contracts. This model is called the Capital Asset Pricing Model (CAPM) in the *Shari'ah* domain and introduces an algorithm.

Chapter 8 discusses Islamic exchange-traded funds (ETFs), which are the best available investment options because they follow the *Shari'ah* rules and can be an efficient way for ethical investors to gain profits without having to disobey their religious rules while trading. The Islamic index and its screening process are shared in sectors across construction, real estate, oil, gas, and telecommunications. Islamic ETFs are a product of the Islamic capital market. Thus, the need to consistently promote capital markets in terms of an alternative for economic growth continues to be a major challenge.

When investments are made in Islamic real estate investment trusts (REITs), investors hold the units. The acquisition of Islamic REITs is done in the form of a pool of assets. *Mudharabah aqad*, or what can be perceived as a trust financing contract, can be understood as an agreement between the investment manager as a *wakil* (agent) of *Shahib al-mal* (the investor) and the property manager. Islamic REITs have been acquiring greater impetus as an alternative channel for *Shari'ah*-compliant investments which are quite feasible. Chapter 9 discusses that there are plenty of opportunities available for the expansion of Islamic or *Shari'ah*-compliant REITs in respect of Islamic asset management in the world financial market.

Chapter 10 looks at financial futures (stock index futures), warrants, and options from an Islamic perspective. It also explores the difficulties of structuring these assets as a part of Islamic capital markets and attempts to provide solutions.

Chapter 11 describes the major functions performed by the Islamic money market and how it allows its participants to perform similar operations to those of conventional money market participants – the exception being that the tools utilised while performing these operations must be in complete compliance with *Shari'ah* principles. The topics covered in depth in this chapter include the commodity *murabahah*, investment, Islamic negotiable instruments of deposit (INID), negotiable Islamic debt certificate (NIDC), and Islamic accepted bill (IAB).

Over the last decade, the relatively young Islamic debt securities markets (*Sukuk*) have expanded to more than $1 trillion and are still developing and expanding at a rate of around 20% every year. Chapter 12 arguably serves as a unique reference tool for critical concerns regarding *Sukuk* markets which can be found in major financial hubs such as Kuala Lumpur, London, and Zurich. In this chapter, the distinctions between *Sukuk* and traditional bonds are clearly defined subjecting to the form, design, and use of proceeds. The ultimate purpose is to support activities which are genuine and eventually facilitate the development of the economy.

As a one-of-a-kind *Shari'ah*-compliant impact-investing instruments, the newly emergent green *Sukuk* has shown strong growth prospects to support environmental initiatives. Chapter 13 explores green *Sukuk*, asset-backed financial products designed to finance renewable energy and environmental projects, among other things. Several countries and corporate sectors have already taken the lead in using green *Sukuk* to fund renewable energy projects. Investors have responded with a multi-fold oversubscription to all green *Sukuk* issuances. As finance mechanisms in the area of asset management, green *Sukuk* and green project trends represent a new route for the United Nations' Sustainable Development Goal (SDG) of creating economic value.

Chapter 14 discusses Basel standards I, II and III. It explains why cohesive international best practices and range of standards for Islamic banking supervision and regulation are required to ensure a legal framework for the proper functioning and supervision of Islamic banks and financial institutions, and simultaneously, for properly managing their risks, information disclosures and corporate governance. While numerous leading Islamic financial institutions operating worldwide have accepted IFSB and AAOIFI standards, significant work has to be done on an international level to standardise Islamic financial products and regulations.

The world of Islamic finance has indeed remained relatively puzzled over the new products of speculating blockchain and cryptocurrencies while investors and financial institutions around the world have been considering adopting digital currencies via technology like blockchain for quite some time. Chapter 15 discusses the impact of digital currencies on Islamic finance and raises concerns about its adoption as money and/or an exchange medium. The possibilities of digital currencies being *Shari'ah*-compliant are also discussed.

The establishment of a nascent Islamic FinTech ecosystem has caused the global FinTech revolution to impact Islamic finance. Chapter 16 examines the broader FinTech environment, focusing on nine key FinTech technologies that provide important customer financial services as well as back-office operational support and efficiencies. Islamic FinTech also applies these technologies to the global Islamic finance market's fundamental propositions, comprising Islamic capital markets, *Takaful* (Islamic insurance), Islamic banking, and other Islamic financial institutions.

Several international Islamic institutions have been established for promoting the global expansion of Islamic financial markets. Chapters 17 through 20 explain the purpose formation and roles played by the AAOIFI, the IFSB, the IIRA, and the International Islamic Liquidity Management Corporation (IILMC).

Chapter 21 concludes the book with a discussion of Islamic finance and its markets and the global development of Islamic financial services in the Middle East, South and Southeast Asia, Europe, and North America. This chapter also explains the challenges and opportunities of this ecological niche market of the Islamic financial markets and institutions as they move forward.

This book has been written under the textbook project of the Deanship of Research Oversight and Coordination (Project no. BW191003 dated 02/01/2020) and under the management of the Interdisciplinary Research Centre (IRC) for Finance and Digital Economy of the King Fahd University of Petroleum and Minerals, Dhahran, Saudi Arabia. Although it is intended for university freshmen in economics and finance departments, this book ought to be a study course in Islamic finance only after the students have gone through thorough training in mainstream financial theory. This legitimises a theoretical and empirical study. These students should have completed courses to the level of intermediate finance courses. Besides these areas of preparation, the student is also expected to use the business-related terminologies in Islamic finance perspectives.

It is hoped that this work in the authentic Islamic financial and scientific worldview of Islamic law (*Shari'ah*) and its applications will act as a substantive learning input in wide erudition to the world of learning. There ought not to be simply a constrained use by students and scholars alone. Key features of the book include the following:

1. The book provides a comprehensive presentation of topics including theoretical foundations, Islamic financial markets, products, issues relating to regulation, risk management, Basel standards, standard-setting bodies like AAOIFI and IFSB, and international Islamic infrastructure institutions.
2. Each chapter opens with a statement of learning objectives. Chapters integrate mainstream and Islamic perspectives to provide students with real-world financial structures and examples.
3. To consolidate students' learning, relevant case studies are provided where necessary to help them build their knowledge of real-world issues to better understand what is happening around them.
4. The language is kept simple to enable a quick understanding of the complex concepts.
5. Tables, diagrams and figures are included to improve the understanding of students and keep them interested in the materials.
6. A glossary is provided, and review questions are included at the end of each chapter to recap what students have learned from the text. Further, we will provide instructors' material on demand in due course, including PowerPoint slides of all chapters of the textbook, along with test bank questions and activities with appropriate answers.

We hope that the book will enter the realm of the important, groundbreaking, and distinctive books of learning and scholarship for all in the areas of Islamic capital markets and Islamic asset management.

Lecturers and students will benefit from comprehensive literature that covers most of the topics related to Islamic financial markets and institutions. Sorting out every important issue from a large body of literature and fitting it into a book with limited scope is a time-consuming and challenging endeavor. Moreover, Islamic finance is a new but growing discipline. More work needs to be done in the area of Islamic financial markets, and we hope to see some young academic pursuers of Islamic finance come forward to produce more textbooks in Islamic finance. Some inconsistencies and flaws are unavoidable due to the vastness and complexity of the task at hand. No human effort can be ideal in terms of coverage and achievement of goals. The contributors have attempted to do some justice to the project's goal, although they do not claim to be perfect. Only time will tell what the future holds in terms of possibilities and failures.

Last but not the least, our God the Almighty deserves all the gratitude and praise, the one who has bestowed us with the wealth of belief (*Iman*) and an understating in the knowledge field (*ilm*).

On behalf of the textbook project Islamic Financial Markets and Institutions,

Dr. Abul Hassan
IRC Finance and Digital Economy
King Fahd University of Petroleum and Minerals
Dhahran, Saudi Arabia

ACKNOWLEDGEMENT

None of this would have been possible without the graces and blessings of God. We are indeed immensely thankful for His divine guidance and infinite generosity. At the same time, we would like to extend our gratitude to all the people without whose help this book could not have been completed.

We would like to specially thank the Deanship of Research Oversight and Coordination, King Fahd University of Petroleum and Minerals (KFUPM), Dhahran, Saudi Arabia, for providing us with the permission to write this book under their textbook grant project (Project no. BW191003 dated 02/01/2020). Special thanks to Dr. Abdullah Sultan, Dean; Dr. Suhail Al-Dharrab, Assistant Dean; Mr. Mohammed Fasiuddin, Technical Research Officer; and Dr. Mouheddin Al Haffar, Research Specialist of the Deanship of Research Oversight and Coordination, KFUPM for extending necessary technical support from time to time to complete the project.

We are equally indebted and thankful to Dr. Hesham J. Merdad, Dean of the KFUPM Business School. Under his dynamic leadership, the promotion of research and learning processes is taking place in the KFUPM Business School, and outcome of this book benefits from his logistics assistance.

The book has been written under the management of the IRC Finance and Digital Economy, KFUPM, who made our endeavour more exciting. We would like to thank Dr. Mousa Albashrawi, Director of the IRC Finance and Digital Economy, KFUPM. He inarguably accelerated the pace to complete the manuscript.

We would also like to thank Professor Khurshid Ahmad, former Chairman of the Islamic Foundation, UK; Dr. M. Manazir Ahsan, current Chairman of the Islamic Foundation, UK, and the Board of Trustees of Markfield Institute of Higher Education, UK; and Dr. Umer Chapra, Senior Advisor to the Islamic Research and Training Institute (Islamic Development Bank, Jeddah, Saudi Arabia), all of whom have mentored and encouraged us in writing this book.

No less important is our duty to express deep gratitude to Kristina Abbotts, Senior Editor of Economics, Finance and Business for Routledge and Christiana Mandizha for their extremely professional support and for bringing this book project to publication.

Sincere thanks to everyone at the IRC Finance and Digital Economy, KFUPM, especially Mr. Sultan Al Rashedi, for inspiring and cooperating with us.

Also, we extend our heartiest thanks to Mr. Md Sarwar M Haque, from the Preparatory Department of the KFUPM, for extending technical support to this book.

Please accept our sincerest apologies if we have missed anyone.

GLOSSARY

Al-bay trading
Al-ghunm bil ghurm 'there is no return without risk'
Al-kharaj bil damam 'profit is accompanied with responsibility'
Amanah honesty
Bai'al-Salam purchase made on advance
Dar'ul mafasid muqoddam min jalbil masholih use of option in
Dayn bi-dyan sale of debt
Fatawah legal opinion
Fiqh Islamic jurisprudence
Fiqh al muamalat Islamic commercial law
Gharar uncertainty/ambiguity
Gharar fahish major uncertainty
Gharar Yasir minor uncertainty
Halal permissible
Haram prohibited
Hawalah a contract which allows a debtor to transfer his/her debt obligation to a third party who owes the former a debt
Ijarah lease
Ijma consent of opinion of the Islamic scholars
Ijtihad independent reasoning based on Islamic laws
Istisna construction finance
Li al-akthar hukm al-kul opinion accepted by the majority
Maisir (mysir) a transaction tantamount to gambling
Maslahah public interest
Mu'amalat law of transaction
Mudarabah trust financing
Mudarib entrepreneur

Murabahah cost plus
Musharaka partnership
Qiyas principles of analogy applied in the interpretation of *Shari'ah*
Qoidah fiqhi legal maxim
Rabb al-mal capital ownership
Ras al maal premium from *Takaful* contributors
Riba usury or interest
Riba al-fadl excess interest
Riba al-nasiah interest by deferment
Salam forward contract
Shahib al-mal real investor
Shari'ah Islamic law
Sharika al-milk joint ownership of property
Sharikat al-'aqd joint ownership of contract
Sukuk Islamic bonds
Sukuk al-ijarah *Sukuk* based on lease
Sukuk al-murabahah *Sukuk* based on deferred payment
Sukuk al-musharaka *Sukuk* based on partnership
Sunnah tradition of the Prophet Mohammed (peace be upon him)
Taawun mutual assistance
Taawuni cooperative model of *Takaful*
Tabarru donation
Takaful Islamic insurance
Tawarruq a product structure by which a buyer can get cash immediately
Ummah community
Uqud Al-Isytirak profit-sharing agreement
Uqud Al-Mu'awadat a contract of an exchange of goods and services
Usul basis or root
Wadiah safe custody
Wadiah yad Amanah guarantee of safe custody
Wadiah yad Dhamanah guarantee of safekeeping
Wakalah agency
Wakil agent
Waqf endowment
Zakah almsgiving (annual requirement to pay charity 2.5% of savings)

1

UNDERSTANDING PRINCIPLES AND CONCEPTS OF ISLAMIC FINANCE

Learning Objectives

On completing this chapter, learners will be able to:

- Describe Islamic finance
- Understand the functions and role of Islamic finance
- Distinguish between equity and debt instruments
- Explain the characteristics of conventional and Islamic financial systems
- Analyse the *Shari'ah* rulings of currency for currency and foods for foods
- Comprehend the major contracts used in Islamic finance.

1.1 Introduction

Shari'ah (or Islamic law) is the crux on which financial activities are shaped in Islamic finance. Investments in Islamic finance have to be approved as per the principles of *Shari'ah*. The foundation of Islam as a religious practice paved the way for Islamic banking and finance. However, the establishment of Islamic finance as a formal financial structure can be traced to the 20th century. The difference in ideology between Islamic and conventional finance is quite evident, owing to certain sets of principles used by conventional finance that are absolutely banned under *Sharia* law.

1.1-1 Islamic Finance Principles

Islamic finance works in absolute accordance with *Sharia* law. The conceptualisation of contemporary Islamic finance is based on several prohibitions that are not

DOI: 10.4324/9780429321207-1

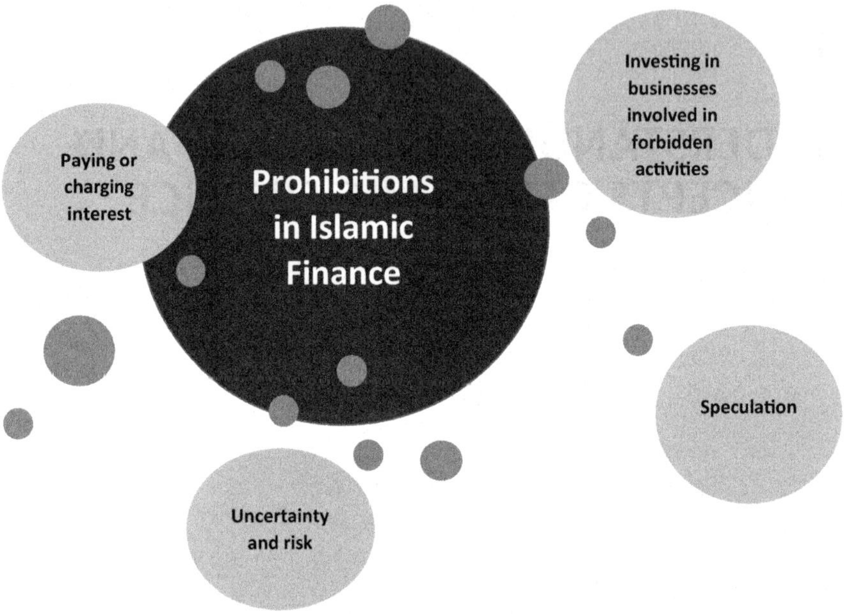

FIGURE 1.1 Main principles of Islamic finance.

necessarily illegal in the countries where Islamic financial institutions are actively operational (Figure 1.1):

1. Paying or charging interest: The idea of lending money by imposing interest rates is considered a means of exploitation in Islam. *Sharia* law prohibits *usury (riba)* or any form of interest to be charged on money lent because this practice benefits the lender over the borrower.
2. Investing in businesses that are involved in forbidden activities: Islamic economics mandates that human activity be productive. The practical use of Islamic finance stems from a religious morality that puts certain boundaries on human desires. Investing in these restricted activities is considered convenient for human society. Any kind of involvement in tobacco, pork products, alcohol, speculation, gambling with monetary or non-monetary assets (*maisir*), armaments, pornography or destructive weapons is entirely forbidden.
3. Speculation (*maisir*): The term *maisir* refers to speculation or gambling of any form or kind. *Sharia* law completely prohibits *maisir* as a practice by financial institutions. Hence, no contracts or deals can be made where the ownership of goods relies on future uncertainty.
4. Uncertainty and risk (*gharar*): Along with uncertainty, *Sharia* also prohibits the idea of contract dealings that involve huge proportions of risk. *Gharar* is a measure of how legitimate is the risk or uncertainty in investments. The

practice of *gharar* involves short selling and enclosing contracts based on derivatives, both of which do not comply with *Sharia* principles.

Apart from the prohibitions mentioned above, two other principles crucial to Islamic finance are discussed:

- Material finality of the transaction: The ultimate reason for every transaction has to be backed by economic exchange.
- Profit/loss sharing: Profit and loss in any transaction of any financial contract have to be shared by the parties involved. This furthers the idea that no person or institution can benefit at the expense of other parties.

The proclamation of Islamic finance as an 'ethical' approach paints a positive image among existing market structures. The foundation of Islam eventually brought Islamic finance into existence, but it was in the 20th century that Islamic financial structures developed into a formal system. The current annual growth rate of Islamic finance is estimated to be around 15%–20%, while Islamic financial institutions are estimated to contribute a worth of more than US$2.5 trillion.

The demand for financial products and services has led the Islamic finance market to grow and evolve dramatically over the last four decades. Nonetheless, Islamic finance is still growing exponentially subject to newer involvements of several companies that want to participate and offer their services in the Islamic way of trade.

Believers in Islam constitute one-quarter of the global population – between 1.5 and 1.8 billion people. It is estimated that over 60% of this population resides in Asia and the Middle East, while about 20% live in North Africa. Table 1.1 depicts the geographical spread of the Muslim population in terms of the percentage of every country's population.

A common misconception perceived among people is that the practice of Islam as a way of life is limited to the Middle East and Southeast Asia. It is undeniable that large numbers of Muslims reside in these regions, but at the same time, a considerable number of Muslims live outside these regions. Tables 1.1 and 1.2 are indicative of the distribution of Muslims regionally and country-wise. Again, in a

TABLE 1.1 Muslim Population Percentage by Region

Region	*Estimated Muslim Population in 2009 (in Thousands)*	*Percentage of Population That Is Muslim*	*Percentage of World Muslim Population*
Asia Pacific	972,537	24.1	61.9
Middle East and North Africa	315,322	91.2	20.1
Sub-Saharan Africa	240,632	30.1	15.3
Europe	38,112	5.2	2.4
Americas	4,596	0.5	0.3
World	**1,571,199**	**22.9**	**100**

Source: Miller (2009) ref. Pew Research Centre.

TABLE 1.2 Countries With Largest Numbers of Muslims

Countries	*Estimated 2009 Muslim Population in 2009 (in Thousands)*	*Percentage of Population That Is Muslim*	*Percentage of World Muslim Population*
Indonesia	202,867	88.2	12.9
Pakistan	174,082	96.3	11.1
India	160,945	13.4	10.3
Bangladesh	145,312	89.6	9.3
Egypt	78,513	94.6	5.0
Nigeria	78,056	50.4	5.0
Iran	73,777	99.4	4.7
Turkey*	73,619	~98.0	4.7
Algeria	34,199	98.0	2.2
Morocco*	31,993	~99.0	~2.0
Saudi Arabia	24,949	~97.0	~2.0
China	21,667	1.6	1.4
Malaysia	16,581	60.4	1.1
Russia	16,482	11.7	1.0
Germany	4,026	~5.0	<1
France	3,554	~6.0	<1
United Arab Emirates	3,504	76.2	0.2
Sri Lanka	1,711	8.5	0.1
United Kingdom	1,647	2.7	0.1

* The data for Turkey and Morocco have been primarily obtained from general population surveys. The reliability of these surveys is far less than of censuses or large-scale demographic and health surveys to estimate minority-majority ratios. Hence, the percentage of the Muslim population of these two countries has been rounded to the nearest integer.

wider context globally, the shares of Islamic finance are relatively smaller. However, experts have reported that the present growth rate ranging between 15% and 20% is not symbolic of a downtrend in the long term or even in the immediate term. Estimates suggest that the Islamic finance industry is supposed to hit US$3.7 trillion by the end of 2024. The consistent growth of this finance structure is facilitated by governmental interventions across the globe. The intention has been to witness the development of Islamic finance in the world market. As an example, the UK government regulated its stamp duties to bring changes that facilitated the growth of the Islamic mortgage market and the promise of the issue of UK sovereign *Sukuk* (bond). This example shows the public acknowledgement of the UK government towards the development of Islamic finance. Presenting Islamic ethical features to a society which is contemporary needed the moulding of Islamic finance into a form which is both modern and innovative and yet does not take away from the basics of how Islamic finance syncs its reality to the present. Hence, the nature of Islamic finance is distinctive.

1.1–2 Islamic Financial Practice

Believers of Islam strongly believe that Islam originated from revelation, a self-evident premise. The notion was to direct humanity in getting hold of its potential as collective morale to be able to come in terms of understanding its worth. What followed next was the structuring of a system, called the *Shari'ah*. *Shari'ah* is the directive system, the pathway for believers of Islam to be guided in whatever they do. It consists of principles, guiding rules, commandments and prohibitions under Islam that would help them deliver their potential into an ethically purposive outcome. *Shari'ah* is inclusive not only of belief systems or moral conduct but also practical rulings valid under law. Islam vouches for the fact that life's completion is rendered properly by the culmination of both legal bindings and good moral behaviour. The amalgamation of value-based morals into law in certain contracts can be observed in the form of *Amanah* (honesty) in *Murabahah* (mark-up) financing. The strict punctuality to be maintained during the payment of debt or asset delivery can be observed to understand the blending of moral codes of conduct in commercial transactions, the failure of which can lead to legal trouble (Usmani, 2002).

1.1–3 What Does Islamic Finance Stand For?

Islamic finance as a term emphasises all kinds of financial trade and business involvements which are in absolute harmony with the *Shari'ah*. When we talk about the conventional finance or banking structure, the banker-customer relationship is always that of a debtor-creditor, as this system is solely reliant on issuing deposits from and providing loans to the common mass. Unlike the *Shari'ah* code of conduct, the conventional banking system largely depends on giving or receiving interest. This interest-based financial system yields monetary profits through the deposition of money itself. A basic example is found in the fixed deposit product of a conventional bank. The borrower has to pay back the original amount of the loan and, additionally, a particular fixed amount of interest levied by the bank (i.e. the lender body). Evidence of unethical principles can be traced to different non-banking businesses and trading of other conventional financial products and services. This includes the insurance and capital markets, which are found to practice *Gharar* or uncertainty in insurance invested and interest charged on conventional bonds and securities. The practice of *Gharar* is totally prohibited in *Shari'ah* law. In the context of investing in insurance, there is no security that the insurer provides. Thus, there is no certainty of time within which the premium amount would materialise. Nor is there any idea of how much money the premium would develop into by the end of the policy term. Conventional ways of financial trading are also inclusive of buying and selling goods and services that are strictly banned under *Shari'ah* law. These practices include trading non-halal food items like pork or other non-slaughtered animals or animals not slaughtered as per Islamic principles. Alcohol, services related to pornography, entertainment or gambling are prohibited as well. The difference in approach between the conventional financial system and the Islamic way of banking and finance can be looked at from two perspectives:

- Contractual structure perspective (based on interest levied or uncertainty involved in financial dealings)
- Transactional perspective (financial deals consisting of producing, selling or distributing goods and services that do not legally comply with *Shari'ah* principles).

1.2 The Components of Islamic Finance

1.2-1 Banking and Riba *(Interest)*

If one aspect of Islamic finance has to be highlighted for its huge growth rate, it has to be Islamic banking, solely because of its uniqueness in approach which the conventional banking system can never match. The idea that money creates more money is the ultimate basis for money to exist in the form of premiums through interest or *usury*. This practice, called *Riba*, can be understood as the antithesis of Islamic finance because the Islamic financial system has banned any such use since its inception. Money in Islam is not objectified as a source to generate more money. Putting price tag on money itself is not the Islamic way of financial dealing. To Islam, money is a medium. It is used as an exchange, a store of value and a unit of measurement. Since money cannot beget more money on its own, the idea is to design a pathway between money and profit but not to use this as an excuse to charge interest.

1.2-2 Islamic Banking

The whole pitch of Islamic banking is contrary to what conventional banking believes in, a lender-borrower relationship. The relationship of the bank with the users of funds can be studied in terms of vendor and purchaser, investor and entrepreneur, principal and agent, lessor and lessee, transferor and transferee, and between partners in a business venture. Figures 1.2 and 1.3 are suggestive of the key differences in relationships between Islamic and conventional banks and how

Conventional Finance	*Islamic Banking/Finance*
1. The benefits of strategic partnerships fail to be maximised	1. Depositor-custodian relationship 2. Lender-borrower relationship (but free from *riba*/interest) 3. Investor-entrepreneur relationship

FIGURE 1.2 Difference in deposit/liability for contractual relationship.

Conventional Finance/Banking	*Islamic Finance/Banking*
1. The benefits of strategic alliances fail to be maximised	1. Purchaser-seller relationship 2. Lessee-lessor relationship 3. Principal-agent relationship 4. Entrepreneur-investor relationship

FIGURE 1.3 Difference in financing/asset for contractual relationship.

the former does not engage in any interest-based compliances like the provision of loans but rather uses alternative financial contracts for banking purposes.

1.2–3 Takaful *(Islamic Insurance)*

The Islamic financial system prohibits the practice of *Gharar*, or uncertainty in kind or form. Under the Islamic insurance policy or *Takaful*, the insurer or the insurance company is not supposed to provide any kind of indemnity to the insured. The premium deposited by the policyholders and the indemnity paid by the insurer is not accounted by any certainty. This practice does not sync with *Shari'ah* principles and hence is not permissible at all. In the context of conventional insurance schemes, companies offering life insurance take into consideration certain aspects like the average life expectancy and high-risk customers when setting their rates so that the return of gains is ensured for the companies. The acceptance of uncertainty through the Islamic perspective is observed only through gratuity or a unilateral contract like donation, which is why *Takaful* has introduced donation among participants or policyholders as an alternative to the indemnity provision for a life insurance premium as used in conventional schemes. Donation, characterised by a unilateral idea, validates the morale of the *Shari'ah* and is thus effective in accepting and tolerating uncertainties because the purpose is not to gain commercially.

1.2–4 Islamic Capital Markets

Islamic capital markets (ICMs), comprising equity investments and fixed income instruments (like *Sukuk*), should be consciously kept away from conventional components based on both contractual and transactional perspectives. Avoidance should not be limited to interest and uncertainty but also to other issues like gambling, investments in illegal activities and capital-guaranteed elements in equity-based products and services. Even if the goal for both the ideologies of Islamic finance and conventional finance is economic gains, the pathway is wholly different and distinctive.

The ICM is a component of the overall Islamic financial markets. It is crucial in generating economic growth for a country. The ICM acts as a complementary feature to the Islamic banking system in making sure that the scope of Islamic financial markets increases manifold globally.

The increase of wealth among Muslim investors (particularly from nations like Bahrain, Kuwait, Oman, Qatar, Saudi Arabia, and the United Arab Emirates, which constitute the Gulf Cooperation Council) is catalysing the growth of the ICM. The growth rate of the ICM, at present is estimated to be between 12% and 15% annually. The sector accounts for 27% of global Islamic financial service industry (IFSI) asset, worth about US$591.9 billion. Despite the record of a slower growth rate in 2018 in comparison to 2017, *Sukuk* remains dominating the ICM sector. This is primarily because of the strong sovereign and multilateral issuances in major Islamic finance markets to provide for the respective budgetary expenditures, as well as first new issuances in other jurisdictions. A comparative analysis of the global equity markets during the same time frame clearly shows the decline of asset value by 8.5% in 2018 as opposed to 2017. An array of reasons is deemed to be causing this downfall, an important one being the moderation in economic growth and recurring geopolitical challenges which happen to tighten the grip of international liquidity factors. The 2019 year-end estimated value of Islamic assets is US$1.5 trillion, 25% of which is constituted by the ICM.

1.3 The Principal Features of Islamic Finance

The distinctive nature of Islamic finance system in contrast with its conventional counterpart can be analysed through the following features.

1.3–1 Interest Free

Islamic banking identifies itself as an interest-free financial system. Every kind of banking business and financial activity will have to mandatorily apply the no-interest policy. Under Islamic law, the concept of interest emerges on account of exchange deals between two similar usurious items or assets (e.g. money for money or main food for main food). In the context of banking, interest is generated through the practice of lending money. The application of interest generation in conventional banking is achieved through premium. Islamic banking structure, on the other hand, prohibits this practice of issuing interest in any kind or form, be it cash or kind. In the Islamic banking system, advertisements of gifts for prospective saving and current account holders based on a *Wadiah* (safekeeping) or *Qard* (loan) contract, is strictly banned.

1.3–2 The Need for Underlying Assets

The role that the Islamic bank plays is that of a seller or a service or usufruct vendor or lessor, which is why an underlying asset is a prerequisite for banking businesses based on sale or lease. Without underlying assets, the contract will be considered legally ineffective. When observed under the conventional banking system, assets do not act as a necessity. Assets are considered important only in terms of collateral security wherein the asset purchased using the loan money may be charged or assigned as security in favour of the bank. However, it should be carefully noted that transactions on loans are not based on asset amount.

1.3-3 Avoiding Uncertainty or Gambling

Islamic financial institutions (IFIs) have made it a mandate for all kinds of transactions to be free from uncertainty (*Gharar*) and gambling (*Maisir*). The practice of *Gharar* in business dealings or contracts is likely to give rise to fallouts as a result of misinterpretation or invalid rationale by one or more parties. On the other hand, gambling, often viewed as a zero-sum game, is believed to benefit one party over the other and is strictly against the ethical principle of the Islamic law.

1.3-4 Profit and Loss Sharing

The allowance of sharing profits and losses has been made possible in Islamic banking activities. The customers get to taste the share of profit by the bank on the basis of proportions or on the basis of an agreement of a profit-sharing ratio done beforehand. A *Mudarabah* contract will lead the bank to take charge of its losses, whereas a *Musharaka* contract will lead to the sharing of losses between the bank and the customer(s). This concept is in direct contrast to fixed-income products. It must be kept in mind that Islamic banking is neither an equity-based market nor representative of the stock market. Profit and loss sharing is exclusive to the Islamic banking market only.

1.3-5 Shari'ah *Based*

Islamic finance revolves around *Shari'ah*-based principles. In order to fully activate and regulate the implementation of the principles in different frameworks, a supervisory board known as the *Shari'ah* advisory board has been established. The role of this body is to act as an advisory agency for the IFIs, Islamic insurance companies, Islamic funds, and other kinds of financial institutions offering financial products and services. Supervisory in nature, the role of the board is primarily directed toward guiding the IFIs in designing their institutional frameworks per *Shari'ah*. No institution can claim to venture into any form of Islamic financial business without forming a board or committee that consists of qualified scholars who are not only distinctly recognised but also have the relevant skills to guide the institution as per *Shari'ah*.

1.4 Why Islamic Finance?

Well-being and prosperity are the ultimate goals around which principles of Islamic finance are conceptualised. The idea of Islamic finance is to accomplish quality along with quantity and not just remain limited to the latter. A financial company running under the Islamic financial system has to equally value the customer. Based on the concept of promoting and accomplishing equality which can be observed from its basic principles of risk sharing and ethical conduct, Islamic finance prohibits any kind of violation of rights as per the law.

All in all, choosing an Islamic approach to finance can work as an impetus for economic development as well as diversification. With the component of sharing profits and losses, Islamic finance aims to protect and vitalise the micro, small and medium enterprises, thereby helping their economic growth, as a result of which the well-being of the society at large is organically served. Subsequently, this alternative form of financing can stimulate the expansion and improvement of the product range offered.

1.4-1 The Benefits of Islamic Finance

According to Abdulkader et al. (2005), Islamic finance strongly stands as a beneficial approach to finance because of the following reasons:

- It is based on real assets.
- Profits and losses are shared.
- Joint ventures or partnerships in companies are offered.
- Financial justice is promoted.
- The well-being of people and nature act as crucial deciding factors for planning development.

1.4-2 What Does Islamic Finance Offer?

More often than not, the micro, small and medium enterprises are not given due importance in the economic scenario of a region. The Islamic financial system, on the other hand, provides capital to the private sector for the development of micro, small and medium enterprises. Any kind of development initiative must be designed on the core principles of prosperity, equality, and partnership. The same applies to that of the relationship between the entrepreneur and the bank. The development of emerging markets is strongly influenced by the growth of the micro, small and medium enterprises since these are largely responsible for the creation of jobs, generation of income, promotion of economic growth, stabilising the social scenario and eventually building up to the development of the private sector. This is primarily why Islamic finance chooses to support the development of these enterprises through the provision of financial services and offerings. Islamic finance extends its offerings to services like current accounts, credit cards, internet banking, and so on for enhancing better growth possibilities.

A different way of analysing the countervalues is when the exchange of these two assets is subjected to the same amount or quantity of the two countervalues. Here, there is a mandate for the two entities to be of the same type. If this failed, it

Subject Matter	*Shari'ah Requirements*
Same currency (e.g. riyal for riyal, dinar for dinar, dollar for dollar)	• Spot transaction • Equal amount
Different currencies (e.g. riyal for dinar, pound for dollar, dinar for dirham)	• Spot transaction

FIGURE 1.4 *Shari'ah* rulings of currency for currency.

Subject Matter	*Shari'ah Requirements*
Same food item (e.g. barley for barley)	• Spot transaction • Equal amount
Different food items (e.g. barley for wheat)	• Spot transaction

FIGURE 1.5 *Shari'ah* rulings of food items for food items.

Interest (Riba 1)	*Interest (Riba 2)*
Exchange occurs between two similar *riba*-based items for different countervalues and for deferred exchange. For instance, 1,000 riyal for 1,200 riyal being exchanged for one another on a deferred basis.	Exchange occurs between two dissimilar *riba*-based items for deferred exchange. For instance, 1,000 riyal is exchanged for 1,000 dirham on deferred exchange.

FIGURE 1.6 Theory of interest (*riba*) in Islamic finance.

would ultimately pave the way for practicing *Riba* in the form of *Riba al-fadl* (Figure 1.6), because then there would be an excess of one of the countervalues. In case of the difference in type or form, such as pounds for dollars or wheat for barley, the requirement to have the same quantity is not applicable. This tradition acts as the founding principle for making sure currency exchange is approved as per the prevailing rate of exchange. For example, the spot basis applied for the exchange of £1,000 for $3,000. Situations like that of a forward currency exchange which does not sync with this traditional mandate and causes deferment of the exchange or delivery are strictly prohibited.

1.4–3 Profit and Loss Sharing

The concept of profit and loss sharing is pivotal to the Islamic financial system. As an approach, it is one of a kind where IFIs are supposed to share the profit margin and losses incurred in financial transactions with the depositors as well as the fund users, based on either the *Mudarabah* contract or *Musharaka* contract. In addition to being compliant with *Shari'ah* principles, both these contracts are generally opted for in countries over other ideologies and have been among the most frequently used financial contracts since medieval times.

Under the *musharaka* contract, the facilitation was made to ensure the joint ownership of property (*sharika al-milk*) or a commercial enterprise (*sharikat al-'aqd*). The intent of this contract is to establish an agreement on the capital shares as per the project's planning by both parties. The implementation and management of the project and profits earned are mutually shared between the two parties as per the norms settled in the agreement. On similar grounds, losses incurred are mutually shared in proportion as per the contribution of capital amount.

IFIs play the managerial role, while depositors serve as the capital providers subjected to the *Mudarabah* contract either through their savings account or investment account. Under the *Mudarabah* contract, depositors will have to share the profit with the bank on the basis of a precise ratio, while losses incurred will be borne entirely by them in terms of money. The banks, on the other hand, will lose their time, work, effort and expected profit.

As per the norms of the *mudarabah* contract, the capital's owner or *rabb al-mal* (this can be the bank or the customer) provides money to the applicant or *mudarib* (this can be the entrepreneur or the bank in the case of indirect financing), who in turn commits to the management of the amount with the purpose of intending to make profit. There will be a division of profits between the parties based on a fixed percentage as agreed upon in the contract. The profit forms a part of the total income and thus isn't fixed as such. When the same module is applied for indirect financing, the agent acquiring the capital can establish a *mudarabah* contract with a third party. This will then get invested in productive activities (double-tier *mudarabah*). The management of mutual funds and the structuring of *Sukuk* are among the most popular financial contracts that *Mudarabah* contracts are used for. This is how sharing of profits and losses forms a distinctive feature of the Islamic banking system in contrast to the conventional banking system.

1.5 Real Assets Over Monetary Assets in Islamic Finance

The idea of creating more money through money itself does not comply with the principles of Islamic law, and thus, direct dealing with money is legally prohibited under Islamic finance. Money must be generated through investments of money into real business activities. Figure 1.7 explains the entire trading paradigm. IFIs play the role of sellers, lessors, or partners to customers, as and when the need arises in order to facilitate their financing needs. Money has switched from a commodity only to an enabling entity for the facilitation of trading, leasing and investment, as explained in Figure 1.7.

Financing trade, lease or investment activities has been made possible by pooling the money collected through various Islamic accounts and/or shareholders' funds.

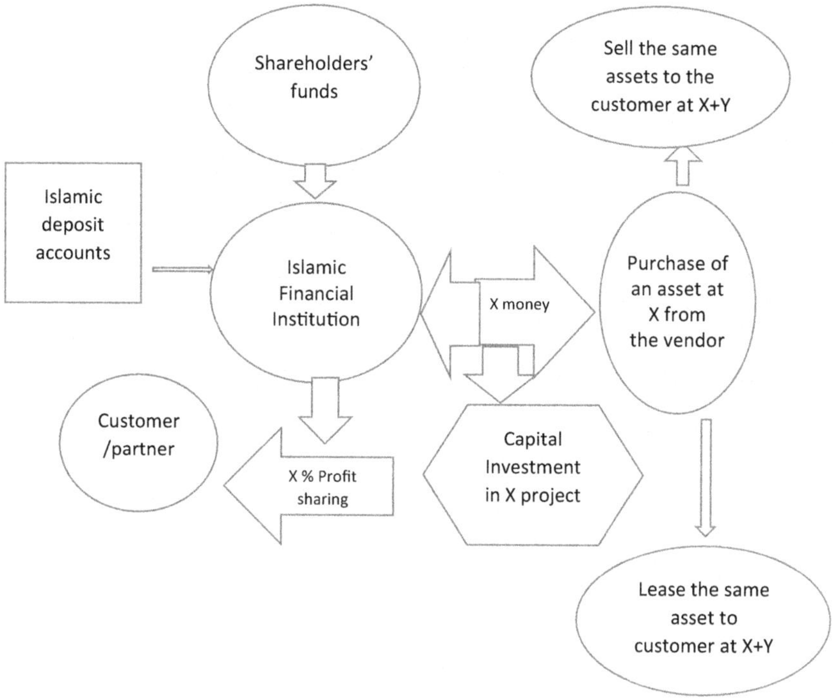

FIGURE 1.7 Money in Islamic finance.

To put forth a micro analysis, the money gets transferred into real economic stock to be able to generate further income. Thus, dealing with real assets over monetary assets has proved to develop profit as an outcome for IFIs.

1.6 Major Contracts Used in Islamic Finance

The development of Islamic products is characterised by the major contracts, as follows:

- *Mudarabah* (trust financing)
- *Musharaka* (profit and loss sharing joint venture)
- *Murabahah* (cost plus)
- *Ijarah* (leasing)
- *Istisna* (manufacturing an asset)
- *Salam* (advance payment sale)
- *Wadiah* (safekeeping)
- *Wakalah* (agency)

1.6-1 Mudarabah *(Trust Financing)*

Under a *Mudarabah* financing contract, there has to be an agreement where both the parties decide on sharing profits of the venture being financed. It is only then that the bank approves to finance the entrepreneur. When individuals make deposits to the bank, the amount equates to being an investment which will eventually be used by the bank to enable profits from its trading activities (e.g. financing of individuals and businesses). The *Mudarabah* contract will ensure that the bank gives the depositor a share of its profits as a return of the investment depending on a pre-agreed ratio.

1.6-2 Musharaka *(Profit and Loss Sharing Joint Venture)*

Under a *Musharaka* contract, all involved partners contribute capital in the form of a collective venture and eventually share the profit and loss on a pro rata basis. The major types of these joint ventures are:

- Diminishing partnership: Mostly used while acquiring properties, this particular venture is agreed upon when the bank and investor collectively buy a property. The bank eventually transfers its equity portion in the property to the investor in exchange for payments.
- Permanent *musharaka*: Mostly used for long-term finance projects, this particular venture does not include a specific end date and remains functional till the time the participating parties agree to cease operations.

1.6-3 Murabahah *(Cost Plus)*

Murabahah financing constitutes quite a considerable segment of Islamic financing equally subjected to both short-term and long-term assets. Extensively used in asset financing, a *murabahah* contract refers to a cost plus mark-up transaction between the parties. This contract entails an arrangement among three parties, where the customer's order is placed with the financial institution for purchasing goods from a supplier. A deposit amount in the form of security might be paid by the customer to the financial institution involved, while the amount of financing outstanding can be secured either in the form of collateral or a guarantee. The goods are bought from the supplier by the financial institution and then eventually sold to the customer at a price including mark-up with a fixed credit period.

1.6-4 Ijarah *(Leasing)*

This particular financial contract involves payments in the form of purchasing and rental exchanges, wherein the property owner acts as the lessor leasing the same property to the lessee. Ownership of property gets transferred to the lessee only on account of the property being purchased.

1.6–5 Istisna *(Manufacturing an Asset)*

As per the norms of Islamic finance, *Istisna* refers to a long-term financial contract, agreeing to which a party has to undertake manufacturing, building or constructing assets. Under this financial agreement, manufacturers or producers have to ensure the completion and delivery of assets to the customer. Unlike *Salam*, where an advance payment has to be made, an *Istisna* contract is widely chosen for its flexible nature, as customers can choose to pay in installments during the course of a project, at delivery or even after the completed project is delivered to them. The use of *Istisna* is prevalent mostly in projects relating to infrastructure. Popular examples are power plants, factories, roads, schools, hospitals, and building and residential developments. The producer or manufacturer, the bank (i.e. the financier) and the customer (i.e. the purchaser of goods) are the major parties in an *Istisna* contract.

1.6–6 Salam *(Advance Payment Sale)*

A financial agreement made under a *Salam* contract would require the full payment for the purchased commodity to be made in advance in exchange for the deferment of the delivery date to another date in the future.

This method of financial dealing is applied when the product has the possibility to undergo a price hike. This contract benefits the buyer, as it enables the buyer to purchase the product or service at a price lower than the anticipated increased rate. Since the delivery is scheduled in the future, it must be ensured that the features of the commodity offered for sale are put up with full clarity to avoid all sorts of ambiguities. The detailed description of the object to be sold forms the basis upon which the agreement is sealed. Under the *Salam* financing mode of trade, it is the bank that makes the payment to the seller or exporter, who in turn produces and/or delivers the goods.

In some financial agreements, the financier will act as the seller as well as the buyer. This particular mode of financial contract made under *Salam* is addressed as the 'parallel *Salam*'.

In contracts that are compliant with the *Salam*, the IFI buys the *Salam* asset from the seller in exchange of full advance payment and schedules a delivery date in the future. The IFI can then play the role of a seller and enter into a *Salam* contract with another party for a shorter period of asset delivery. This is where the parallel *Salam* comes into play. It is this parallel *Salam*, or the spread between the first and second *Salam* contract, which helps the IFI in earning profit.

Salam is chiefly characterised by the following principles:

- A forward purchase of a commodity is made.
- Payments are made in advance at the beginning of the contract period.
- Products received at the end of the contract period must be identifiable as per the details upon which the agreement was made.

- In case the contract is not able to be completed as per specifications in the agreement, remedies must be made available.
- Parallel *Salam* is useful for financing the ultimate producer, as the IFI is neither the ultimate producer nor the user.

1.6–7 Wadiah *(Safekeeping)*

Wadiah is synonymous with the ideas of trust, custody, deposit, and safekeeping. The *Wadiah* contract is as per the norms of Islamic finance, wherein a depositor deposits funds or assets with an Islamic bank with the intent of safekeeping. This contract is often characterised by a fee charged by the bank in ensuring the safe custody of the person's funds or/and assets.

Primarily, *Wadiah* can be observed through the two following forms:

- *Wadiah yad Amanah*, where properties are deposited on the basis of trust (guarantee safe custody)
- *Wadiah yad Dhamanah*, where savings are deposited with the guarantee of safekeeping.

Wadiah has evolved from the traditional concept of *Amanah*, where assets used to be handed over to one person by the other with the sole motive of keeping them safe and secured. *Wadiah* as a financial practice has been widely implemented in several Islamic countries, such as Malaysia and Bangladesh (Hosen and Nahrwai, 2012). Islamic banks charge an account maintenance fee for *Wadiah* accounts, which in turn helps them to maintain the administrative costs incurred by the bank in managing the assets or funds in safe custody.

Some of the features of Wadiah bank accounts are the following:

- It is a product that does not bear profit and loss.
- The return of the full amount on demand/maturity is guaranteed by the bank at its own risk. Here, no risk is shared by the depositor.
- Upon the approval of the depositor, the bank can invest this deposited fund. As for profits earned, the bank might have to share the profit with the depositors if such a decision has been taken by the senior management concerned.
- A fee amount is applicable for the maintenance of the accounts.

1.6–8 Wakalah *(Agency)*

Wakalah corresponds to a financial contract between an agent and a principal. This contract gives authority to an agent to provide services in exchange for a payment or fee (*Ujrah*). For example, an importer, applying for a letter of credit based on *Wakalah*, will authorise the bank to issue the letter of credit on their behalf to the exporter's bank. The issuing bank will then play the role of an agent to process the issuance of the letter of credit for which a fee imposition is made on the importer for rendering the services.

Wakalah is characterised by major principles:

- There is involvement of an agency contract between an agent and principal.
- It facilitates transactions.
- The agent is paid a fee (*ujrah*) in exchange for its services.

1.7 Conclusion

Islamic banking is a banking system which revolves around the principles of *Shari'ah*. If one studies the timeline of evolution of Islamic banking from its inception, it becomes evident why it is acknowledged as a distinguished and respected financial structure in the context of the international financial system. To put it into simple words, an awakened Islamic economic thought has to be credited for the consistent growth of Islamic finance. At the same time, the rising demand from customers for services and products have equally supplemented that growth.

The benefits that the Islamic financial industry offers have drawn not only the Muslim participants but also non-Muslim participants into the international market structure. *Shari'ah*-compliant financial products are reported to be around US$3 trillion in the global market. As per the London-based International Financial Services (McKenzie, 2010, January), *Shari'ah*-compliant assets rose 40% from $549 billion in 2006 to US$758 billion in 2007, followed by a 25% hike by the end of 2008 to hit $951 billion. IFIs have been simultaneously growing at 15%–20% p.a. – a growth rate that far exceeds that of the conventional financial industry. The passing years are witness to the growth and evolution of Islamic finance and how it has gained momentum on a global scale. Financial institutions all over the world, including conventional financial institutions, have launched their own Islamic financial products through Islamic windows in trying to keep up with the pace of growing demand for *Shari'ah*-based products and services.

In order to remain competitive in the mainstream global economy, the Islamic financial industry has to cultivate certain practices which in turn can enhance their transparency and make them credible in potential markets worldwide. This might also require the need to be more accepting of different kinds of interpretations of *Shari'ah* principles between regions as well as between institutions. Regulatory oversight should be enriched. All these measures can collectively work wonders for strengthening the appeal and amplifying the credibility of the Islamic financial system as a suitable alternative to the mainstream financial system in the long run. Since a trading agreement is a mandate for every financial transaction, the Islamic financial system offering *Shari'ah*-based products and services might appear to be more complicated in comparison with mainstream financial systems. Sustainable equivalents over mainstream financial instruments, like corporate treasury and derivative products, are still lacking. Innovation is another aspect that the Islamic financial industry has to work on. The hindrance to innovation is largely impacted by the limited number of *Shari'ah* board members (*Shari'ah* scholars) able to vet financial products for *Shari'ah* compliance.

Review Questions

1. Briefly elaborate on the principles of Islamic finance.
2. Discuss the components and functions of financial institutions.
3. What are the salient features of Islamic finance?
4. What are the important features of Islamic banking and finance?
5. Why opt for Islamic finance, and what does it offer?
6. What are the *Shari'ah* rulings of currency for currency?
7. What are the *Shari'ah* rulings of food items for food items?
8. What are the differences between money and the capital market?

References

Abdulkader, T, Stella, C and Bryan K (2005), *Structuring Islamic Finance Transactions*, London: Euromoney Books

Hosen, M and Nahrwai, A (2012), Comparative Analysis of Islamic Banking Products Between Malaysia and Indonesia, *International Journal of Academic Research in Economics and Management Sciences*, 1(2), 120–143.

McKenzie, D (2010), *IFSL Research: Islamic Finance 2010*, International Financial Services, London, retrieved from www.ifsl.org.uk (Access date February 9, 2010).

Miller, T, ed (2009), *Mapping the Global Muslim Population: A Report on the Size and Distribution of the World's Muslim Population*, Pew Research Center, retrieved from www.pewforum.org/2009/10/07/mapping-the-global-muslim-population/

Usmani, MT (2002), *An Introduction to Islamic Finance*, The Hague: Kluwer Law International

2

PRIMARY AND SECONDARY MARKETS

Learning Objectives

On completing this chapter, learners will be able to:

- Comprehend the organisational structure of the primary market
- Recognise the differences between primary and secondary markets
- Comprehend and motivate the advantage of listing shares in the stock exchange
- Understand contemporary stock trading
- Explain the role and functions of the stock market
- Identify the challenges in promoting secondary markets for Islamic financial markets
- Analyse the causes of liquidity problems in the secondary market in ongoing structural issues for Islamic financial institutions.

2.1 Introduction

Financial markets are generally characterised by the presence of primary markets but do not always necessarily include secondary markets. In the context of savings deposits a primary market is always found, but at the same time, these financial instruments cannot be sold off by the deposit holders. Securities that can be marketed generally give rise to secondary markets. Listed equities are marketable, and hence equity markets are inclusive of primary as well as secondary markets. Newly formed equities are generally issued in primary equity markets, while secondary markets serve as platforms to trade the existing securities. Therefore, the issuing companies in primary market issues are funded to the extent of the number of shares issued in terms of the price of the shares (Handtke, 2012).

DOI: 10.4324/9780429321207-2

The functional system of both the primary and secondary markets are explained in the following sections.

2.1-1 Primary Market

The primary market is not characterised by the presence of a physical market structure, as is Wall Street. Under the financial market structure, individuals and institutions issue and trade securities. Unlike the secondary market structure, which is based on the selling and buying of securities from each other, primary markets are tasked with the initial public trading of stocks and bonds. Here, investors directly purchase securities from banks held accountable for underwriting the initial public offering (IPO). An IPO is a process by which a company transitions into a publicly traded company by offering equities to investors. The IPO, a financial method that enhances fundraising in the company, also enables investors to invest in a company for the first time. Another financial method, called the further public offer (FPO), helps to raise additional funds from the public. The FPO allows fresh equities to be offered by existing listed companies.

Unlisted shares are characterised by a forthright primary market. For a new company, its owners could conveniently hire accountants or lawyers to create the shares and put the funds (share value) in the respective company's bank account. In case there is any requirement for more funding, the company might design a prospectus and approach investors. If the deal is deemed successful (i.e. investors accept it), shares will be placed with them while the raised funds would be put in the respective bank account.

For a listed company, the primary market structure is hassle free. Henceforth, the concept of primary markets is elaborated based on the following features:

- Economic role of the primary market
- Advantages of listing
- Conditions that are to be considered for listing
- Categories of companies that list
- Listed products other than shares
- Processes of listing
- The prospectus
- Share underwriting issue
- Additional resources of primary market issue of registered equity
- Raising of capital.

2.1-1-1 Economic Function of the Primary Market

A buyer investing in equities does so with an assumed risk. Economically, primary equity markets are conceptualised to provide gains by directing the funds that are in surplus into a productive investment subjected to a price that corresponds to the same estimated risk. The perceived risk and expected return

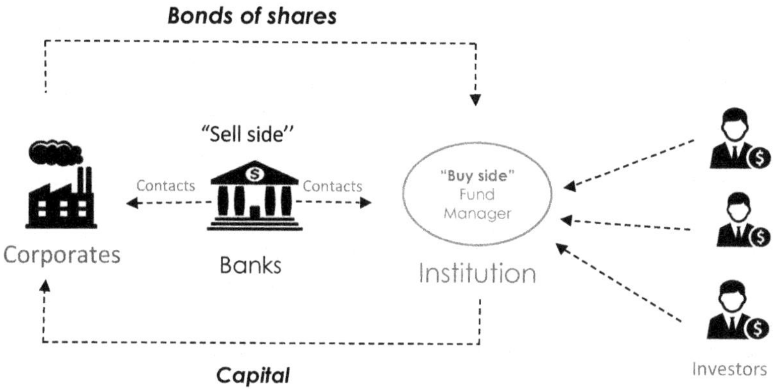

FIGURE 2.1 Primary markets.

ensure the functionality of the issue paid price and, at the same time, factually put forth the simultaneous existence of secondary markets required for equity trading. This is how we observe the intertwined nature of primary and secondary markets.

A majority of companies choose to list their shares on an exchange with the motive to avail the acquired (permanent) capital for long-term investment (additions to a production facility and/or equipment) which is supposed to produce a considerable return for the company, thereby benefitting its shareholders. In case of the absence of secondary markets for equities, this capital will cease to be conveniently available.

Thus, the secondary market is seen to provide an exit mechanism for the investment (keeping in mind several short-term investments). To add to this is its genuine evidence in terms of correct pricing. The equity market is largely drawn by professional investors or 'institutions', while smaller investors are reliant on these 'professional large investors' for determining the market pricing range and keeping it in check.

Investors can buy business shares after the company sets up its issue price and creates its IPO. Trading activities of the capital markets are distinctively different for primary markets and secondary markets.

2.1-1-2 Raising Funds From the Primary Market

Certain ways through which companies collect funds from the primary market include the following:

1. Public issue. Popularly known as one of the most efficient methods, the company uses an IPO as a medium to fundraise. To facilitate trading activities, the securities are listed on a stock exchange to be issued to the general public.

2. Rights issue. Under the rights issue, a company can offer more shares to its existing shareholders. The number of shares offered is generally on a pro rata basis and mostly at a price lower than the existing market price. The sole intent here is to generate more capital by offering discounted price rates.
3. Preferential allotment. Under the system of preferential allotment, the market price does not actively determine the price rate of shares that the listed company chooses to issue shares at. The company would preferably issue shares to certain individuals at any price without the market price impacting the share price. Here, the company acts as the sole decision maker in allotting shares.

2.1-2 Secondary Market

All kinds of existing shares and Islamic (or *Sukuk*) bonds are traded among investors in a secondary market. As we have already mentioned, securities initially traded in the primary market are followed up by being traded on the secondary market. The New York Stock Exchange (NYSE), the Nasdaq, S&P Islamic indices, Dow Jones Islamic market indices and all other global exchanges constitute the major indices in a secondary market that investors decide to trade on. Securities on the secondary market are traded without any involvement or intervention of the issuing companies.

The transactional process of trading between a buyer and a seller is facilitated by the stock exchange. The issuing company remains uninvolved in the sale of its securities.

Take as an example an investor wanting to purchase shares of British Petroleum on the secondary market. The purchasing order would acquire the particular shares not from the company but from a different investor. Simultaneously, anyone selling on the secondary market is selling their shares to another investor. We can further understand the secondary market through four operational categories:

- Auction markets
- Dealer markets
- Broker's markets
- Exchange markets.

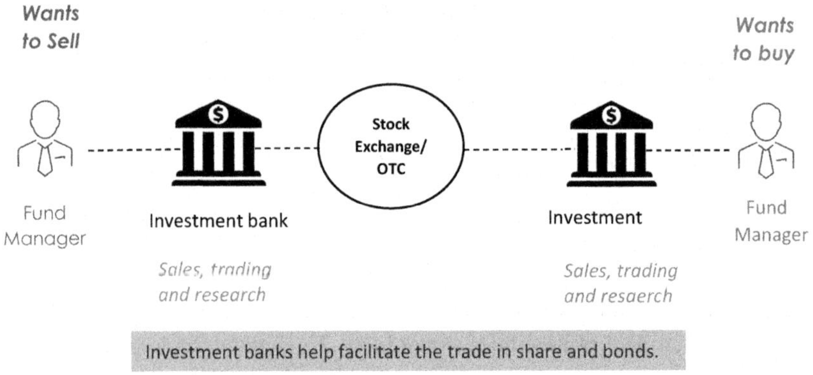

FIGURE 2.2 Secondary markets.

TABLE 2.1 Difference Between Primary and Secondary Markets

Primary Market	*Secondary Market*
Here, the issuance of fresh shares is done in the market. Synonymously known as the new issue market, one of its major components is the IPO.	Here, trading is made of shares, the issuance of which has been already done and already existing. It is synonymously referred to as the after issue market.
The company gets to keep the amount received from issuing shares for their business expansion purposes.	The company does not get anything, owing to the fact that the amount invested by the buyer of shares ultimately goes to the seller.
The issuance of securities is done at a uniform price for all investors participating in the offering.	The exchange of securities takes place between buyers and sellers. Trade is facilitated by stock exchanges.
No liquidity is provided by the primary market for the stock.	Liquidity is provided for the stock by the secondary market.
Underwriters act as intermediaries.	Brokers act as intermediaries.
Here, securities can be sold just once.	Here, there is no restriction on the number of times that securities can be sold.

Sources: Handtke (2012); Chen et al. (2013).

2.1-2-1 Auction Market

As a category of the secondary market, auction markets can be explained in the form of announcements made by participants in order to consistently bid and ask for prices they are comfortable with. These auctions are most likely to occur between investors wanting to buy and sell. Business intent is not an underlying reason for these auctions. During the auctioning, prices become a more concrete figure, as this process entails everyone involved declaring their terms, thereby enhancing market efficiency. The NYSE is a quite popular auction market.

In an auction market scenario, the coming together of the buyers and sellers eventually leads to a justified price range for everyone, making it beneficial for investors as they do not have to go on a quest for seeking out the best price on the secondary market. In an ideal world, buyers and sellers will be submitting competitive offers at the same time. After every bid is submitted, the auction market will analyse and find out the highest price that a buyer is willing to pay and the minimum a seller is willing to accept. Transactions are declared successful once the bids and offers match each other.

2.1-2-2 Dealer Market

The overview of auction markets makes it evident that convergence of investors is a mandatory requirement for their operational efficiency. Dealer markets, on the other hand, entail transactions that happen electronically through individual markets. This can be illustrated through the functionality of one of the most popular dealer markets, Nasdaq in New York. Dealers have to maintain an inventory of securities set to be traded with other investors at a moment's notice. Dealers would then declare a price range at which they are initially willing to buy or sell specific securities. To ensure clarity and remain transparent, they will subject their own capital at risk by providing liquidity for subsequent investors. In return, dealers reap profits based on the spreads that securities are bought and sold for.

Prices are displayed by dealers so that the process is equally transparent to and for everyone. This transparent approach happens to develop competition. And it is this competitiveness that largely influences this dealer market in theoretically providing investors with the best possible prices.

Dealer markets are more active in currency and bonds than in stocks. Dealer markets can be equally preferred for futures and options, or other standardised contracts and derivatives. The foreign exchange market is generally operated through dealers while the banks and currency exchanges act as the dealer intermediaries.

2.1-2-3 Broker Market

The operational effectiveness of a broker market is deemed successful if both the buyer and seller find themselves counterparties. A dealer can play the role of a counterparty, but it must be also noted that the more time is taken to find an appropriate / better / perfect counterparty, the more likely it is to generate less liquidity in brokered markets as an outcome.

In the traditional era, stock markets were brokered. Stockbrokers would try to look for an appropriate counterparty for their clients on the trading floor. This image portrayed here is relevant to the stereotypical projection of the famous Wall Street, where men and women in different coloured jackets would yell at each other while continuously noting their clients' orders on pieces of paper.

Broker markets are generally used for all kinds of securities, particularly those with initial issues. An IPO, launched through an investment bank, would broker the issue in trying to find subscribers. This seems equally applicable for certain bond issues that are relatively more recent. Brokered markets are also the right fit for tailored or custom products.

2.1-2-4 Exchanges

In a market structure characterised by exchange, execution of trade occurs in terms of mostly automated exchanges on the basis of order books matching buyers and sellers. Stocks are no longer brokered but automated. In case the buyers and sellers cannot come together in terms of price, then the trade is called off.

Automated exchanges are more convenient and favourable at the same time since there is no involvement of brokers or dealer intermediaries and these exchanges provide a central location for buyers and sellers to find their own counterparties. Automated exchanges are mostly applied for standardised securities inclusive of stocks, bonds, futures, contracts, and options. The characteristics of securities traded on exchanges are:

- Contract or lot size
- Time need to execute the entire contract
- Tick size
- Terms of delivery
- Quality.

In the context of stock exchanges or bond exchanges, the exchange is mostly characterised by the contract size, tick size and trading duration (which particularly happens to be immediate execution). Contract sizes might require a minimum. For example, a specific exchange could entail stocks to be purchased in lots of 100. The lowest denomination of a currency is generally identified as the tick size. For example, in US stock exchanges, the lowest tick in price is a cent. A contract tick size would then be $1 ($0.01 × 100 shares per lot).

Delivery terms and quality are chiefly used in commodity exchanges and with derivatives inclusive of assets having these characteristics. This can be understood with examples of gold and diamonds, both being typically characterised by their qualities and ratings. If a physical asset is dealt with, it must be in a deliverable form so that it can be easily transferred to the buyer or contract holder. All these characteristics essentially make the dealer market the most liquid of all markets.

2.1-2-5 Stock Market in the Secondary Market

In a secondary market system, any kind of public market used to issue, buy, and sell stocks being traded on a stock exchange is generally identified as a stock market. Stocks are synonymous with equities and represent fractional ownership in a company. Stock markets let investors purchase and sell ownership of such invisible assets. On grounds of stock markets functioning efficiently, companies gain opportunities to access capital from the public swiftly. This in turn plays a crucial role in holistic economic development (Handtke, 2012).

2.1–2–5–1 Objectives of the Stock Market

Functionally, stock markets serve two important purposes. Primarily, they provide capital or funds to companies to facilitate their business expansion. To understand this better, we can take the example of a company issuing $1 million in shares of stock that were initially sold for $10 per share. This would then provide the company with $10 million of capital that it can eventually use to expand its business. One must note that the stock offering is generally managed by an investment bank in exchange for a standard applicable fee, which is be paid by the company and is generally deducted from the capital amount. Stock markets become an ideal way for companies to expand their businesses because they do not have to take the pressure of incurring loans and paying interest charges on that loan by conveniently offering stock shares instead of borrowing from banks (Akerlof, 1970).

Another purpose of stock markets is how investors who purchase stocks have an opportunity to gain shares in the profits of publicly traded companies. Profits from purchasing stocks can be availed in different ways. The first is through regular dividends paid by some particular stocks. Investing in these stocks would ensure a particular amount of money per share depending on the entire stock owned. Second, investors can sell an initially purchased stock at an increased stock price and earn a profit. For example, an investor selling a stock at $15 per share who had initially bought the same stock at $10 per share generates a 50% profit on their initial investment just by selling their shares.

2.1–2–5–2 Contemporary Stock Trading: The Shifting Face of Worldwide Stock Exchanges

Over the spread of two centuries or more, the NYSE happened to successfully dominate within its domestic periphery, and its growth is symbolic of the simultaneous expansion of the US economy. The LSE (London Stock Exchange), on the other hand, has dominated the European market for stock trading. However, the NYSE became home to a continually expanding number of large companies. Countries such as France and Germany started building their own stock exchanges modelled on the LSE or NYSE.

The 20th century eventually witnessed the expansion of stock trading into different exchanges, particularly the Nasdaq, which rapidly growing tech companies opted for at one and every go. The technology sector boom of the 1980s and 1990s can equally be credited for the increased importance of the Nasdaq. As a first of its kind, the exchange of trades through the Nasdaq took place electronically on a web of computers. Electronic trading transitioned the entire process into a more efficient one, cutting down not only on time but also on costs. The rise in demand of the Nasdaq along with stock exchanges from the financial hub of Asia (particularly Beijing, Malaysia, Hong Kong and Tokyo) provided strict competition for the NYSE. This is why the NYSE eventually integrated with Euronext, formed in 2000 through the merger of the Brussels, Amsterdam, and Paris exchanges. The NYSE/Euronext merger, established in 2007, is reputed to be the first transatlantic exchange.

2.1–2–5–3 Stock Market Indexes

Several stock market indexes are used as indicators to track, analyse and comprehend the overall performance of the stock market. Stock indexes are designed in the form of a constitution of selective stocks acting as performance indicators for comprehending the overall performance of stocks. Trading of stock market indexes take place in the form of options and possible contracts in the future which are further traded on regulated exchanges. Some of the major stock market indexes include the Dow Jones Industrial Average (DJIA), the Dow Jones Islamic Market Index, the Standard & Poor's 500 Index (S&P 500), the S&P Islamic Index, the Financial Times Stock Exchange 100 Index (FTSE 100), the FTSE Global Islamic Index, the Nikkei 225 Index, the Nasdaq Composite Index, and the Hang Seng Index.

2.2 Bull and Bear Markets

Bull and bear markets constitute two basic conceptual trade ideologies. A 'bull market' is mainly characterised by the rise in prices of stocks, thereby being more likely to ensure prosperity for most investors. Here, a larger proportion of stock investors make up the buyers instead of short sellers. This is the type of market most investors prosper in, as the majority of stock investors are buyers rather than short sellers. In a 'bear market', stock prices are characterised by a consistent decline.

2.3 Short Selling

Bear markets can facilitate investors making profits, but only in terms of short selling. As a practice, short selling allows the investor to borrow stock. The investor would then sell the borrowed stock shares in the secondary market and receive a certain amount from the sale of that stock. As soon as the share prices hit a downfall, the investors purchase stocks in the market and return the broker the equal number of stocks borrowed, with the difference now being that the price rate per share has depreciated. This results in developing profits for the investors. An example illustrates the functional capacity of short selling with more clarity. An investor has anticipated that company A's stock, priced at US$20 per share, is likely to go down. The investor can place a margin deposit to the broker to be able to borrow 100 shares of this stock. The investor in turn sells off these shares at the same price range of US$20 per share and earns US$2,000. Now when the price range hits a downfall of, say, US$10 per share, the investor immediately purchases 100 such shares, amounting to a purchase of US$1,000, and returns the same to its broker, thereby earning a handsome profit of US$1,000.

2.4 Two Basic Strategies: Value Investing and Growth Investing

Investors and analysts can choose from innumerable methods to selectively pick stocks. However, all of these options come under two basic stock buying strategies: value investing and growth investing (Brancaccio et al., 2017).

In the value investing strategy, value investors usually invest in well-established companies that have shown consistent profits over a long period of time and might also offer regular dividend income. Unlike growth investing that is based on a riskier edge, value investors attempt to purchase stocks by finding the stock price to be an undervalued bargain.

In the growth investing strategy, growth investors are on the lookout for companies with an exceptionally high growth potential, the intent being able to develop and mature maximum appreciation in share price. Unlike value investing which focuses more on dividend income, growth investors willingly prefer to opt for risk investing in relatively younger companies, such as technology stocks and construction stocks, owing to their potential capacities in developing exponential growth.

2.5 Conclusion

Investors find navigating the financial markets quite a daunting experience, whether they have been trading since ages or are considerably recent in the trading business. The operational approach of all these markets mostly prevails on self-sustenance by developing independent methods. To add to this is the massive volume of these markets. The complex structures and varied operational approaches often seem to intimidate investors; nevertheless, the same reasons should not prevent investors from investing. To be able to learn about the market system and be able to evolve into an efficient investor, one has to pause and reconsider the dynamics of each market structure without falling for the hustle culture. Once they are well acquainted with the nitty gritty of the trade, the knowledge gained can help them develop a powerful foundational base for each investment portfolio. Investors who have done their due diligence at present can breathe a sigh of relief in their upcoming years. The individual differences between a primary market and a secondary market must not trigger arguments but rather be acknowledged as a learning experience.

Islamic markets are not characterised by a separate primary market; hence they rely on the structure of the conventional primary market system for issuing common stocks and *Sukuk*. The role of 'liquidity' is imperative in maintaining the functional efficiency of an Islamic secondary market through methodical and effective distribution of economic resources in allocating capital and risk productively, generating accuracy and disseminating issuer-specific information and effectiveness of the Islamic secondary market (Ibrahim, 2019).

Further, liquidity in the secondary market is an ongoing structural issue for Islamic financial institutions as a result of the scarcity of high-quality liquid assets and an underdeveloped secondary market for *Sukuk* (Islamic bonds), owing to both commercial purposes and difficulties arising out of necessary *Shari'ah* compliance. The stopping of short-term *Sukuk* issuance in certain jurisdictions, such as Malaysia in 2015, also affected the liquidity of the secondary market, according to the Islamic Financial Services Board (Ibrahim, 2019).

Financial architecture and infrastructure have critical roles to play. The secondary market can achieve the needed depth if the focus is more internationally centered. This means that Islamic financial contracts, which form an important element of the Islamic financial architecture, need to be looked at to address the structuring issues emerging from a lack of consensus.

Review Questions

1. Explain the definition of a primary market.
2. Explain the definition of a secondary market.
3. What are the differences between primary and secondary markets?
4. What are the methods of stock listing?
5. What are the functional differences between a stock exchange and a stock market?
6. Explain the roles played by the stock exchange in terms of raising capital.
7. Describe the challenges in promoting secondary markets for Islamic financial markets.

References

Akerlof, GA (1970), The Market for 'Lemons': Quality Uncertainty and the Market Mechanism, *The Quarterly Journal of Economics*, 84(3), 488–500

Brancaccio, G, Li, D and Schurhoff, N (2017), *Learning by Trading: The Case of the US Market for Municipal Bonds*, Working Paper, Princeton: Princeton University

Chen, J, Esteban, S and Shum, M (2013), When Do Secondary Markets Harm Firms?, *American Economic Review*, 103(7), 2911–2934

Handtke, E (2012), *Primary and Secondary Market*, Working Paper No. 741, New York: Levy Economics Institute of Bard College, retrieved from www.levyinstitute.org/pubs/wp_741.pdf (Access date March 2019)

Ibrahim, A (2019, June 5), Islamic Secondary Markets, *Islamic Finance News*, retrieved from www.researchgate.net/publication/345433685_Islamic_secondary_markets (Access date September 25, 2020)

3

ISLAMIC CAPITAL MARKET

Learning Objectives

On completing this chapter, learners will be able to:

- Apply the *Shari'ah* principles governing operation of the Islamic capital market and relate the knowledge to actual operations
- Understand the knowledge underpinning Islamic finance to illustrate the distinctive characteristics of various Islamic capital market products
- Discuss the screening of Islamic stocks
- Examine the liquidity issues in the Islamic capital market.

3.1 Introduction

A capital market is a market for issuing and sale of stocks, bonds, or similar securities to boost long-term capital. The term 'capital market' applies to any financial market where debt and equity are ordered and supplied. A capital market facilitates investors to find a platform for making their investments and facilitates both investors and borrowers by directing funds from those with excess funds to those in need of such funds. Companies and governments obtain funds from the capital market.

In contrast, an Islamic capital market is such a market where *Shari'ah*-compliant financial assets are transacted. It functions parallel to the traditional market and facilitates investors to find *Shari'ah*-compliant investment opportunities. The Islamic capital market is divided into debt capital markets and equity capital markets. Also, Islamic capital markets are classed into primary markets and secondary markets. In the primary market, an investor buys securities which are released for the first time. Like the conventional financial market, Islamic primary capital markets are important for the capital development of an economy. However, existing securities are bought and sold in the secondary market.

DOI: 10.4324/9780429321207-3

In an Islamic capital market (ICM), market operations are carried out in ways that do not clash with the business ethics of Islam. Here, there is a declaration of *Shari'ah* law, where the market is free from events prohibited by *Shari'ah*, such as usury (*riba*), gambling (*maisir*), and ambiguity (*gharar*).

The Islamic capital market (ICM) is a component of the overall Islamic financial markets. It plays an important role in generating economic growth for a country. The ICM functions as a parallel market to the conventional capital market and plays a complementary role to the Islamic banking system in broadening and deepening the Islamic financial markets in the world.

The growth of wealth among Muslim investors (especially from the Gulf Cooperation Council [Bahrain, Kuwait, Oman, Qatar, Saudi Arabia, and the United Arab Emirates]) is encouraging the development of the Islamic capital market (ICM). The current growth rate of ICM products is between 12% and 15% annually. This sector accounts for 27% of global Islamic financial assets, worth about US$591.9 billion. *Sukuk* (Islamic bonds), despite recording a slower growth in 2018 compared to 2017, still dominates the ICM sector because of strong sovereign and multilateral issuances securities in the key Islamic financial markets to support respective budgetary expenditures, as well as first new issuances in other jurisdictions. If we compare the trend observed in the global equity markets over the same period, the assets of Islamic funds declined in 2018 by 8.5% compared to 2017 due to, among other reasons, moderation in economic growth, ongoing geopolitical challenges, and increasing international liquidity. In total, Islamic assets are worth an estimated US$1.5 trillion, and about 25% of that amount was tied to the Islamic capital market in the year 2019.

3.2 Products in ICM

There are different products in the Islamic capital market. This is the financial market for financial assets where debt and equity issued by companies are traded. Trading of funds in the capital market makes possible the construction of factories, highways, schools, and other infrastructure which requires huge financing. The most important borrowers in the capital market are businesses of all sizes that issue long-term instruments representing claims against their future revenues in order to cover the purchase of equipment and the construction of new facilities. The products of the capital market can be classified:

1. Islamic exchange traded fund
2. Shares and quasi equity
3. Bonds and *Sukuk*
4. Commercial paper.

Figure 3.1 presents a general overview of the Islamic capital market.

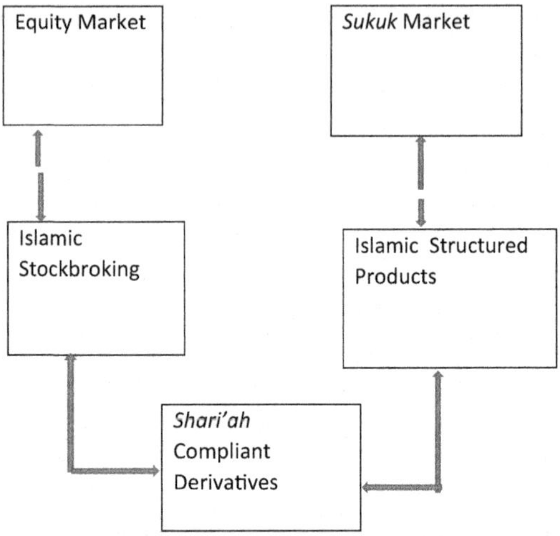

FIGURE 3.1 Structure of the Islamic capital market.

3.3 Classification of the Islamic Capital Market

The Islamic capital market is divided into the primary and secondary market.

1. Primary market: In the Islamic primary market, new issues of Islamic equity and debt products are arranged in the form of entirely new flotations or issues of shares/securities, or in the form of an offer to existing investors. In either case, the organisation concerned raises new cash in exchange of the issue of securities. In a company the securities may take the form of share (equity) or Islamic bond (or *Sukuk*), whereas governments invariably issue sovereign *Sukuk*. Having a public quotation on a stock exchange is a prime advantage to listed firms or companies when they need to raise more capital.
2. Secondary market: In the secondary market, Islamic financial assets which have already been issued in the past are exchanged or traded among investors. The secondary market allows owners of shares and *Sukuk* to sell their holdings readily, hence assuring them a degree of liquidity that helps to sell and buy securities. In this process, investors feel confident that their investment will not be locked in; rather, the securities can be more readily converted into cash. This signifies that the function of the Islamic platform of secondary market is to facilitate the continuous reallocation of Islamic financial assets among the various investors. This also allows the investors to diversify their stocks or financial assets.

Following are the seven key products in the Islamic capital market:

1. Ordinary stocks: These are common stocks or shares which characterise the basic voting rights of shareholders within a company or corporation. The

owner of an ordinary share is generally eligible to one vote per share. Through the system of ordinary stocks, equal ownership is created evident with the system of issuing shares in agreement with shareholder having percentage ownership in the firm.

2. Preferred stocks: Preferred stock is an element of share capital that should have any combination of elements not acquired by common stock together with properties of both an equity and a debt instrument. It is usually seen as a hybrid. Most preferred shares offer fixed dividends, whereas common stocks do not. Preferred stock shareholders do not have voting rights, whereas common stock shareholders do.
3. Mutual funds: These are investment vehicles comprising funds collected from small investors for investment in securities such as stocks, bonds, money market instruments, and other such assets. Qualified fund managers are appointed to manage these funds and distribute the fund's investments with the aim of generating income for the fund's investors.
4. Single stock futures: In this type of product, contracts are made between two market participants, where a buyer agrees to pay a required price for several shares of one stock at a slated time in the future. In this method, the seller's responsibility is to provide the stock at an agreed price at that future date.
5. *Mudarabah Sukuk*: Documents in a *mudarabah* contract representing ownership in assets are managed on the basis of *Mudarabah*. One indispensable form of profit-sharing in Islamic finance in a *mudarabah* agreement lies on a foundation done by a contract between entrepreneurs. and capital providers. With the formation of an enterprise targeted towards generating a profit, and both parties share profit on an pre-agreed ratio. The requirement is that if the company goes into loss, the capital provider bears these losses, while the entrepreneur only receives no reward in this situation.
6. *Ijara Sukuk*: The basic concept of *Ijara Sukuk* is that the holders of an asset belong to investors and are allowed to collect a fee in return for leasing that asset. In sum, this is basically a lease or rental contract allowing the right to make use of an asset in return of payment.
7. *Musharaka Sukuk*: These are the deeds that are declarative of the possession of the holder of a tangible asset that belongs to the private companies, corporations or governments. Up until the maturity of the *Sukuk*, any variations in price of the asset would concern the holders of *Musharaka Sukuk*.

Figure 3.2 shows the stock exchanges that currently trade Islamic capital market instruments.

3.4 Understanding *Shari'ah* Screening

The sustained interest in Islamic capital market products and the greater number of players have resulted in its growth. This constant growth has resulted in a boost in the market capitalisation of *Shari'ah*-compliant stocks and the net asset value (NAV) of *Shari'ah*-compliant mutual funds.

Market	*Description*	*Securities Traded*
Jakarta Stock Exchange	Holding company that lists more than 500 companies	*Sukuk*, *Shari'ah*-compliant equities and conventional financial products
Bursa Malaysia (MYX)	Kuala Lumpur–based exchange Standing company that lists almost 1,000 companies	Islamic securities and conventional capital market products
Labuan International Financial Exchange (LFX)	An offshore exchange based in Malaysia launched in 2000 and operating 24/7	*Sukuk* and Islamic funds
London Stock Exchange (LSE)	Largest stock exchange in the world; possessor of the alternative investment market (AIM), which includes on its list *Shari'ah*-compliant firms	*Sukuk*, equity funds and Islamic exchange-traded funds (ETFs)
Luxembourg Stock Exchange	The first European exchange to transact *Sukuk* (the Islamic bonds), documents sold to investors that represent possession of a tangible asset, project, business, service or joint venture	*Sukuk*, *Shari'ah*-compliant funds
Nasdaq Dubai	An exchange providing services to Western, Middle Eastern, European, and East Asian investors; a leading exchange for *Sukuk* in the Middle East	*Shari'ah*-compliant stocks, Islamic funds including mutual funds, Islamic (ETFs) and Islamic real estate investment trusts
London Stock Exchange	Based in London	*Sukuk*, Islamic funds
Tadawul (Saudi Arabian stock exchange)	Situated in Riyadh; listing companies operating in industries involving oil and gas, food, agriculture, banking and other financial sectors.	Stocks, IETFs, mutual funds and *Sukuk*

FIGURE 3.2 Stock exchanges that currently trade Islamic capital market instruments.

A vital driver of this growth seems to be the high level of market confidence of the market players and investors who are active in the Islamic capital market's *Shari'ah* governance participations.

3.4–1 Screening Methodology

A comprehensive *Shari'ah* stock screening methodology in Islamic finance offers a higher level of assurance and certainly about the *Shari'ah* compliance of the companies registered on the stock exchange. Unlike in the conventional market,

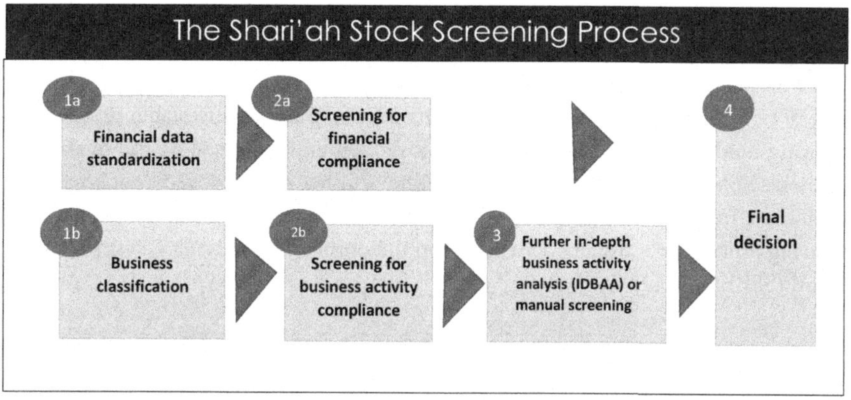

FIGURE 3.3 *Shari'ah* stock screening process.

transactions in the Islamic capital market are made only in methods that do not conflict with *Shari'ah* law. This demands a particular stock screening process to detect and record *Shari'ah*-investable companies. This procedure is called *Shari'ah* stock screening. In the Islamic capital market, the *Shari'ah* stock screening methodology was instituted as early as 1996 by Dow Jones USA and named the Dow Jones Islamic Global Market Index.

The *Shari'ah* corporate governance structure in the Islamic financial market is unique, as it has accepted a centralised method. This differs from the market style followed by the international markets and it ascertains *Shari'ah* matters. In a consolidated approach, the financial market authority sets up the standard of *Shari'ah* prerequisites to be approved through Islamic scholars' opinions (*fatwas*) announced by the *Shari'ah* supervisory board. In a market style, financial institutions or market players issue their own *fatwas* given by their *Shari'ah* supervisory boards; meanwhile, the financial authority monitors the compliance.

3.4–2 Shari'ah *Stock Screening*

The *Shari'ah* stock screening process involves the filtering of data and examining the information included in the listed corporation's latest published annual report. This program demonstrates the attempt to harmonise the *Shari'ah* stock screening standards with global hopes and to spur on capital inflows, particularly from investors in the Asian and Middle East. The screening methodology has been implementing the practice of global *Shari'ah* index contributors such as the Dow Jones Islamic Market Index, FTSE Global Islamic Index, and MSCI Shari'ah Index.

The design of the current *Shari'ah* stock screening methodology includes the test of a company's core business pursuit and its financial ratios, as well as the measurement of the public image and perception of the company. The test portion is typically known as the quantitative test, and the qualitative assessment portion is known as the qualitative test. To be a *Shari'ah*-investable company, it must pass both tests.

In its practice component, the *Shari'ah* stock screening methodology employs several tiers of filtering procedures to create a list of *Shari'ah*-investable stocks. The filtering method begins with the quantitative elements followed by the qualitative elements. The quantitative filtering procedure follows the approved benchmarks in both the core business pursuit and the financial ratios of the firms. The qualitative filtering procedure is usually dependent on the opinions of the *Shari'ah* supervisory board (SSB).

3.4-3 Screening Business Activities

Traditionally, three types of business endeavours are required to filter in the *Shari'ah* screening process: (1) business activities allowable under *Shari'ah*, (2) business activities not permissible under *Shari'ah*, and (3) mixed activities.

1. Business activities allowable under *Shari'ah* include the provision of lawful needs, goods and services, such as food, education, garments, furniture and healthcare. Further, the companies under investment should operate according to Islamic financial rules; that is, free of any forbidden (*haram*) financial practices involving
    - Interest (*riba*)
    - Gambling and pure games of chance (*maisir*)
    - Excessive risk and speculations (*gharar*)
    - Any other forbidden component in commercial dealings.
2. Business activities not permissible under *Shari'ah* include conventional insurance and banking, gambling, liquor and liquor-associated activities, pork and pork-connected businesses, non-*halal* beverages and food, *Shari'ah* non-compliant entertainment, tobacco and tobacco-associated businesses, and other businesses that are believed to be *Shari'ah* non-compliant.
3. Mixed activities are a blend of both allowable and non-permissible business activities. While it is straightforward to filter allowable and non-permissible stocks under *Shari'ah*, the challenge remains in the mixed class.

3.4-4 Qualitative and Quantitative Screening Criteria

Shari'ah screening methods have been approved by the Accounting and Auditing Organization for Islamic Financial Institutions (AAOIFI), which is a standard-setting body in the fields of accounting and auditing for Islamic financial institutions. The *Shari'ah* screening methods provide procedures to screen companies that do not conform with *Shari'ah* principles in their businesses. The criteria eliminate the companies whose financing norms do not meet the lowest possible acceptable levels (Table 3.1).

TABLE 3.1 Comparison of *Shari'ah* Screening Methodology

S&P Dow Jones	*FTSE*
Stocks or securities are first screened by employing a sector-wise screening, and then a stock-based ratio screening system.	Utilising the following screening methodology: Industry activity screening followed by financial ratio screening

According to the AAOAFI, there are two types of *Shari'ah* screening: business sector screening and financial ratio screening / quantitative screening.

3.4-4-1 Business Sector Screens

Shari'ah screening contributors, such as the FTSE Global Islamic Index, Dow Jones Global Islamic Market Index, and S&P Shari'ah Index, consider both the qualitative and quantitative aspects. The quantitative aspect is looking for the contribution of *Shari'ah* non-compliant businesses to the whole revenue and profit before tax of the unit. The qualitative standpoint, on the other hand, reflects the public sensitivity and the image of the firm's businesses from the point of view of Islamic teaching. The following qualitative screenings are not allowable under *Shari'ah* and therefore, do not qualify for *Shari'ah*-compliant investing:

- Alcohol, tobacco, and pork-related products
- Companies linked to financial interest (*riba*)
- Non-*halal* leisure (e.g. non-*halal* hotels, cinema/movie theatres, gambling, music, pornography)
- Weapons/arms and ammunition
- Traditional financial services (e.g. insurance, interest banking)
- Biotechnology companies engaged in human or animal genetic engineering.

A company should satisfy that at least 95% of its gross revenues are created by businesses other than those stated in these screening criteria. Some *Shari'ah* scholars have also prevented some printing and media sector firms (e.g. *Playboy* magazine and nude photographs), excluding newspapers. One common reason for the elimination of firms from the above stated industries through qualitative screening is that humans are instructed to participate in good things and work for virtue. The products of several of the industries stated above have been explicitly outlawed in Islamic teachings.

3.4-4-2 Financial Ratio Screening/Quantitative Screening

The objective of financial ratio screens is to eliminate firms that do not conform to a minimum appropriate level of leverage, receivables, and interest income. The

TABLE 3.2 Comparison of Quantitative *Shari'ah* Screening

S&P Dow Jones	*FTSE*
Sector screens Income from the following tainted sources should not exceed 5% of revenue: – Alcohol – Tobacco – Pork-related products – Traditional financial services – Weapons/arms and ammunition – Unlawful entertainment (e.g. hotels, casinos, cinemas, pornography) **Accounting-based screens** Debt or impure interest income of all of the following must be less than 33%: – Total debt divided by trailing 24-month average market capitalisation – The sum of a firm's cash and interest-bearing securities divided by trailing 24-month average market capitalisation – Account receivables divided by trailing 24-month average market capitalisation (Hassan and Mollah, 2018)	**Business-related screening** The following business-related activities are *Shari'ah* non-compliant: – Traditional finance – Alcohol or any activity related to alcohol – Pork-related products and food-production, packaging and processing, or any activity related to pork – Unlawful entertainment (e.g. casinos, haram hotel businesses, gambling) – Tobacco, weapons, arms and defence manufacturing **Financial ratio screening** The following are considered *Shariah*-compliant: – Debt is less than 33.33% of total assets – Cash and interest-bearing items are less than 33.33% of total assets – Accounts receivable and cash are less than 50% of total assets – Total interest and non-compliant business income must not exceed 5% of total revenue (Hassan and Mollah, 2018)

financial ratio measurements system has developed over time (Table 3.2). Corresponding to the AAOIFI, a company would develop various *Shari'ah* standards which are acceptable for *Shari'ah*-compliant investments if a company meets the following criteria in terms of level of debt, receivables or financial interest (*riba*) income:

- Conventional debt/total assets < 30%
- [(Cash + interest-bearing deposits)/total assets] < 30%
- [(Total interest income + income from non-compliant activities)/total revenues] < 5%
- Accounts receivable/total assets < 45%.

(AAOIFI Shari'ah Standard No. 21)

The above figures show how diverse is the *Shari'ah* screening methodology implemented by S&P Dow Jones and FTSE. Other than sector screening and financial ratio criteria, some rules are seen also as a cleansing mechanism to purify investments that are corrupted and so fall under prohibited activities. The cleansing process is usually accomplished by the individual investors, even though in some cases, the Islamic funds/stocks may perform the job on behalf of their investors.

For example, if a certain portion of the income from interest-bearing accounts (forbidden by *Shari'ah*) is contained in the income of the firm, the proportion of such income in the dividend given to the shareholder must be distributed to charity and must not be held by the shareholders. This is known as purification or dividend cleansing.

3.5 Flow of Funds in the Islamic Capital Market

There are two major components in the matter of choice of financial architecture: bank based and market based. Market-based systems are exemplified by substantial and active capital markets where firms are able to raise external funds by issuing equity and debt securities. On the other hand, bank-based systems are characterised by Islamic financial institution (IFI) systems where the banks are the major source of external finance. The Islamic capital market precludes the components of interest and replace profits in investments based on a profit-sharing ratio. In the average business, there are some consumers who have income which is more than their expenditures. Such individuals are identified as savings surplus units (SSUs). These individuals are mandated to pay *Zakah* (alms) on their surplus wealth endowment every year that their wealth is above the *Nisab* (the minimum amount that a Muslim must have before being obliged to give *Zakah*). Therefore, to escape a reduction in wealth and to get any genuine return on their surplus savings, these SSUs have to make investments in the real economy.

In the Islamic or *Shari'ah* asset market, savings deficient units (SDU) have:

$$\left(Y_t - C_t\right) < 0 \text{ for consumers and } K_t < C_t \text{ for firms}$$

where
Y = earnings or incomes at the time t
C = cost at the time t
K = investment at time t

For generating finance, firms will offer investments to SSUs at a particular profit-sharing ratio. No fixed stipulated increment on investment is offered to SSUs, be they individuals or financial institutions. On the other hand, in the case of the SDU, it happens the opposite.

The factors that determine the offered profit-sharing ratio include the following:

- Sum of capital required
- Period of investing
- Incentive to variability ratio of the investment undertaking.

It may be noted that the larger the capital investing and the length of investment undertaking, the greater will be the extended in profit-sharing ratio. Although there should be a higher reward-to-variability ratio, there may also be a smaller amount offered in the profit-sharing ratio. The Islamic equity financing–centred capital market does not have an inherent conflict between savings and investments. Both respond uniformly to the internal intensity of the investment activity (i.e. reward-to-variability ratio).

In Figure 3.4, the curve along the horizontal line indicates the SDU demand for capital investing. On the other hand, in Figure 3.5 the upward sloping line illustrates the SSU supply of investable funds at the various levels of profit-sharing ratios. Equilibrium will occur where the profit-sharing ratio is equivalent: the amount of capital financed by the investors will be equal to the capital investment companies need. Generally, the higher the capital requirement, the longer duration of investment, and the lower Sharpe ratio theory will oblige the companies to offer a higher profit-sharing ratio.

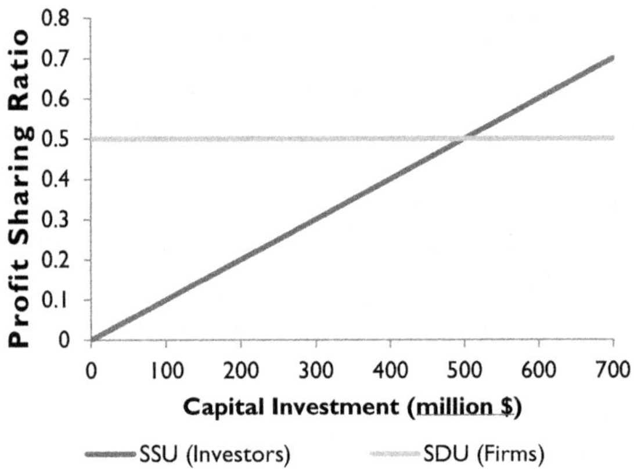

FIGURE 3.4 *Shari'ah*-based asset market.

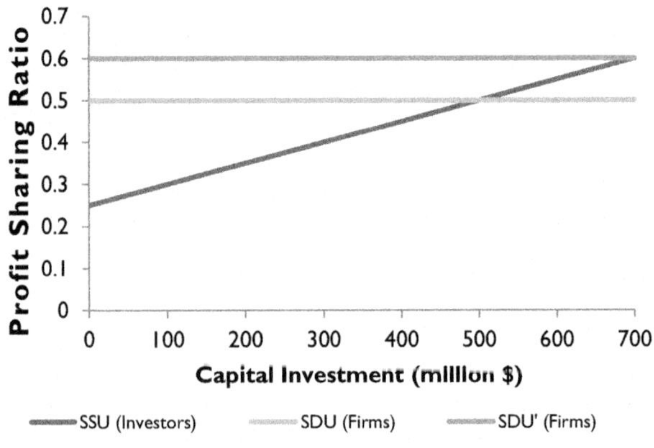

FIGURE 3.5 *Shari'ah*-based asset market.

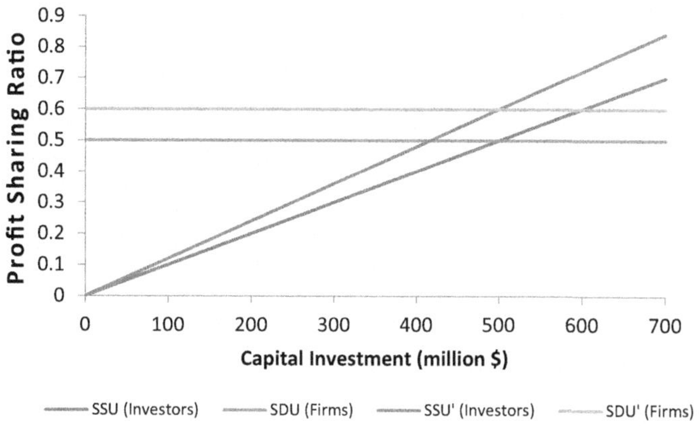

FIGURE 3.6 *Shari'ah*-based asset market.

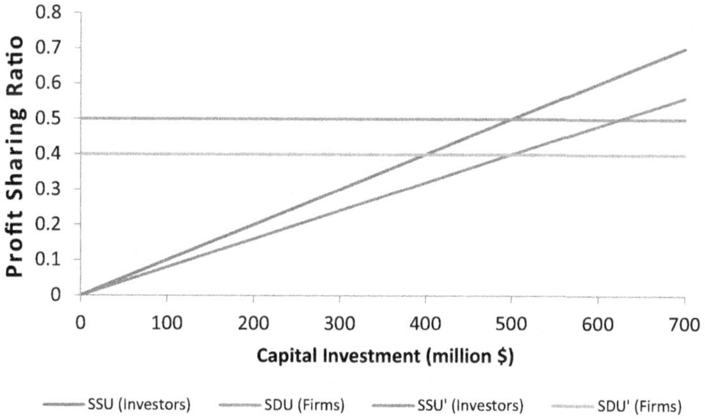

FIGURE 3.7 *Shari'ah*-based asset market.

Then again, greater impatience of customers would make indifference curves steeper; henceforth the SSU curve would shift on the left and show it steeper. Further, the SSU would become steeper because of higher risk aversion. Therefore, companies will have to react by raising the profit-sharing ratio for inducing patient and risk-averse consumers to take part in capital investments. Figures 3.6 and 3.7 show the rightward and leftward shift, respectively, in the SSU investment supply curve. In view of this, the prior assessment shows that improvement in the profit-loss sharing ratio can perform the asset allocation function in the Islamic capital market.

3.6 Liquidity Issues in the Islamic Capital Market

Like all investors, those investing in Islamic assets should manage liquidity so they can feel self-confident about meeting their current and future financial obligations.

However, investors in the Islamic capital market may face the following concerns that investors in traditional assets do not face.

Islamic capital product growth is slow as compared to traditional financial product development. Therefore, Islamic investors do not have as much highly liquid investment options as traditional investors do. There are three causes for this:

1. The market share for Islamic investments is still small compared to the conventional capital markets.
2. Islamic investments must conform with *Shari'ah*, which involves screening processes involving arguments among scholars that may be quite time-consuming.
3. Investors occasionally lack access to the Islamic capital market. For instance, since there is a lack of financial infrastructure, a customer in UK may not be capable to gain access to the US-based Islamic asset market as easily as they can enter the traditional market. For want of market access, they will lack the ability to turn their investments into cash as rapidly as they can in the traditional markets.

3.7 Regulatory and Legal Frameworks of the Islamic Capital Market

The Islamic capital market is regulated and regulated by regulatory bodies like government regulation formulated in the line with the IFSB and AAOIFI standards. Because the Islamic capital market is in its infancy, regulation in this aspect is also in development. Usually, the conventional capital market authority in any particular country supervises the Islamic capital market as well. Even though Islamic capital markets have *Shari'ah* supervisory boards that are particularly responsible for *Shari'ah*-related matters of Islamic capital market business, all IFIs need to be regulated and monitored carefully. This is vital to protect the funds of investors against the breakdowns of intermediaries and to ensure redistributive policies and prevent financial crime (Ibrahim, 2020). The regulatory goal might be attained through the regulation of securities and financial institutions and through efficient corporate governance at the top. The uniqueness of IFIs makes establishing the standards and regulations of their control a formidable task. This describes the justification for divergent opinions with respect to developing a structure for supervising and regulating Islamic financial institutions (Jobst et al., 2008, Hassan and Mollah, 2018).

However, there is advancement in this area, as a number of global Islamic financial infrastructure institutions are making efforts to harmonise the functions of different IFIs across the world. These institutions are the Accounting and Auditing Organization for Islamic Financial Institutions (AAOIFI), the Islamic Financial Services Board (IFSB), the Liquidity Management Centre (LMC), the International Islamic Financial Market (IIFM), the International Liquidity Islamic Management Corporation (ILIM), and the International Islamic Rating Agency (ISRA, 2011).

Given the importance of the Islamic capital market in economic growth and development, it is critical to shield the market with a legal framework. This will guarantee that nobody confiscates the advantage of the system ambiguities to misuse them. Moreover, there is a solid association between legal protection for financiers and economic development. Likewise, successful legal protection over the enforcement of legal guidelines has a substantial influence on the size of the capital market (Ibrahim, 2020). In other words, outstanding legal rules implementation will lead to the growth and advancement of the Islamic capital market.

3.8 Conclusion

Considering that Islamic financial businesses are subjected to distinct rules separate from the ones appropriate to traditional business operations, there are several challenges being encountered by the Islamic capital market. For instance, in many circumstances, the Islamic capital market has had to conform with the regulatory requirements meant for the traditional system, which has a completely separate underlying approach and objectives. In addition, it should be mentioned that the fairly young Islamic capital market is functioning in the similar environment with its long-standing traditional counterpart, which has been in the arena for centuries.

This chapter highlighted the principles and tenets of Islamic capital which is fast growing mostly because capital market products like Islamic equities and *Sukuk* have a lot of promise that is yet to be exploited. In structuring the different products of the Islamic capital market, there are some ethical norms protected in the Islamic legal procedure that must be ensured. For example, while designing *Sukuk*, it is essential that *Shari'ah* issues are carefully examined. One of the important components of the popularity of the Islamic capital market is *Sukuk*. Likewise, the international Islamic infrastructure institutions are making relentless efforts in instituting Islamic financial standards, regulations and rules with a view to standardise the Islamic market functions globally.

Review Questions

1. Define the Islamic capital market, and state the types of Islamic capital markets that are in operation.
2. What are the Islamic capital market products?
3. Discuss in brief the *Shari'ah* stock process.
4. Compare the stock screening processes between S&P Dow Jones and the FTSE Islamic Index.
5. Discuss liquidity issues in the Islamic capital market.
6. Why is regulation essential for development of the Islamic capital market?

References

Hassan, A and Mollah, S (2018), *Islamic Finance: Ethical Underpinnings, Products and Institutions*, Cham: Palgrave Macmillan

Ibrahim, M (2020), Islamic Banking and Banking Performance in Malaysia: An Empirical Analysis, *Journal of Islamic Monetary Economics and Finance*, 6(3), 487–502

ISRA (2011), *Islamic Financial System*, Kuala Lumpur: International Shari'ah Research Academy for Islamic Finance

Jobst, A, Kunzel, P, Mills, P and Sy, A (2008), Islamic Bond Issuance: What Sovereign Debt Managers Need to Know, *International Journal of Islamic and Middle Eastern Finance and Management*, 1(4), 330–344

4

ISLAMIC EQUITY MARKETS

Learning Objectives

On completing this chapter, learners will be able to:

- Comprehend the concept of Islamic equity and its features
- Explain the types of Islamic equity funds
- Know the global market share of Islamic equity funds
- Learn how to invest in Islamic equities
- Understand Islamic equity indices
- Calculate pricing and valuation of Islamic equities
- Measure the risk of Islamic equity funds.

4.1 Introduction

Conventional financial structures had miserably fallen prey to the ills of the financial crisis as largely witnessed during the subprime market crash of 2007–2008. The *Shari'ah*-compliant Islamic financial system has been evolving since its inception, and it is from the mid-1970s that Islamic finance started embracing modern aspects, thereby rising to the pinnacle of being a successful alternative to existing conventional finance structures. Tenets of *Shari'ah* preach the idea of risk-sharing and advocate the usage of *Mudarabah* and *Musharaka* as profit-sharing instruments instead of financial contracts based on interest.

Risk-sharing is an upholding idea for people in Islamic finance. The ultimate premise is fixated on the equitable and productive sharing of risks, which is not only bounded to the Islamic financial system but also happens to be equally possible for the economy at large. Primarily, equity markets stand to be ideal for practising

DOI: 10.4324/9780429321207-4

risk-sharing. It is undeniably true that stock markets comprise risk-sharing components. To speak from a global perspective, equity markets remain mostly well organised. These markets have been long thriving and are often regulated. A considerable population of Islamic jurists considers investing in modern joint-stock corporations based on the approval of *Shari'ah* norms.

Principles of *Shari'ah* are strictly adhered to while screening the stocks for their acceptability. The screening ensures whether Islamic ethical investors would invest in these equities owing to the nature of stocks, if and only in harmony with *Shari'ah* tenets. Norms of *Shari'ah* imply that any firm involved in tobacco, alcohol, gambling and gaming, conventional insurance and interest-based finance will be excluded from an Islamic portfolio. Domains like entertainment, hotels, and weapons are equally excluded from being considered eligible for investments by ethical investors. Additionally, the application of financial ratios helps in maintaining limits on financial transactions based on interest. These transactions could be in any form of interest-based debt, interest income, cash or other receivables. Funds and portfolios of investors essentially need to be *Shari'ah* compliant. The consistent growth of the investment category of Islamic finance is not only determined by its growing company shares but also the growth in its equity instruments, which is evident from the emergence of unit trusts or mutual funds, real estate investment trusts (REITs), exchange-traded funds (ETFs), venture capital funds, investment funds and structured products depending on *Shari'ah* indices. Islamic equity products have to be characteristically put together in accordance with the ideas of *Shari'ah* principles.

4.2 Types of Islamic Equity

Islam believes in social justice and thus advocates the idea of involvement of investors and entrepreneurs in economic activities that could generate profits or/and losses. In doing so, two of the most broadly used equity products are detailed below.

4.2-1 Mudarabah *Products*

When a financial contract is made under the *Mudarabah* format, it becomes the responsibility of the entrepreneur to manage economic activities which could be property construction, any business or even a joint venture. The capital for making the management possible is provided by the financier. If profit is generated as a result of this economic activity, both the financier and the entrepreneur get to hold a share of the proceeds, whereas on accounts of incurring financial losses, only the financier becomes the bearer. The effort and time put forth by the entrepreneur in managing the economic activity are considered to be his part of the losses. On grounds of proven mismanagement of the economic activity which might have played a key role in the whole loss, the entrepreneur could be subjected to bear financial losses as well.

4.2–2 Musharaka *Products*

When a financial contract is made under the *Musharaka* format, there is an involvement of both the parties, the one investing capital and the other as the entrepreneur. As a part of this joint venture, both parties are subjected to share profit or/ and bear losses as an outcome of the economic activity.

4.3 *Shari'ah* Recognise the Joint-Stock Companies and Trading of Shares in the Secondary Market

Two or more legal persons involved in a business entity constitute a joint-stock corporation. For every financial contribution, the company issues certificates (as an acknowledgement of ownership of stocks) to the contributor. Stocks can be further sold off at any point after that point, resulting in the eventual transfer of ownership of the stocks of the shareholders. *Shari'ah* laws in regard to finance, particularly in equity markets, have been observed to embrace modern concepts without having to give up on their ethical roots. In this context, the Organisation of Islamic Cooperation (OIC) Islamic *Fiqh* Academy has approved share companies, and in the course of doing so has accepted two Western legal concepts: artificial personality and limited liability (ISRA, 2011). When secondary markets are to be considered, sharing of trades form an important prerequisite to ensure liquidity and overall appeal of equity markets. If seen from the traditional Islamic viewpoint, the law approves of trading of products and services which are tangible except for those that aren't *Shari'ah* compliant, as are *Riba, Maisir and Gharar.*

4.3–1 Islamic Investment Funds

Islamic investment funds constitute funds that have to be necessarily *Shari'ah* compliant. Here, investors come together and contribute in a joint venture where they pool their surplus money to be able to generate profits. On subscribing to Islamic investment funds and Islamic mutual funds, subscribers are issued a certificate as a written record of their subscriptions. This document is often termed a certification share and unit trust, mutual fund and so forth. A few of the Islamic investment funds are discussed below.

4.3–2 Shari'ah-*Compliant Stocks*

The name *Shari'ah*-compliant stocks are itself suggestive of the fact that the securities as well as the company's principles are being checked in accordance with *Shari'ah* tenets and only then are approved for investment. The securities are generally that of a public-listed company, its compliance being in harmony with *Shari'ah* principles assured in all possible categories: primary business, investment activities, and financial position. The Islamic stock index providers (such as Dow Jones, S&P, and

MSCI) are responsible for ensuring the classification of these securities by applying both qualitative as well as quantitative approaches. The use of these methods helps in determining the benchmarks for business activities and financial ratios, which further helps in evaluating the *Shari'ah* status of the same securities.

4.3–3 Islamic Mutual Funds

The functional approach of Islamic mutual funds is similar to that of a conventional fund; the only distinguishable characteristic is that funds are deployed in *Shari'ah*-compliant investments only.

To explain *Shari'ah*-compliant investments in simpler terms, they are funds which are designed on the basis of the principles of Islam (i.e. they are free of *Riba* [interest] and *Gharar* [speculation]). Investments in Islamic mutual funds are made in shares of joint stock companies, and the resulting profits are earned through capital gains in the shares.

4.3–4 Mixed Islamic Funds

Mixed Islamic funds allow subscriptions to be made under different types of investments comprising equities, leasing, commodities, and the like. The share of mixed Islamic funds is subjected to negotiation in the market, considering the fact that tangible assets of the fund constitute 51% or more, whereas liquidity and debts constitute 49% or less.

In 2019, Malaysia had 440 Islamic funds estimated at $32 billion. In the global context, Islamic funds represented $140 billion in the same year. Iran became the fastest-growing Islamic fund asset market worldwide. Out of the non-Muslim countries venturing into the domain of offering investment funds, the United States and Luxembourg were the most active.

Investments in Islamic equities come with an assurance that the funds are being used in purchasing assets that are *Shari'ah* compliant. Apart from this advantage, investments made in Islamic equities have other benefits as well. Some of these include the following:

- Transparency: To be in compliance with *Shari'ah* tenets is one of the major objectives of the Islamic equity funds, and this demands a high level of transparency from the fund managers subject to the kinds of industries and companies they would invest in.
- Financial screening: Screening is inevitable to ensure that equity assets are in full sync with *Shari'ah* laws. In doing so, a company's financials and the amount of debt they carry are taken into consideration. Often considered more conservative than conventional equity funds, Islamic equity funds would not invest in firms that possess high debt amounts, so as to avoid higher risks.
- Diversification: Investments made in funds (Islamic or conventional) buying assets from a diverse set of companies help in reducing the risk of losing capital during any disaster or the company going bankrupt and such other similar conditions.

TABLE 4.1 Global Market Share in Islamic Asset Management

Country	*Share in Islamic Fund Assets (2019, in %)*
Malaysia	31.7
Ireland	8.6
United States	5.3
Luxembourg	4.8
Indonesia	3.0
Kuwait	2.5
South Africa	2.4
Pakistan	2.3
Saudi Arabia	1.3
Jersey	0.5
Cayman Islands	0.3
United Arab Emirates	0.3
Others	37.1

Source: Islamic Financial Services Stability Report (2020).

TABLE 4.2 Number of Islamic Funds Outstanding Worldwide, 2019

Country	*Number of Islamic Funds*
Malaysia	440
Iran	165
United States	6
Luxembourg	161
Indonesia	234
Kuwait	18
South Africa	118
Pakistan	178
Saudi Arabia	206

Source: Statistics.com (2020).

- Liquidity: Islamic investors choose to invest in funds rather than make fixed-term investments because of the liquidity benefit offered in the former case. This means that in adverse situations when the investor would need his cash back, the process is easier. Having said so, it also must be remembered that all kinds of Islamic investments, including those of Islamic funds, are comparatively less liquid than their conventional counterparts.

4.3–5 Islamic Assets Under Management

In Islamic investment literature, when a group of investors puts their resources into a fund and purchases stock collectively, it becomes crucial for that fund to be managed. This activity is defined as fund management. More often than not, a manager is recruited to manage the fund. The collective purchasing decision is taken primarily because the investors might not be able to individually buy the stock. Both commercial banks and investment banks ensure the provision of fund management services. At present, the number of investment banks offering these services is comparatively larger than commercial banks. As Islamic finance is asset based, fund management is more likely to be a better business strategy for Islamic financial institutions (IFIs) than commercial banking. In 2018, approximately 323 Islamic funds were reported to be offering *Shari'ah*-compliant products in the low risk/moderate return, balanced risk/return, and high risk/high return categories and operating in Saudi Arabia, Bahrain, Kuwait, Qatar, Pakistan, Malaysia, Singapore, Germany, the United States, the United Kingdom, and Ireland. These are primarily equity funds and mutual funds, while a few of them are into real estate, hybrid funds or *Takaful* funds.

Managing funds comes in two different ways: the *Mudarabah* basis or through an agency. The *Mudarabah* system comprises the manager or the *mudarib*, who earns a share of the realised profit as a part of agreement made before. If funds are managed via an agency, the manager is paid a fee or some part of the net asset value of the fund. Based on the usage and kinds of returns, Islamic investment funds can be classified in multiple ways. The categories include equity funds, *Ijarah* funds, commodity funds, *Murabahah* funds, and mixed funds. Their usages are vastly different from one another. For instance, proceeds of the equity funds are invested in the shares of joint stock companies, and any returns as capital gains or dividends are paid back to the shareholders on a pro rata basis, whereas *Ijarah* funds are used to buy assets that can be leased. The lease income is divided among subscribers to the fund. *Ijarah Sukuk* can be traded in the secondary market, and the new buyer gets hold of all the rights and obligations of the seller. On the other hand, commodity funds can be used to purchase commodities for resale. The profits generated from funds are distributed among subscribers.

Murabahah funds can be described as closed-ended funds that cannot be resold in the secondary market, the sole reason being that Islamic banks do not have tangible assets. Mixed funds are used to purchase different sets of assets which could be equities and commodities and assets for leasing. The trading of mixed funds is possible only when 51% of their assets are tangible and the rest intangible.

The development of *Shari'ah*-compliant products serve the purpose of equity and debt securitisation along with being used as derivatives. Places for banking, brokering, investment and *Shari'ah* advisory services have put up rules adhering to the principles of Islamic tenets.

Equity financing is crucial to Islamic financing. Profit-sharing agreements called *Uqud Al-Isytirak* (including *mudarabah* and *musharaka*) facilitated the process and accomplishment of equity financing.

The two types of equity financing instruments are

- *Mudarabah*, or profit sharing
- *Musharaka*, or profit and loss sharing.

The traditional interest-based approach of debt financing does not comply with *Shari'ah* principles. In Islam, debt financing is attained when an existing asset is made the subject of a sale or purchase contract. Such a contract is known as *Uqud Al-Mu'awadat* (a contract in which parties make an exchange of goods and services).

The familiar Islamic debt instruments are:

- The *Murabahah*, or trade with mark-up or cost plus
- *Ijarah*, or lease contracts
- *Bai 'al-Salam*, or purchases made in advance
- *Istisna*, or purchase order.

In *Ijarah*, two different types of leasing are recognised as per *Shari'ah*: operating lease and finance lease.

4.3–6 Growth in Islamic Funds Assets

The global reach of functional *Shari'ah*-compliant mutual funds within *Shari'ah*-compliant asset management has reached more than 1,410. The overall global Islamic assets under management are estimated to be at US$110 billion (Table 4.3).

In the context of the Islamic financial market structure, *Sukuk* refers to a debt instrument representing a proportionate ownership of the underlying asset. This underlying physical asset is generally financed using Islamic trade and lease (*Ijarah*) modes of financing. The funding from the asset comes from issuing participation certificates (*Sukuk*) to the investors. Returns of these assets are generated in the form of profit on sale or rentals on the usage of assets which are paid to the issuer of *Sukuk*.

Sukuk makes an exceptional contribution to the total assets of Islamic finance industry, the value of which scaled up to US$426 billion in 2017. Overall, 19 countries observed *Sukuk* issuances, amounting to US$85 billion in 2017. Among

TABLE 4.3 Growth in Islamic Funds Assets

Year	*Islamic Funds (Billion US$)*	*Sukuk (Billion US$)*
2012	46	260
2013	54	284
2014	59	299
2015	66	342
2016	91	345
2017	110	426

Source: Thomson Reuters Report (2017).

these, agency *Sukuk* constituted a share of 6%, whereas sovereign issuances and corporate issuances constituted shares of 31% and 63%, respectively.

4.4 Characteristics of Islamic Equity

The first and foremost characteristic of a business is that it has to be *halal*, meaning that businesses will not include prohibited activities like gambling, the sale of alcohol or any financial dealings involving the practice of *riba* and *gharar*. However, one might question the authenticity of practicing halal for the entire business, and relatedly, what would happen if the main business is *halal* but some parts of the same are involved in interest-based activities. Some Islamic scholars disapprove of the purchase and sale of such stocks because these business activities imply that the shareholders agree to be a part of these practices which do not stand in full accord with *Shari'ah* laws. However, in today's context, it is nearly impossible to find companies which are 100% *Shari'ah* compliant in the sense that every aspect of their business is in full conformity to *Shari'ah*. If a strict operational definition of what is meant by lawful or ethical business is framed, it would result in a very narrow universe of *Shari'ah*-compliant stocks that an individual can invest in. Several *Shari'ah* scholars put forth arguments on a joint-stock company being different from a partnership. For the former, shareholders who are owners do not hold much power in influencing the decisions of the company compared to one that is based on a partnership model. Therefore, the decisions taken by the company cannot be wholly attributed to individual shareholders. Hence, many scholars are of the opinion that if certain parts of the business are involved in non-permissible activities, it does not necessarily make the whole business illegal. Therefore, *Shari'ah* decisions on compliant equities do consider the current realities of the society. In a market where the regulatory framework is more established, this is clearly defined with regard to *Shari'ah* compliances. Examples in this context could be cited from regulatory authorities in the criteria of the Dow Jones Islamic Index in the United States and Meezan Islamic Fund in Pakistan that constitute their standards. Even if these two standards have different levels of stringency, the results arising from their individual screening processes are not likely to be substantially different (ISRA).

Conformity to *Shari'ah* principles is not only limited to funds being invested in legal activities but also extends to if and how these same funds are structured in harmony with *Shari'ah*. This means that every financial product must abide by underlying principles that are associated with the concepts or contracts of the products that *Shari'ah* talks about. This also includes the *Shari'ah* endorsement and certification processes (Safiullah and Shamsuddin, 2019).

Profits earned through a fixed return on capital must be shared on a pro rata basis. No guarantee can be ensured on the principal or rate of profit. The principles of profit-and-loss sharing will be based on either of the contracts made: *mudarabah* or *musharaka*.

Negotiation of shares becomes possible depending on the liquid assets owned by the company. If all or a substantial proportion of the assets are in liquid form, they cannot be bought or sold off except at par value. This means that ownership interest is related to ownership of a real business. The reflection of the same can be easily identified in the existence of real assets. If shares are inclusive of only money assets, the money cannot be traded except at par value. This requirement is representative of an important *Shari'ah* principle that money has to be used as a medium of exchange and not as a means to earn more money.

4.5 Islamic Equity Market Indexes

The most promising feature of all established equity capital markets worldwide is the equity market index. It is a number, the computation of which takes place in real time to reflect the current price level of its designated components. It is generally used as a benchmark or an indicator of the performance of a given stock exchange. Media reports the performance of the equity markets by quoting these indexes (or indices). Financial analysts and stock market observers often use these indices during their discussions. Some of the well-known Islamic indices include the Dow Jones Islamic Market Index, the Standard & Poor's Islamic Index, and the FTSE Islamic Index.

Equity market indexes serve the following key roles:

1. As a measure of the overall performance of an equity market, indices are considered to be representative of the strength of a financial system as well as the economy. The relationship shared between index levels and general economic conditions is generally that of a positive one. When there is a positive economic outlook, indices tend to be on the upward trend.
2. Indexes are often used directly in certain investment instruments (e.g. index-linked mutual funds and funds based on trading exchanges). The asset composition of such funds depends directly on the make-up of the related index. Thus, the performance of the said index funds typically tracks the performance of the index in question closely.
3. Indexes are also used as the benchmark or reference point in accountability and measuring of performance of assets or fund managers. The return performance of funds is often compared directly against the performance of indexes. Hence, if a fund outperforms a given established index, the fund automatically is viewed positively by investors and the market.
4. One measure of the risk of a stock is the stock's beta. A common method of computing beta is via regression of the stock's historical returns against the corresponding historical returns of an index. Beta measures systematic risk, as defined by the capital asset pricing model (CAPM). A stock's beta is an important variable in investment or portfolio decision-making.

4.5-1 Relative Performance of Islamic and Conventional Indexes

Sacrifices need not be made by Muslim investors on financial performances to be able to participate in Islamic capital market investments that are in full accord with *Shari'ah* ethics. Global evidence from cross-country studies suggests that the systematic risk and lower volatility rate of Islamic indices help them outdo their conventional counterparts, particularly during crisis periods. Table 4.4 shows that Islamic indices have outperformed conventional market indices subjected to annual returns, the only exception being that of emerging markets. Even during the financial crisis of 2007–2010, Islamic indices did not have a lower annual standard deviation (SD) of returns. Here, the exceptions are S&P 500 and S&P Europe. However, it was during the post-crisis period from 2011 to 2016 that Islamic indices suffered a lower SD and coefficient of variation.

Table 4.3 portrays how post the financial crisis of 2007–2010, Islamic indexes recovered quite well and in fact, more than the conventional market indices. However, Islamic indexes are seen to have a lower coefficient of variation and hence, a higher reward to variability ratio.

TABLE 4.4 Comparative Performance Between Islamic and Conventional Indexes

Measures/Groups	*Annualised Return (%)*			*Annualised Standard Deviation (%)*			*Coefficient of Variation*		
Islamic	07–16	07–10	11–16	07–16	07–10	11–16	07–16	07–10	11–16
S&P Developed Shari'ah	6.24	1.65	8.53	17.42	23.47	13.41	2.79	14.25	1.57
S&P Global Shari'ah	5.74	1.63	7.79	17.23	23.41	13.10	3.00	14.36	1.68
S&P Emerging Shari'ah	1.36	2.36	0.85	20.04	28.20	14.33	14.78	11.92	16.82
S&P 500 Shari'ah	9.88	6.37	12.14	19.67	25.40	14.89	1.99	3.99	1.23
S&P Europe 350 Shari'ah	8.05	4.94	10.03	19.14	23.61	15.64	2.38	4.78	1.56
Conventional	07–16	07–10	11–16	07–16	07–10	11–16	07–16	07–10	11–16
S&P Developed Index	5.89	1.94	8.42	17.70	22.75	13.53	3.01	11.75	1.61
S&P Global Index	5.66	2.92	7.42	17.54	22.62	13.31	3.10	7.76	1.79
S&P Emerging Index	4.85	13.24	−0.52	20.14	26.04	15.21	4.16	1.97	−29.22
S&P 500 Index	9.09	3.14	12.91	25.64	27.89	24 14	5.39	8.87	4.19
S&P Europe 350 Index	5.51	−0.35	9.26	20.95	25.52	17.42	3.80	−73.71	1.88

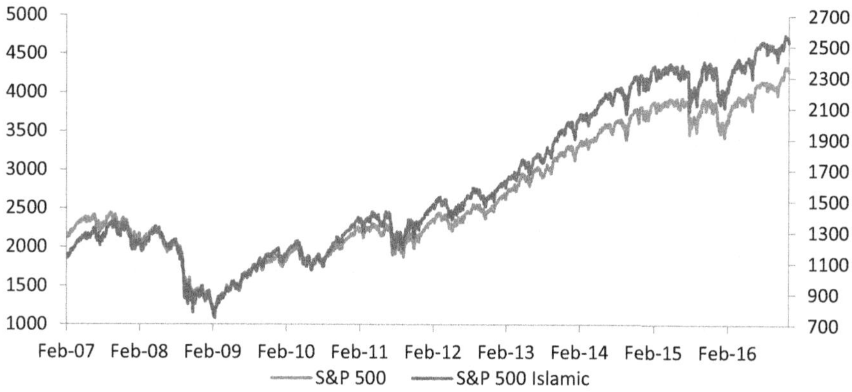

FIGURE 4.1 Daily closing values of S&P 500 Islamic and S&P 500 conventional indexes.

Figure 4.1 shows that the correlation between both indices was 0.9895 during 2007–2016. In the formal co-integration test, the results are that the values of S&P 500 Islamic and S&P 500 conventional indexes are co-integrated, thereby concluding that there is a long-term relationship between the two indexes.

4.5–2 Significance of Islamic Equity Investments

Investors are mostly on the lookout for equity investments, as they have a better ability to share in the profits and growth of a firm. An investor's stake in the company in terms of proportion of the company's shares is represented through equity. When lifetime resources are not needed for current consumption, Islamic equity investments aid in their growth overtime. A proper analysis of risks and returns has to be the prerequisite before making any decision on investments because investors desire more returns and less risk. When risk arises, most risk-averse investors will prefer a proportionately higher increase in returns for the constant increase in risk, as illustrated in Figure 4.2. The goal for an investor in equity investments is to attain the highest possible returns for a specific risk or to reduce the risk of achieving a given target level of return.

According to Markowitz portfolio theory (1952), risk appears in two forms: diversifiable risk and non-diversifiable risk. Diversifiable risk is non-systematic, firm-specific risk and can be reduced through portfolio diversification comprising financial assets that have less than perfect correlation. Non-diversifiable risk, on the other hand, is a systematic risk that cannot be reduced through further diversification.

Figure 4.3 shows how the increase in the number of stocks in the portfolio tends to reduce unsystematic risk. A well-diversified portfolio has only systematic risk. It must be kept in mind that a risky portfolio of less than perfectly correlated assets tends to offer better risk/return opportunities as compared to the individual

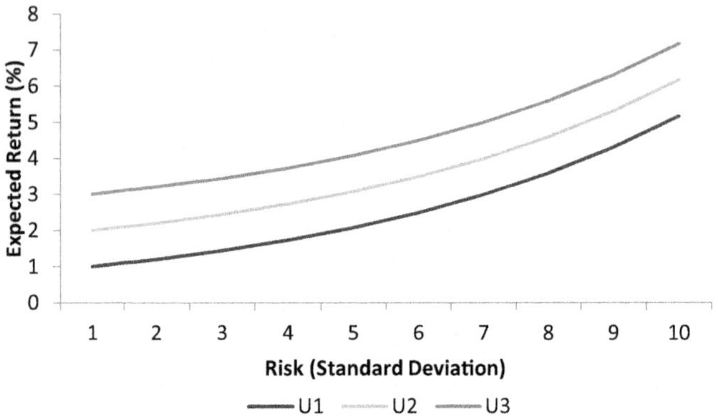

FIGURE 4.2 Risk/return preferences of investor in utility curve.

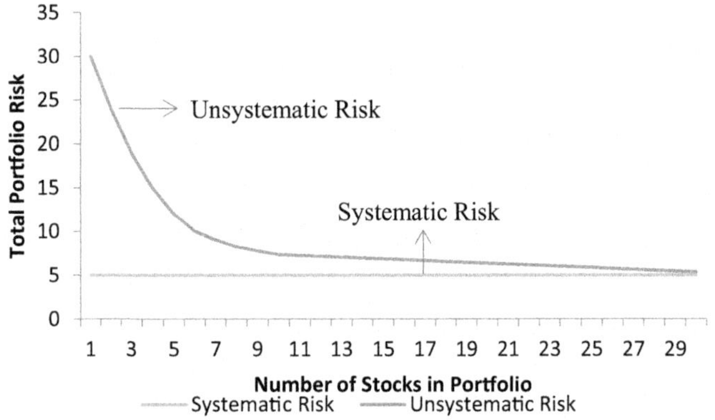

FIGURE 4.3 Risk of overall portfolio of securities.

constituent of securities on their own. This is why when some stocks move downwards, others rise upwards and help in the reduction of overall risk.

Further, according to Markowitz portfolio theory (1952), investors assess investment opportunities in terms of return and risk. Because the expected utility of investors is a decreasing function of risk (risk aversion) and an increasing function of return, investors' preferences are represented by the indifference curve. The indifference curve represents those risk and return combinations for which the investor is indifferent (i.e. obtains the same utility).

Corresponding to the modern portfolio theory, investors analyse investment opportunities in terms of return and risk. According to Markowitz (1952), an efficient portfolio has the highest return subjecting to a specific level of risk, or alternatively, no other portfolio will have a low risk for the specific return level. Along with an efficient frontier, the preferences of investors about risk and return, the equilibrium can be illustrated where the investor chooses an optimal portfolio

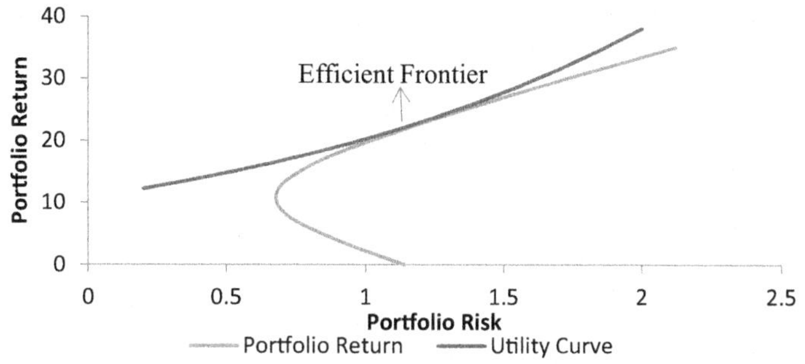

FIGURE 4.4 Investor choices optimal portfolio.

as portrayed in Figure 4.4. An optimal portfolio on an efficient frontier is one that is tangent to the investor's indifferent curve.

Opting for the optimum portfolio of the risky assets depends on the liking of individual investors. This justifies the reality of Islamic funds. Islamic portfolios are inclusive of growing and small-cap stocks. On the other hand, value and mid-cap stocks are dealt with under conventional portfolios (Girard and Hassan, 2008).

The traditional nature of Islamic equity investment acts as an impetus to make people feel assured of protection against risk extremes and excessive volatility in the conventional equity market. This is primarily why and how Islamic finance has witnessed exceptional growth over the years. Portfolio diversification and strategies subject to hedging constitute the chief distinguishable characteristics between Islamic finance and conventional finance. For Islamic ethical investors with surplus endowments, the available investment avenues would include *Shari'ah*-compliant investments, mutual fund investments, and direct equity investments.

4.6 Price and Valuation of Equity

4.6–1 Using Price-to-Earnings Ratio to Evaluate Stock

The price-to-earnings ratio (P/E ratio) can be defined as the ratio for valuing a company that measures its current share price relative to its earnings per share (EPS is a company's net profit divided by the number of the common shares outstanding). The P/E ratio is often termed the price multiple or the earnings multiple. Investors and analysts use the P/E ratio for determining the relative value of a company's shares subject to comparisons that are reasonable as well as relevant. At the same time, the P/E ratio helps to evaluate a company against its own historical record or to compare aggregate markets against one another or over a considerable period of time.

Price-to-earnings (P/E) ratio = Market value per share / Earnings per share (EPS)

To determine the P/E value, one needs to divide the current stock price by the earnings per share (EPS). An example is illustrated below.

Al Rajhi Bank in Saudi Arabia closed the financial year of 2020 showing the following data:

EPS = US$2.72
Share price = US$25.21
Al-Rajhi's P/E = US$9.27

The data tells us that Al-Rajhi Bank was trading at approximately nine times earnings. However, the 9.27 P/E by itself does not serve as a significant determining factor unless it is compared with something else. A relevant comparison could be made to that of the stock's industry group, a benchmark index, or the historical P/E range of a stock.

Al-Rajhi's P/E was lower than the S&P 500, which typically averages around 15 times earnings. However, it is crucial that the company's P/E must be compared to those of its peers. For example, SABIC had a P/E of $10.76 by the end of 2020. In comparison, Al-Rajhi's P/E scored a little above 9, whereas SABIC's P/E reached almost 11; the former's stock does not appear to be undervalued when put in comparison with the larger market structure.

4.6–2 Price-to-Earnings Ratio and Return on Equity

A company generating more for shareholders will excel in P/E because the P/E is what the shareholders are willing to pay for every dollar earned. On the other hand, the return on equity (ROE) is the return that is generated on the company's equity. In this context, equity corresponds to the summation of share capital of the company along with its retained earnings.

4.6–3 Price-to-Book Ratio and Return on Equity

The ultimate use of the price-to-book ratio (P/B ratio) is done by companies to comparatively analyse a firm's market capitalisation against its book value. This can be defined as an equity valuation ratio. This is a comparison of the market value (stock price per share) to the book value (equity of shareholders). The P/B ratio is expressed in terms of multiple values, which gives us clarity on the number of times book value stock investors are willing to pay for acquiring a company's stock. The company's stock price per share gets divided by its book value per share to get the P/B ratio.

The book value of an asset is synonymous to its carrying value on the balance sheet. The calculation of the same is done by companies by acquiring the asset against the depreciation that has accumulated (Gitman and Zutter, 2014). Book value can be simultaneously defined as the tangible total asset value of a company calculated by deducting intangible assets (e.g. patents, goodwill, and liabilities) from overall assets. The definition can be further explained as the deduction of liabilities shown on the company's balance sheet as a per-share estimate of the liquidation value of the company from its overall recorded assets. The initial outlay of an investment can project book value in terms of the net or gross expenses, such as trading costs, sales taxes, and service charges.

Price-to-book ratio = Market price per share / Book value per share

Value investors have been preferring the P/B ratio for ages, as have market analysts. As per traditional standards, a value under 1.0 is considered a good P/B for value investors, indicating a potentially undervalued stock. However, value investors might opt for stocks with a P/B value under 3.0 as their benchmark.

4.6–4 Return on Equity

Return on equity (ROE) is the measure of a company's annual return (net income) divided by the value of its total shareholders' equity. The ROE is always expressed as a percentage (e.g. 10%). As an alternative method, dividing the firm's dividend growth rate by the retention rate of its earnings (1 – dividend payout ratio) can also help in deriving the ROE. This derivation is a two-part ratio owing to calculating the income statement and the balance sheet together. Here, a comparison is made of net income or profit to the shareholders' equity. The number acts as a representative of the total return on equity capital and depicts the capacity of the firm to generate profits out of equity investments. To put it in simple words, the ROE measures the profits made for each dollar from shareholders' equity. The straightforward calculation of P/B and ROE is shown below:

Price-to-book ratio = Stock price / Shareholder's equity per share
Return on equity = Net income / Average shareholder's equity

The company's latest balance sheet can help in determining the per-share equity figure through the division of shareholders' equity by the number of outstanding shares. Companies with high growth rates are supposed to have high P/B ratios. An example can be taken in the form of a case study of IBM showing the effects of ROE on P/B ratios. IBM's ROE was recorded at 25% in 1983, and its stock traded at three times its book value. However, due to its decreased ROE in 1992 to negative values, it had to trade at book value.

It must be noted that a high P/B ratio does not in any form ensure higher ROE, but it does under certain circumstances. Investors opt for companies offering better ROE. The preference yields into higher company prices. This makes it clear that a low P/B ratio can be observed as an undesirable ROE and return on assets (ROA).

4.6-5 Equity Value and Enterprise Value

The term 'equity value' is popularly known as the market value of equity or market capitalisation. It can be explained in terms of the entire value of the company that becomes attributable to equity investors. A company's share price is multiplied by its number of outstanding shares to attain the equity value. A derivation is made by starting with the company's enterprise value:

Equity value = Share value × Number of shares outstanding

Alternatively,

Equity value = Enterprise value – Debt and debt equivalent – Non-controlling interest – Preferred stock + Cash and cash equivalent

Calculation of equity value from enterprise value will entail deducting debt and debt equivalents, non-controlling interest and preferred stock, and adding cash and cash equivalents. Debt and debt equivalents, non-controlling interest, and preferred stock are deducted because these are representative of other shareholders' shares. The add-ons of cash and cash equivalents are included because any amount of cash remaining after paying off other shareholders is available to equity shareholders, and equity value primarily emphasises what is available to equity shareholders.

4.6-6 Difference Between Market Value of Equity and Book Value of Equity

The equity value of a company cannot be considered synonymous to its book value. The calculation is done by multiplying a company's share price by its number of shares outstanding, whereas book value or shareholders' equity can be calculated as the difference between a company's assets and its liabilities.

The equity value of a company which witnesses healthy growth consistently over the years reaches far ahead of book value, owing to the increased market value of the company's shares. In this regard, equity value is always greater than or equal to zero, because both the share price and the number of shares outstanding can never be negative. Book value can be positive, negative or zero.

4.6-7 Basic Equity Value Versus Diluted Equity Value

A company's share price is multiplied by the number of basic shares outstanding to produce the basic equity value. Any effect of dilution occurring due to securities that are dilutive in nature is not included in the calculation of basic shares outstanding. These securities are inclusive of stock options, restricted and performance stock units, preferred stock, warrants, and debt which is convertible. Basic shares outstanding can be formulated as follows:

Shares outstanding = Issued stocks – Treasury stock

The treasury stock method is primarily used for calculating the dilutive effect of these securities (shares). Outstanding shares are indicative of investor or institutional ownership in a company. On exercising convertible securities, outstanding shares along with additional shares are included in fully diluted shares. Here, the surplus number of shares needs to be added on because of the dilutive effect of securities on the basic securities outstanding.

From the perspective of a valuation amidst an acquisition, money securities are paid off by the buyers and thus, diluted shares outstanding must be used with equity value or when calculating enterprise value because this serves as a stronger determining factor to come up to the cost of acquiring a firm. Once these securities are paid off by the buyers, they convert the same into additional shares for the buyer's, thereby raising the acquisition cost of the company.

4.7 Understanding Measuring of Risks

In an economic context, risk can be defined as the probability of the actual return from an investment turning out to be different from that of the expected return. Therefore, it is imperative to understand the development and social processes as driving forces in modulating risk, because the expected value of the results of one or multiple future events is influenced by risk undertaken. A theoretical perspective might say that the results could be positive or negative, but more often than not, the emphasis is put on the potential harm arising out of a future event. This harm can take the shape of an incurring cost (known as downside risk) or the inability to make any profit (known as upside risk). Financially, the idea of risk corresponds to the idea of losing some, most or, in some cases, the entire amount of one's initial investment. The calculation of the standard deviation of the historical or average return of a specific investment is often considered as an insight in gaining some historical measure of risk. Broadly, two categories of risks include financial risk, which is market dependent and determined by various factors of the market, and operational risk, which occurs as an outcome of fraudulent behaviour (ISRA, 2011).

The relationship between risk and return has to be observed as a crucial ideology in the domain of investment science. Risk rises if the potential return is deemed to be of greater value. This is manifested in the free-market pricing principle of an instrument. Effective demand for a more secure instrument hikes up its price and, simultaneously, lowers the return. Meanwhile, weak demand for a riskier instrument drops its price but elevates its potential return. For example, a UK treasury bond, being a sovereign bond, is considered to be one of the safest investments in comparison to corporate bonds, but the provision of returns is at a lower rate. The justification for this is that a corporation is much more likely to default than the UK government. In order to be appealing to investors, the bond-issuing corporations have to offer a higher rate of returns owing to the higher risk in corporate bonds.

4.7–1 Classifications of Risks

Besides the above-mentioned measures of risk, risk management can be broadly categorised into two types: systematic and unsystematic risk.

4.7-1-1 Systematic Risk

Unpredictable and undiversifiable in nature, systematic risk impacts the entire market of the security. However, hedging can assure risk mitigation. Political upheaval can be an excellent example by which to observe systematic risk. Multiple financial markets including bonds, stocks, and currency markets are affected as a result of political disruption. An investor can protect himself from being at the suffering end of this particular risk by purchasing put options in the market itself.

4.7-1-2 Unsystematic Risk

Unsystematic risk is itself identified as diversifiable risk. Primarily associated with a company or sector, the mitigation of this risk is made possible through asset diversification. The attribution of this risk is specific to a particular stock or industry. For example, an investor has to assume risks corresponding to both the oil industry as well as the company before purchasing oil stocks.

The example can be elaborated in an attempt to comprehend risk undertaking with more clarity. An investor in an oil company can be of the opinion that the downfall of oil prices might affect the company. The investor, to safeguard his position, might purchase from put options on crude oil or on the company. Alternatively, the investor might undertake diversified risks by purchasing stocks in retail or airline companies in an effort to diminish risks. In this way, the investor mitigates certain parts of the risk so as to protect its exposure to the oil industry. If the investor does not consider proper risk management, the investor could end up losing overall investments owing to a sudden downfall of the company's stock and oil price, resulting in adverse impacts on its investment portfolio.

4.7-2 Common Measures of Risk

Risk management forms the crux of investment decision-making. The process entails identification of risks and simultaneously analysing the amount of risk involved in an investment, which results in either acceptance of that risk or taking steps to ensure its mitigation. Some of the common measures of risk include standard deviation, beta, value at risk (VaR), and conditional value at risk (CVaR). The measures are described below.

4.7-2-1 Standard Deviation

The standard deviation helps in measuring the dispersion of data from its expected value. The standard deviation method is helpful in making an investment decision where the amount of historical volatility corresponding with an investment subjected to its annual return rate has to be measured. It acts as an indicator of how much the current return is deviating from its anticipated historical normal returns. Stocks having high standard deviation encounter higher volatility, and thus a higher level of risk is subjected to the return of stock(s).

4.7-2-2 Sharpe Ratio

The Sharpe ratio helps in measuring the performances as modelled by corresponding risks. This method is applied with the removal of return rate on a risk-free investment, like that of the UK treasury bill from the experienced rate of return. It is further divided by the associated investment's standard deviation, thereby becoming indicative of whether an investment's return happens because of wise investing or the assumption of surplus risk.

The Sortino ratio can be viewed as an alternative form of the Sharpe ratio under which the effects of upward price movements on standard deviation are directly removed. This is done to switch the emphasis on the distribution of returns that are below the target or required return. With the Sortino ratio, there is a simultaneous replacement of the risk-free rate with the required return in the numerator of the formula. This helps in making the formula the return of the portfolio less than the required return, divided by the distribution of returns below the target or required return.

Apart from the Sortino ratio, one also needs to observe another variant of the Sharpe ratio, known as the Treynor ratio. In the context of the latter, a portfolio's beta or correlation that the portfolio has with the rest of the market is used. Beta can be understood as the measurement of how volatile and risky a particular investment stands to be in comparison with the entire market. The aim of applying the Treynor ratio is to determine whether compensation is being made to an investor who is involved in taking additional risk beyond the inherent risk of the market. The Treynor ratio formula is the return of the portfolio less the risk-free rate, divided by the portfolio's beta.

4.7-2-3 Beta

Beta constitutes another familiar measuring indicator of risk. The amount of systematic risk an individual security or an industrial sector has subjecting to the whole stock market is measured using beta. The market is at a beta of 1 and helps in measuring the risk of a security. If a security's beta is equivalent to 1, the security's price moves in time step with the market. A market is considered more volatile if the security's beta is greater than 1 and less volatile if the security's beta is less than 1. For example, a security is considered 50% more volatile than the market if its beta is theoretically subjected to 1.5.

4.7-2-4 Value at Risk (VaR)

Value at risk (VaR) is a statistical measure used in assessing levels of risk associated with a portfolio or company. Using the VaR method can help in determining the maximum potential loss with a more confident approach for a specified period. For example, a portfolio of investments having a one-year 10% VaR of US$6 million would mean that there is a 10% chance of losing more than US$6 million over the time period of one year.

4.7-2-5 Conditional Value at Risk (CVaR)

Conditional value at risk (CVaR) is another risk-measuring method which is generally used in assessing the tail risk of an investment. This method is primarily used as an extension to the VaR. The CVaR assesses the probability of a break in the VaR with greater assurance. Furthermore, it analyses what happens to an investment beyond its maximum loss threshold. This measure is more sensitive to events that happen at the tail end of a distribution, termed as the tail risk. For example, a risk manager is of the opinion that the average loss on a US$12 million investment for the worst 1% is a possible outcome. Henceforth, the CVaR, also known as the expected shortfall, is US$12 million for the 1% tail.

4.7-2-6 R-squared

As a statistical measure, R-squared helps in determining the percentage of a fund portfolio or a security's movements in terms of a benchmark index. The US treasury bill acts as the benchmark for fixed-income securities and bond funds. The S&P 500 Index acts as the benchmark for all sorts of equities and equity funds.

R-squared values range from 0 to 100. As per Stein (2018), a mutual fund with an R-squared value ranging between 85 and 100 indicates a performance record which is closely correlated to the index. On the other hand, a fund rated 70 or lower does not perform like the index. Funds having high R-squared ratios are often criticised by most financial analysts as being 'closet' index funds, and thus, mutual fund investors should keep away from this specific category.

4.8 Can Screening of Islamic Stocks Induce Another Risk for Investors?

Because *Shari'ah* principles in investment promote transparency and the sharing of risks and profit and loss, *Shari'ah* screening could help in the reduction of much of these risks that usually emanate from the larger universe in financial investment (ISRA, 2011).

Yet, practitioners often point to the existence of *Shari'ah* risks to include, among others, the complexity of structuring a product to be compliant. This becomes a reality because there exist potential risks that the product may not be approved as targeted and hence the associated costs involved in such undertaking. *Shari'ah* risks may also refer to the different jurisdictions governing different Islamic products and the risks that some products are not accepted in certain markets purely on the basis of *Shari'ah* issues. This could also ensue from the possibility that certain authorities in certain jurisdictions may declare an Islamic product '*Shari'ah* non-compliant' based on new information or line of interpretation.

4.9 Conclusion

Islamic equity revolves around the primary notion of sharing risks as well as rewards. *Mudarabah* and *musharaka* are strong pillars of financial instruments in operationalising Islamic equity. Today's Islamic jurists have approved of modern-day corporations and the secondary market trading of shares. Conventional theories of finance are mostly relied on in regard to equity valuation, thereby indicating a research gap that needs to be fulfilled through Islamic inputs on equity valuation. Financial practices such as preference shares and stock index futures are approved by some *Shari'ah* jurisdictions irrespective of objections and alternative opinions put forth by other jurists. Unit trusts or mutual funds, real estate investment trusts (REITs) and exchange-traded funds (ETFs) equally act as salient instruments in Islamic equity and possess great potential to eventually develop the Islamic capital market. The *Shari'ah* stock-screening process includes two major components: sector screening and financial screening. The stock-screening process raises the issue of dividend purification. The *Shari'ah* stock-screening process is of a dynamic nature because there are still a number of ongoing issues that initiate debates around them. The dynamism provides a huge scope for improvement. All in all, equity market indices and their functionalities in Islamic equity markets are paramount.

Review Questions

1. What is an Islamic equity?
2. What are the types of Islamic equity funds?
3. What are the characteristics of Islamic equity investment?
4. Why is the Islamic benchmark used in comparing Islamic equity performance?
5. How are the earnings per share, return on equity, price-to-book ratio and price-to-earning ratio calculated?
6. Define beta, R-square and value at risk.

References

Girard, E and Hassan, M (2008), Is There a Cost to Faith Based Investing: Evidence from FTSE Islamic Indices, *Journal of Investing*, 17(4), 112–121

Gitman, L and Zutter, C (2014), *Principles of Managerial Finance*, New Yok: Pearson

IFSB (2020), *Islamic Financial Service Feasibility Report 2020*, Kuala Lumpur: Islamic Financial Service Board

ISRA (2011), *Islamic Financial System*, Kuala Lumpur: International Shari'ah Research Academy for Islamic Finance

Markowitz, H (1952), Portfolio Selection, *Journal of Finance*, 7(1), 71–91

Safiullah, Md and Shamsuddin, A (2019), Risk-Adjusted Efficiency and Corporate Governance: Evidence from Islamic and Conventional Banks, *Journal of Corporate Finance*, 55(C), 105–140

Statistics.com (2020), retrieved from www.statista.com/statistics/1092680/worldwide-number-of-islamic-funds-outstanding-by-country/ (Access date March 21, 2021)

Stein, W (2018), *The Morningstar Dictionary- R-Squire*, retrieved from www.morningstar.com/articles/873622/the-morningstar-dictionary-r-squared (Access date January 2, 2019)

Thomson Reuters Report (2017), *Islamic Finance Development Report 2017*, #IFDI2017, Islamic Corporation for the Development of the Private Sector (ICD)-Thomson Reuters.

5

INVESTMENT IN ISLAMIC MUTUAL FUNDS

A Vehicle for Mobilisation of Small Savings

Learning Objectives

On completing this chapter, learners will be able to:

- Explain Islamic mutual funds and their corresponding features
- Describe the types of Islamic mutual funds
- Understand net asset value (NAV) and how to calculate it
- Differentiate between swing pricing and fair value pricing
- Know how to perform Islamic screening
- Learn about the roles of *Shari'ah* supervisors in Islamic mutual funds
- Understand how to invest in Islamic mutual funds.

5.1 Introduction

Islamic investment has to be understood as investments in financial services and products which are in sync with principles of *Shari'ah* (or the Islamic law, as prescribed in the Qur'an and Sunnah). The *Shari'ah* principles hold the following points as important parameters required for Islamic investments:

- The sectors which are approved for investments have to be necessarily in sync with the Islamic law. No kind of profit can be earned from activities that are prohibited in Islam. This prohibited list includes sectors such as alcohol production, gambling and pornography. At the same time, any investment in a financial prospect/institution which is interest (*riba*) oriented is equally prohibited.
- The creation of wealth should be produced as an outcome of a partnership between the investor and the user of capital. This must be inclusive of mutual

DOI: 10.4324/9780429321207-5

sharing of rewards and risks. It must be noted that returns on invested capital if predetermined as in the case of interest-based returns provided by bank deposits, do not align with *Shari'ah*. Islamic law approves of returns on invested capital only when it is earned as in the case of profits generated by the capital amount.

Islamic mutual funds are quite similar when observed alongside conventional mutual funds. The key difference is that the former follows the mandate of complying with *Shari'ah* principles. As mentioned above, *Shari'ah* or the Islamic law does not approve of practices such as *Riba* (charging interest), *Maisir* (gambling and games of chance), and *Gharar* (uncertainty). The law holds strictly that these practices cannot be implemented in any kind or form in financial transactions, not even in mutual funds. When talking about the scenario of Islamic mutual fund portfolios, *Shari'ah* principles imperatively form the deciding factor for the allocation and investment of assets, their investment, and trading practices. The law also extends to income distribution which is further supervised and finalised based on the opinions of some *Shari'ah* scholars.

Over the last few years, mutual funds have catalysed in mobilising savings, particularly from the small household sector. It can be seen as an investment vehicle used by which different investors, both small and large, collectively bring in their funds as per the directive guidance of an investment or fund manager. Islamic mutual funds can be thought of as a co-partnership between the public and financial institutions. Thus, these provide an excellent opportunity, especially for small investors who do not have access to the capital market, to actively take part in the economic development of the country. Islamic mutual funds have ultimately become a mechanism through which surplus funds available with the public are diverted to the Islamic capital market. Alternatively, these funds constitute one of the collective *Shari'ah* compliance investments which benefit not only in the form of spreading risks but also optimising returns. A beneficial feature of the Islamic mutual fund is how small investors who could not diversify their portfolios, essentially because of the lack of knowledge, get a chance to do so.

5.2 Types of Islamic Mutual Funds

Before heading toward investing in any Islamic mutual fund company or asset management company, it is imperative to understand the different types of Islamic mutual funds available. This would help the investor in analysing the need to invest in one or more categories as per their financial objective. Depending on principal investments, Islamic mutual funds are broadly classified into four types:

- Islamic money market funds
- Islamic stock or equity funds
- *Sukuk* or fixed income funds
- Islamic hybrid funds.

These funds are further detailed as follows:

- Islamic money market funds: These Islamic mutual funds mature in a comparatively shorter time and come with a high credit quality. They offer fixed-income securities and thus are mostly used to invest in Islamic money market instruments. Money market funds act as a substitute for saving accounts. The Islamic treasury bills or other short-term securities which are generally issued by a corporation can be taken as examples of this category of mutual funds.
- Islamic stock or equity funds: After their compliance with *Shari'ah* principles has been approved, these funds cater to investments made in common stocks, both domestic or/and foreign. Islamic equity funds are classified on the basis of market capitalisation and the style of their investments (i.e. their growth stock or value stock).
- *Sukuk* funds: These funds are primarily used for making investments in Islamic fixed-income securities such as *Sukuk*. Depending on who the *Sukuk* is being issued by, it can be classified into several types. *Sukuk* issued by the government is known as government *Sukuk*, *Sukuk* issued by the municipalities is referred to as municipal *Sukuk*, and *Sukuk* issued by corporations is called corporate *Sukuk*. The classification of *Sukuk* is not limited to issuer based. The further categorisation of *Sukuk* funds is dependent on the time it takes for these funds to mature. They are classified into short-, intermediate- and long-term *Sukuk funds*. Furthermore, classifications can be also made depending on whether the *Sukuk* is being issued domestically or through foreign means.

Market capitalisation, simply known as market cap, is the value of a company's stock. It is the number of shares outstanding multiplied by the market price of a certain stock. Within its own periphery, market capitalisation is broadly classified into four major categories:

- Micro capitalisation
- Small capitalisation
- Mid capitalisation
- Large capitalisation.

This classification is likely to differ from one country to another. For example, if the market capitalisation in the United States is more than US$10 billion, the stocks can be considered in the large cap. These stocks are considerably higher priced and are primarily offered by big companies or blue chip companies. If the market capitalisation is below US$2 billion, the stocks are considered in the small cap. If the market capitalisation is below US$300 million, the stocks are considered in the mid cap. Emerging companies are mostly included in the small cap and micro cap. Here, the associated risks are higher than those of the mid cap.

The Islamic stock fund can be additionally categorised depending on whether the stock is coming from the domestic market or international market. A certain amount of risk exposure is associated with the stocks coming from the international market, as the country from which the stock is being issued has to be taken into consideration. The manager has to equally focus on the exchange rate. An entirely different category of Islamic mutual funds is being constituted as a result of the combination of *Sukuk* Islamic stocks and Islamic money market funds, which are known as Islamic hybrid funds. The ultimate purpose of these funds is risk prevention while providing both income and capital appreciation. The other purpose that these funds serve is to provide investors with a single mutual fund that is capable of amalgamating the objectives for growth as well as income. The diversification in turn serves as an assurance of the funds performing well in the downturns of the stock market, thereby protecting against a big loss. It must be simultaneously known that during the bull market, these funds perform less well than other stock funds.

5.3 Calculation of Net Asset Value in Islamic Mutual Funds

An important prerequisite that enriches the process of decision-making before investing in a stock is knowing how an investment is priced. To have a better understanding, one must get hold of the knowledge of the net asset value, or NAV. NAV can be understood as the computation of the total market value of the investments held by the fund excluding its liabilities and expenses. At the end of each day, mutual funds conventionally price shares of the fund based on the NAV.

Net asset value (sometimes called the 'net asset') corresponds to the current market value of funds minus the fund's liabilities. This amount will then be divided by the number of funds outstanding. Every time the stock exchange market is open, this value has to be computed regularly. The mutual fund assets are paid by the investors in terms of units. The price that an investor pays per unit is called par value or face value. For instance, the investor pays $10 per unit. The price keeps on changing regularly, which is why it is referred to as marked to market. An example can be used to understand this concept with clarity. Assuming there are two investors, Fahad and Abdullah, who invest US$10,000 and US$90,000, respectively, summing up to a total investment of US$100,000 subjected to a price per unit of US$10. Here, Fahad is supposed to get 1,000 units and Ahmad 9,000 units. As NAV is the total amount over total outstanding shares (units), the NAV would amount to US$10 as an outcome of US$100,000/10,000.

Another example can be used in this context. The fund manager allocates a total of US$102,000 in two equity funds: Islamic mutual funds A and B. Let's assume he spends each of the 100 units of Fund A at US$50 (the total would be US$50,000) and each of the 100 units of Fund B at US$400 (the total would be US$40,000), and he keeps the remaining US$10,000 (see Table 5.1).

TABLE 5.1 Islamic Mutual Funds A and B (Before Price Increase)

Name of Stock	*Number of Unit*	*Price*	*Value*
Islamic Mutual Fund A (IMF A)	100	500	50,000
Islamic Mutual Fund B (IMF B)	100	400	40,000
Remaining Cash			10,000
Total			100,000

Source: Omar et al. (2013).

5.3-1 Swing Pricing

In order to pass on the trading costs to those who are purchasing and selling within their accounts, the fund provider might have to adjust the NAV, and this is exactly where swing pricing occurs. The design of swing pricing helps in protecting the value of the accounts of longer-term shareholders from being eroded by the transactional activities of others within the same fund.

If a fund's net inflows or outflows happen to exceed a pre-set level as determined by the fund provider, the implementation of swing pricing comes into play. In all such situations, the provider calculates the NAV as normal prior to adjusting it by the designated swing factor. An example can be used in this regard to understand the applicability of swing pricing. Let's say Al Rajhi Fund has a price of $20 per share and the fund's provider sets a swing factor of 0.1% of the NAV for net flows above or below 5% of the prior day's price. In this case, if the net inflow that the fund experiences are 10% of NAV, the price of the fund would be adjusted upward to US$20.02 (US$20 + (US$20 × 0.1%)). The same situation might occur with a 10% outflow except that the price would be adjusted downward to US$19.98. On account of the net flow being less than 10%, swing pricing cannot be implemented, and the fund's price remains at US$20.

5.3-2 Difference Between Swing Pricing and Fair Value Pricing

More often than not, swing pricing is considered similar to fair value pricing, but in reality, these two are inherently different. In fair value pricing, if the most recently traded price is considered out of date or stale, an adjustment of a security's price is made to an estimated current value. Contrary to that, in swing pricing, the NAV of the fund is adjusted to account for the costs of high-volume buying or selling. It must be noted that fair value pricing occurs at the security level while swing pricing occurs at the portfolio level.

5.4 Islamic Investment Criteria

Screening of companies is an essential criterion before Islamic investments are made in Islamic mutual funds. Islamic investments are based on two types of screenings, as explained below.

5.4–1 Qualitative Screens

Qualitative screens constitute the general rules that *Shari'ah* scholars abide by in identifying whether the purpose of an investment should be declared as *halal* (lawful) or *haram* (prohibited).

Qualitative screenings can further be divided into two types:

1. Industry screening, which involves determining whether the company in an industry is prohibited according to Islamic norms. Industries related to *haram* or unlawful activities are related to alcohol production, *riba*-based financial institutions, gambling and entertainment.
2. Business practices, which are involved in determining whether the company is being exploitative in its relationship with customers and suppliers or has unethical approaches with regard to its trading practices.

5.4–2 Quantitative Screens

Just like qualitative screenings, quantitative screenings too constitute certain general rules followed by *Shari'ah* scholars in determining whether the purpose of an investment should be declared as *halal* (lawful) or *haram* (prohibited). The *Shari'ah* board members of the Dow Jones Islamic Index have set up certain guidelines that should be followed for quantitative screenings. These guidelines are discussed below.

- Debt/asset ratio, which helps in determining whether a company has borrowed funds on interest or not. This further helps in determining whether the interest is fixed or at a floating rate. It is quite evident that Islamic law does not approve of any form of interest-based debt. However, as per the saying of the Islamic legal principle, *li al-akthar hukm al-kul* ('the verdict is won by the opinion of the majority') and other such opinions of scholars, a company would not enjoy the status of a permissible investment if debt financing escalates more than 33% of its capital (as per the *Shari'ah* board members of the Dow Jones Islamic Index).
- Interest-related income, which helps in determining if the company generates any kind of interest or interest-related income. This includes companies who put their surplus funds in investments, thereby yielding interest income. This is how their business is not centred on earning interest only. *Shari'ah* makes it an important criteria that no income can be generated from interest-related sources.
- Monetary assets can be identified as the substantial portions of a company's assets which are monetary in their nature. These assets include accounts receivable and liquid assets like that of bank accounts and marketable securities. Certain varied minimums are set for the ratio of illiquid assets (assets that are not in the form of money) for making an investment permissible. According to the principle of *li al-akthar hukm al-kul*, the minimum is sometimes set at 51%. According to others, a ratio of illiquid assets to total assets that can be accepted is kept at 33%.

5.5 Trading and Investing Practices

Under Islamic law, the selection criteria are not limited to the selection of securities only. Investing and trading practices are equally based on *Shari'ah* principles, and so are Islamic mutual funds (Jaffer, 2004). These practices are inclusive of the following:

- Investable funds must be free of interest-based debt: To finance investments, the investor is not allowed to borrow on interest. Thus, he cannot opt for trading on margin (i.e. borrowing for purchasing shares). For financing their investments, conventional funds such as hedge funds, arbitrage funds, and leveraged buyout (LBO) funds borrow in massive quantities and are thus prohibited for Islamic investors.
- Prohibition of speculation: The practice of making investments on the basis of short-term speculations as practiced by conventional investors is prohibited under Islamic law. As a Muslim, sound analysis of the investment has to be given grave importance before making the final decision of investing. Well-timed trading is definitely important to reap the benefits of market prices, but at the same time, these considerations should not be based on ignoring the fundamental value of the companies in which the investor has decided to invest.

5.6 Growing Importance of Islamic Mutual Funds

As a means of providing capital information, Islamic mutual funds are crucial to the development of the Islamic capital market. Individual savers purchasing shares in Islamic mutual funds benefit from this investment as they get hold of the opportunity to acquire access to capital market investment. This in turn helps them in synchronising their long-term liabilities. This can be observed as retirement and education with long-term investment assets (Islamic stocks and *Sukuk*). It becomes quite evident that the Islamic mutual fund industry has the potential to mature and develop globally. This could help in developing the necessary link between private savings and its prospective Islamic capital market. The domestic nature of Islamic mutual funds can conveniently enhance the liquidity and stability of the prospective Islamic capital market in Muslim countries. Islamic mutual funds will eventually provide the means for global investors in aligning their assets and liabilities in a better way.

An Islamic mutual fund is a pool of capital that has been managed for individuals for investing their surplus money. Investors get to enjoy dual advantages of their funds. One is that the funds are managed by specialised investment institutions. The second is the complete assurance that the funds are *Shari'ah* compliant. It gets to regulate its selection of investments, its own operations, and its trading practices owing to its strict adherence to *Shari'ah* investment principles.

5.7 Investment Process of Islamic Mutual Funds

To be able to achieve the right outcomes, keeping in consideration that the Islamic investing industry is flourishing, the emphasis is put on strategies for re-assessing asset allocation, development, and strategic thinking. Equal importance has to be given in the selection of the right Islamic mutual fund manager because this person will be eventually responsible for running a robust selection process in determining which Islamic mutual funds to invest in. To put forth the objective in most simple words, Islamic mutual fund strategies which deliver the best risk-adjusted returns in a sustainable and *Shari'ah*-compliant manner have to be identified. Depending on the unique contribution a strategy offers to the risk and return properties of the total portfolio, funds are selected alongside.

The initial process of investment begins through the applications of screenings, both qualitative and quantitative. Screenings through large sets of data from the investible universe help in sorting and identifying attributes which are indicative of the potential to deliver strong risk adjusted returns. Certain quantitative attributes in this regard include tracking error, win/loss ratio, historical alpha, information ratio, and the Sharpe ratio. On the other hand, qualitative attributes include concentration levels, ownership structures, style biases, liquidity, and funds under management.

One must be essentially aware of the consequences subjected to randomly dismissing large segments of the market in the process of filtering the Islamic mutual fund management universe. Researchers have been able to identify attributes that could help in concealing them from traditional screening measures, and in the course of doing so, the process happens to remain flexible as well as responsive. Additionally, the screening process must undergo continuous and consistent interaction with the market to be able to source ideas through direct referrals and contact with managers. On the universe getting minimised, the process of reviewing begins. This is generally based on extensive desktop research in order to identify potential competitive advantages. Historical performance attribution is used in this process. This enables investors in determining the breadth, strength and consistency of stock selection. Analysts should equally focus on assessing certain qualitative aspects like that of the investment team, available resources, process, and strategy and risk management.

Strategies which qualify the initial research processes are then subjected to extensive due diligence for assessing their compliance with *Shari'ah* principles and their suitability for active use. During the desktop research, it becomes very important for confirming with those attributes and competitive advantages. This step equally entails the consultant and analyst in making a qualitative assessment on how sustainable these attributes stand to be while syncing up with the requirement of being quantitatively aligned. These perspectives are based on extensive on-site reviews, direct contact with the investment team, assessment of financial models and a review of back-office and compliance processes. It is undoubtedly a dynamic process in terms of its approach and applicability. At the same time, the formerly rated strategies are continuously reassessed on their relative worth or appealing approaches. As already mentioned, quantitative measures are being used for monitoring the portfolios after making the respective investments.

A 'buy list' or a list of 'preferred' strategies becomes the output of the process. This collectively represents the universe in which consultants build portfolios. Each asset class will typically have between three to four managers, thereby demonstrating the capacity for delivering strong risk-adjusted returns. This also includes a cluster of favourable qualitative and quantitative attributes. Strategies rated 'strong' are typically back-up managers should the preferred group be at capacity, downgraded or unavailable for one reason or another. Proactive management of the research agenda is inevitable. The research agenda should simultaneously seek to challenge existing views on preferred managers. The process needs to have a futuristic vision and must be able to entirely utilise the available qualitative and quantitative inputs.

5.8 Asset Growth and Investment Allocation

Islamic asset management claims to have more than 1,410 functional funds operating worldwide. Table 5.2 shows how by the end of 2017, the total global Islamic assets under management (AUM) stood at US$110 billion. According to the Eurekahedge (2019) Global Islamic Fund Database, the number of live and obsolete *Shari'ah*-compliant funds operating globally in different countries is 828. With these funds, the investors get access to financial markets inside a framework that is deemed ethical as per the financial legal framework of Islam. These funds depict a moderate growth of the wider Islamic finance industry and reached the US$2 trillion mark by the end of 2015. By the end of 2017, 516 live Islamic funds were operating, out of which 88% of the strategies are represented by mutual fund/unit trusts (367 funds), equities (25 funds), investment trusts (23 funds), structured products (22 funds) and closed-ended investment companies (CEIC) (15 funds). The value of Islamic funds outstanding globally subjecting to mutual funds amounted to US$97 billion by the end of 2018. There are 261 global Islamic fund managers involved in managing funds of this size. Six funds are greater than $1 billion (see Table 5.2).

The average minimum investment size for Islamic funds is estimated at $1.087 billion. It has to be noted that almost half of the *Shari'ah*-compliant funds invest with a Middle East/Africa mandate, followed by 33% of investments made in Asia Pacific and 26% with a global mandate. Most of these funds are based in either the GCC countries or Southeast Asia followed by the United Kingdom.

According to Eurekahedge (2019), 440 Islamic funds (38.5% of assets form the largest number worldwide) were operational in Malaysia. Saudi Arabia with 206 Islamic funds having 28% of the total Islamic assets followed up next. However, Islamic

TABLE 5.2 Islamic Funds Asset Growth

Year	*Islamic Funds (Billion US$)*	*Sukuk (Billion US$)*
2012	46	260
2013	54	284
2014	59	299
2015	66	342
2016	91	345
2017	110	426
2023	325	783

Source: Thomson Reuters Report (2018).

TABLE 5.3 Number of Islamic Funds Outstanding Worldwide, 2019

Country	*Number of Islamic Funds*
Malaysia	440
Saudi Arabia	206
United States	6
Luxembourg	161
Indonesia	234
Kuwait	18
South Africa	118
Pakistan	178
Iran	165

Source: Statistics.com (2020).

funds have not enjoyed the popularity that other conventional funds enjoy. Islamic funds are still developing and have the potential for further growth. A lot of Muslim majority jurisdictions with a functioning Islamic finance regulatory framework and banking sector still have small Islamic funds segments. Five out of the available 28 jurisdictions account for more than 90% of the total assets under management. Islamic funds scale in a limited way, as they are mostly concentrated in Saudi Arabia, Malaysia and Iran (see Table 5.3). With an approximate $36 billion in Islamic fund assets, the GCC region held the largest value in 2019. Equity assets constitute the most popular Islamic fund asset. The total value of assets under management of the Islamic funds sector has been substantially soaring higher with the support attained by the growth in equity markets (Statistics.com, 2020).

By the end of December 2018, the value of investment allocation of Islamic funds outstanding globally amounted to US$97 billion (see Table 5.4). It is anticipated that by 2024, the total value of outstanding Islamic funds will amount to about US$216 billion (Statistics.com, 2020).

5.9 Comparative Performance of Islamic and Conventional Indices

Investors investing in Islamic mutual funds have to mandatorily apply both the Islamic sector and financial criteria for evaluating the funds before making their investments. This ensures that the selected funds absolutely align with their value system and beliefs. It is often perceived that the mandate of applying the screen criteria in Islamic investment is likely to affect the performance of the Islamic funds' returns in a negative way. It becomes quite evident through literature that the screening criteria adopted to eliminate *Shari'ah* non-compliant company stocks results in a subset of a sufficient number of companies for effective diversification without affecting the performance of the Islamic mutual funds' return. Certain empirical studies such as Hassan (2005) and Rana and Akhtar (2015) have depicted that the expected returns of Islamic portfolios are higher than the expected returns of

TABLE 5.4 Investment Allocation of Islamic Funds Globally, as of 2018

Asset Class	*Investment Allocation of Funds (in billion US$)*
Islamic mutual funds	97
Exchange-traded funds	9
Insurance funds	2
Pension funds	0.37

Source: Statistics.com (2020).

conventional portfolios. Islamic and conventional indices chosen in this context are developed, global, emerging, Standard & Poor's (S&P) 500, and S&P Europe.

Table 5.5 highlights the annualised returns, annualised standard deviation and coefficient of variation statistics for five Islamic indices and five conventional indices. The table is equally indicative of the fact that Islamic indices happened to outperform conventional market indices in terms of annualised returns throughout the entire

TABLE 5.5 Return and Standard Deviation (SD) of Islamic and Conventional Indices

Measures/Groups	*Annualised Return (%)*			*Annualised Standard Deviation (%)*			*Coefficient of Variation*		
Islamic	07–16	07–10	11–16	07–16	07–10	11–16	07–16	07–10	11–16
S&P Developed Shari'ah	6.24	1.65	8.53	17.42	23.47	13.41	2.79	14.25	1.57
S&P Global Shari'ah	5.74	1.63	7.79	17.23	23.41	13.10	3.00	14.36	1.68
S&P Emerging Shari'ah	1.36	2.36	0.85	20.04	28.20	14.33	14.78	11.92	16.82
S&P 500 Shari'ah	9.88	6.37	12.14	19.67	25.40	14.89	1.99	3.99	1.23
S&P Europe 350 Shari'ah	8.05	4.94	10.03	19.14	23.61	15.64	2.38	4.78	1.56
Conventional	07–16	07–10	11–16	07–16	07–10	11–16	07–16	07–10	11–16
S&P Developed Index	5.89	1.94	8.42	17.70	22.75	13.53	3.01	11.75	1.61
S&P Global Index	5.66	2.92	7.42	17.54	22.62	13.31	3.10	7.76	1.79
S&P Emerging Index	4.85	13.24	−0.52	20.14	26.04	15.21	4.16	1.97	−29.22
S&P 500 Index	9.09	3.14	12.91	25.64	27.89	24.14	5.39	8.87	4.19
S&P Europe 350 Index	5.51	−0.35	9.26	20.95	25.52	17.42	3.80	−73.71	1.88

period, the only exception being the emerging markets. During the financial crunch of 2007–2010, Islamic indices did not have a lower coefficient of variation apart from Europe. Simultaneously, Islamic indices did not have a lower annualised standard deviation during the same phase of the financial crisis. Here, the exceptions were S&P 500 and S&P Europe. However, Islamic indices were observed to have a lower standard deviation and coefficient of variation post the financial crisis period, particularly between 2011 and 2016. This hints that Islamic indices recovered positively, even more than conventional indices, after the global financial crisis of 2007–2009. Results as shown in Table 5.5 show that Islamic market indices of Islamic funds and equities are superior to conventional market indices, adjusting for the variability of returns.

5.10 Conclusion

It is now evident that Islamic mutual funds can only invest in assets and securities that are entirely aligned with *Shari'ah* principles and guidelines. Sales and marketing practices need to be given proper attention to be able to popularise Islamic mutual funds. The ethical mandate of these funds should not be avoided as *Shari'ah* forms the moral crux on which Islamic finance has been designed. Certain anecdotal evidence claims of unethical practices have been observed while selling Islamic mutual fund products. This is mainly done to trigger emotionally by displacing rational thinking. Any kind of misleading representation and/or lack of complete disclosure in the form of declaring generalised statements about potential returns must be weeded out. Islamic mutual funds are required to be wholly ethical. Thus, the distribution channels should directly address any lack of proper explanation and the implications of fee structures. The lack of proper investor education about the realities in terms of risks and the long-term investment horizon of Islamic mutual funds must be addressed alongside.

Review Questions

1. Define Islamic mutual fund and their types.
2. Let the total number of outstanding shares (units) be 10,000. Based on this, answer the following:

    a. Calculate the NAV.
    b. If the price of IMF A escalates to 450 and that of IMF B goes up to 400, calculate the new NAV.

3. Explain the criteria for Islamic screening.
4. Explain the investment strategies of Islamic mutual funds.

References

Eurekahedge (2019), *Islamic Funds Database*, retrieved from www.eurekahedge.com/NewsAndEvents/News/1733/Hedge-Fund-Report-March-2018 (Access date February 11, 2019)

Hassan, A (2005), *Evaluating the Performance of Managed Funds: The Cases of Equity, Ethical Funds and Islamic Indexes*, PhD Thesis, Durham University, Durham

Jaffer, S (2004), *Islamic Asset Management: Forming the Future of Shari'ah Compliant Investment Strategy*, London: Euromoney Books

Omar, A, Abduh, M and Sukmana, R (2013), *Fundamentals of Islamic Money and Islamic Capital Markets*, Singapore: John Wiley and Sons, Wiley Finance Series

Rana, M and Akhtar, W (2015), Performance of Islamic and Conventional Stock Indices: Empirical Evidence from Emerging Economy, *Empirical Innovation*, 1(1), 15–24

Statistics.com (2020), retrieved from www.statista.com/statistics/1092680/worldwide-number-of-islamic-funds-outstanding-by-country/ (Access date March 21, 2021)

Thomson Reuters Report (2018). *Islamic Finance Development Report 2018*, Building Momentum, #IFDI2018, Islamic Corporation for the Development of the Private Sector (ICD) - Thomson Reuters

6

INVESTMENT IN ISLAMIC PRIVATE EQUITY

Learning Objectives

On completing this chapter, learners will be able to:

- Understand Islamic private equity and its difference from conventional private equity
- Comprehend the structure of Islamic private equity
- Examine the deal and Islamic screening criteria of funds
- Recognise the growth of Islamic private equity funds
- Know the benefit Islamic private equity investors get from their investments.

6.1 Introduction

One of the incredible corporate experiences of the past 20 years has been the development of private equity. Previously, private equity was well known as venture capital. Private equity is currently perhaps at the very much part of corporate finance and occurs in mergers and acquisitions (M&A) events globally. What was apparent only a few years back as a substitute asset class on the borders of uncontrolled financial capitalism is today a conventional and accepted *Shari'ah*-compliant investment avenue, offering competitive returns not only for private equity authorities and their investors but also for shareholders, managers, and suppliers of debt finance alike. In reality, the notion of private equity does not negate *Shari'ah* norms or Islamic laws of contracts. Thus, it is very uncomplicated to carry out ordinary private equity actions in a *Shari'ah*-compliant way, with purchase targets ethically screened, debt-to-equity, and income ratios curved surrounded by the required *Shari'ah* limits. In this sense, *Shari'ah*-compliant investing may be employed for the acquisition and financing (Hassan and Mollah, 2018).

DOI: 10.4324/9780429321207-6

The main principles behind Islamic private equity are *musharaka*, *mudarabah* and *wakalah*. The *musharaka* or *mudarabah* principles are applied in order to enable the pooling of the investors' funds into a limited partnership arrangement. *Mudarabah* principles are applied in the case where the fund manager does not invest in the said arrangement. Based on these principles, the terms of an agreement between the investors and the fund manager shall include a profit-sharing arrangement and risk sharing in proportion to capital contribution as the case may be. On the other hand, the *wakalah* arrangement is set between the investors in managing the fund.

6.2 Venture Capital Versus Private Equity

Normally, venture capital is described as a firm that invests in early on-stage start-ups, while private equity is a company that invests in later-stage firms, including stock market–registered companies (Al-Rifai and Khan, 2000). Nevertheless, both type of capital has similar investment styles. They invest in a firm in exchange for equity in the company. Venture capital is truly a subgroup of private equity investing. Private equity assets include distressed investments, leveraged buyouts, and mezzanine capital. Due to the financial crises that occur from time to time, venture capital companies have been extra conservative, so therefore, many venture capitalists are financing more in matured-stage companies where the risks are smaller.

Additionally, the boundaries between venture capital and private equity financing have been obscured by an enhanced contest in the capital markets. The enhanced stress on the part of fund managers, investment adviser, and capital suppliers to put funds is at an all-time high. This boosted contest among investors has compelled both private equity and venture capital firms to increase their corresponding horizons to capture more opportunities (Hassan and Mollah, 2018).

6.3 Structuring Islamic Private Equity

Private equity companies are normally structured as partnerships with two key elements: the 'limited partnership', which is the provider of the capital, and the 'general partnership', in which the management team is responsible for taking investment decisions. The limited partnership gives the funding, permitting the general partnership to draw down as needed for investments that will meet the decided profile. Occasionally, limited partnership capital suppliers set an obstacle rate, which signifies a minimum investment return goal. The proceeds in surplus of this are divided with the general partnership at a predetermined rate.

It is noted that some Middle East–centred private equity assets use a sell-down model in which the limited partnership is embodied by a conglomerate of usually tiered high–net worth investors. The general partnership recognises the target, accepts the due diligence, reaches an agreement on principal terms and conditions with the financier's group, and then initiates the acquisition. Usually, the general partnership marks up the price prior to selling down the stake to the different financiers on prior fixed terms.

In constructing private equity for Islamic investors, a couple of matters need to be considered. First, Islamic financiers perform their investment endeavours in agreement with *Shari'ah* law. *Shari'ah* disallows the paying or charging of interest (*riba*); investment in specific prohibited businesses such as mainstream financial services, armaments, gambling (*maisir*), and alcohol; contractual uncertainty (*gharar*); and the guaranteed of a fixed return in investing.

The most vital principle of Islamic finance is that business should be based on profit and loss sharing, using instruments like *musharaka* and *mudarabah* modes of finance. As cited in *Shari'ah* principles, not only profit but also losses must be shared between the *rabbul maal* (investor) and *mudarib* (entrepreneur) in a *musharaka* contract in proportionately to their invested capital, while sharing the profit should be decided at agreed levels. Thus, the Islamic model of financing is built on profit and loss sharing through equitable contractual and financial arrangements. The private equity company offers a natural *musharaka*-based solution with a sustained track record of achievement in the standard system.

It must be noted here that constructing a *Shari'ah*-compliant private equity fund typically involves management conforming with the standards set out by the *Shari'ah* supervisory board. Islamic private equity fund documents, such as the private placement memorandum and limited partnership agreement, normally contain rules of conformity which control the management to use the funds supplied by the Islamic financiers. It is normal to contain investment principles based on *Shari'ah* law; for example, investment in any avenue must be only in lawful (*halal*) companies. The *Shari'ah* supervisory board should have sanction rights on the proposed investments of the fund and should oversee the fund's continuing fulfilment of its investment policies.

Furthermore, the fund operations are designed in such a manner that its cash flow begins from the financiers to a fund and in turn to the target company. The members of the *Shari'ah* supervisory board (SSB) play the role of advisers who model mechanisms and clauses to meet up the obligations of the *Shari'ah* in general and the principles of *mudarabah* or *musharaka* the paths of profit and loss sharing (PLS) partnerships and *wakalah* in particular. These forms of private equity products attract Islamic investors.

In the *musharaka* type of private equity (Figure 6.1), there is a party who sponsors the private equity fund, offering the management, and another party is the investor, who gives cash to the fund. There is also an alternative structure which is called *mudarabah*. Using the *musharaka* mode of finance is best fitted to the requirements set by local laws and the required tax transparency. Additionally, this structure can be closed ended or open ended. Basically, nearly all Islamic private equity forms are closed ended, which is often understood as *Shari'ah* compliant.

But this type of Islamic private equity may differ from a stand-alone corporation with an external or internal management team to a deal fund designed holding the funds, which is handled by an outside asset management firm. This kind of designed product may play a role as a limited partnership or general partner in an inclusive partnership structure.

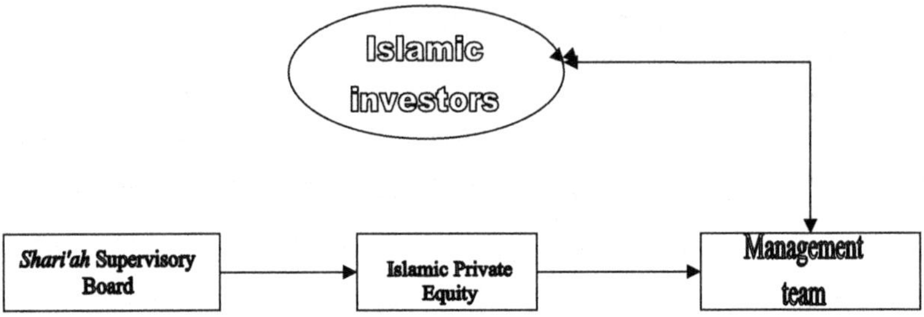

FIGURE 6.1 Design of Islamic private equity fund.

6.4 Deal and *Shari'ah* Screening Process

Islamic private equity is medium- or long-term finance, typically from three to seven financial years, delivering earnings for an equity stake in possibly high-growth businesses. Throughout the holding period, the aim of the private equity company is to enhance the high yield of the company to increase value upon exit.

Thus, the legal structure and jurisdiction of the private equity funds are vital. Consideration should be given not only to the kinds of fund products presented in the host state of the Islamic private equity, but also need to see the potential of funds that would be marketed to investors in their home dominions, and further the form of investments they are permitted to venture into in the territories of the target companies. Also, it is crucial to think about cross-jurisdictional matters between private equity and investors of funds and targeted companies in the local market.

The ultimate outcome of what legal vehicle to apply for the Islamic private equity would be motivated by, amongst other things, the infrastructure is accessible in any specific jurisdiction, tax obligations, and certain *Shari'ah* constraints. Following primary fundraising, the developer of the Islamic private equity is typically the general partner of the managing team. The managing team should detect the target corporations, perform due diligence analyses, acquire the contract with investors and take on the preliminary equity acquisition at the targeted company. Also, the general partner is accountable to manage targeted companies and eventually carry out the exit policy on behalf of the Islamic private equity fund.

The targeted companies should be detected through communications within the Islamic private equity association, seeking the targeted companies and sector track. In the process, thorough due diligence on financial and non-financial issues, anticipated return on financing, timing and synergy would help to pull out Islamic investments. Minor corporations with the possibility of considerable growth should be high on the list of selecting Islamic private equity firms. Although SMEs (small and medium enterprises) have little interest in leverage, there is still a significant scope of mediation for asserting and structuring *Shari'ah*-compliant products.

Most of the time, when a general partnership of a traditional private equity firm accepts an Islamic financier into its fund, then it must adopt a *Shari'ah*-compliant investment strategy which contains *Shari'ah*-based fund documentations. Put through a fine tuning by the SSB of the Islamic private equity company, these should exclude:

- *Riba* (interest) based banking and other financial services transactions
- Business with gaming, gambling casinos, lotteries, and related unlawful activities
- Pork and pork-related products
- Engagement in pornography or obscenity in any form
- Engagement in the unlawful entertainment business, such as immoral films, video, theatre, cinema, and so forth
- Traditional insurance
- Arms industry
- Alcoholic beverages or related products
- Intoxicant products such as tobacco and harmful drugs
- Environmentally destructive activities.

In the international financial market, the traditional financial system dominates the market; in that sense, it is extremely challenging to focus on companies that are entirely *Shari'ah* compliant. So, investing in the stock market–registered public companies where it is usually admitted that any prohibited income of a *Shari'ah* non-compliant targeted company that does not exceed the norm of 5%–15% (dependent on the approval of the *Shari'ah* board scholars) of total gross income should be considered as marginal or incidental. Nearly all *Shari'ah* scholars have accepted and recognised the following financial ratios or screening criteria of stock-listed companies:

- Total debt: Removes investment in businesses when total interest-based debt divided by 12-month average market capitalisation exceeds or is equal to 33%.
- Total interest-bearing securities and cash: Removes investments when total cash and interest-bearing securities divided by 12-month average market capitalisation exceeds or is equal to 33%.
- Accounts receivable: Removes investments in target companies if accounts receivable divided by total assets is greater than or equal to 33%.

Although the screening criteria of Islamic market indices have been designed by the Standard & Poor's Islamic Index, the Dow Jones Islamic Market Index, and many other Islamic indices in Asian markets for the stock market–registered companies, they can also be employed to private equity investment criteria. In fact, these *Shari'ah* norms of financial ratios are applied by some private equity investors in the United Kingdom and United States (Mughal, 2007; Hassan and Mollah, 2018).

Prohibited income comes from unlawful activities which are against the *Shari'ah*. Therefore, in investment activities unlawful income must be eliminated, or at least it needs to be minimised. Further, private equity fund documentations also require alteration to stop the fund manager from charging financial interest or *riba* on monies. To some extent, Shari'ah screening criteria provide guidelines to screen companies conducting non-Shari'ah–compliant business activities. However, some Islamic investors would tolerate interest income, subject to the condition that such income should not exceed 5% of the total income of the private equity fund or portfolio of a company. In a way, such financiers will 'purify' this income by giving it to a charitable foundation.

Apart from this, for certain Islamic investors, there will also be a need to address issues in relation to the exercise by the fund of redemption rights and liquidation preferences attaching to preference shares, which may not be acceptable in a form familiar to Western investors.

The usage of interest-bearing debt at both the stage of any special purpose vehicle financing and a portfolio-level company in the merger and acquisition (M&A) arrangement should be concerned particularly with Islamic investors on the *Shari'ah* injunction on *riba*. In theory, *Shari'ah*-compliant private equity funds are controlled with respect to leveraging their assets in comparison to traditional private equity funds. Dependent upon the legal opinion of the relevant SSB, leveraging should be completely prohibited or accepted to a certain extent as per Islamic rulings. For example, the SSB may permit the private equity fund to make use of leverage within a specific limit, such as 33% of the balance sheet of the targeted firm.

However, Islamic private equity funds should also compete with traditional private equity funds in the matter of their rate of returns, besides the expectation of Islamic investors that their money must be invested in such *Shari'ah*-based products that would provide competitive yields. This involves also their fund may be leveraged its investments to a specific extent. To make sure that leverage is *Shari'ah* compliant, one should use those *Shari'ah*-based structures that are typically used for acquisition in financing by employing modes of finance like *ijarah wa iktina* (lease and purchase transaction) or *murabahah*. These forms of products are always put through the authorisation of the SSB. Moreover, they should be examined from the local legal perspective on the subject of feasibility and avoidance of unfavourable tax effects (Mughal, 2007).

6.5 Choice of Investment in Islamic Private Equity

An investor essentially has three choices when considering an investment in private equity. Investment may be made a direct investment, through a fund of funds, or through investment in a private equity.

6.5–1 Direct Investment

Direct investment happens when the private equity investors directly participate in the investment company to enable the investors to confirm *Shari'ah* compliance of the investment. It involves a commitment of time and resources by the investors to understand and analysis the target investments.

6.5–2 *Fund of Funds*

Investing through a structured fund, such as a fund which consists of a portfolio of professionally selected and managed companies, provides a better spread of risk as compared to direct investment. However, this approach needs strong governance and a clearer statement of policy in respect of the underlying investments' compliance with the principles of *Shari'ah*. On the other hand, the fund manager needs to maintain a balance with different types of funds and focus on investing in the funds and focus on investing in the funds that will be in the top 25% for their types. One way of selecting the funds is the use of fund of funds, which can be multi-investor or single investor. The choice of funds will be made upon advice of the fund of funds advisor. This approach offers diversification in terms of measures, sector, geography, investment stage and strategy that could possibly reduce risk.

6.5–3 *Private Equity Funds*

The difference among the funds is basically the investment strategy and focus, for instance at what stage the fund is invested, geographic or sector specification, and the preferred form of investment. For an Islamic private equity fund, the composition of a *Shari'ah* supervisory board is necessary in order to ensure that all management and investment strategies of the funds are *Shari'ah* compliant.

The Islamic financial market could successfully pioneer a form of financing similar to conventional private equity, but addressed with Islamic tenets firmly in place, to result in the best of both practices. Partnering with established European and US firms presents an attractive proposition for many Middle Eastern Islamic investors. *Musharaka* or equity financing, if the price and structure are right, could provide a useful source of diversified funding for private equity firms.

6.6 Factors of Benefit From Islamic Private Equity

Islamic finance takes to rebuild the economic system on the Islamic foundations governing wider society. The Islamic private equity sector has observed remarkable growth in recent years. This section is based on *Shari'ah* principles and signifies a credible, competitive alternative to mainstream private equity and has potential for growth in the area of Islamic asset management (Yunis, 2006) There is a continuing convergence of three facilitating factors necessary for the advantages of Islamic private equity to be fully roused for the first time.

6.6–1 *Continuing Convergence*

6.6–1–1 Demand

There is increased awareness of and attention to Islamic investments, both from Muslim and non-Muslim investors seeking to take the lead in an economic life as envisaged in Islamic business ethics, and non-Muslim institutions looking to tap a growth market. Also, the Islamic private equity sector currently looks at the capacity for returns equivalent to conventional investments.

6.6-1-2 Process

Capital flows into the Muslim countries, especially the GCC, have expected extraordinary proportions. Hydrocarbon revenues are projected to top $8 trillion by 2030.

6.6-1-3 Support

The governments' and regulatory backing are observed in the Muslim countries, which have ensued in the operational environment for Islamic finance turn out to be gradually more supportive and flexible.

6.6-2 Delivering

With these circumstances in place, there are four purposes for bridging the size of the investment cycle, and providing an answer to why Islamic private equity would be thought of as a key element of this new financial paradigm:

1. There is a near symmetry between Islamic financial prescriptions and private equity. Both of them are participatory in nature, resulting in income from asset-supported, enterprise investment and engaging equitable distribution of risks and rewards.
2. Neither Islamic private equity financiers nor their investee firms should be reliant on debt financing. The Islamic prerequisite is that productive and financial flows are jointly offering desirable degrees of financial stability and resilience.
3. There is an expanding channel of *Shari'ah*-compliant financial deals on hand, and currently *Shari'ah*-compliant investors have the benefit of quick liquidity to achieve them. Real demand for Islamic investment solutions currently comprises all phases of the financial ecosystem, from business owners to limited partners. Islamic private equity is also optimally placed to help non-collateralised start-ups and regularly conservative GCC family organisations.
4. Islamic private equity investors should apply the similar value addition instruments as conventional private equity investing to their investee firms, subject to the condition that these modes of financing do not breach the basic tenets of *Shari'ah* (Mughal, 2007).

Tools in management care and global connectivity have long been indicated to be vital in driving financial business growth, and Islamic private equity gives weight to the significance of corporate governance particularly in the GCC, where an ethos of full business transparency remains to progress and cultivate. In effect, Islamic investors should well deliver yet closer support, due to their demand to safeguard continual *Shari'ah* compliance.

6.6–3 Activating

Islamic private equity is instantly receptive to use by *Shari'ah*-compliant financiers. There are negligible differences in several areas between conventional forms of private equity and Islamic private equity which remain either characteristic sources of competitiveness in plummeting leverage and refining corporate transparency or do not inevitably create a disadvantage in deal flow. The similarities, on the other hand, principally among them the support and creation of world-class businesses, are fascinating. Corresponding to the three enablers which have set aside the sector to start its early growth, there remain four important drivers which should be addressed if the profits of *Shari'ah*-compliant private equity are to be stimulated and maintained.

1. Business standardisation: Standards enhance transparency and enable the integration of Islamic finance into the international marketplace. They also simplify internal *Shari'ah* screening, extend clarity of obligations and rights; and lower the costs – substantial progress towards competitiveness with traditional investors.
2. Financial engineering: Current private equity is a difficult phenomenon and requires the development of creative tools. Innovation should also be in appealing to broader interest critically for the long-standing sustainability and competitiveness of Islamic investment, even though this should not result in erosion of *Shari'ah* authenticity.
3. Market education: Islamic private equity should be explained with clarity. Investors should build a track record and present concrete illustrations of value addition; the matter should not only distinguish between Islamic and conventional investment but also implicitly distinguish value-adding Islamic private equity investing from those which may not add value.
4. Human capital: There is a supply-and-demand disparity for skilled experts, with talent extremely monetised. Education and training should also be improved.

Islamic private equity should be the right product for the proper time and provides benefits during the course of the investment cycle. Assumed that the financial doctrines of Islam seeks to distribute wealth equitable, with a vital matter for economic justice, socio-economic impact of effective *Shari'ah*-compliant investing might be immense.

6.7 Growth of Islamic Private Equity

In the sphere of Islamic corporate finance, private equity also offers an appealing outlet for *musharaka*-based investing in the institutional Islamic funds to culminate in an ever-increasing trend of Islamic banks should be involved in private equity deals by introducing their own private equity funds. The extensive market for private equity in the Muslim countries in general, and the Middle East countries in particular, has been unexploited. Most of the Middle Eastern Islamic banks and giant individual investors have had surplus liquidity over the current year and, thus, the significance of private equity in the Middle Eastern region has been steadily recognised. The funds handled by private equity companies in 2011 were around US$41 billion and reached the end of 2020 at US$140 billion.

Islamic private fundraising constructs a small part of total private equity fundraising in Islamic areas. The aggregate capital raised up by Islamic funds has declined in recent years. In 2019, US$0.05 billion was raised from a single fund compared to US$0.6 billion raised through funds in 2018 (Table 6.1). After the collapse of Arbah Capital in 2019, the popular Islamic private equity funds in the space including Arbaaj Global Investment House, Fajr Capital, Gulf Capital, Injazat Capital, Investcorp, Sana Capital and a few captive Islamic private equity funds that are functioned by the key Islamic banks in the GCC and SE Asian counties.

Islamic private equity concentrates on acquiring bulk stakes in privately held *Shari'ah*-compliant firms. By doing this, it allows investors to retain control and safeguard the company's observance to *Shari'ah* principles. Islamic private equity offers investors ethical investment products presenting portfolio diversification, high performance, excellent risk-adjusted returns and various investment avenues. Traditional private equity and Islamic investment share many common principles. Both of them are founded on investing in the real economy and on the basis of sharing risks and rewards via partnership contracts. Further, traditional private equity holds a long-term position on investments and falls into line with the interests of stakeholders, which are also amongst the fundamental ethics of Islamic investment.

On its face, Islamic private equity appears to be deterring in contrast to conventional private equity. Actually, on the investment side, there are certainly some limitations in terms of businesses (e.g. alcohol, tobacco, and leisure-related activities are prohibited industries), in addition to certain financial strictures such as the usage of debt instruments and investment in businesses with extraordinary leverage. Still, such impediments should in the majority of cases be overcome by advanced structuring, for instance by way of repaying the portfolio firm's conventional debt

TABLE 6.1 Islamic Private Equity Fundraising, 2015–2019

Year	*Number of Funds Closed*	*Aggregate Capital Raised (Billion US$)*
2015	3	0.27
2016	1	0.32
2017	3	0.19
2018	4	0.60
2019	1	0.05

Source: Salam Gateway.

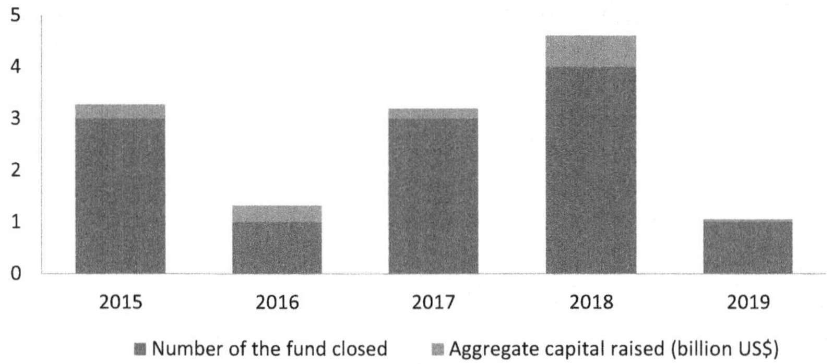

FIGURE 6.2 Islamic private equity fundraising 2015–2019.

Source: Salam Gateway.

and refinancing it via a *Shari'ah*-compliant form such as a *Murabahah* contract, along with other solutions.

Islamic private equity promises to be a developing field both within the Islamic finance and private equity space over the upcoming years. So far, there are only a few Islamic private equity funds in the market. Still, the reputation of these funds is expanding enormously. The Islamic private equity funds declared outstripped US$4 billion during the year 2009–2010 and have grown threefold as of December 2021, showing strong growth and demonstrating investor demand (Figure 6.2). Contemplating the growth in assets globally and GCC Islamic banks and financial institutions, it is estimated that during the year 2015–2019 Islamic private equity industry was worth US$1.43 billion by the end of the year 2019.

While Islamic investment follows high Islamic ethical standards, it has been appealing to an increasing number of non-Muslim investors, together with Muslims investors aiming at a significantly larger investor base than traditional private equity. The latest research has noticed that a significant number of venture capital funds and private equity funds have been successful in *Shari'ah* compliance tests, with only minimal adjustments done to the investment strategies of these funds (Hassan and Mollah, 2018).

6.8 Prospects of Islamic Private Equity in the Global Markets

As of December 2019, according to a report of the Eurekahedge Islamic funds databased (it maintains 112 different products in its database estimated for over 20% of the total universe, projected at 550 funds across all asset classes), with other types of assets, containing real estate funds, demonstrating 330 (60%, leasing funds being a 10% subset) and 220 private equity funds (40%). It shows that Islamic private equity has been raised up by the investment and advisory company COREcap, which launched its first $150 million in the year 2008 and later also projected continuous growth. COREcap Islamic Private Equity Fund I (CIPEF I) has invested in the *Shari'ah*-compliant private equity in the Middle East and North Africa (MENA) region. Corresponding to the Emerging Markets Private Equity Association (EMPEA), Capital International Private Equity Fund-IV (CIPEF VI) is targeted to raise $2.5 billion, which is the largest worldwide emerging markets private equity fund closed in the last five years (Babar, 2012). Through the total corpus, CIPEF VI was aiming at 15–20 investment funds and would focus on roughly 16 of the 138 emerging market countries in the globe. Thus far it has already dedicated nearly 20% of capital from CIPEF VI in several investment avenues (Babar, 2012). Most prominent private equity investors in the Middle East, including Gulf Finance House and Investment Dar of Kuwait, Investcorp of Bahrain, Shuaa Capital and Millennium Private Equity of Dubai, have involved themselves in the private equity market which signifies constant importance of the sector.

Malaysia has also developed as a popular country for private equity investing, with an ample population of 27 million and a robust global business community. iSpring Capital Sdn Bhd and Actis Capital LLP in Malaysia are important private equity companies in Kuala Lumpur.

Indonesia, Southeast Asia's leading economy, is gradually developing an attractive investment environment for private equity companies. With a population of more than 235 million and a strong real GDP growth level over the past decade, it offers some exciting investment chances in areas such as telecommunications and financial services. Indonesia also is abundant in natural resources, providing rise to its own set of associated investment prospects. But there are only a small number of private equity companies operating in Indonesia currently. Saratoga Capital, Quvat Management and TPG-affiliate Northstar Pacific Partners Affinity Equity Partners are operational in Indonesia. The latter is a new buyout firm set up in Jakarta which concentrates on leveraged buyouts and managed investments on a careful basis.

Islamic private equity in Europe and the United States presently does not have many companies but they invest in large volume of traditional private equity. While Islamic finance and Islamic private equity are growing by around 10% per year, the funds offered for Islamic investors are far fewer than conventional private equity funds (Mughal, 2007). To encourage this industry, governments of western countries should understand more and offer a better ecosystem for *Shari'ah*-compliant investing. The UK, Germany and, lately, France are well ahead of the others by solving some unfavourable tax concerns for *Shari'ah*-compliant mode of transactions. Businesses dealing such as private equity, *Sukuk*, and Islamic mortgages which are *Shari'ah* compatible, viable and enforceable of local law and offering satisfactory tax treatment have been growing popularity in the western market.

Private equity has arisen a long way in the worldwide financial market. The essence of entrepreneurship which remains at private equity's core area, it appears fair to forecast that it would stay on as principal to the twin areas of corporate finance and M&A for several years to come. Also, private equity is an important asset class for Islamic investors because of its natural fitting with the *Shari'ah* principles. Both private equity and Islamic investment share some common principles:

both of them give priority to invest in the real economy and on the matter of risk sharing and rewards through partnership. Further, private equity holds a long-term position on investing and lines up with the interests of stakeholders, and these characteristic are also amongst the fundamental principles of Islamic investment. With this suitable ethical investment product for Islamic financiers comes portfolio diversification, high performance, higher risk-adjusted returns and distinct investment opportunities.

Even though there are only a handful Islamic private equity funds in the market, it assures to be one of the fastest-growing areas both within Islamic finance and private equity space over the coming years. Islamic private equity concentrates on buying majority stakes in the private-sector *Shari'ah*-compliant companies. As a result, it allows investors to retain control and make sure the company's loyalty to *Shari'ah* principles. Most investment companies have either their own SSB, while some Islamic private equity companies acquire the *Shari'ah* rulings from independent *Shari'ah* scholars (Yousfi, 2012).

Muslim countries are growing their economies, and edging into retail in addition to the SME market stays a key challenge. Conceivably this is a sector that Islamic finance could pioneer by adjusting early-stage private equity systems to the owner-managed small and medium business market. This is the area which belongs to a majority of the grassroots business community in the sector.

6.9 Conclusion

Islamic finance, like private equity, remains to have strong growth. Islamic private equity offers an appealing outlet for *musharaka*-based investments as institutional Islamic funds, culminating in an expanding trend of Islamic banks being involved in private equity deals by creating their own private equity funds or employing a sell-down model.

However, Islamic banks have to be cautious that the private equity model needs a broader approach beyond financial engineering to incorporate improvement in operation as this is a vital area for driving value. In order to efficiently participate in private equity deals, Islamic banks should ensure that they have the proper resources, employ experienced individuals with established track records or contemplate partnering with active boutiques or deploy a fund-of-funds style.

In the developed market like the United Kingdom and the United States, the crossover into retail along with the SME market stays a key challenge. Maybe this is a sector that Islamic finance should pioneer by adjusting early-stage private equity methods to the owner-managed business (US$2.08 million value level market). This is an area which needs a majority of the developed economies' business community grassroots to remain. The Islamic finance sector and its experts could effectively pioneer a form of financing similar to traditional private equity, but addressed with Islamic principles firmly in place, to effect in the best ofboth practices. The prospect to innovate as opposite to emulate has never been more prime, as the sector is developing and has not yet secured its structures. To establish a new identity embedded in strong financial achievement and to replace the current model will lead to a long way in distinguishing Islamic finance and adding reliability to the industry. This is what the assets class of private equity funds has succeeded to do in the traditional sphere, and as such, the Islamic finance industry at large would be a great hope and encouragement in the knowledge that parallel to equity-based success is attainable in its own market.

However, private equity in general and Islamic private equity, in particular, are yet in their growing stages. The competitors in the industry confront with lack of information and academic research, as accessible market data is seldom inconsistent and incomplete. Furthermore, there is only a couple of professionals who are well trained in the standards of *Shari'ah* law and their use, especially when it comes to the designing of new structures and products.

What is required to speed up the Islamic private equity funds' development in particular is experienced and knowledgeable human capital, in addition to a higher level of *Shari'ah* standardisation across countries, disciplines, and products of the all-inclusive Islamic finance space. Crucial success factors on the micro level include client relationship management, product development skill, and effectiveness, both in terms of pricing and quality among others. In this perspective, innovation is crucial, as it allows individual competitors and the businesses as a whole to draw the link between Islamic financial and conventional products by constructing the latter in loyalty to Shari'ah laws. Also at its core, private equity stays one of the most effective means of making corporate value and embodies around one-quarter of all M&A in the area of corporate finance internationally.

Review Questions

1. An investor essentially has three choices when considering investing in private equity. What are these choices?
2. What should be the duties of the *Shari'ah* advisor of Islamic private equity?
3. Discuss the future growth of Islamic private equity.
4. Why should Islamic private equity be considered a key component of the alternative financial paradigm?
5. What are the key drivers which must be addressed if the benefits of *Shari'ah*-compliant private equity are to be enhanced?

References

Al-Rifai, T and Khan, A (2000), *The Role of Venture Capital in Contemporary Islamic Finance*, The International Investor/ABNAMRO, retrieved from https://ibir-api.hbku.edu.qa/sites/default/files/2019-10/The-Role-of-Venture-Capital-in-Contemporary-Islamic-Finance.pdf

Babar, K (2012, May 10), Capital International Private Equity Funds (CIPEF) Raises $3 Billion Emerging Markets Fund, *The Economic Times*, retrieved from https://economictimes.indiatimes.com/industry/banking/finance/capital-international-private-equity-funds-cipef-raises-3-billion-emerging-markets-fund/articleshow/13080760.cms?utm_source=contentofinterest&utm_medium=text&utm_campaign=cppst

Hassan, A and Mollah, S (2018), *Islamic Finance: Ethical Underpinnings, Products and Institutions*, Cham: Palgrave Macmillan

Mughal, UF (2007), No Pain, No Gain: The State of the Industry in Light of an American Islamic Private Equity Transaction, *Chicago Journal of International Law*, 7(2), 469–494

Yousfi, O (2012), *Islamic Private Equity: What Is New*, retrieved from http://ssrn.com/abstract=1985389 (Access date December 2017)

Yunis (2006), Growth of Private Equity Funds Using Islamic Finance, *Islamic Finance News*, retrieved from www.islamicfinancenews.com (Access date November 3, 2017)

7

CAPITAL ASSET PRICING MODEL IN THE *SHARI'AH* DOMAIN

Learning Objectives

On completing this chapter, learners will be able to:

- Describe the relationship between systematic risk and expected return of assets particularly stocks
- Know the disadvantage of traditional CAPM
- Define capital asset pricing in the Islamic domain
- Understand why the capital asset pricing model (CAPM) is required in Islamic finance and the *Shari'ah* viewpoint on the assumption of the CAPM

7.1 Introduction

The Islamic financial approach is not restricted to banking but includes capital growth, capital markets, and all other types of financial intermediation. Explaining the system as *riba* or free from financial interest is likely to create confusion among the people who do know about the Islamic principle of business. The moral foundation of an Islamic financial system moves beyond the interface of factors of production and economic behaviour. While the traditional financial system aims primarily at the economic and financial facets of businesses, the Islamic financial system stresses the moral, social, ethical, and religious aspects to develop equality and fairness for the welfare of the entire society. The Islamic financial system may be fully appreciated only in the framework of principles of Islamic business ethics in the matters of wealth distribution, economic justice, social responsibility, work ethics and the role of the government. The theory of Islamic finance is instituted on the definite prohibition of the payment or receipt

DOI: 10.4324/9780429321207-7

of any predetermined and guaranteed rate of return. The style of Islamic investment is transformed with the growth of business range and gaining popularity all over the globe for these businesses free of *riba* (interest), *maisir* (gambling) and *gharar* (excessive uncertain).

Equity- or partnership-based firms (*musharaka*) have given financiers an opportunity to invest their money in the relatively large amounts in various companies. A rational financier is all the time risk averse, meaning they intend to boost their wealth by reducing risk. Therefore, a rational financier will never place their all eggs in one basket and will choose to spread risk by selecting a set of securities (portfolio) which would raise their return by lowering the risk (Levy and Markowitz, 1979).

7.1–1 Efficient Frontier

In his seminal article, "Portfolio Selection" (Markowitz, 1952), he did some pioneering work for modern portfolio theory. The part of the minimum-variance curve that lies above and to the right of the overall minimum variance portfolio is called the Markowitz efficient frontier, as it includes all portfolios that rational, risk-averse financiers would select. Investors would monitor the slope of the efficient frontier and the variation of return per unit at the minimum level of risk. As an investor moves to higher levels of risk, the resulting rise in return begins to reduce. The slope starts to flatten (Figure 7.1). It means investors cannot achieve ever-growing returns as they take more risk – somewhat becoming contrary. Also in a point, investors may go through a diminishing of potential returns as portfolio risk is enhanced (Analyst, 2020). The events can be described using the slope of the efficient frontier.

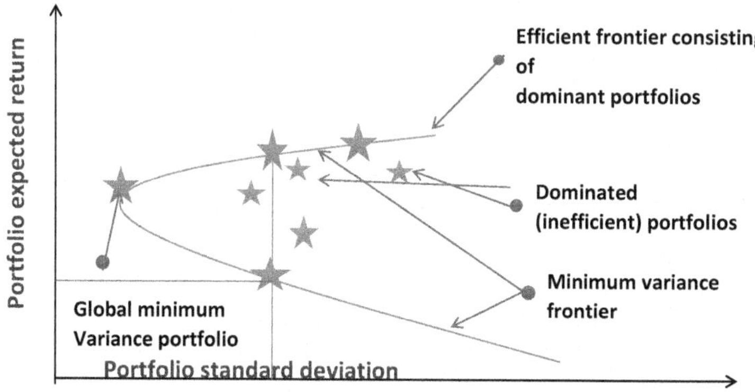

FIGURE 7.1 Slope of efficient frontier.

Source: Analyst (2020).

Example 1

Which statement best which explains the global minimum-variance portfolio?

A. The global minimum variance portfolio provides financiers the maximum amount of return.
B. The global minimum variance portfolio provides investors the lowest risk portfolio made up of risky assets.
C. The global minimum variance portfolio remains to the right of the efficient frontier.

Solution: The answer is B.

The global minimum variance portfolio reaches the far left of the efficient frontier and is a portfolio of risky assets that is exposed to the minimum risk for an investor. The financial market includes all risky assets or anything that has value – bonds, stocks, real estate, human capital, commodities – these are assets well defined in an efficient market. However, it is true that not all market assets are investable. But there are hundreds of thousands of individual financial securities which make up the market that are investable and tradeable. An average investor expects more concerned with their regional or country's stock market as a measure of the efficient market.

In the 'efficient frontier', the capital market line (CML) is a unique case of the capital allocation line – the line that makes up the allotment between a risk-free asset and a risky portfolio for a financier. In the case of the CML, the risk portfolio is the market portfolio (Figure 7.2). Where an investor has defined 'the market' to be their domestic stock market index, the anticipated return of the market is stated as the anticipated return of that index. In that case, the risk-return attributes for the potential risk asset's portfolios may be plotted to create a Markowitz efficient frontier. Where the line from the risk-free asset touches and is tangential to the Markowitz portfolio, this situation is described as the point of a portfolio. The

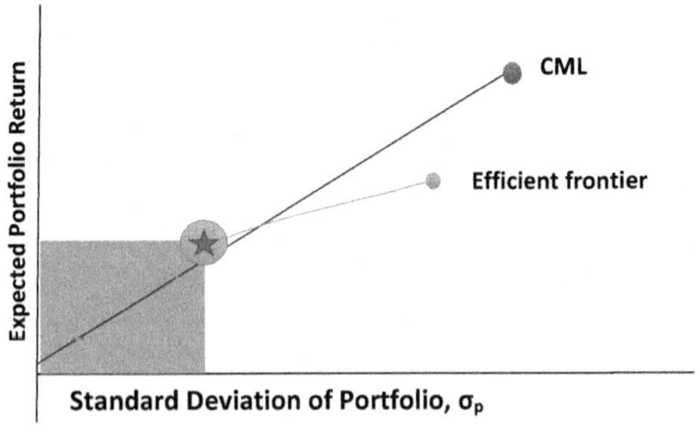

FIGURE 7.2 Capital market line.

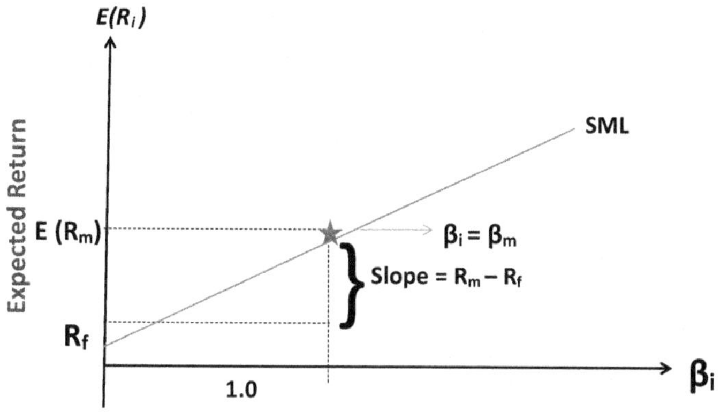

FIGURE 7.3 Security market line representing capital asset pricing line, indicating beta.

line joining the risk-free asset with the market portfolio is called CML, which is illustrated in Figure 7.2 (Analyst, 2020).

This phenomena can be written in the following equation:

$$E(R_p) = \left[\frac{R_f + \{E(R_m) - R_f\}}{\sigma_m}\right] \times \sigma_p$$

This is the form of an equation of a straight line where the intercept is R_f and the slope is $E[(R_m) - R_f]/\sigma_m$. This is the CML line, which has a positive slope as the market return is greater than the risk-free return. Based on this, Sharpe (1966) developed the security market line (SML) and the capital asset pricing line (CAPM) which are discussed below.

The SML is the graphical description of the CAPM, with beta indicating systematic risk on the x-axis and anticipated return on the y-axis. The SML intersects the y-axis at the risk-free rate, and the slope of the line is the market risk premium, $R_m - R_f$ (Figure 7.3).

Example 2

An overpriced security would highly possible plot:

A. Beneath the SML
B. On the SML
C. Over the SML

Solution: The answer is A. If the security lies on top of the SML, it is under-priced (go long). If the security lies beneath the SML, it is overpriced (go short).

7.1–2 Disadvantages of CAPM

A major disadvantage of CAPM is that it is hard to determine a beta. The return calculation CAPM involves the investors to assess a beta value that indicates the equity or share being invested in. It might be tricky and time consuming to assess an exact beta value. In almost all cases, a proxy value of beta is used.

Another disadvantage in employing the CAPM in investment appraisal is the assumption of a single-period time horizon at odds with the multiple period nature of investment appraisal. While CAPM variables would be assumed constant in the ensuing future periods, evidence shows that this is not true in the real investment world.

7.2 Previous Studies on CAPM in the *Shari'ah* Domain

There are some studies on conventional CAPM, and those studies explained why it is not practical to apply CAPM in the Islamic financial system with modifications. Tomkins and Abdul Karim (1987) said that *Shari'ah* rules are drawn from the Qur'an and tradition of the Prophet Mohammed (peace be upon him), which prohibit *riba* (interest) and assured return from the capital and indicate that no minimum premium in the form of a risk-free rate of return occurs in the Islamic financial system. The CAPM equation is as follows:

$$R_j = \beta_j\left(R_m\right)$$

where
R_j = the expected return of the security j
β_j = the systemic risk of security j
R_m = the return of the market index.

Further, El-Ashker (1987) then replaces the *Zakah* rate with the risk-free rate of return. El-Ashker argues that the *Zakah* rate is the minimum rate of return utilised to draw financiers to investment activities that provide the objective to employ *Zakah*. If the investor's secured return fails to use *Zakah*, then the investor will prefer to spend their capital in its place of engaging in investment activities. According to El-Ashker, the equation for the CAPM model would be as follows:

$$R_j = Z + \beta_j\left(R_m - Z\right)R_j = Z + \beta_j\left(R_m - Z\right)R_j = Z + \beta_j\left(R_m - Z\right)$$

where
R_j = the expected return on share or equity
Z = the *Zakah* rate
R_m = the market return
β_j = the systematic risk for every share or equity.

As a different method to the mentioned point, Selim (2008) uses a method of Islamic finance that is built on profit and loss sharing in contrast with the traditional

CAPM developed by Sharpe (1964) and describes the expected return from the investment as given below:

$$R_I' = \frac{(1-\alpha)\left[\pi E + kR_f\right]}{K}$$

where

R_I' = the anticipated return on the investment

α = the share of investment partner built on the method of profit and loss sharing

πE = the financial profit of the investment

kR_f = the capital opportunity cost.

A study was conducted by Shaikh (2010) with the sample data from around 38 years of a group of most important economies. His results appear that GDP is influenced by differences in the interest rate, affecting both to go in a similar direction. The GDP growth rate is used worldwide for indexing of loans. In actuality, Shaikh focused on the relationship between the nominal GDP (NGDP) growth rate and a company's loan and indicated that the NGDP growth rate would be employed in financial models for valuation functions. Shaikh replaced the NGDP growth ratio for the risk-free rate of return in the CAPM. So Shaikh's developed CAPM equation would therefore be as follows:

$$R_j = NGDP_g + \beta_j\left(R_m - NGDP_g\right)$$

The model developed by Shaikh (2010) is as consumption CAPM.

Hanif (2011) described that r_f (risk free) comprises two components: the first is the actual r_f and the second is the inflation cost. Here r_f indicates the cost of money which is the rate of interest and a value for use of the money. Corresponding to the *Shari'ah* law, money is the trade facilitator and not a commodity as the traditional system states and so does not justify any benefit until the same money is not invested in a real business. The time value of money is thus not accepted by the Islamic scholars and as a result, it comes within a similar class as financial interest (*Riba*). The second factor of r_f is the cost of inflation. In the fiat money method, inflation in the economy decreases the buying ability of money, and capital would be reduced consequently. Hanif (2011) believed that in a *Shari'ah*-compatible financial system, the financier should get a minimum premium equal to the inflation rate. He explained the *Shari'ah* compatible asset pricing model would be designed as follows:

$$R_j = N + \beta_j\left(R_m - N\right)$$

where

R_j = the anticipated return on the share or equity

N = the inflation rate

R_m = the mean return on the market portfolio

β_j = the systematic risk for each share or equity.

The study Pouryani (2015) developed expanded the traditional CAPM employing *Shari'ah* rules in functioning Islamic financial system which may be termed a value-based pricing model (on the total asset basis), a design in underlying financial processes in the Islamic system which is built on the basis of Islamic contracts.

Further, Hazny et al. (2020) introduced a model of Islamic financial asset pricing. This *Shari'ah*-conforming CAPM is a revision of the conventional CAPM that integrates principles of Islamic finance and incorporates other Islamic variables such as the purification of unlawful income from investments (*riba, maisir* and *gharar*), the prohibition of short selling, and *Zakah*.

7.3 *Shari'ah* Viewpoints on the Assumption of Traditional CAPM

The CAPM is a demand-side model that is built on maximising the investor's utility function and believes in the market equilibrium. The model is dependent on a set of assumptions built by Markowitz (1952) with a number of extra assumptions set by Sharpe (1964). Based on Elton et al. (2014), the assumptions are as follows: there is no transaction cost; the assets are substantially divisible; individual income tax is absent; an investor should not distress the price of a stock by their selling and buying activities; investors' choices are solely in terms of expected values and variance of returns; unlimited short sales are permissible; there is unlimited borrowing and lending at the riskless rate; and the similarity of expectations and all financial assets is marketable. In what happens next, there is presentation of an outline of the assumptions under which the CAPM has been developed, in terms of *Shari'ah* conformity. Certain of these assumptions might appear impractical, but such an explanation of realism makes the CAPM further workable from a mathematical standpoint (Hazny et al., 2017).

7.3-1 No Operation Cost

The CAPM assumes 'no transaction cost' to decrease the complication of the model (Elton et al., 2014). The 'no transaction cost' belief is not contrary to any principles of *Shari'ah* and finance. Yet, it is prudent to point out that the presence of transaction cost affects significant errors when various transactions are presented as in uninterrupted-time models (Steinbach, 2001). In the perspective of *Shari'ah*, these errors may possibly take the lead to a violation of the ethics of Islamic finance where the outcomes of the model might be misleading or deplorable due to speculative (*maisir*) and severe uncertainties (*gharar*) in findings.

7.3-2 No Personal Income Tax

In CAPM it is believed that there is no individual income tax. This belief is not contrary to the principles of *Shari'ah*, as there is no provision of direct income tax in Islamic laws. But, the Islamic economic system has a concept of *Zakah* – a sacred tax for all Muslims who meet the necessary norms of wealth, that is only imposed on the surplus wealth and not on income.

7.3–3 Divisibility and Saleability of Asset

The CAPM assumes that the assets are infinitely separable and saleable. In reality, it is not continually feasible to buy only a unit of an asset, and financiers are not always in the situation of perfect liquidity. But, this assumption is aimed for simplification of the model and consistent with the ethics of *Shari'ah* and Islamic finance. Various research shows that relaxing of these assumptions indicates robust empirical results.

7.3–4 Investors' Choices Are Exclusively in Terms of Variance (Risk) and Expected Return

In all anticipated returns, covariance should and variance would be known in advance so that investors would take decisions solely on the basis of variance and expected return. Corresponding to Rosly (2005), this is, in fact, in line with the Islamic principles of *al-ghorm bil ghonm* ('there is no return without risk') and *al-kharaj bil damam* ('profit comes with responsibility'). In circumstance, *Shari'ah* maxim of *al-ghorm bil ghonm* is appealed to call the investors to take part in ventures connecting both risk and return such as *al-bay* (trading); *salam* (forward contract); *ijarah* (hire, lease or rent); *mudarabah* (quiet partnership), where one of the parties delivers capital and the other gives their technical know-how or skill to conduct a particular type of business; and the *musharaka* (joint partnership business) type of contract is based on more than two persons doing business on a partnership basis.

7.3–5 Short Sales Violate Islamic Ethics

The assumption of short sales makes the CAPM simpler for its arithmetic derivation. This belief implies that assets might be held in an arbitrary sum of money – negative and positive. Dusuki and Abozaid (2008) examined the subject of a short sale in which an asset is selling but the investor does not hold, and it clearly violates the ethics of Islamic finance, which is called *bay' al ma'dum* ('selling what the seller does not own'). The profit from this type of business is considered *riba* and therefore not *Shari'ah* compatible. The component of speculation (*maisir*) is implicated in short sales, hence it implies that short selling is undesirable in Islamic finance.

7.3–6 Homogeneousness of Expectation

The traditional CAPM model believes all financiers have similar hopes about expected returns, correlation coefficients among assets, and variances (risks) of assets. In the existence of homogeneous beliefs, investors have an equal optimal portfolio. However, in Islamic finance, investors are urged to trade in *Shari'ah*-compatible funds to receive profit in the generally agreed manner (*al-ribh al-ma'ruf*) and consist of risk (Islahi, 1988). Therefore, it is acceptable to assume that investors maintain consistent expectations in the market. Thus, each asset would have a market price, and it would be considered the appropriate price when investors have a similar expectation. Additionally, *Shari'ah* permits detecting the price corresponding to the market price (Hassan et al., 2005), and this should take the lead to mutual consent, and eventually homogeneous beliefs could be attained.

7.3–7 Unrestricted Borrowing and Lending at a Risk-Free Rate

This assumption is extremely important in designing the CAPM model since this assumption advances to a piecewise linear association between beta for efficient portfolios and expected return. In the matter of Islamic finance, the ban of interest (*riba*) takes the lead to the non-existence of risk-free asset, and therefore, it needs to eliminate the risk-free rate from *Shari'ah*-based investment. But there are issues that this assumption might be applied as per *Shari'ah*; for example, the usage of Islamic financial assets that might be similar to risk-free assets such as Islamic bonds (*Sukuk*). Omar et al. (2010) suggested using three-month Islamic T-bills as a proxy for risk-free assets.

7.3–8 A Financier Should Not Change the Price of a Stock by Buying and Selling Activities

The homogeneity of anticipation indicates that investors are price takers, since a single investor may not change the price of stock by the act of buying and selling. In Islamic finance, financiers may not influence the price of their transactions. Therefore, the homogeneous expectation hypothesis in the conventional CAPM is maintained, and investors should constantly choose an optimal portfolio. Thus, based on the above considerations, it is presumed that the majority of the assumptions in the conventional CAPM and mean variance analysis of Markowitz are not inconsistent with any ethics of Islamic finance, and therefore at this point it has conformity with *Shari'ah*.

7.4 Traditional CAPM Undesirable in Islamic Finance

In view of the preceding explanation, the CAPM model with such an investment space is not appropriate for the clarification of returns on Islamic financial instruments because of the restrictions forced by *Shari'ah* in dealing with interest (*riba*) and participation of unlawful (*haram*) businesses (Hakim et al., 2016). The market portfolio of the CAPM model includes the stocks of both unlawful (*haram*) and lawful (*halal*) businesses and is therefore not permitted in investment choices for ethical investing. The Qur'ānic prohibitions draw up the realm of Muslims' investment endeavours. Further, the injunction of *riba* stops interest-holding risk-free assets from the investment universe and prevention of participating in *haram* (unlawful) businesses, which necessitates reorganisation of the market portfolio in the light of Islamic ethics. Under these situations, the real questions appearing are:

1. Is the CAPM model appropriate for clarifying returns on assets in the Islamic investment universe?
2. If it is the case, then what is required to make it relevant in the Islamic financial universe?

To answer these questions, an alternative version of CAPM is needed for *Shari'ah*-compliant investment universes that is entirely in conformity with the principles of Islamic business ethics. Over the years, a few *Shari'ah*-compatible Islamic financial instruments that provide several styles of investment demand for investors have been established. Since Islamic financial instruments vary from conventional financial instruments in relation to their legal structure and the nature of transactions, it is imperative that asset pricing models originally structured for conventional financial instruments are modified so that some alternative CAPM model should be made applicable to Islamic financial instruments (Jobst, 2007). Additionally, sustainability of the desirability of Islamic financial instruments is conditional on investors' ability to properly evaluate their risk-return dynamics. Acknowledging the demand for asset pricing models that not only are built on the investment options allowed by *Shari'ah* but also may be efficient in securing the true nature of the risk and return dynamics of Islamic financial instruments is to accept the shortcomings of CAPM affirmation of the adequacy of market portfolio in justifying stock returns, which in fact may lead to the advent of multifactor asset pricing models. But, the multifactor asset pricing models acknowledge the domination of market portfolio in justifying returns of risky assets (Fama and French, 1996; Carhart, 1997; Pastor and Stambaugh, 2003). Therefore, it is required to consider focusing on developing a useful CAPM model that holds to the tenets of *Shari'ah* and should be suitable for investors in the Islamic financial market.

7.5 The Proposed CAPM in the Islamic Domain

The proposed *Shari'ah*-based CAPM model is examined from two aspects: risk-free rate of return and valuation based on stock supply and demand in turn as market value. In this model, asset valuation is done on the basis of market value, and it needs brief clarification. In stock markets, stock prices are regulated by market value (i.e. supply and demand), and here it is sometimes not clear to sellers and buyers what they have owned and what they have sold. This occurs because of manipulation of security price and speculation in the market. Consequently, the genuine nature of traded documents fade away by the speculators in the market that influence at security the prices artificially. In fact, a market-based pricing system on which market value is based paves the way for and leads the stock market speculators to use all stock in trading as their means of unethical income. However, it should be acknowledged that the pricing of securities as such sets the grounds for performance of unethical games which affects the restraint of information for some investors. This type of phenomenon in market price manipulation and speculators generates such income that is unlawful from the point of view of Islamic business ethics.

Therefore, it is seen that the market-based valuation of stocks takes the lead in manipulation and speculation of security prices. It also affects potential funds to deviate from their principal route and enter into a money vortex, even though this makes income for lenders and speculators in the money market. Not only does this type of manipulation decrease the growth of production and employment, but also it increases financial imbalance which in turn creates inflation and unemployment in the economy. The allocation of income and wealth thus becomes unfair due to speculation (at the same time with *riba*-based transactions), and such imbalance creates the ground for economic problems. So investors observe excessive volatility in the stocks market from time to time – the worst of which happened in the New York stock market during 1929–1933, in which stocks dropped their nominal value by up to 60%. Therefore, market-based pricing of stocks as such neither indicates the actual value of stocks nor the outperformance of their issuance companies. Therefore, market-based pricing is not considered in line with the goals of the Islamic financial system, and thus the views of many Islamic scholars in respect of asset-based pricing is considered helpful. In this respect, the analysis of Khan (1982) indicated that the real price of stocks in the Islamic stocks market is correctly anticipated to be defined as follows:

> Actual value of assets in a production unit
> = Nominal stock value – loss (if any) + aggregated profits or resources – aggregated loss/total number of stocks
> = actual stock value in the Islamic stock market

As a result of the aforesaid paragraphs, market-based pricing does not comply with *Shari'ah* in the Islamic financial system. Consequently, the value of a firm's assets along with the profit from market movement is to be considered in the valuation of securities. It is thus considered that instead of using market value for capital asset pricing, a factor that does directly affect the firm's assets and performance is used instead, in which case the Islamic business ethics will be more closely look like. Certainly, the valuation of every share built on the share's acquired interest is supported by an asset, and as a result it generates artificial volatility in the supply and demand of stocks in the market. It must be noted that in the Islamic ethical environment and for the matter of information transparency, Islamic business ethics does not accept any form of artificially created risk.

However, first given that investments associated with profit and loss sharing (PLS) risk are genuine, the Islamic market allows such risks. To attain the pricing of securities based on real value, the profit to total assets ratio (π/A) is used to build up the *Shari'ah*-compliant CAPM (Pouryani, 2015). In this type of model, the actual value reflects the firm's assets and its operation to make use of these assets, represented by the following equation.

$$R_j = F\left(\frac{\pi}{A}\right)$$

The second element is equity risk premium specified as $(R_m - R_f)$ in the traditional CAPM. Because in the traditional CAPM it is presumed that the anticipated return on non-market assets is equivalent to the risk-free rate of return, the beta risk premium is equal to the anticipated return on the market portfolio minus the risk-free rate of return.

In the Islamic financial market, financial instruments are based on Islamic contracts which are divided into fixed income and variable rate of return as discussed previously. Because of the underlying structure of the Islamic financial system, in fact *Shari'ah* ethics govern all market mechanisms. In an Islamic financial market system that operates as a whole entity in the market that exhibits natural fluctuations in supply and demand, the weighted average rate of Islamic contracts with volatile income can be regarded as the return on non-market assets. The equity risk premium should then be assessed from the variation in the investment rate of return (profit to total asset ratio). On the other hand, the weighted average for fixed-income contracts should be replaced with the risk-free rate of return as the model intercept.

Application of the first and second aspects hereby examined (i.e. replacement of profit to asset ratio with market return) and replacement of the weighted average rate for Islamic contracts with volatile income with the return for non-market assets develops the anticipated *Shari'ah*-compliant CAPM model in the line of Pouryani (2015), as follows.

$$R_j = R' + \beta_j\left\{\left(\left(\frac{\pi}{A}\right)_j - R''_f\right)\right\}$$

R_j is the anticipated return of the security and R' is the weighted average *murabaḥa* rate for the fixed-income contract, which is the intercept of the model and the risk-free rate of return replaced in the CAPM. This is the appropriate choice, since some Islamic contracts such as *murabaha* (cost plus) have fixed and pre-defined income. R''_f is the weighted average rate for the contract of volatile income. In the CAPM, this rate explains the rate of return for non-market assets. It is believed that the financial system functions as an entire entity and the investment take place in the form of Islamic law of contracts. The rate of return in an Islamic contract is believed to be one of the crucial choice making principles, leading to the withdrawal of capital if a significant variation occurs between the return on non-market assets and assets at hand in the market. This dilemma has been kept in mind, and the weighted average rate of return in an Islamic contract with volatile income is deemed as the rate of return for non-market assets. The investment rate of return (profit divided by total asset) is $(\pi / A)_j$, and β_j is the systematic risk of j security. This element explains the sensitivity of each share to its rate of return. Greater beta indicates that a larger return generates at the price of experiencing higher risk.

7.6 Benefits of the *Shari'ah*-Compliant Model in Contrast With the Traditional CAPM

Figures 7.4 and 7.5 show the advantages of the proposed *Shari'ah*-compliant CAPM which are explained in detail as follows:

1. In the conventional CAPM, market-based pricing is exercised and return on equity is matched with return on the equities market. Actually, beta is calculated from the sensitivity of every share in relation to the market return.
2. In the current model, the crucial role portrayed by every firm's interest rate in the valuation of securities requires the evaluation of firms against their competitors. Even though it is recognised that the rate of investment return (profit to total asset ratio) varies between different projects in the short term, these rates (under fixed conditions) be likely to get closer and even at a level in the

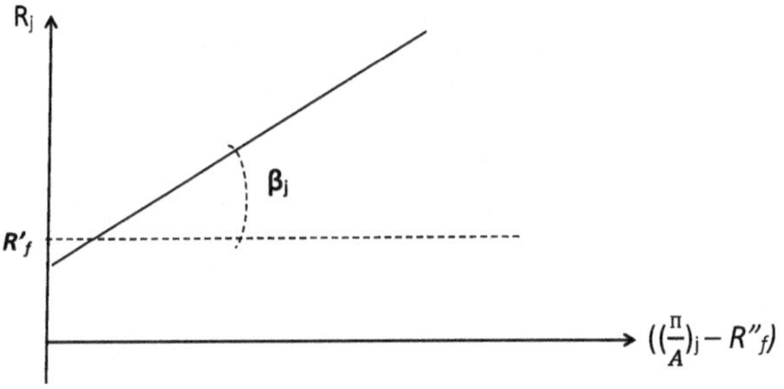

FIGURE 7.4 Composition of expected return and beta risk premium in the proposed model.

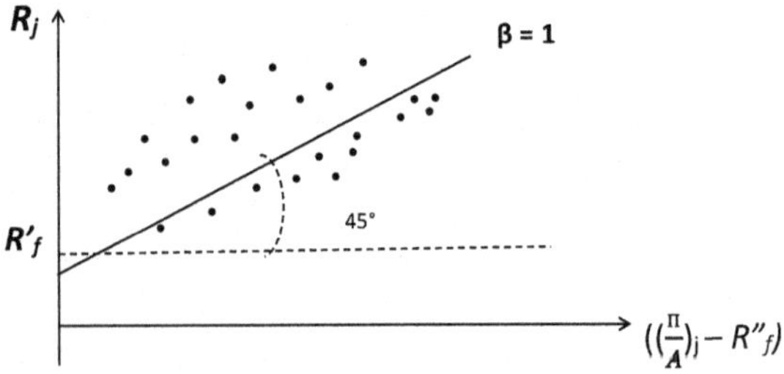

FIGURE 7.5 Merging of the investment rate of return in the planned model around the 45-degree line (β = 1).

> long term under competitive circumstances. This is due to the access of new production units in the financial services industry or as a result of increased production of the current production unit. On the other hand, companies providing the market profit-making skills difference between the various businesses in the long term, the exit and entry of firms in a free market, but projects are not self-governing from each other in the eyes of statistics and finally, given the law of large numbers, the investment rates of return (π / A) for these companies attain and beta becomes equal to 1. In other terms, basic assumptions concerning the Islamic financial market in the competitive market conditions and dependency of various projects on each other lead to (π / A) ratios which are not much different from each other and converge in the long run for the several firms in the Islamic financial system, when beta is equal to 1.

On the contrary, the rate of return in the Islamic law of contracts with fixed income declines gradually in modest market conditions and converges to a minimum ($min\ R'$) that is equal to the time value of money. At this juncture, the question may be raised: does the time value of money involve or have any role in the Islamic economy? It is obvious that Islamic economics do not have time value of money on its own. It means that the time value of money is equals zero (0). But appreciation of credit sales by Islamic financial institutions (IFIs) suggests that there is a presence of time money value. In credit transactions, for example, the cash price of a good is p_0 at the present time, and given goods are transported at the present time and the price received in the future, the let payable price would be p^t as such $p_t > p_0$ (Pouryani, 2015). According to the assertion hereby presented, $p_t - p_0$indicates that the seller receives a value greater than the cash price of the goods which are transported to the buyer at present time or sometime after the supply time. The time break between the transfer of goods to the buyer and the price received by the seller is equal to t . In other words, money has a time value in the traditional economic method, and the time value of money is the interest rate calculated is $((M_t - M_0) / M_0)$.

According to *Shari'ah* laws, however, there is no time value of money concept, but time holds money value. Therefore, the time value of money is zero in the

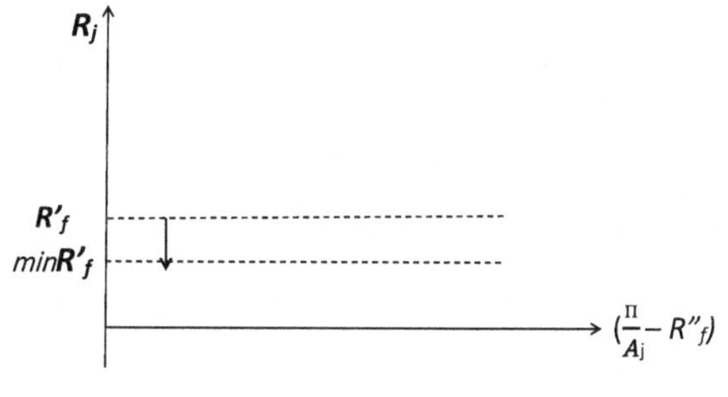

FIGURE 7.6 Intercept for the suggested model in the long term.

Islamic economy. The money value of time may be measured through the relationship $((P_t - p_0) / p_0)$. Indeed, some Islamic economists and *Shari'ah* scholars did not make this difference.

Because of exclusion of interest (*riba*), denial of speculation, and prohibition of hoarding in Islamic finance, the unlawful transaction of money is no longer in the market. Therefore, the demand and supply sides leave no further room for revision other than in extraordinary circumstances. At this point, the virtual money market bounces its place to the demand and supply of real capital. Together with the management tool in the Islamic stocks market, it will lead to reduced speculative buying or selling in the market when real value replaces market value. This also impedes artificial variations on stocks demand as forced by the dealer of speculative exchange. As a result, additional artificial risk in the market is stopped. It is assumed that all risk is natural and under Islamic assumptions (which command no money market or speculative buying or selling of money or stock), therefore no artificial risk prevails in the financial market.

Correspondingly, the pricing of stocks in the projected in the *Shari'ah*-conforming model is designed on the basis of the economic profit of the company where the entire economy is regulated based on *Shari'ah*. Hence under this argument, the financing of firms by Islamic financial institutions (IFIs) does comply with *Shari'ah*, in this case, firms run via *mudarabah* or *musharaka* contracts (profit and loss sharing contracts) in which the IFI is the firm's partner with entrepreneur where depositors and firms share their profit. As a result, the production firm does not consider costs as interest (*riba*) but as owners of a firm. In other way, under the Islamic economic system, the head-to-head point for Islamic firms is lesser in comparison with its counterparts. Therefore, companies are funded via partnership (*musharaka* or *mudarabah*) contracts which acquire more profit under similar conditions. It is thus anticipated that equal risk of the proposed model generates a greater return, as shown in Figure 7.7.

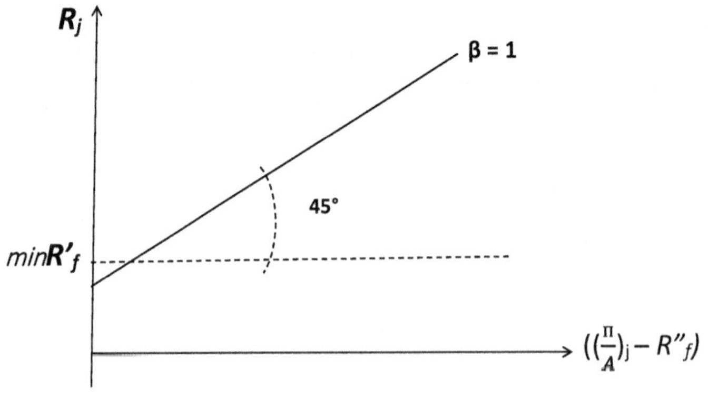

FIGURE 7.7 Composition of expected return and risk premium in the planned model in the long term.

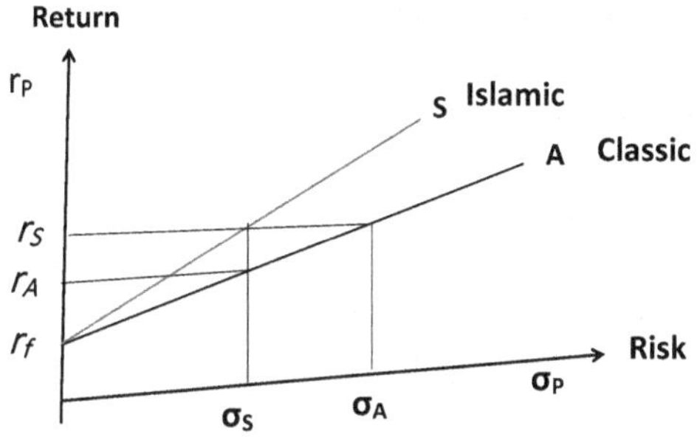

FIGURE 7.8 Composition of expected return and portfolio risk in the conventional (A) and Islamic (S) models.

In view of the foregoing, it is anticipated that the gradient of the proposed model goes beyond the traditional model under Islamic financial market conditions, and at this condition, equal return of the proposed model would endure with lower risk in comparison to the conventional model. A comparison is shown between $r_f A$ and $r_f S$ in Figure 7.8, which carries an expected rate of return in which $r_f : \sigma \text{S} < \sigma \text{A}$.

Based on the evidence from Figure 7.8, it can be confirmed that for every specific risk σS, the anticipated rate of return in the Islamic model (rS) is greater than the projected rate of return in the traditional CAPM (rA): $rS > r$.

7.7 Conclusion

A theoretical extension of the CAPM in the Islamic domain has been done through the portrayal of Islamic business ethics rules that runs the Islamic financial system, value-based pricing of capital assets, and the importance of the Islamic law of contracts in Islamic finance and also application in the CAPM. Finally, market-based pricing is not acknowledged as in line with the aims of the Islamic financial market. As a substitute, asset-based pricing is reflected as appropriate, according to the opinions of many Islamic intellectuals (e.g. Hakim et al., 2016; Khan, 1982). Therefore, the value of a firm's assets and the profit it acquires through its investment activities may be deemed appropriate in the valuation of security or stocks. It is therefore recommended that CAPM model should be based on the application of factors that bring direct impact from the profit sharing system stemming from the effective application of the company's assets, as a result the *Shari'ah* rules are intensely prospered.

To realise the value-based pricing of securities or stocks, the profit to total asset ratio π / A method is utilised. Assuming that all market forces are ruled by the principles of Islamic economics, where the Islamic financial system functions as a whole unit competitive market. The weighted average rate of return in Islamic law of contract with volatile income is deemed as the return of non-market assets; therefore equity risk premiums should be assessed from the variance in the investment rate of return (profit to total asset ratio). The weighted average of Islamic law of contract with fixed income should be replaced with the risk-free rate of return in place of the model's intercept.

This chapter provides a model to equip with a contemporary form of knowledge by introducing an algorithm and *Shari'ah*-compliant CAPM that is missing in the literature of Islamic investment. It offers a novel method in pricing Islamic investable assets in compliance with *Shari'ah*, which has been replicated from a contemporary financial theory of Markowitz's MVA (mean variance analysis) and capital asset pricing model (CAPM).

Review Questions

1. What is the CAPM used to measure?
2. What is Markowitz's efficient frontier?
3. What are risk-free assets and their risk-return characteristics?
4. Why is the *Shari'ah*-compliant CAPM needed in Islamic finance?
5. What are the *Shari'ah* views on the assumption of CAPM?
6. What is the relationship between systematic risk and expected return in Islamic investments?
7. What are some shortcomings to beta that receive much criticism?

References

Analyst (2020), *Evaluation of Portfolio Theory Efficient Frontier to SML*, retrieved from https://analystprep.com/blog/evolution-of-portfolio-theory-efficient-frontier-to-sml/ (Access date March 2, 2021)

Carhart, MM (1997), On Persistence in Mutual Fund Performance, *Journal of Finance*, LII(1), 57–82

Dusuki, A and Abozaid, A (2008), Fiqh Issues in Short Selling as Implemented in the Islamic Capital Market in Malaysia, *Journal of King Abdulaziz University-Islamic Economics*, 21(2), 63–78

El-Ashker, A (1987), *The Islamic Business Enterprise*, London: Croom Helm

Elton, E, Gruber, M, Brown, S and Goetzmann, W (2014), *Modern Portfolio Theory and Investment Analysis*, 9th ed, New York: John Wiley and Sons

Fama, EF and French, KR (1996), Multifactor Explanations of Asset Pricing Anomalies, *The Journal of Finance*, 51, 55–84

Hakim, S, Hamid, Z and Meera, A (2016), Capital Asset Pricing and Pricing of Islamic Financial Instruments, *JKAU: Islamic Economics*, 29(1), 21–39

Hanif, M (2011), Risk and Return Under *Shari'ah* Framework: An Attempt to Develop *Shari'ah, Pakistan Journal of Commerce and Social*, 5(2)

Hassan, A, Antoniou, A and Paudyal, K (2005), Impact of Ethical Screening on Investment Performance: The Case of the Dow Jones Islamic Index, *Islamic Economic Studies*, 12(1), 67–97

Hazny, M, Hasim, H and Yusof, A (2017), Mathematical Modelling of a Shari'ah-Compliant Capital Asset Pricing Model, *Journal of Islamic Accounting and Business Research*, 1(1), 90–109

Hazny, M, Hasim, H and Yusof, A (2020), Mathematical Modelling of a Shari'ah Compliant Asset Pricing Model, *Journal of Islamic Accounting and Business Research*, 11(1), 90–109
Islahi, A (1988), *Economic Concepts of Ibn Taimiyah*, Leicester: The Islamic Foundation
Jobst, A (2007), The Economics of Islamic Finance and Securitization, *Journal of Structured Finance*, 13(1), 6–27
Levy, H and Markowitz, HM (1979), Approximating Expected Utility by a Function of Mean and Variance, *American Economic Review*, 69, 308–317
Markowitz, H (1952), Portfolio Selection, *Journal of Finance*, 7(1), 77–91
Khan, M (1982), Inflation and the Islamic Economy: A Closed Economy Model, in *Monetary and Fiscal Economics of Islam*, edited by M. Ariff, Jeddah: ICRIE
Omar, M, Noor, A, Meera, A, Manap, T, Majid, M and Zain, S (2010), *Research Paper: Islamic Pricing Benchmark*. International Shari'ah Research Academy for Islamic Finance (ISRA), 17
Pastor, L and Stambaugh, R (2003), Liquidity Risk and Expected Stock Returns, *Journal of Political Economy*, 111(3), 642–685
Pouryani, S (2015), Providing Recommendations on Capital Asset Pricing Model (CAPM) on the Basis of Islamic Assumptions, *International Journal of Scientific Management and Development*, 3(5), 341–349
Rosly, S (2005), *Critical Issues in Islamic Banking and Financial Markets*, Kuala Lumpur: Dinamas Publishing
Selim, T (2008), An Islamic Capital Asset Pricing Model, *Humanomics*, 24(2), 122–129
Shaikh, S (2010), *Proposal for a New Economic Framework Based on Islamic Principles*, Karachi: Institute of Business Administration
Sharpe, W (1964), Capital Asset Prices: A Theory of Market Equilibrium under Conditions of Risk, *Journal of Finance*, 19, 425–442
Sharpe, W (1966), Mutual Fund Performance, *Journal of Business*, 39(1), 119–138
Steinbach, M (2001), Markowitz Revisited: Mean-Variance Models in Financial Portfolio Analysis, *SIAM Review*, 43(1), 31–85
Tomkins, C and Abdul Karim, RA (1987), The Shari'ah and its Implications for Islamic Financial Analysis: An Opportunity to Study Interactions Among Society, Organization, and Accounting, *American Journal of Islam and Society*, 4(1), 101–115

8

ISLAMIC EXCHANGE-TRADED FUNDS

Learning Objectives

On completing this chapter, learners will be able to:

- Understand the differences between exchange traded funds (ETF) and Islamic ETFs
- Identify the advantages and risks associated with ETFs
- Know the parties engaged in the management of ETFs
- Differentiate between ETFs and stocks
- Explain the process of Islamic ETFs
- Describe the global trends of Islamic ETFs.

8.1 Introduction

Exchange-traded funds (ETF) are marketable securities that are based on a specific index, asset, or group of assets, such as the S&P 500, treasury, gold, and other commodities or a currency rate. Similar to a stock, the price of an ETF rises and falls throughout a market session in tandem with the index or assets it represents. The job of the fund manager is to match the performance of the underlying assets by making appropriate investments that track accordingly.

ETFs provide investors and traders an opportunity to participate in markets that would otherwise be too difficult or costly to piece together on their own. Taking a position in an ETF of the Financial Times Stock Exchange (FTSE) 100 index, for example, with one transaction is much easier and more affordable than buying all the components of the FTSE 100, which would need to be properly weighted and ultimately unwound when exiting. ETFs also offer precise control over entry and exit strategies that is not possible with multiple, individual stocks or a security with inter-day price changes, as in the case of a mutual fund or unit trust.

DOI: 10.4324/9780429321207-8

ETFs have been created to allow investors to participate in new industries and segments like cryptocurrencies and marijuana, which reduces the risk of investing in these untested areas. ETFs will continue to grow as popularity of the vehicle increases. Treasury, currency, and commodity ETFs make these asset classes available to a broader pool of investors who would traditionally be less likely to hold these assets. On the opposite, ETFs are another class of these products which work in opposition to the assets' movements. In other ways, they appreciate if the underlying asset declines in value, for instance, which allows bearish investors a unique opportunity to profit from a market with waning momentum.

8.2 Common Type of ETFs

A larger proportion of ETFs are based on indexes which are quite likely to follow and represent certain index benchmarks like that of the Dow Jones Islamic Market Index. Possibly based on stocks and irrespective of the underlying asset, an index ETF assists in tracking index performance by taking into consideration the entire or a particular index sample (Hill et al., 2015). An example can be given of the top 500 companies listed on the New York Stock (NYS) market based on the dimension of their size, being responsibly tracked by the MSCI Islamic Index. An ETF tracking the Amana MF will typically hold all 50 stocks in the same proportion as the Index.

8.2-1 Equity ETFs

Equity ETFs are responsible for tracking an index of equities. An investor can opt for ETFs which cover large and/or small businesses or stocks from a particular country. Using equity ETFs can help the investor direct towards well-performing sectors at that given time. Sectors could range from tech stocks to Islamic banking stocks, both of which are quite familiar to investors.

8.2-2 Bond/Fixed Income ETFs

Diversification of an investor's portfolio is imperative to wiser investing even if this does not entirely ensure portfolio protection from risks in the market. Diversifying investments into bonds and fixed-income ETFs does not in any way guarantee returns or eradicate chances for incurring losses. Professional conventional investors still choose to invest in fixed-income and bond ETFs because these promise steady returns and simultaneously have lower risks associated with them as compared to equity ETFs.

8.2-3 Commodity ETFs

Commodities like gold, silver or oil are comparatively more difficult to access than stocks. ETFs of these commodities act as an effective alternative to stocks, thereby helping in the diversification of an investor's portfolio as well as its corresponding risks. It must be kept in mind that the transparency of commodity ETFs is lower than that of index or stock ETFs. Most of the time, the ownership of the underlying asset is not direct. For example, gold ETFs will entail the usage of derivatives that help in tracking the underlying price of the commodity. However, this is equally risky, for it might involve a counterparty risk, such as an ETF which directly owns the underlying asset (Hill et al., 2015). Counterparty risk can be explained as the risk that the counterparty to a derivative might be unable or unwilling to perform its payment obligations.

8.2–4 Currency ETFs

Currency ETFs involve making investments in a single currency (e.g. the UK pound) or in a basket of currencies. The investment by the ETF will be directly made in the currency, or derivates will be used for the same. Simultaneously, a mix of the two can be also used. An investor needs to be more careful regarding the purchasing choices they make while using the derivative method as this potentially brings in more risk. If the investor believes in hedging the portfolio or thinks that the underlying currency is about to strengthen, only then should they purchase currency ETFs. (Hedging constitutes to be one of the most important risk management strategies applied to be able to offset losses in investments.) ETFs investing in markets overseas might have supposedly 'hedged' against currency risk. The primary investment strategy of a fund might be partly inclusive of currency hedging. Currency hedging is also done in share classes where derivatives are used by funds to be able to hedge currency risk, even if this usage might bring in a potential risk of contagion (also known as spill-over of risk and liabilities) to other share classes in that fund.

8.2–5 Specialty ETFs

Apart from the above-mentioned funds, two other types of funds are observed to be active in recent times: leveraged funds and inverse funds. These specialty ETFs are designed to sync to very specific needs (BlackRock, 2019) and are inclusive of provisions of greater growth potential but are simultaneously subjected to higher risk.

- Inverse funds rise when the target index goes down (e.g. investors short selling a stock when its price comes down).
- Leveraged funds are used to reap maximum returns by borrowing more money (leverage) to invest. Investors can determine these ETFs by emphasising on how much they are leveraged for. An instance can be 2X borrowing an extra US$1 for every US$1 investors put into the fund.

8.3 Factors Investing in ETFs

An investment approach involved in specifying drivers of return across asset classes can be summed up as factor investing. Overall these years, factors have been in regular use by managers and institutional investors in managing investment portfolios. Ruled-based ETFs, popularly known as 'Smart Beta', are the way to gain access to these factors. As a collective of investment strategies, 'Smart Beta' emphasises the use of alternative index construction rules to traditional market capitalisation-based indices. Additionally, it also focuses on capturing investment factors and pinpointing market inefficiencies, ideally based on rules and in an entirely transparent way (BlackRock, 2019).

8.3-1 ETF Creation and Redemption

Aps (authorised participants) are large, specialised investors involved in a mechanism which regulates the supply of conventional ETF shares. This mechanism consists of creation and redemption.

8.3-1-1 ETF Creation

In situations where additional shares are to be issued by an ETF, the AP would purchase shares of the stocks from the index, the S&P 500, tracked by the fund. The AP would then sell or exchange the shares to the ETF for new ETF shares at the same price they had bought the shares, earlier. The AP would eventually generate profit by selling the ETF shares in the market. Creation involves this process of the AP selling stocks to the ETF sponsor to get shares in ETF as returns (Figure 8.1).

8.3-1-2 Creation When Shares Trade at a Premium

An accounting mechanism that helps in determining the overall asset value or stock value in an ETF is net asset value (NAV). As an example, an ETF having a share price of US$101 at the closing market is investing in stocks of FTSE 500. If the stock value per share of what the ETF owns is at US$100, the fund being traded at US$101 per share is considered to be a premium to the fund's NAV.

$$\text{Net asset value (NAV)} = \text{Value of assets} - \text{Value of liabilities}$$

An incentive that the authorised participant enjoys is to be able to bring the ETF share price back into equilibrium with the fund's NAV. For this, the AP would have to purchase stock shares that it wants from the market to be compiled in its portfolio and sell them to the fund in return for ETF shares. An example in this regard would be an AP purchasing stocks worth US$100 per share in the open market and instead receiving ETF shares that are being traded at US$101 per share in the open

Exchange-Traded Funds	*Mutual Funds*	*Stocks*
These are a type of index funds that track a basket of securities.	Mutual funds are pooled investments into bonds, securities and other instruments that provide returns.	Stocks are securities that provide returns based on performance.
Here, trading is done at a premium or at a loss to the net asset value of the fund.	Here, trading is done at the net asset value of the entire fund.	Stock returns occur on the basis of their actual performance in the markets.
The trading in the markets is done during regular hours, very similar to that of stocks.	Redemption can be made only at the end of a trading day.	Here, too, trading is done during regular market hours.
Since no marketing fee is charged, some ETFs can be purchased commission-free and are less expensive than mutual funds.	A majority of mutual funds are more expensive than ETFs because they charge administration and marketing fees; some do not charge large fees.	Stocks can be purchased commission free on some platforms and mostly do not have corresponding charges associated with them after purchase.
No actual involvement of securities is involved here.	Here, the ownership of securities is done in their basket.	Here, securities are physically owned.
Here, risk is diversified by tracking various companies in a sector or industry in a single fund.	Here, risk is diversified by creating a portfolio that spans multiple asset classes and security instruments.	Here, risk is concentrated in a stock's performance.
ETF trading occurs in-kind, meaning they cannot be redeemed for cash.	Mutual fund shares can be redeemed for money at the fund's net asset value for that day.	Stocks are bought and sold in cash.
ETF share exchanges are treated as in-kind distributions, which is why they are the most tax-efficient among all three types of financial instruments.	Tax benefits are offered by mutual funds when they return capital or include certain types of tax-exempt bonds in their portfolio.	Stocks are taxed at ordinary income tax rates or at capital gains rates.

FIGURE 8.1 ETFs versus mutual funds versus stocks.

Source: Hill et al. (2015).

market. This constitutes the process of creation and thereby elevates the quantity of ETF shares in the market. Given that everything continues to remain uniform, the number of shares available in the market will bring down the ETF price and put forth shares in line with the fund's NAV.

8.4-3-2 ETF Redemption

Redemption constitutes a process through which the number of ETF shares is reduced. An AP who purchases ETF shares in the open market and eventually sells them back to the ETF sponsor in exchange for individual stock shares that the AP can sell on the open market results in causing redemption (Figure 8.1).

The demand in the market acts as the determining factor for whether creation or redemption takes place and the particular amount associated with each of these activity. Additionally, the ETF being traded at a discount or premium to the value of the fund's assets equally influences creation or redemption.

8.4-3-3 Redemption When Shares Trade at a Discount

An example is illustrated here. Let's consider an ETF holding the stocks in the MSCI 2000 small-cap index and being traded at US$99 per share at present. If the stock value that ETF is holding in the fund is US$100 per share, then the ETF is being traded at a discount to its NAV. To be able to bring back the ETF's share price to equilibrium or its NAV, an AP will have to purchase ETF shares in the open market and sell them back to the ETF in return for shares of the underlying stock portfolio. Here, the AP can buy stock worth of US$100 in exchange for ETF shares it purchased for US$99. This process is defined as redemption, which in turn decreases the supply of ETF shares on the market. When the supply of ETF shares drops, the price should rise up and get closer to its NAV (Figure 8.1).

8.3-2 Not Free From Risk

Investments made in ETFs do not ensure the absence of risks in any way. Certain risks associated with ETFs are briefly mentioned below:

- Market risk: Economic conditions can largely influence stock prices. Political scenarios are equally responsible for impacting ETFs. As a basket of securities, the performance of the ETFs depends on the performance of its component securities. These are represented in the benchmark index.
- Tracking error: The performance of the underlying index might not be actively tracked by the performance of ETFs.
- Discount or premium: The exchange of the ETF's unit price might be traded either at a discount or premium to its NAV.

Investors who might have already decided on the investment objective and strategy are more likely to face these risks. Investors need to primarily decide whether the ETFs they want to purchase are aimed at short-term or long-term gains. Second, information on the index that ETFs are tracking has to be well known. An example can be taken of the energy sector where investors can follow the movement of, let's say, the world oil price. The third crucial thing that needs to be focused on is to trace information about the company's performing status. This is imperative for investors for early identification of several indicators, like that of profitability and/or solvability of a company, which might directly or indirectly affect the index. These instances stand as some primary ways through which these risks can be possibly terminated.

8.4 Process of ETF

The investment objective of the fund is generally determined by the sponsor of an actively managed ETF. Securities have to be traded at their discretion, which is very similar to that of an actively managed mutual fund. An example can be taken that of a sponsor attempting to achieve investment objectives by outperforming a segment of the market or using a portfolio of stocks, bonds or other assets to invest in a specific sector.

The chief functionaries of an EFT are briefly stated as follows (Omar et al., 2015):

1. Manager: The one who is responsible for managing the ETF so that it can be in line with the trust deed and securities laws.
2. Trustee: The one who acts as the custodian of the asset of ETF. Additionally, it is the trustee's role to ensure the administration of ETF is synced with the trust deed and laws of securities. At the same time, the interests of the ETF unit holders have to be safeguarded by the trustee.
3. Participating dealer: The entity which aids in the facilitation of in-kind creation and redemption of the ETF units. The participating dealer simultaneously acts as the liquidity provider.
4. Other liquidity providers (if any). These aid in providing liquidity to the ETF.
5. Investors: The ones who invest in the ETF units, mostly through the medium of brokers.

Selecting a particular Islamic index to be used as a benchmark is one of the first and most crucial steps among others during the creation of the ETF unit. Sets of securities will vary for every Islamic index, and also the screening criteria will vary.

Let us analyse a situation to understand the concepts with more clarity. Individuals / companies / participating dealers need to initially have the perfect basket of securities within the Islamic index in order to be able to create $1 million in ETF funds. This perfect basket has to be delivered by the dealers to the trustee for the latter to be able to create the $1 million units of Islamic EFT.

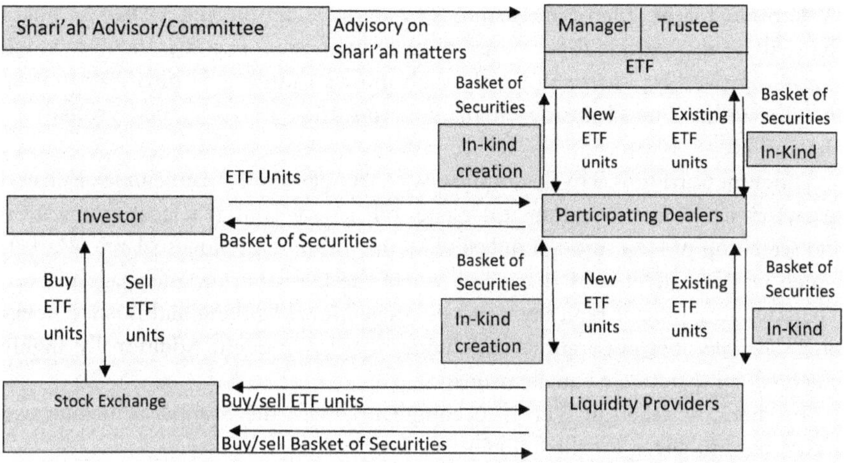

FIGURE 8.2 Process of EFT.

Thus, this is addressed not in terms of cash subscriptions but in kind. Hence, the ETF units represent the underlying shares, as the shares act as the founding criteria for the creation of the ETFs. This unit of ETFs will be returned to the participating dealers and in due course, being purchased by the investors through liquidity providers (Figure 8.2). After owning the ETF units, investors can then trade them via a secondary market where cash transactions will take place. During redemption, the participating dealers will assemble the specified number of ETF units and deliver to the manager and trustee. As an exchange, the perfect basket will be returned to the participating dealer.

8.5 Islamic Exchange-Traded Funds

The ETFs that follow the principles of Islamic investing rules are also known as *Shari'ah*-compliant ETFs. Islamic ETFs come under the category of socially responsible investments under ESG, the category of investment options available to the investors that are based on the environmental, social, and governance factors. ESG investments are often used for describing investment types such as 'socially responsible investing' and 'sustainable investing', which are accepted in the Islamic investing universe. Islamic ETFs are the best available investment options as they follow the *Shari'ah* rules and can be an efficient way of gaining profits for Muslim investors without having to disobey their religious rules while trading to gain profits.

Islamic funds are based on many requirements that they must follow. Some of the major requirements for an ETF in order to become an Islamic ETF is that it should mandatorily avoid making investments where a major portion of the income is derived from the trading of alcohol, services related to pornography, gambling, military equipment or weapons, and products associated with pork.

Another major rule of an Islamic ETF requires appointing a *Shari'ah* board that will be responsible for conducting an annual *Shari'ah* audit. Income which is not approved by *Shari'ah* (e.g. through interest) undergoes purification during this audit. The cleansing entails donating the interest-earned profits to a charity.

Different portfolios actively dominate a variety of sectors. Islamic index is shared in sectors across construction, real estate, oil, gas, as well as telecommunication and screening process through indexes like that of the Dow Jones Islamic Market, which was not affected by the meltdown of the US subprime mortgage market. The screening process typically removes conventional banking and finance stocks since *Shari'ah* does not approve of activities that pay interest. Additionally, highly indebted companies are equally banned.

To check whether an ETF is in compliance with the *Shari'ah* principles, we would have to check for the following factors:

Shari'ah-compliant constituents: For an ETF to be declared *Shari'ah*-compliant, its constituents must be in harmony with *Shari'ah* principles. This refers to all kinds of shares and assets which an ETF consists of.

Compliance with *Shari'ah* screening: All ETFs should go through regular screenings to ensure ongoing *Shari'ah* compliance. The screening criteria that should be satisfied by an ETF to be compliant with *Shari'ah* principles are:

- The screening must be associated with a business activity.
- The screening must correspond to financial requirements.

Business activity screening: If found to be involved in any of the following activities, companies will be filtered based on being non-compliant with *Shari'ah*:

- Traditional banking and investments which constitute conventional financial services.
- Any form of trade involving risks and *Gharar* (uncertainty).
- Activities that involve gambling, *Qimar* (betting and wagering) or *Maisir* (gambling and speculation).
- Activities that are related to alcohol and other prohibited beverages.
- Activities that are directly linked with products that are associated with pork and non-halal food production. Packaging, processing, marketing or any activity that is linked to unlawful consumables is equally banned.
- Goods and services that are involved in tobacco-related products.
- Activities related to the illegal adult industry (e.g. pornography).
- Entertainment activities (e.g. music, movies).

If a company qualifies all of these criteria, its business activity screening is successful, and it is then subjected to a financial ratio screening process.

8.5-1 Financial Ratio Screening

The financial ratio screening process requires the following:

- Income from the activities which do not happen to sync with *Shari'ah* principles and are involved with interest must not surpass 5% of total revenue.
- Interest-related deposits must not exceed 30% of the market capitalisation.
- Interest-bearing debt must not exceed 30% of the market capitalisation.
- Thirty percent of the overall asset value in the market should be occupied by debt-free assets subjecting to cash directly.

8.6 Tracking a *Shari'ah*-Compliant Index

Traditional indices are generally tracked by conventional ETFs. It is necessary for an Islamic ETF to track an Islamic index to be in compliance with *Shari'ah* principles. An Islamic ETF is allowed to track indices that adhere to *Shari'ah* principles.

8.6-1 Compliance With Shari'ah *Principles for Gold, Silver and Currencies*

Any ETF which is composed of constituents such as gold, silver or currency must be in compliance with the *Shari'ah* principles of trading gold, silver and currencies. Gold can be sold in exchange for silver irrespective of their differences in the weight of the countervalues. Gold is equally approved to be sold for currencies at a price which is mutually agreed. In both of these trading situations, the countervalues exchanged must correspond strictly to the principles of S*hari'ah.*

Gold can be sold for something which doesn't come under gold, silver or currencies. These might include commodities, services and so on. There is neither a price range as such, nor is there any requirement of immediate exchange of the countervalues.

When gold is sold for gold, silver, or currencies, the two countervalues have to be delivered physically and/or constructively during the session. On gold being sold for anything other than the ones mentioned, one of the countervalues might be approved for deferment. It must be noted that the deferment of both the countervalues while selling gold, such as in forwards and futures, is not allowed.

When trading with *Shari'ah*-compliant ETFs, it is imperative that one ensures that the principles of *Shari'ah* have been adhered to with complete accuracy. The general set of principles includes the following:

- The object of sale must be in an existing state during the time of its sale. If a commodity/product has been sold not in its existing form, *Shari'ah* law wouldn't approve the sale even if the sale was decided on mutual consent.
- The seller should be the original owner of the sale object when the sale is being made.

- The sale object should be in the physical possession of the owner during the sale.
- The sale should be done at the same time and cannot be postponed to a future date. Even if both the seller and buyer are willing to make the sale event in the future, it would be against the principles.
- Any sale object that is being sold by the seller should have to possess some value. Any sale of an object or a thing that is of no value should not be sold.
- Only usable objects can be sold during the time of sale, and *haram* objects cannot be sold.
- The object should be familiar to the seller.
- Any type of sold commodity should not be bought by an individual, and the buyer should not take any chances in that.
- The price of the object should be certain, and any sale involving in uncertain prices will not be considered as a sale.
- The sale should be regardless of any disparities and discrimination. The sale should be unconditional such that any person who is willing to buy the object can be able to purchase it for the same price as others.

8.7 Islamic EFTs in the Global Market

Javelin Investment Management is credited with launching the first US-based Islamic ETFs (Islamic Finance News, 2009, July 3). They are considered similar in their approach as the socially responsible funds as they keep away from companies dealing in alcohol and gaming. These funds are involved in tracking the Dow Jones Islamic Market (DJIM) Titans 100 index. Comprising 100 non-US companies, it is being traded in 18 trading currencies in 23 countries. The UM

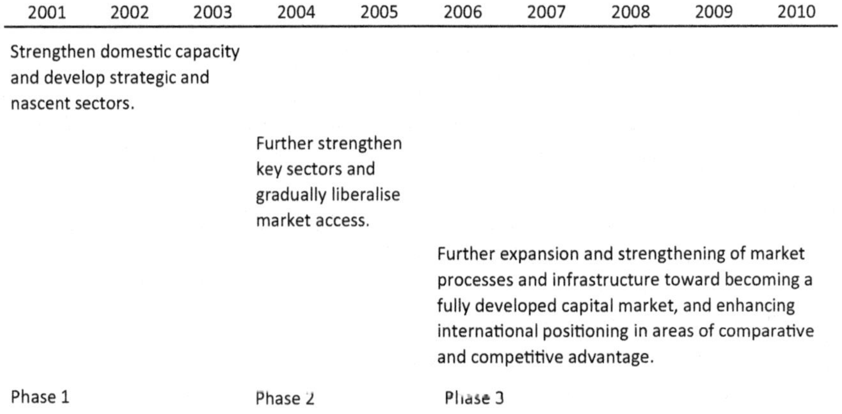
2001
2002
2003
2004
2005
2006
2007
2008
2009
2010
Strengthen domestic capacity and develop strategic and nascent sectors.
Further strengthen key sectors and gradually liberalise market access.
Further expansion and strengthening of market processes and infrastructure toward becoming a fully developed capital market, and enhancing international positioning in areas of comparative and competitive advantage.
Phase 1
Phase 2
Phase 3

FIGURE 8.3 Islamic ETF trends.

Source: ISRA Bulletin (2009, April).

Financial and Jovian Capital managed the first Islamic ETFs in Canada by tracking the performances of the S&P/TSX Shari'ah Index (Islamic Finance News, 2009, July 24).

It was in 2008 that the first listing of iShares FTSE 100 ETFs took place in the London Stock Exchange (LSE). Certain *Shari'ah*-compliant ETFs are traded in LSE in several currencies. Initially, ETFs are being tracked by iShares based on the MSCI World Islamic, MSCI USA Islamic, and MSCI Emerging Markets Islamic indices. Simultaneously, db x-trackers (Deutsche Bank index trackers) popularly known as the ETF arm of Deutsche Bank, offers Islamic ETFs based on the S&P Japan 500 Shari'ah, S&P 500 Shari'ah, S&P Europe 350 Shari'ah, and Dow Jones Islamic Market Titans indices (Islamic Finance News, 2010, October 13). The year 2007 witnessed a vital step, as Reliance *Shari'ah* BeES was launched on the Bombay Stock Exchange (now the BSE; ISRA Bulletin, 2009). As a *Shari'ah*-compliant ETF, Reliance *Shari'ah* BeES refers to an open-ended index scheme that tracks the Nifty 50 *Shari'ah* index.

Malaysia, in Asia witnessed the launch of Islamic ETF instruments on 22 January 2008 and became listed in Bursa Malaysia on 31 January 2008. This ETF project got pushed forward by the Malaysian government through the participation and coordination of several stakeholders such as government linked investment companies (GLICs). Known as the MyETF Dow Jones Islamic Market Malaysia Titans or simply MyETF-DJIM25, it is valued at 840 million RM. Considered as a market capitalisation–weighted and free-float-adjusted index, DJIM comprises 25 *Shari'ah*-compliant securities of companies listed on Bursa Securities, Kuala Lumpur. This fund ensures benefit by enabling the GLICs in divesting their interest in government-linked companies (GLCs) by selling off a portion of their portfolio to the ETFs in exchange for units. It is equally involved in the promotion of greater retail participation in the equity market. When the fund was introduced, the market capitalisation of the 25 constituent companies totalled 30% of the Malaysian stock market.

8.8 Islamic ETFs in Comparison

On the basis of the aforementioned guidelines, an ETF can be classified as an Islamic ETF and be assured of its eligibility to be traded by an Islamic investor. There are multiple ETFs that adhere to *Shari'ah* principles and are thus available to invest in *Shari'ah*-compliant way. Certain famous Islamic ETFs provided by S&P Dow Jones are S&P Global Healthcare Shari'ah, S&P Global Infrastructure Shari'ah, S&P Developed Large and Mid-Cap Shari'ah, S&P Developed Small Cap Shari'ah and the S&P Developed BMI Shari'ah Index.

When one opts for a *Shari'ah*-compliant or Islamic ETF, several other factors need to be considered apart from the underlying index's methodology and that particular ETF's performance. Table 8.1 depicts a detailed list of well-performing *Shari'ah*-compliant ETFs ranked by fund size subject to several parameters based on size, cost, age, income, domicile and replication.

TABLE 8.1 Some of the Best-Performing *Shari'ah*-Compliant ETFs in Comparison

Fund Provider	*Fund Size (Million EUR)*	*Total Expenses (TER) in %*	*Use of Profits*	*Fund Domicile*	*Replication Method*
iShares MSCI USA Islamic UCITS ETF IE00B296QM64	145	0.50% p.a.	Ireland	Ireland	Optimised sampling
iShares MSCI World Islamic UCITS ETF IE00B27YCN58	278	0.60% p.a.	Distributing	Ireland	Optimised sampling
iShares MSCI Emerging Markets Islamic UCITS ETF IE00B27YCP72	98	0.85% p.a.	Distributing	Ireland	Full replication
HANetf Almalia Sanlam Active Shari'ah Global Equity UCITS ETF IE00BMYMHS24	6	0.99% p.a.	Distributing	Ireland	Sampling

Source: justETF.com (as of 31 August 2021; calculations in euros including dividends).

8.9 Return Comparison of Islamic ETFs

Table 8.2 projects the returns of some of the best-performing *Shari'ah*-compliant or Islamic ETFs in comparison. All returns as depicted in Table 8.2 are inclusive of dividends as of month end. Not only the return but also the reference date on which the investors conduct the comparison is crucial.

8.10 Cases of Three US-Based *Halal* ETFs

In 2019, the launch of three new products to the Islamic financing market in the United States took place. These were HLAL, SPUS, and SPSK. All three are exchange-traded funds (ETFs) which hold assets like a mutual fund but can be traded like stocks, making them more liquid. How are these new players performing in the market, and how do they compare with other options and benchmarks?

SPSK, the only one of the three which invests in *Sukuk*, provides an option for investors looking to gain *Shari'ah*-compliant fixed-income exposure for a fraction of the cost of traditional individual *Sukuk* certificates, and for a lower fee than the traditional *Sukuk* mutual funds. The fund has gained a return of 0.45% year to date (YTD), compared to the mutual funds Amana Participation and Azzad Wise Capital, which are at 1.09% and 0.61% YTD, respectively. Unlike mutual funds, however, SPSK can be tracked in real time and requires no lock-in period or minimum amount to invest.

TABLE 8.2 Returns of Some of the Best-Performing *Shari'ah*-Compliant ETFs in Comparison

Islamic Exchange-Traded Funds (ETF)	*1 month (%)*	*3 months (%)*	*6 months (%)*	*1 year (%)*	*3 years (%)*
iShares MSCI USA Islamic UCITS ETF	2.65	9.31	19.12	28.87	36.86
iShares MSCI World Islamic UCITS ETF	2.04	6.97	16.62	27.78	33.35
iShares MSCI Emerging Markets Islamic UCITS ETF	2.80	2.37	3.41	19.86	31.59
HANetf Almalia Sanlam Active Shari'ah Global ETF	0.66	3.54	11.27		

Source: justETF.com (as of 31 August 2021; calculations in euros including dividends).

On the other hand, HLAL and SPUS both invest in *Shari'ah*-compliant equities. HLAL tracks the FTSE *Shari'ah* USA Index and has gained a return of 3.48% YTD. SPUS tracks the S&P 500 *Shari'ah* Industry Exclusions Index and has gained a return of 5.74% YTD. This figure is even higher than the S&P 500 Index, which over the same period produced a return of 4.62%.

It is interesting to note that while equity investors have long touted the S&P 500 Index as the benchmark to beat, the five-year performance of the S&P 500 *Shari'ah* Industry Exclusions Index (established to adhere to AAOIFI scholarly guidelines) has been better than the S&P 500 itself. This may come as a surprise to those who doubt the ability of *Shari'ah*-compliant investments to deliver returns comparable to the broader market. However, it is not an anomaly. Some restrictive Christian funds (e.g. BIBL and CATH) have similarly been performing better than the S&P 500, which may say something regarding the usefulness of extra caution and restrictions in investment models (Walji, 2020).

8.11 Conclusion

The Islamic ETF is a product of the Islamic capital market. Thus, the need to consistently promote capital markets in terms of an alternative for economic growth constitutes to be a major challenge. Businesses issuing *Sukuk* and shares form one aspect of the Islamic capital market which witnesses the diversification of products. It is equally important for investors to have the option of being able to purchase Islamic finance products subject to their individual investment choices. If investors opt out from making investments in the Islamic capital market and rather choose to deposit their money in banks, it will result in fewer active businesses participating in the capital market.

A lot of things need to be done in the context of the Islamic ETFs. Education and promoting awareness of Islamic ETFs should be conducted consistently owing to the fact that Islamic ETFs are considerably new in comparison to other existing investment instruments. It is a time-consuming process to authentically convince investors about Islamic ETFs being *Shari'ah* compliant and these ETFs being holders of lower risk. Thus, the Islamic exchange-traded (index) fund has to be promoted systematically.

Review Questions

1. What are the differences between ETFs and mutual funds?
2. Describe the benefits and the risk of Islamic ETFs.
3. What are the differences between conventional ETFs and Islamic ETFs?
4. Explain the process of Islamic ETFs.

References

BlackRock (2019), *Different Types of ETF*, retrieved from www.blackrock.com/sg/en/etfs-simplified/types-of-etfs (Access date March 20, 2020)

Hill, J, Nadig, D and Hougan, M (2015), *A Comprehensive Guide to Exchange Traded Funds (ETFs)*, London: CFA Institute

Islamic Finance News, July 3, 2009, No. 3, p. 4

Islamic Finance News, July 24, 2009, No. 4, p. 3

Islamic Finance News, October 13, 2010, No. 20, p. 6

ISRA Bulletin, vol. 3, August 2009, 3799

Omar, A, Abduh, M and Sukmana, R (2015), *Fundamentals of Islamic Money and Capital Markets*, Singapore: Wiley

Walji, A (2020, February 26), Examining the New Halal ETFs, *Islamic Finance News*, p. 17, retrieved from https://shariaportfolio.com/wp-content/uploads/2020/02/v17i08-17-Examining-the-new-Halal-ETFs.pdf (Access date March 25, 2020)

9

ISLAMIC REAL ESTATE INVESTMENT TRUSTS

Learning Objectives

On completing this chapter, learners will be able to:

- Compare the characteristics, classifications, and basic forms of public and private real estate investments
- Know and understand the types of REITs
- Explain the advantages and disadvantages of investing in real estate
- Differentiate between conventional and Islamic REITs
- Describe the structure of Islamic REITs.

9.1 Introduction

Real estate investment trusts (REITs) are vehicles that are in ownership of real estate assets. Having said that, REITs are equally involved in operating the portfolio of income-generating real estate. The development of REITs has been done in parallel to that of unit trusts, also making an allowance for the accumulation of funds from multiple investors. The structural composition of REITs benefits retail investors in ways more than one. They get to enter and experience exposure to a pool of real estate assets without much difficulty. The diversity of the assets along with higher liquidity are equally beneficially. On the other hand, direct investing does not have all these advantages. A majority of REITs are listed publicly. More than 90% of their earnings have been declared as dividends for fulfilling the advantages granted to REITs by the securities regulator. With REITs, one gets access to a stable source of income. This income is recurrent in nature. Unlike serving as an investment avenue where capital gains are reaped, REITs can be perceived more

DOI: 10.4324/9780429321207-9

like a yield pay. When making investments, the emphasis of REIT is primarily on properties of a particular category.

To put it up in simple words, REITs are companies who are in ownership of income-producing real estate and are most likely to be operating the same as well. This real estate includes apartments, warehouses, self-storage facilities, malls, and hotels. A majority of REITs have a track record for paying large and growing dividends. However, the growth potential will contain a considerable amount of risk. The risk is subjected to variation owing to the type of REIT.

9.2 How Do REITs Operate?

In 1960, real estate investment trusts were developed by the US Congress with the purpose of offering ownership of equity stakes to individual investors. The ownership of these equity stakes would be in large-scale real estate companies; the process is similar to that of owning stakes in other businesses. With this move, investors could conveniently purchase and trade a diversified real estate portfolio.

A set of standards was developed by the US Internal Revenue Service (IRS). These standards, shown here, need to be fulfilled by REITs:

- At least 90% of the taxable income has to be returned annually in terms of shareholder dividends. This makes it quite appealing for investors to invest in REITs.
- A minimum of 75% of overall assets has to be invested in real estate or cash.
- A minimum of 75% of gross income is received from real estate. This might be in the form of real property rents, interest on mortgages financing the original property, or from sales of real estate.
- One hundred shareholders, at a minimum, have to be actively present after the first year of the REIT's existence.
- Not more than 50% of shares can be held by five individuals or fewer subjecting to the last half of the taxable year.

By abiding by these regulatory guidelines, REITs are free from having to pay taxes at the corporate level. With this, they are able to conveniently get involved in financing real estate in a less expensive way when compared to that of non-REIT companies. This signifies that over a particular period of time, REITs have the potential to grow quite large and eventually pay out larger dividends.

9.3 Kinds of REITs

REITs can be broadly categorised into three types on the basis of their investment holdings: equity, mortgage, and hybrid. Each of them is further sub-divided into three types on the basis of the process of purchasing the respective investments. These sub-divisions are publicly traded REITs, public non-traded REITs and private REITs. The types of REITs are characteristically different from one another and simultaneously have different types of risks associated with them.

9.3-1 Types of REITs on the Basis of Investment Holdings

Equity REITs: The operational format of equity REITs matches that of a landlord. They are in ownership of the underlying real estate. They provide for the maintenance of the same. As they make reinvestments in the property, rent checks are simultaneously fetched. Every activity in association with managing the property comes attached with its ownership.

Mortgage REITs: Mortgage REITs (mREITs) do not possess the ownership of the underlying property. The debt securities backed by the property are owned by mREITs. Let us consider an example in this regard. Suppose a family takes out a mortgage on a house. The mortgage would be purchased from the original lender by the mREIT, and the monthly payments would be collected for a period of time. In the context of this example, the family is in ownership of the property and also oversees the operational dimension of the property. It must be noted that mortgage REITs have significantly more risk associated with them when compared to equity REIT cousins. With more risk, they are more likely to pay out higher dividends.

Hybrid REITs: Hybrid REITs can be understood as a blend of both equity and mortgage REITs. Hybrid REITs are in ownership of real estate properties as commercial property mortgages in their portfolio. They are equally involved as operational entities of these properties.

9.3-2 Types of REITs on the Basis of Trading Status

9.3-2-1 Publicly Traded REITs

The name itself is suggestive of the fact that the trading of publicly traded REITs is done on an exchange like stocks and ETFs. These REITs can be availed or bought through an ordinary brokerage account. The National Association of Real Estate Investment Trusts (NAREIT) claimed that the US market consists of more than 200 publicly traded REITs. The governance standards of publicly traded REITs are most likely to be better in different aspects, particularly on transparency. The most liquid stocks are simultaneously offered by them implying that investors can purchase and sell the REITs' stock faster without much difficulty as compared to selling and investing a retail property by itself. A lot of investors purchase and sell only publicly traded REITs owing to all the benefits associated with them.

9.3-2-2 Publicly Non-traded REITs

The registration of these publicly non-traded REITs is done with the Securities Exchange Commission (SEC). However, these are not available on an exchange.

Publicly non-traded REITs are bought from a broker who makes public non-traded offerings. An example can be taken of an online real estate broker such as Fundrise. A database is maintained online by the NAREIT. Investors can use this virtual database for reaching REITs based on the status of listing. Owing to the fact that these REITs are not publicly traded, their nature is not liquid at all, which is most likely to continue for a time period of eight years or more, as per claimed by the Financial Industry Regulatory Authority (FIRA). It can become equally difficult to understand the valuation of these non-traded REITs. The SEC has even warned that most of the time, these REITs do not estimate their value for investors until 18 months after the end of their offering. Timewise, this is most likely to be in the form of years after someone has made investments.

9.3–3 Private REITs

Private REITs are not listed. This makes it essentially difficult to estimate their value and tradable possibilities. However, they are simultaneously exempted from SEC registration. There are fewer requirements of disclosure for private REITs. This again makes it difficult to analyse their performance. The limitations associated with these REITs make them less appealing to most investors. These REITs have additional risks because of which they become even less appealing. When compared to publicly traded REITs, the minimum amount required to initiate

TABLE 9.1 Best-Performing REIT Stocks, as Updated in November 2021

Symbol	*Company*	*REIT performance (1-year total return)*	*Share price*
DBRG	Digital Bridge	258%	$6.98
SKT	Tanger Factory Outlet Centers, Inc.	170.7%	$17.09
CPLG	CorePoint Lodging	151.9%	$13.78
RHP	Ryman Hospitality Properties, Inc.	137.2%	$78.08
SPG	Simon Property Group	126.7%	$134.03

Sources: NARIET, Morningstar, and ETF.com.

TABLE 9.2 Best-Performing REIT Mutual Funds, as Updated in November 2021

Symbol	*Company*	*Year return to November 2021*	*Gross expense ratio*
IVRIX	VY Clarion Real Estate I	43.30%	0.68%
IVRSX	VY Clarion Real Estate S	42.96%	0.93%
IVRTX	VY Clarion Real Estate S2	42.82%	1.08%
PJEQX	PGIM US Real Estate R6	40.52%	1%
PJEZX	PGIM US Real Estate Z	40.44%	1%

Sources: NARIET, Morningstar, and ETF.com.

TABLE 9.3 Best-Performing REIT ETFs, as Updated in November 2021

Symbol	*Company*	*Year return to November 2021*	*Gross expense ratio*
EWRE	Invesco S&P 500 Equal Weight Real Estate ETF	39.29%	0.4%
REZ	iShares Residential and Multisector Real Estate ETF	35.87%	0.48%
XLRE	Real Estate Select Sector SPDR Fund	34.49%	0.12%
PPTY	US Diversified Real Estate ETF	32.66%	0.49%
VNQ	Vanguard Real Estate ETF	31.32%	0.12%

Sources: NARIET, Morningstar, and ETF.com.

Note: All data used are up to date as of November 2021.

trading in both public non-traded REITs and private REITs is higher, particularly US$25,000 or more. The fees are also steeper for both of these REITs, unlike publicly traded REITs. This is why private REITs and several non-traded REITs are open only to accredited investors with a net of US$1 million. Or else to investors whose annual income in each of the past two years amounts to a minimum of US$200,000 if single or US$300,000 if married.

According to NAREIT, within two decades until December 2019, the FTSE NAREIT All Equity REITs index involved in collecting data on all publicly traded equity REITs exceeded in performance in comparison to the Russell 1000, a stock market index of large-cap stocks. The REIT-indexed investments put forth that it has a total return of 11.6% annually in comparison to 6.29% of the Russell 1000.

9.4 Islamic Real Estate Investment

We know the real estate investment trust (REIT) is a collective investment scheme in real estate which is a combination of the best features of real estate as well as trust funds. Now, let us understand the Islamic real estate investment trust. The Islamic REIT can be perceived in terms of an Islamic version of the conventional REIT. To put it simply, real estate has been quite an appealing sector for *Shari'ah*-compliant investment after Islamic REITs were established in the market. It is no hidden fact that *Sukuk*, or what we would generally perceive as Islamic bonds, occupy the market as the most dominant financing source for Islamic REITs. According to the findings of Parsa and Muwlazadeh (2010), the United Kingdom has been marked as the most favoured location in Europe for making *Shari'ah*-compliant real estate investment, followed by France and Germany. The determining factors that the authors used for the listing the success rate of the financial product were political environment, human capital and expertise, regulative and legislative framework, and institutional frameworks. Let us consider another study related to *Shari'ah*-compliant real estate investments in Asia. A research survey was conducted by Ibrahim et al., (2009) with *Shari'ah*-compliant property investment stakeholders in three jurisdictions: Singapore, Bahrain, and Dubai. As per the findings of the research, *Shari'ah*-compliant property investment is distinctively different from conventional property investment in two major aspects. The first involves how the compliance is being monitored, and the second involves regulations and the processes of how portfolios are being selected. They ultimately remain the same as their counterparts in terms of managing portfolios and paying dividends (Ibrahim et al., 2009). Therefore, monitoring the compliance with *Shari'ah* requirements is imperative for the operational and developmental aspects of *Shari'ah*-compliant real estate investments.

9.5 *Shari'ah* Guidelines for Real Estate Investment Trusts

The fundamental importance of monitoring *Shari'ah* requirements is imperative in *Shari'ah*-compliant real estate investments. This is inclusive of the Islamic REITs as well. Figure 9.1 depicts the major concepts and structural formats of Islamic REITs. This is where the *Shari'ah* advisory committee plays a vital role. The committee and the REIT managers guide and monitor the level of *Shari'ah* compliance for the operational activities in Islamic REITs (Chuweni, 2018). When we take the example of Malaysia, Islamic REITs must meet the mandates of the Securities Commission Act 1993 and work in accordance with the guidelines on Islamic real estate investment trusts (Islamic REITs guidelines) (Securities Commission Malaysia, 2016). Chuweni (2018) also put forth a discussion on issues and challenges of

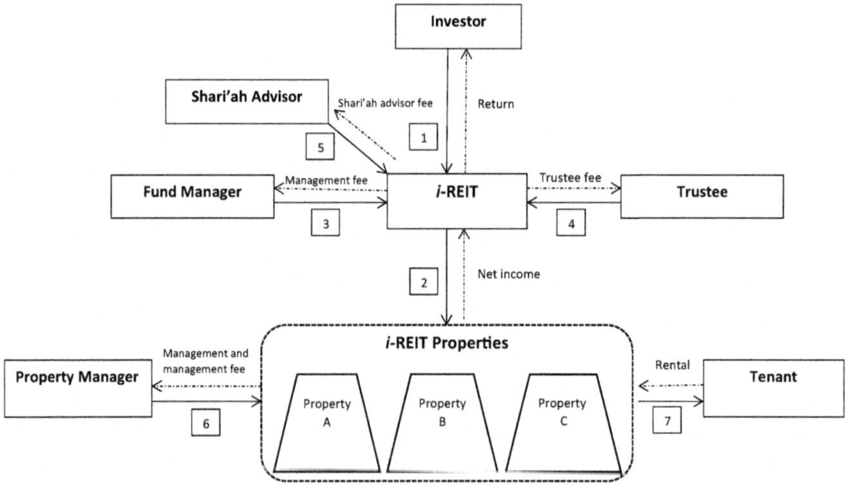

FIGURE 9.1 Structure of Islamic REITs.

Source: Bursa Malaysia (2015).

Islamic REITs and pointed out there is more room for enhancing and standardising *Shari'ah* guidelines of REITs globally, with special reference to the screening methodologies adopted.

Thomas (2014) pointed out two differences in the policies overseeing *Shari'ah* compliance that were put into effect by Malaysian and Singaporean Islamic REITs. The first is the percentage of distribution of non-*Shari'ah* income. The benchmark is kept at 20% of the gross revenue by Malaysian Islamic REITs, while in Singapore, the benchmark is kept at 5% of its gross revenue (Thomas, 2014). For financing, Malaysian Islamic REITs are forbidden to take up any conventional loan. Meanwhile, allowance is made for Singapore's Sabana *Shari'ah*-compliant REIT to be involved in a conventional loan, provided that it cannot surpass one-third of the net asset value or market capital (Figure 9.1). The allowance, however, is subject only to the non-availability of *Shari'ah*-compliant products in the market (Thomas, 2014).

9.5-1 Features That Define Islamic REITs

The features that define Islamic real estate investment trusts include the following:

1. When investments are made in Islamic REITs, it is done by investors holding the units.
2. The acquisition of Islamic REIT is in the form of pool of assets.
3. The management and administration of Islamic REITs is done by a manager.
4. The trustee plays the role of being the custodian of the fund.
5. A *Shari'ah* committee offers advice on any aspect that is associated to *Shari'ah*.
6. The property manager's role is to maintain and manage the services of the real estate.
7. The real estate is rented by tenants.

9.6 Contracts in Islamic REITs

When contracts in Islamic REITs are being talked about, preference is given to the *Mudharabah aqad*, or what can be perceived as a trust financing contract. This contract can be understood as an agreement between the investment manager as a *wakil* (agent) of *Shahib al-mal* (investor) and the property manager. The preference given to this contract is primarily because of the following reasons:

1. Profits are shared between the investor (*Shahib al-mal*) and the investee (property manager). The agency of the investment manager acts as the means through which the sharing is accomplished. The sharing is in accordance with respective proportions as agreed upon by both parties. It is simultaneously consented upon that no fixed return to the investor is guaranteed.
2. The risk shared by the investor will be in proportion of the contribution they made in terms of capital.

3. No such risk of loss to investment will be borne by the property manager provided that they have done their work with due diligence and have not neglected any of it.

In context of another contract, termed *ijarah aqad*, the investor (*Shahib al-mal*) receives rental payments from the property manager for the use of the property. The payment is received through the investment manager. The property manager can choose to put the property on sub-lease for different tenants. The rental pricing for the tenants might be a sum of the cost and margin. *Ijarah aqad* is advantageous because the return received by the investor is relatively constant while the property manager bears the spread risk.

If the property manager happened to be the former owner of the commercial property before its purchase by Islamic REIT, the *ijarah aqad* sale and leaseback become applicable. This is because the owner of the property had sold it to the REIT, after which it leased it back from the respective REIT.

Let us now discuss the *wakala bil-ujrah* (agency for fees) contract. Here, the agreement is made between investor and its agent (investment manager and custody bank). The conduct of the contract takes place through a *Shari'ah*-compliant mutual fund, characteristically similar to an Islamic REIT. The investment manager is provided with a mandatory guideline by the investor. As per the requirement of the guideline, the investment manager has to invest on behalf of the investor in strict compliance with the terms and conditions mentioned in the prospectus (for public REIT) or the information memorandum (for private REIT).

9.7 Prohibitions in REITs Under *Shari'ah*

Islamic REITs have to also follow certain prohibitions in accordance with *Shari'ah* norms, as follows (Bursha Malaysia, 2015).

1. In a general context, hotels and resorts of all kinds are forbidden, with an exception only for those that are operational in full adherence to *Shari'ah*.
2. Any kind of financial service that is based on *riba* is not allowed. This is an implication of *riba*-based financial services. This might consist of tenants of a mall. Any kind or form of financial transaction that involves *riba*-based use by a REIT is prohibited. This might include conventional loans undertaken for new property acquisition.
3. Conventional insurance is forbidden; for example, conventional insurance as tenants of an office building or REITs using conventional insurance for insuring the building.
4. Prohibition is made against several substances, such as alcohol, tobacco (based on *fatwa*), gaming, gambling and other goods and services that can be categorised as *haram* under Islamic law. This is also an implication that involvement in these activities will also act as determining factor for forbidding tenants, the example of which was taken earlier. The ban on goods and services can

be done if they are found to have *mudarat* (a harmful effect) on the general public.

9.8 Development of Global *Sharia*-Compliant REITs

Asia's highest *Shari'ah*-compliant investment potential is credited to be identified in Southeast Asia, wherein ultimate preferences are given to Malaysia and Singapore for these *Shari'ah*-compliant funds (Ibrahim et al., 2009). In one of the research studies by Ibrahim et al. (2009), more than 60% of respondents have claimed that the right platform for *Shari'ah*-compliant funds in Malaysia. The factors making Malaysia the preferred end point are primarily its political environment, institutional framework, legal framework, human capital, and expertise in *Shari'ah* investment. Malaysia is a pioneering model and has attained global leadership in *Shari'ah*-compliant real estate investment since the inception of Islamic REITs in November 2005. This has been followed by several other countries including Singapore and those in the GCC (Chuweni, 2018).

TABLE 9.4 The Major Milestones of Global Islamic REITs

Year	*Key Achievements*
2005	The introduction of Malaysian Islamic REITs guidelines
2006	Malaysian Al'Aqar KPJ REIT listed as the first Islamic REIT
2007	Malaysian Al Hadharah Boustead REIT was listed
2008	• Malaysian Axis REIT reclassified into an Islamic REIT • Kuwait launched Al Mahrab Tower REIT
2009	The establishment of • Qatar's Regency REIT • Bahrain's Inovest REIT
2010	Singapore's Sabana *Sharia*-compliant REIT was listed
2011	UAE's Emirates REIT was introduced
2013	The listing of KLCC Stapled Securities on Bursa Malaysia as the first *Sharia*-compliant stapled REIT structure
2014	• Delisting of Malaysian Al-Hadharah Boustead REIT • UAE's Emirates REIT shares were listed on Nasdaq • Bahrain's Al Salam Asian REIT fund was introduced
2015	The listing of Malaysian Al Salam REIT
2016	Bahrain's first listed *Sharia*-compliant REIT, namely Eskan Bank Realty Income Trust
2017	• Entrance of two UAE REITs into the market, namely Residential REIT and Etihad REIT • Oman at the stage of finalising the draft guideline for REITs
2019	Manulife Shari'ah Global REITs Fund • Jersey Cell company Structures Islamic REITs in UK
2021	• MENA countries adopted Islamic REITs structured by Jersey

Sources: Authors' compilation and Chuweni (2018).

Table 9.4 shows the major milestones for global *Shari'ah*-compliant REITs from 2005 to 2017.

9.8–1 GCC's Shari'ah-*Compliant REITs*

Several regulations have played an influential role in positively developing the Islamic REITs in the Gulf Region in the present day (Mcaughtry, 2016). In 2008, Al Mahrab Tower REIT was launched in Kuwait. This was followed by the establishment of Regency REIT in Qatar and Inovest REIT in Bahrain, both of which took place in 2009 (Maierbrugger, 2015). In 2014, a second Islamic REIT called the Al Salam Asian REIT fund was launched in Bahrain. (Maierbrugger, 2015). The establishment of Emirates REITs took place in 2011 and also was listed on Nasdaq Dubai in April 2014. It was a property portfolio of the commercial, retail, and education sectors (Al Jazira Capital, 2014). In 2016, approval of the first listed *Shari'ah*-compliant REIT, Eskan Bank Realty Income Trust, was done by Bahrain. The emphasis here was on the retail sector (Islamic Finance News, 2016). In 2017, the UAE put forth two new REITs in the market: Residential REIT and Etihad.

REIT (Islamic Finance News, 2017a, 2017b) Equitativa and partners with Al Hamra Real Estate Development and National Bond were collectively involved in launching the Residential REIT (Islamic Finance News, 2017a). Meanwhile, Abu Dhabi Financial Group launched the Etihad REIT (Islamic Finance News, 2017b). The Residential REIT is accredited to be the first UAE *Shari'ah*-compliant residential REIT, while the Etihad REIT is characterised of being a diversified REIT comprising a blend of retail, residential, warehousing and staff accommodation as their main property portfolios (Islamic Finance News, 2017b). In 2017, Oman happened to launch Islamic REITs (Islamic Finance News, 2017a).

9.8–2 Malaysian Shari'ah-*Compliant REITs*

Table 9.5 shows that the largest global Islamic REIT is in Malaysia, followed by Kuwait, Qatar, Bahrain, United Arab Emirates (US$501 million), and Singapore (US$377.2 million; Chuweni, 2018). Table 9.5 also shows that the market capitalisation of the Malaysian REIT (M-REIT) industry has had a considerably large-scale hike, increasing from RM5.25 billion in 2007 to RM44.19 billion in 2016. Currently, 18 Malaysian REITs are listed on Bursa Malaysia. Four out of the 18 are *Shari'ah*-compliant: Axis REIT, Al-Aqar Healthcare REIT, the stapled KLCCP REIT, and Al-Salam REIT.

The first Islamic REIT to be listed was Al-'Aqar KPJ REIT. Here, the underlying assets are properties in association with healthcare. These assets comprise private hospitals and nursing colleges (Al-'Aqar Healthcare REIT, 2014). On 8 February 2007, the Al Hadharah Boustead REIT was listed on the main board which has its special emphasis on plantation assets, especially the oil palm estate and palm oil mills (Al-Hadharah Boustead REIT, 2012). It must be carefully noted that Al Hadharah Boustead REIT was later removed from the list Bursa Malaysia

TABLE 9.5 Global Islamic REITs, to December 2014

Country	*REIT Name*	*Date Esta-blished*	*Listed*	*Market Cap (US$)*	*Percentage of Asian Market*	*Percentage of Global Market*
Malaysia	Al-'Aqar Healthcare REIT	2006	Yes	5 billion	96	85
	Axis REIT	2005	Yes			
	KLCC REIT	2013	Yes			
GCC	Arabian REIT	2006	No	501 million	NA	9
	Al Mahrab Tower REIT	2008	No			
	Inovest REIT	2009	No			
	Emirates REIT	2010	Yes			
Singapore	Sabana REIT	2010	Yes	377.2 million	4	6
United States	Standard & Poor's (S&P) Global REIT Shari'ah ETE	2020	Yes			
Total in Asia				5.3 billion		
Total Global				5.8782 billion		

Source: Chuweni (2018).

in 2014 because it chose privatisation. KLCC Property Holdings was listed on the main board of Bursa Malaysia in 2005. On 9 May 2013, it went on to undertake a corporate restructuring exercise (KLCCP Stapled Group, 2016) following the completion of which KLCC REIT acquired the prominent Petronas Twin Tower, Menara ExxonMobil, and Menara 3 Petronas for its portfolios. Considering up to 31 December 2016, the largest and the first *Shari'ah*-compliant tacked REIT structure in Malaysia was the KLCC REIT. Its assets are worth beyond RM9.6 billion, and the market capitalisation amounts to RM14.9 billion (KLCCP Stapled Group, 2016).

When talking about the reclassification from a conventional REIT into an Islamic REIT, is credited to be the first Malaysian REIT to be undergone the process. Up until 11 December 2008, the investments of Axis REIT had been largely in industrial and commercial properties (Axis Real Estate Investment Trust, 2014). The company's reason for reclassification was to broaden its investor base. It wanted to grasp the demand arriving from Muslim investors and not stay limited only to conventional investors. It must be understood the demand from Muslim investors represents one-quarter of the world's population (Axis Real Estate Investment Trust, 2014). An extraordinary response to Malaysian Islamic REITs was recorded when the over-subscriptions were made for acquiring the initial public offering for Al-Salām REIT (Al-Salām REIT, 2015). This clearly implied a relatively greater demand for *Shari'ah* asset classes (Islamic Finance News, 2015). Listed in September 2015, Al-Salām REIT can be perceived as a diversified REIT, the primary focus of which ranges from commercial, retail and office to food and beverages, restaurants and industrial assets (Chuweni, 2018).

9.8–3 Singaporean Shari'ah-*Compliant REITs*

On 26 November 2010, Sabana *Shari'ah* Compliant Industrial REIT was listed on the Singapore Exchange Securities Trading Limited. It went on to become the first listed *Shari'ah*-compliant REIT in Singapore (Sabana *Shari'ah* Compliant Industrial REIT, 2016). The *Shari'ah*-compliant standard as per the GCC was adopted by Sabana REIT, in accordance of which 5% of its gross revenue is forbidden in the non-permissible activities. At present, Sabana's quarterly non-permissible rental income is lower than 0.1% in adherence made to the *Shari'ah* investment compliance of the GCC standard. Up until 31 December 2016, the valuation of its property portfolio was at $1 billion, the major proportion of which is in industrial sectors such as warehousing, logistics and industrial assets (Sabana Shari'ah Compliant Industrial REIT, 2016).

9.8–4 The United Kingdom and the Middle East and North Africa

Inward investments have been in practice for quite a long time in the United Kingdom and *Shari'ah*-compliant structured real estate products commonly have been used to hold UK real estate. Middle East and North Africa (MENA) investors have been inclined in structuring their investments in UK's real estate. An increase in the interest of MENA investors in using Jersey Cell companies as investment vehicles has been observed. This is primarily because of the many options that investors get the opportunity to choose. The options comprise a range of property portfolios under one management dimension.

Shari'ah-compliant funding for MENA investors willing to invest in UK real estate is readily available in the UK. At present, there are five fully *Shari'ah*-compliant banks licensed in the UK: Al Rayan Bank, the Bank of London and the Middle East, Gatehouse Bank, QIB (UK) and Abu Dhabi Islamic Bank (Collas-Crill, 2021).

In the context of transactions made under Islamic financing, the involvement of a commodity Murabaha product is essential. However, MENA investors can avail of other products as well. This is inclusive of *Ijarah* (a type of lease) and *Musharaka* (an investment partnership). In the context of asset classes, the popularity of commercial properties is prominent, and so is for the buy-to-let properties and build-to-rent developments. Over the last years, a shift from retail property (other than supermarkets) towards logistics (mainly warehouses) and industrial property has been observed.

Investors have become more confident now in seeking valuable opportunities outside of London, as a result of which regional centres such as Birmingham, Manchester, and Liverpool have become more popular in recent years. The assets in these regions offer more attractive prices and are even able to develop higher yields (Collas-Crill, 2021).

9.8-5 REITs in the United States

On 30 December 2020, the Standard & Poor's (S&P) Global REIT Shari'ah ETE (ticker: SPRE) was launched on the New York Stock Exchange. It helps in tracking the S&P Global Shari'ah All REIT Capped Index, the design of which is aimed to measure all *Shari'ah*-compliant constituents of the S&P Global REIT Index. This has become an integral benchmark of publicly traded equity REITs listed in developed markets as well as emerging markets. SPRE is curated on the basis of the S&P Global Shari'ah All REIT Capped Index. The index works in accordance with *Shari'ah*-compliant parameters as per the guidelines provided by the S&P Shari'ah Supervisory Board. The fund does not include REITs that are involved in attending to industries such as alcohol, tobacco, pork-related products, conventional financial services (banking, insurance, etc.), weapons and defence, and entertainment (hotels, casinos/gambling, cinema, pornography, music, etc.). This also extends to companies that are involved in financial services based on interest (or *riba*; Global Newswire, 2021).

The consideration of financials is deemed eligible owing to the company being integrated as an Islamic financial institution; for instance, Islamic banks and *Takaful* insurance companies. It has to be sincerely taken into note that income generated from forbidden sources or industries as mentioned earlier cannot exceed 5% of revenue. After delisting REITs whose primary business activities are in forbidden and unacceptable sectors, the remaining ones are evaluated in accordance with several financial ratio filters. The filters are determined on the basis of criteria pertaining to *Shari'ah*. This does not include the REITs whose total debt divided by average market capitalisation and account receivables divided by average market capitalisation exceed 30%.

The ESG characteristics in SPRE ETF are predominantly strong. One of these characteristics is carbon intensity per value invested (million tons Co2e/$1 million invested) at only 11.21. The expense ratio of SPRE is 0.69%. S&P Funds announced its collaboration with the team at Tidal ETF Services so as to put forth its funds to market (Global Newswire, 2021).

9.8-6 A Case Study: Manulife Shari'ah Global REIT Fund

This fund is aimed at providing regular income and capital appreciation by making investments in Islamic real estate investment trusts (REITs). If income distribution is made, it is to be done in form of cash or additional units that are to be reinvested into the fund. Approval of the unit's holder is to be sought before a change of the investment objective of the fund.

9.8-6-1 Investor Profile

This fund is best suited to investors who are keen on having an investment exposure by the means of a diversified portfolio of global Islamic REITs, so that regular income can be generated and potential capital appreciation is sought for a medium to long term. This fund is suited to investors preferring *Shari'ah*-compliant investments.

Manulife Investment Management (US) Limited holds the position of being the fund manager at Manulife, while the position of trustee is held by HSBC (Malaysia) Trustee Berhad (Manulife Investment Management, 2021).

9.8-6-2 Fund Information

As of 31 October 2021, the NAV/unit (US$ Class) is US$ 0.5992. Fund size is US$ 86.07 million units in circulation $542.12 million. The fund's launching date was 12 March 2019 and its commencement date was 4 April 2019. The management fee of the fund was up to 1.8% of NAV p.a. while the trustee fee was up to 0.06% of NAV p.a. This does not include foreign custodian fees and charges. Sales charge went up to 5% of NAV p.a. Benchmark of the fund IdealRatings and Global Islamic REITs Malaysia Index (Manulife Investment Management, 2021).

9.8-6-3 Market Overview

The *Shari'ah* global real estate sector posted strong returns for October 2021, outperforming the broader global equity markets (Table 9.6). World equity markets gained ground in October 2021, which represented an impressive showing in a month that is often one of the worst of the year for stocks. The potential reasons for performance were numerous, including the possibility of slow growth plus rising inflation, tighter monetary policy by the world's central banks, ongoing uncertainty regarding China's economy and worries about declining corporate profit margins. Still, equities marched higher on the strength of massive inflows of new investor cash coming into the market.

It must be noted that past performance cannot be used as an indicator for assessing future performance. The performance is calculated on a NAV-to-NAV basis (Manulife Investment Management, 2021).

TABLE 9.6 Total Turnover, to 31 October 2021

	1 month	*6 months*	*YTD*	*1 year*	*2019*	*2020*	*2021*
Fund US$ Class (%)	5.57	10.13	22.61	34.96	4.00	0.82	28.55
Benchmark in US$ (%)	6.21	11.09	21.47	33.76	8.64	0.49	32.61
Fund RM Class (%)	4.41	11.36	26.30	34.58	4.28	-0.91	30.50
Benchmark in Malaysian ringgit (%)	5.06	12.30	25.05	33.30	9.35	-1.18	35.14

Source: Lipper.

During 2021, a resurgence of dividend growth within the REITs sector was observed, as during 2020 some REITs took a conservative approach and reduced or maintained their dividends. As the economic recovery has begun, REITs have begun to increase their respective distributions. REITs valuations continue to trade near or below their respective NAVs, which may lead to an increase in M&A activity. On the other hand, overall, the long-term outlook for Shari'ah global REITs remains positive given the trajectory of the recovery and likely lower-for-longer interest rate environment. Distribution yields within the sector remain attractive compared to other yield-oriented investments. The spread between the yields of REITs and fixed-income securities is well above historical averages (Table 9.6). Therefore, there are attractive opportunities within the REIT market that trade at significant discounts to what is viewed as their intrinsic NAVs (Manulife Investment Management, 2021).

9.9 Conclusion

Islamic REITs have been acquiring greater impetus as an alternative channel for *Shari'ah*-compliant investments which are quite feasible. However, the degree to which this investment vehicle will be able to secure a position in the trillion-dollar Islamic finance industry is yet to be observed and analysed. Numerous REITs are operational in Asia. Bahrain, Saudi Arabia, Singapore and the UAE are working towards the establishment of their real estate sectors. Plenty of opportunities are available for the expansion of Islamic or *Shari'ah*-compliant REITs. They organically sync with Islamic finance, which looks towards accomplishing stability by investing in the real economy. Owing to real estate being a tangible asset, it serves as the preferred asset class among Muslim investors and institutions. Islamic REITs fulfil certain requirements and therefore serve as great choices for affluent global investors. These investors are not only from the Middle East but also from across the world. The major intent and purpose of these investors is in finding viable investment avenues so that their funds can be properly channelled. This is where Islamic REITs can come into play, because with these, investors can be provided selected projects that yield good returns and an income which is stable. The interest that has been particularly shown in the Asia Pacific region across Singapore and Malaysia, along with the launch of multimillion-dollar industrial Islamic REITs in Singapore, make it clear that the GCC will consistently prosper with every passing day.

Review Questions

1. Make a distinction between conventional and Islamic REITs.
2. Describe the structure of Islamic REITs.
3. What are the activities that are forbidden under the Islamic REIT rules?
4. Explain the usage of contracts in Islamic REITs.
5. Why do financiers want to invest in Islamic REITs?

References

Al-'Aqar Healthcare REIT (2014), *Al-'Aqar Healthcare REIT Annual Report*, retrieved from www.alaqar.com.my/index.php/publications (Access date December 28, 2014)

Al-Hadharah Boustead REIT (2012), *Al-Hadharah Boustead REIT Annual Report*, retrieved from https://klse.i3investor.com/financial/annual/5124/31-Dec2012_2753959261.jsp (Access date December 31, 2012)

Al Jazira Capital (2014), *Real Estate Investment Trusts: KSA Real Estate Thematic Report*, retrieved from www.aljaziracapital.com.sa/report_file/ess/SPE165.pdf (Access date June 1, 2015)

Al-Salām REIT (2015), *Al-Salam REIT Annual Report*, retrieved from www.alsalamreit.com.my/ (Access date December 31, 2015)

Axis Real Estate Investment Trust (2014), *Axis Real Estate Investment Trust Annual Report*, retrieved from http://ir.chartnexus.com/axisreit/annual-reports.php

Bursha Malaysia (2015), *Shari'ah Compliant Real Estate Investment Trusts (iREITs)*, retrieved from www.bursamalaysia.com/trade/our_products_services/ustain_market/bursa_malaysia_i/Shari'ah_compliant_real_estate_investment_trusts (Access date May 2, 2021)

Chuweni, N (2018), *Performance Analysis of Malaysian Islamic Real Estate Investment Trust: Management Approach to Best Practices*, PhD Thesis, Queensland University of Technology, Brisbane

Collas-Crill (2021), *Jersey: Ideally Placed for Islamic Investors*, retrieved from www.mondaq.com/jersey/islamic-finance/1119902/ideally-placed-for-islamic-investors (Access date October 12, 2021)

Global Newswire (2021), *SP Launches First Shari'ah REITs EFT*, retrieved from www.salaamgateway.com/story/sp-funds-launches-first-sharia-reit-etf (Access date March 14, 2021)

Ibrahim, MF, Eng, OS and Parsa, A (2009), Shari'ah Property Investment in Asia, *Journal of Real Estate Literature*, 17(2), 233–248

Islamic Finance News (IFN) (2015, September 22), Jcorp's Islamic REIT Attracts Overwhelming Response; Demonstrates High Demand for Shari'ah Asset Classes, *Islamic Finance News (IFN)*

Islamic Finance News (IFN) (2016), Bahrain Approves Maiden Islamic Listed REIT, *Islamic Finance News (IFN)*

Islamic Finance News (IFN) (2017a, February 6), Sharia Compliant REIT Makes Further Inroads in the UAE, IFN Alerts, *Islamic Finance News (IFN)*

Islamic Finance News (IFN) (2017b, April 13), Islamic REITs Riding High on Low Property Prices in the GCC, IFN Alerts, *Islamic Finance News (IFN)*

KLCCP Stapled Group (2016), *KLCCP Stapled Group Annual Report*, retrieved from www.klcc.com.my/investorrelations/annual_reports.php (Access date May 2, 2014)

Maierbrugger, A (2015), Islamic REITs Slowly Get Traction in the Middle East, *Gulf Times*

Manulife Investment Management (2021), *Factsheet Manulife Shari'ah Global REIT Fund*, retrieved from www.manulifeinvestment.com.my/servlet/servlet.FileDownload?file=00P6F00002opppgUAA (Access date November 20, 2021)

Mcaughtry, L (2016), A New Trend in Property Investment: The Growth of Islamic REITs in the Gulf, *Islamic Finance News (IFN)*, 13(48), 9–11

Parsa, ARG and Muwlazadeh, MA (2010), Islamic Finance and Shari'ah Compliant Real Estate Investment, in *Global Trends in Real Estate Finance*, edited by G Newell and K Sieracki, New York: Blackwell Publishing Ltd, pp. 157–189

Sabana Shari'ah Compliant Industrial REIT (2016), *Sabana Shari'ah Compliant Industrial REIT Annual Report*, retrieved from http://sabana.listedcompany.com/ar.html (Access date April 23, 2017)

Securities Commission Malaysia (2016), *List of Listed Real Estate Investment Trust (As at 31 December 2020)*, retrieved from www.sc.com.my/wpcontent/uploads/eng/html/resources/stats/REIT.pdf (Access date May13, 2017)

Thomas, A (2014), *Islamic Fund and Asset Management*, Kuala Lumpur: Islamic Finance Training

10

FINANCIAL FUTURES, STOCK OPTIONS AND WARRANTS IN THE ISLAMIC CAPITAL MARKET

Learning Objectives

On completing this chapter, learners will be able to:

- Define *Shari'ah*-compliant futures, options, and warrants
- Elucidate the characteristics of conventional and *Shari'ah*-compliant futures, options, and warrants
- Explain why Islamic capital markets require derivative products
- Understand the viewpoints and opinions of *Shari'ah* scholars in using derivative products in Islamic financial markets.

10.1 Introduction

During a trade, futures contracts serve as an agreement where allowance is made for producers and commercial operators to determine the price of commodities prior to receiving or delivering the products or services in their physical form. By incorporating these contracts in a trade agreement, multiple varieties of risks get minimised effectively. These contracts help in the facilitation of production planning in agriculture, industry, and commerce. To add to that, they are equally effective in providing marketing facilities for high volumes of trade. According to Kamali (1999), qualified brokers and agents are generally involved in drawing a conclusion of these contracts as their job entails them to carefully take note of market rules on a highly controlled and centralised basis. To assuring the guarantee of the applicability of these contracts in the future, the trading activities on the exchange are supervised by the clearinghouse which manages the solvency of all traders (Khan, 1988).

DOI: 10.4324/9780429321207-10

The integration of futures contracts in a trade agreement under the Islamic commercial law has been subjected to different opinions. Muslim scholars are of the opinion that these contracts lack consistency in conforming to *Shari'ah* principles because of certain reasons, as follows:

1. When the contract is made, the countervalues seem to be absolutely non-existent. During the time of making the agreement in the form of a futures contract, no payment is made and no delivery of goods and services is made. The transaction happens on paper only with the ultimate aim of earning profits on the basis of speculation. At the time of making any contract under *Shari'ah* law, the mandate involves the requirement of at least one of the countervalues (if not both) for the sale to be established as valid. With reference to the use of *Salam*, the buyer generally makes an advance payment but the seller defers the delivery date of the goods to a date in the future. The deferment in this regard is made in terms of the delivery date. Thus, *Shari'ah* does not have any provision for allowing the deferment of the price to be paid as well as the delivery of goods/services.
2. In futures contracts, short selling happens. This implies that the commodities sold by the seller are neither possessed nor owned by the seller irrespective of its existence. A sale is characterised by the transfer of ownership of the product or service sold from the seller to the buyer. Thus, the transfer of ownership of the commodities which are ultimately not owned by the seller cannot happen.
3. Futures contracts do not fully comply with the requirements of being able to take the product's ownership before reselling it. The majority of the transactions in the futures market happen without physical delivery.
4. With both the countervalues being deferred to a future date, these contracts ultimately take the shape of a forbidden sale of one debt for another (*bai al-kali bil-kali*).
5. The element of speculation involved in futures contracts is on the borderline of gambling (*maisir*) and uncertainty (*gharar*), both of which are totally disapproved of by *Shari'ah*. Gambling is simultaneously believed to give rise to volatile prices of commodities in the cash market.

In the case of a contract in the form of an option, a buyer is entitled to the right to purchase or sell a particular quantity of an asset at a fixed price at a particular future date. However, the buyer in no way is obligated to do the same. This right entails the buyer paying a premium which can be defined as an amount paid to the seller by the buyer. The right can be exercised through two primary options. The first one is a call option, which entitles the buyer with the right of purchasing the asset at a set amount and by a particular date. The other one, the put option, entitles the buyer to sell the asset at a fixed price by a future date.

Let us consider an example of a call option (right to buy) in this regard. According to A, company X's stocks are likely to increase in value. In order to be able to purchase the stocks, A has to pay the entire amount or alternatively pay the premium for buying call options. In case there is an increase in the prices, A gets to be benefitted through both of these ways. In case the value of the stocks decreases, A can let options lapse. Therefore, the losses incurred by A are only limited to the premium amount only.

Now, let us consider an example of put option (right to sell) in this regard. Let's say B is in a state of worry and thinks that their stock prices are likely going to decrease. B can choose to sell the stocks or purchase put options. In case if there is a decrease in the prices, the stocks can be sold by B at a fixed price by only paying the premium. In case if there is an increase in the prices, B can choose to let options lapse.

Both of these are instances of simple options.

More often than not, businesses use a combination of put options and call options so as to be able to hedge the risks associated with them, particularly subjected to currency fluctuation as well as against the fluctuation of commodity prices. Combined options allow the premiums to be set up in a way so that they could be cancelled by each other. Let us consider an example in this regard. Let us say, C is concerned about the fact that if the value of the US dollar fluctuates, it might get impacted in performing a contract. For hedging the risk associated with this worry of value fluctuation, a combined option can be purchased by C. A combined option is a blend of both a put option and a call option. Now, if the value of the US dollar escalates, the put options will enable C to purchase for the lower price as compared to the market price, thereby generating enough profit for being able to overcome the loss incurred from the call options and vice versa.

'Stand-alone' options, are the terminology used as a reference for the above-mentioned options owing to their nature of being bought and sold separately in the security markets regularly. 'Embedded options', on the other hand, are options that are not being sold separately but are rather embedded in another product. A cancellation option can be considered an example of an embedded option. A built-in cancellation feature is available in some products enabling either the buyer or the seller to cancel the transaction with no other obligations required. In transactions like this, the premium price does not have to be paid separately as it is already embedded in the price of product itself.

Conventional options under the norms of *Shari'ah* are likely to be disapproved. A larger section of Muslim jurists consider that conventional options cannot be permitted. According to the Islamic Fiqh Academy of the Organization of Islamic Cooperation, 'Since the subject of [option] contracts is neither sum of money, nor a utility, nor a financial right which may be waived, then the contract is not permissible in *Shari'ah*' (Resolution No. 63/7/2001). The opinion of the majority is taken into absolute consideration owing to the following reasons:

1. The nature and the utility of options ultimately lead to *maisir* (gambling).
2. Excessive speculations are being made by using options.
3. The premium paid has not been granted permission.

On a parallel note, an influential minority is of the opinion that options must acquire the approval. The *Shari'ah* board, as an Islamic financial institution (IFI), has incorporated the opinions of the minority by developing options which are *Shari'ah* compliant and can be therefore used as an alternative to conventional options.

Warrant can be defined as a corporate form of security whose features are similar to that of a call option. With a warrant, a holder is entitled to the right to directly purchase shares of common stock from a company at a price which is fixed for a particular period of time. It must be noted that the buyer can in no way be obligated to do the same. The specifications contained in each warrant comprise the number of stock shares that can be purchased by the holder, the exercise price and the date of expiration. Similarly, a lot of the cases comprise warrants being attached to bond when issued. Considering from the viewpoint of investors, warrants can be perceived similar to that of a call option for shares of common stock, as they entitle the holder to purchase common stock at a particular price. According to the company's perspective, warrants and call options are significantly different. The most important distinctive feature between the two is the issuance. The individual issues the call option while the company issues the warrant. On a call option being exercised, there is no involvement of any company and investors purchase common stock from other investors. On a warrant being exercised, the company receives a particular amount while there is an increase in the number of shares outstanding.

The ultimate concern revolves around the fact whether Islamic warrant is characterised by a considerable amount of risk or uncertainty (*gharar*) as a result of speculation of a variety or by taking an analogous attempt. The concern of Islamic scholars around the approval of embedded option (warrant) is based on *gharar*. As per Jobst (2007), an option is considered as *gharar fahish* (mild uncertainty). Embedded option does not provide clarity on the next price of stock. Thus, the decision of an investor in either continuing the contract (exercise) or cancelling it remains undetermined. A section of investors will likely utilise this contract for just speculating a transaction. Under the *qoidah fiqhi* (legal maxim) of '*dar'ul mafasid muqoddam min jalbil masholih*', the use of an option as an Islamic contract is not permitted. The approval of using embedded options is allowed by certain jurists owing to the implicit consideration of the obligations for both parties in the contract with no possibility of transferring the obligations to a third party so as to effectively curb speculative tendencies. Again, it is undoubtedly true that as a result of stipulation, the organised market in options can be simultaneously killed. All in all, the primary concept of option needs to be perceived in terms of a hedge instrument that aims in reducing the risk of loss, particularly during the testing times of the present economic situation. Owing to the fact that the economy fluctuates severely, the option contract is imperative for the interest of public (*maslahah*) as well as for community (*ummah*). The issues associated with *gharar* and *maisir* (gambling) will likely emerge on account of speculation being attempted by a smaller portion of investors. This specific issue cannot be used as a means to generalise the requirement of prohibition on option contract. In the context of legal frameworks and regulations of the economy, options play a crucial role and henceforth must be made permissible.

When drawing a comparison with the components of conventional law of transactions (*mu'amalat*), no such parallel can be obtained for the new age economic phenomenon through futures, options, warrants, and other derivative contracts. An Islamic perspective must be used to analyse their validity of being declared as permissible in terms of transactions. Both their pros and cons must be simultaneously considered.

10.2 Stocks and the Islamic Capital Market

All commercial and financial activities in the Islamic financial market are characterised by their absolute conformity to *Shari'ah* principles. The *Shari'ah* serves as a guiding pillar for a Muslim about how they must lead their life. In a similar proximity, it equally acts as the Islamic religious law being adhered to in determining and conducting all kinds of commercial and financial activities. *Shari'ah* scholars have developed and set the practical rules of *Shari'ah* on the basis of:

- The Qur'an, which is the holy book of Islam and the revealed word of God. (It must be noted that the legal nature of Qur'an does not even amount to 3%.)
- The Sunnah of the Prophet Mohammed (peace be upon him), which has been considered to be the binding authority of his dicta and decisions.
- The *ijma*, or 'consensuses' of the eminent Muslim scholars.
- The *qiyas*, or reasoning and deductive analogies.

The initiative of developing consensuses collectively among *Shari'ah* scholars as well as the scholars of Muslim business communities can be perceived as a relevant aspect of development in this context. This process has given rise to questions, reservations, doubts and dilemmas among a certain section of critics, irrespective of which a degree of *ijma* has been obtained. This has simultaneously benefitted the Islamic finance industry on a larger scale. Among several examples, one instance that has to be unduly mentioned is how the deliberations and unifying and standardising pronouncements and issuances of the OIC Fiqh Academy, Accounting and Auditing Organization for Islamic Financial Institutions (AAOIFI) and the Islamic Financial Services Board (IFSB) have positively impacted the Islamic financial industry.

Common stock in an Islamic financial system is referred to as a *Mudarabah*, which can be equally understood as a profit and loss sharing certificate. The concept of the capital being divided into smaller portions in the form of stocks likely appears to have originated in the initial development stages of conventional economies in the West. On the other hand, Robertson (1933) has been able to trace that origin of stocks dates back to the time of medieval Muslim traders. In common stock, the claim of ownership is represented on a company and stockholders are considered as business owners. At the same time, they receive the entitlement of sharing the rewards of ownership as well as the profits generated in the firm. The ownership rights are extended to the right of being able to elect the directors of a company and vote on crucial issues during stockholders' meetings. It must be noted that the residual risk corresponding to the ownership has to be equally borne by the stockholders. On the occasion of a company getting dissolved, all third party claims must be attended to before the capital in any form is returned to stockholders. On grounds of these features, Islamic scholars and economists are in favour of common stocks being accepted as securities under Islamic law. In 1993, at their seventh meeting, the OIC Islamic Fiqh Academy even approved common stocks as an investment instrument (JIBF, 1994).

Eventually, in 2002, *Shari'ah*-compliant capital market instruments were developed, subjecting to a more modern approach following which it has only accelerated. An amalgamation of several factors has resulted in this process, including:

- The evolution of modern Islamic finance with particular reference to its evolution since the mid-1990s.
- Multilateral institutions like the Islamic Development Bank (IDB), Accounting and Auditing Organization for Islamic Financial Institutions (AAOIFI) and the Islamic Financial Services Board (IFSB) have been putting considerable effort in this context.
- The evolution and development of transactions, particularly from the mid-1990s.

The modern financial system includes two types of capital markets: the stock market and the commodity (derivatives) market. Islamic economy ensures that the stock market works in conformity with the *Shari'ah* morale, which must be an equally imperative mandate in transferring funds from surplus to deficit units. Another key objective of the Islamic stock market is to make sure that there exist the means to attract surplus funds for investments that are worth making. This has to be ensured as per the preferences of the owner subject to the extent of risk involvement, return rate and the period of investment, all of which have to be in full compliance with the ethical rules of conducting businesses under Islamic law.

In the stock market, multiple issues consisting of stock index futures, stock options and warrants are mostly complicated in nature and are thus subject to the scholarly opinions and interpretations from the major schools of Islamic jurisprudence.

10.3 Strategies for Sophisticated Conventional Investors: Stock Options, Warrants and Futures

At present, structured products and derivatives have been significantly contributing to international financial markets. Innovation has been largely integrated and increased in derivative instruments as a result of the investor's appetite for returns, difficult conditions of the capital market and growth of funds management. On the other hand, the Islamic financial sector has been simultaneously witnessing large-scale development. Issuers as well as investors are now exposed to multiple opportunities because *Shari'ah*-compliant products have been currently applying derivatives. At the same time, one must be aware of understanding the primary ideologies of conventional stock options, warrants and futures prior to discussing the problems encountered during the conversion of certain selective derivatives instruments from conventional to *Shari'ah*-compliant products.

10.3-1 Options

Options serve as contracts entitling the holder with the right of buying and selling a certain amount of a particular security at a fixed price within a certain period of time that has been predetermined. The time period refers to the expiration date. The fixed price is also referred to the exercise price or strike price. The expiration of options is scheduled to occur on the third Friday of each month. To be able to get the right to hold an option, a premium amount has to be paid by investors. It must be noted that every option contract is representative of 100 shares of stock. The underlying company does not issue options. The primary four option plays are buying calls, buying puts, selling calls, and selling puts (Hull, 1995).

10.3-1-1 Stock Options

When a contract is made with regard to stock options, its holder gets legally entitled to the right of purchasing a set number of shares of the employer's stock at a fixed price. It must be noted that this right can be availed within a particular time span. It is up to an employer in correspondence with its board of directors in setting specifications such as the number of shares, exercise price and time period for availing of the option, and so forth, all of which pave the way for a stock option to be granted. The option contract can simultaneously include a later date at which it is effective. The exercise price, also known as 'strike price', is the probable amount to be paid by the option holder for purchasing the optioned stock. On the date of granting the option, the exercise price remains equivalent to the value of the stock option on most occasions. In case the stock value increases to become greater than the exercise price after the granting date, employees are entitled to purchase the stock at the exercise price, which is lower in comparison to the market price that other investors are required to pay. The stock can eventually be sold in exchange of cash, thereby generating profit. The stock option holder is not entitled to the rights that the shareholder has, such as voting or dividend rights, except when the exercise and issuance of stock option is done. When the exercise price is paid by the option holder for purchasing shares, a stock option gets exercised. This is also the time when the registration of the stock shares is made in the name of the option holder, thereby leading to the beginning of the shareholder status.

The approval of stock options is primarily ensured with respect to a vesting requirement which implies that a set of conditions must be fulfilled prior to the option becoming exercisable and for the shares to be purchased by the employees. The occurrence of vesting is primarily because of continued employment, referred to as time-based vesting. On the other hand, in a performance-based vesting, there is a mandate for performance goals of an individual and/or company to be achieved as a requirement for vesting. The stated exercise period of stock options represents the time frame within which the exercise of the option must be done. On account of the option not being exercised within the set time frame, it expires. The most widely used exercise period for employee options is a time frame of ten years.

In case of termination of the employment, the exercise period of an employee's option can be completely reduced. This is applicable to the majority of option plans for employees. However, there are certain cases in which the provision of all options in an option plan expires as soon as the termination of employment is made by the employee. Again, there are certain plans that make an allowance for continuation of the options for a shorter time period after termination (e.g. a shorter time period of 90 days). Exceptions can be made owing to specific types of terminations such as, death, disability, or retirement. Normally, employees are supposed to exercise their option after its vesting by paying the value of the exercise price to the employer in a cheque. Certain plans make a facilitation for employees for paying the exercise price not only in cash but through different forms. For instance, the exercise amount can be lent to the employee by the company, or an approval can be made for the employee to deliver previously acquired shares of employer stock so as to be able to pay the exercise price.

10.3-1-2 Making Money With Stock Options

'Spread' is a term used for defining the excess of the stock option's value over the exercise price of the option. Let us consider an example in this regard. The per-unit exercise price of a share is US$10 while its present stock value per share is US$25. Thus, the spread per unit of share becomes 415. The payoff stock options might be termed as 'out of the money', 'at the money', or 'in the money' (Table 10.1).

Here, K is representative of the strike price while S is representative of the current stock price.

An option can be described as 'in-the-money' when the stock value surpasses the exercise price. This implies that the spread generates a positive number.

An option can be described as 'out-of-the-money' when the stock value is lower than the exercise price. This implies that the spread results in a negative number.

An option can be described as 'at-the-money' when the stock value is equivalent to the exercise price. This implies that the spread is nil.

TABLE 10.1 Payoff Stock Options

	Call	*Put*
Out-of-the-money	$K > S$	$K < S$
In-the-money	$K < S$	$K = S$
At-the-money	$K < S$	$K > S$

The similarity of option programs of private companies and public companies can be observed in more ways than one. However, the key distinctive feature lies in exercising of an option by the employee of a private company and the consecutive stock purchasing where a market for the stock is not readily available for the employee.

A genuine concern here is about the process and possibility of generating profit on the option by an employee of a privately held company. Certain private companies can choose to purchase stock from the employee, especially when the employee has put up termination of their employment. Or otherwise, the employee has to wait until the occurrence of a significant event or so, like an initial public offering (IPO) or sale of the company, before being able to acquire profit.

10.3-1-3 Pricing

'Option premium' is the price at which an option is sold. Several factors act as determinants in fixing the option's price or premium (Hull, 1995):

- The underlying stock's price
- The time duration for which the option continues to persist
- The volatile nature of the underlying security
- The exercise or strike price at which the underlying stock is purchased or sold
- Rates of interest (Table 10.2).

Commodity options indeed have their own set of advantages over stock options despite the fact both of these work on similar grounds in terms of stock options. The similarity entitles the buyer with the right of buying or selling a stock option at a price and particular time frame, both predetermined. It must be noted that the right does not signify any form of obligation. The innumerable advantages of commodity options can be observed in terms of diversification, implementation of strategies, and fair pricing.

10.3-2 Warrants

Warrants can be defined as derivative securities where their values are being 'derived', or based on the value of underlying security. Similar to that call options,

TABLE 10.2 Changing Variable, Value of Put and Value of Call

Changing Variable	*Value of Put*	*Value of Call*	*Rationale*
Increased underlying stock price	L_0	H_i	With a call, an allowance is made for the investor in purchasing a security at a price which is predetermined. The investor gains owing to the increase of the underlying security's price. The opposite is applicable for the put option.
Increased volatility	H_i	H_i	When the volatile nature is higher, it is more likely of the security taking a large swing away from the strike price (in either direction).
Increased time until maturity	H_i	H_i	If the time span is longer, there is a greater chance of the investor making more money on the option.
Increased strike price	H_i	L_0	When the strike price is higher, the value of the call option lowers owing to the fact that investors are entitled to the right of purchasing the security at this price. The opposite is applicable for the put option.
Increased interest rates	L_0	H_i	Higher rates of interest are indicative of the lower value of the upcoming strike price (in US dollars) in comparison to the value set by an investor at present. This ultimately becomes similar to setting a lower strike price. So higher interest rates imply the low worth of future investments and more worth of the call. The opposite is applicable for the put option.

warrants entitle the holder with the right to buy a set number of stock shares within a particular time frame and at a price that is predetermined. In consideration of calls, warrant holders hold the expectation for their stock investment prices to escalate. Irrespective of these similar grounds, warrants differ from calls owing to their direct issuance by the corporation whose stock they are based on instead of an independent option writer. A legally binding contract in terms of a 'warrant agreement' specifies all the terms governing the warrant in a comprehensive way. This agreement includes how and when the warrant can be exercised. A corporation issue warrants directly instead of an outside issuer.

10.3–3 Futures Contracts

Futures are almost synonymous with options in their features, with the only exception that in the case of the former, the right of purchasing the underlying financial instrument or commodity (metal, grain, cotton, oil and gas, etc., but not stocks) is exercised by the investor at the settlement date. Thus, futures constitute an obligatory contract making an investor transact with another party. This culminates into unlimited downside risk as it becomes an obligation for investors in fulfilling their end of the transaction irrespective of the current trend of market prices. Investors need not pay a premium for entering into a futures contract, as this entails an agreement for making a transaction at a later date. Therefore, it is crucial for the contract to be sold prior to the date of settlement. By using this method, investors need not worry about the truckload of grain being delivered to them on the very settlement date.

However, futures are advised against investors who are considerably new and inexperienced. Portfolio managers are seen to primarily use these contracts in hedging as well as making speculations. A futures account is needed by an investor for them to start making transactions with this product. Speculations make it evident that the investor is eyeing greater rewards by accepting greater risks. An investor purchases a future with the intent that its eventual payoff might have the potential in outweighing the risk taken. The United States is credited for having not only the largest and the most developed futures market globally but also the one characterised by paramount sophistication. With the financial markets maturing, growing and evolving, new futures markets emerge all the time. The exercise of future contracts is done at a future date which is evident from the term itself. No premium is required for entering into the futures contract. It is only during the expiration that money only changes hands. Options entitle the holder with the right of making transactions, while in futures, parties are obligated to make transactions. Trading derivative securities are complex in nature, which is why investors must have an approved option and futures account prior to making transactions with these products.

In simple terms, hedging can be best described as a strategy used in offsetting risk (Al-Suwailem, 2006). Let us consider an example in this context. A cereal manufacturer is in fear of the rise in costs of the ingredients. In order to 'hedge' the risk, the manufacturer will purchase a futures contract on grain. Here, the futures contract will ensure the current grain price is locked, and thus, increased prices need not be paid later if the prices soar higher.

10.4 *Shari'ah* Prohibits *Maisir, Gharar* and *Dayn bi-dyan*

Shari'ah norms and regulations have been long assumed to cause hindrances in the development of *Shari'ah*-compliant derivative instruments. The key precepts causing these assumptions are:

- If a person is not in ownership of the thing he is willing to sell, it cannot be ultimately sold. This prevents short sales.
- Assets that can be purchased and sold have to be necessarily tangible. This prevents the sale of options and derivatives.

It must be simultaneously noted that *maisir, gharar* and *dayn bi-dyan* are banned under *Shari'ah*. The prohibition on these practices makes it difficult for finding Islamic alternatives to stock index futures, stock options, hedging, and so forth.

Therefore, the issue of *maisir* (or gambling) becomes a problematic reason for designing instruments in an Islamic stock market (Islamic capital market). *Maisir* involves speculation in the stock market, which means trading in securities solely for the purpose of generating short-term profit as a result of the market's uncertainty. Conventional markets accept speculative trading when the levels are moderate. The market becomes more observant when speculators come into play as an immediate emphasis is put on what is happening. This results in the improved liquidity of the trading. Rationale investors are considered to be trading on 'true' information corresponding to the stock while speculators on the other hand are considered to be trading on 'noise'. From a conventional point of view, the interaction between both of these kinds of investors ultimately helps in ensuring market efficiency. Speculation comes with a whole lot of issues. It is only after the resolution of these issues that might help us in contemplating a fully functioning Islamic capital market (stock market).

Speculation is characterised by excessive uncertainty, or *Gharar*, the practice of which is yet again very much unacceptable under *Shari'ah* law. When a party enters into a contract with another party with regard to purchasing or selling stocks with excessive risk involved in the transactional process, such practice is absolutely unacceptable. It can be only applicable when markets are characterised by high volatility. The buyer and the seller must not get involved in a transaction whose outcome is marked by a high level of uncertainty. The risk of a stock is directly proportional to the expectancy of return, which is why market participants are attracted to stocks that have higher risks associated with them. In an Islamic market, stock market regulators are entrusted with the responsibility of determining whether during a period of high price volatility the permission to trade is acceptable or not.

Stock trading simultaneously corresponds to another issue of arranging certain transactions in the form of *Ikrah*. Under it, a party unwilling to make the contract is imposed to make the same. Or else, the imposition of conditions that the party are not ready to accept is done. A conventional lens makes it difficult to identify any such problem in this context. Stocks are purchased and sold by market participants in order to be able to secure positions in derivative markets. Some parties willingly enter into these contracts having full knowledge of the terms and probable outcomes. In light of the traditional trading of stocks, two willing parties are required, which is why this cannot be identified as a problem as per the viewpoint of Islamic law. When options are written on stocks, the contract implies that it can be exercised by the option buyers only on account of being beneficial to them while potentially incurring losses for sellers. It is true that the option's buyer and seller can choose to enter the contract willingly. However, the practice of imposing losses on the seller by the buyer is banned under Islamic law. The loss does not directly correspond to transactions that are not clearly identifiable in products or services but rather corresponds directly to a derivative position, thereby bringing in further difficulties.

The issue of derivatives hovers around the concern of hedging or insurance. The mainstream format of conventional style of insurances is prohibited under the Islamic law. The process of hedging with the use of derivatives is a form of insurance. In order to cater to the protection of underlying investments, investors can opt for purchasing and selling derivatives like that of options and contracts. The point of concern is whether the acceptability of it must be allowed in the Islamic financial market or not. Derivative markets are inclusive of speculation because the functionality of the derivatives market is largely determined based on the interaction between speculators and hedgers.

10.5 Obstacles Encountered During the Practice of Stock Index Futures, Stock Options and Warrants in the Islamic Market

The usage of modern financial institutions such as stock and derivative markets or modern financial instruments such as shares, bonds, futures, options and swaps in an Islamic economy is most likely to give rise to several problems. These hindrances are primarily caused due to the lack of proper clarity of *Shari'ah* norms guiding the possible acceptance of these institutions/instruments. The approval of stock markets in Muslim countries does not act as the qualifying ground of equating these instruments and trading practices of the markets in conformity with *Shari'ah* norms. A large section of Muslim countries approve interest-based banks even though interest is known to be prohibited under Islamic law. In order to evaluate the possibility of accepting any (unclear) element in Islamic financial system, the approach used is of breaking down the larger issue into several smaller components. Each of these smaller components is then further analysed in terms of their *Shari'ah* compliance. The next section attempts to briefly discuss instruments, such as stock index futures, stock options and warrants as per the perspective of Islam.

10.5-1 Stock Index Futures

In order to be able to fine-tune the risk-return profile of their portfolios, equity investors typically opt for utilising stock index futures. Historically speaking, commodity futures have come a long way. However, the familiarity of using financial futures like that of stock index futures hit the markets not before the 1980s. The significant world stock markets are characterised by stock index futures. Under this type of contract, a dollar value of the stock index can be traded by an investor while the delivery can be done in the future. To ensure practicality, cash is used for accomplishing settlement and not the physical delivery of stocks inclusive of index. In order to facilitate the protection against odds of market fluctuations, stock index futures equip their investors with the provision of all possible means. It simultaneously acts as a well-defined hedging device for diversified stock market investors subjecting to the considerable high futures prices in correspondence with the underlying market (Jones, 1996). For being able to hedge the risks, investors should take a stand where their profits and losses in the stock index futures are able to offset changes in the value of their underlying stock portfolio.

For the possibility of stock index futures to be used in an Islamic stock market is primarily based on whether the idea of future delivery of a product/service can be accepted as a practice. Islamic law has certain regulations and restrictions subjecting to an agreement of selling a commodity/service in the future even if it does not entirely prohibit the practice (Kamali, 2005). Let us consider the *Istisna* contract to understand the same. This contract involves manufacturing a commodity where delivery and payment are scheduled for a future date. At the same time, another mandate is that the contract must clearly define the specifications of the commodity. These requirements are not likely to be fulfilled by a stock index future owing to the fact that a dollar value of an index is not really considered a well-defined commodity. When a commodity is not aptly defined in terms of its specifications, doubt and concern arise with regard to its physical delivery. A modern index future ultimately leads to cash exchange, representative of the distinction between the contract's opening and closing price on the day of maturity.

Contemporary futures contracts in all possible forms have been completely dismissed by Islamic economist Chapra (1985). According to his point of view, futures contacts do not lead to the title exchange of the underlying commodity. It must be notably mentioned that title exchange is not allowed under a typical commodity future. He has put forth a factual statement on the possibility of futures users opting to close out their positions before the maturity. This might lead to hedgers not wanting to accept the delivery of a commodity, thereby making the utilisation of futures null and void. We can borrow a statement from the OIC Islamic Fiqh Academy for clearer guidance. As per the statement, permission is not granted to trading in the futures market wherein the contract ends on a converse contract sale as a result of which a settlement is made on the difference in price. A problem encountered with regard to stock index futures price risks is shifted to speculators by the hedgers. All in all, this evidently portrays that futures are dependent on speculation even if it is not acceptable as a fair practice under Islamic law.

The process of hedging involved with futures is aimed at protecting a position in the cash market while the implementation and achievement of the same is largely dependent on the involvement of speculators. Speculators are not supposed to be mandatorily involved in the cash market. Their role is limited to purchasing and selling futures to generate and earn a profit. However, speculators are perceived as crucial components of conventional futures markets owing to their expertise in risk assumption of price fluctuation that hedgers try to avoid. Their simultaneous contribution in the liquidity of the futures market eventually helps in reducing the volatile nature of the market. One must understand that the utility of futures is not limited to speculation solely. Let us understand it through an example. One might trade in common stocks, most likely on the basis of speculation, but that does not make stocks ineffective or invalid as an Islamic financial instrument. What we need is to wipe away speculation. However, eliminating speculation from stock index futures in an Islamic stock market would ultimately result is a contract, difficult for hedgers to use. This in turn would lead to the absence of interaction between speculators and hedgers in the market.

In an Islamic stock market, hedging might be considered acceptable (Al-Suwailem, 2006) owing to the requirement of both the buyer and seller of the stock index future completely aware of their individual positions and not making any kind of speculation. Hedging is aimed for the protection of an underlying investment. Investors opt for hedging as one of the techniques for minimising risk. We can look at an example in this regard. Single stocks and undiversified portfolios are associated with a considerable amount of risk. For eradicating the possibility of encountering these risks, investors opt for holding diversified portfolios of stocks.

To summarise, the argument in favour of using the stock index futures depends on whether they are legitimately used as hedging techniques. The contract being used by speculators does not make its usage invalid. The major hindrance can be seen in terms of the technical nature of the settlement process. Commodity futures characterised by title exchange to a commodity would not give rise to any problem in this respect. Settlement in terms of cash is largely practiced in western conventional markets, thereby dismissing them as possible options by Islamic scholars. If the settlement process is modified in the line with the Islamic business ethics to include the delivery of the basket of stocks, then it could be possibly considered the stock as *Shari'ah* compliant. This is certainly a complicated and time-consuming process, but that does not mean it is impossible to create such a contract. An example in this regard can be taken that of the Dow Jones Islamic Index fund. As a stock index future, it is traded on the New York Stock Exchange while equally entailing the physical delivery of stock.

10.5-2 Stock Options

Stock options, or simply equity options, are another complex option from the lens of the Islamic stock exchange. Investors in developed financial markets can choose from multiple exchange-traded and over-the-counter (OTC) options. Exchange-traded options are standardised contracts, the trading of which is done on the derivatives exchange. OTC options, on the other hand, are individual contracts, the negotiation of which is done with financial institutions.

Good flexibility of the terms of OTC options is available, which is why we have emphasised exchange-traded stock options here. Characterised by a straightforward approach, these contracts can be conveniently used in the exploration of issues from an Islamic viewpoint (Al-Amine, 2005). With a stock option, the holder is entitled to the right of purchasing or selling a particular company's stock at a set price within a certain time span. This does not signify that holder of an option is obligated to buy or sell the stock. Meanwhile, if a decision is taken by the holder to exercise that right, the seller/buyer is obligated to sell/buy the stock.

Let us now dive deeper into the reasons that make investors opt for stock options and whether using the same can be justified through the lens of an Islamic stock market. Strategically, a call option can be purchased on a company's shares. For ensuring the life of the option, a corresponding claim on the underlying stock can be controlled by the investor. The premium paid becomes the cost, which remains still lower than the cost of purchasing the stock. With the anticipation that the price of the stock is likely to escalate, the buyer hopes for being provided a profit on the option. In case the price of the stock remains unchanged or suffers a downfall, the loss incurred is known beforehand, since loss is equivalent to the premium paid. This simple instance makes it evident that a call buyer is in anticipation of the stock price to rise, while the seller of the call is in the expectation of the price to either come down or stay unchanged. It is quite difficult for this simple call option strategy to be justified through the lens of Islamic law. When the buyer and the writer of the call are neither in hold of the underlying stock nor show any intent in holding it, the speculative tendency of their involvement is clearly portrayed. They utilise the trading options for the sole purpose of generating returns from price movements. A simple hedging strategy is followed when the writer of the call option holds the underlying stock. The premium obtained helps in providing protection against the downfall in the stock price. In this situation, the writer needs to have full confidence about the price not escalating or otherwise, the chance of facing major losses is possible. The hedger can avail of several hedging strategies for being provided better protection. However, these hedging strategies are far more complex in nature.

On the parallel front, the buyer of a put is in anticipation of the stock price to hit a downfall so as to acquire the profit from this transaction. Contradictorily, the seller of a put option has an opposing viewpoint. The transaction can be interpreted in terms of absolute speculation, particularly when both parties do not remain involved in the underlying stock. The put's buyer might co-exist as a hedger if they are holding the underlying stock in their portfolio. The investor not only purchases the stock but also purchases a put written on the stock at the same time. This strategy serves as a provision of a form of insurance against the downfall in the price since the investor has the ability to sell the stock at a higher price than that of the market price.

The use of options as a hedging tool is again very difficult to be justified through an Islamic perspective. The issue is quite synonymous to that of a stock index futures cash exchange used for establishing settlement. The provision of delivery of shares at the exercise date is theoretically possible with stock options but in reality, this is hardly practiced. Traded options are regarded as part of the review of new financial instruments (JIBF, 1994) under the consideration of the 7th Council of the OIC Islamic Fiqh Academy. Options have been observed to lead to issues of multiple interpretations. Thus, the reports of the OIC Islamic Fiqh Academy do not provide relevant clarity on whether they are granted.

However, Elgari (1994) puts forth an opinion in favour of stock options being possible to be accepted under Islamic law on grounds of the seller of a call and the buyer of a put holding the underlying stock. According to his recommendations, standardised European-style options which can be exercised only during expiration can be utilised. This can help in reducing flexibility as well as speculative possibilities.

10.5–3 Warrants

Warrants can be understood as a particular type of call option. Generally, corporations issue warrants by entitling their holders the right to subscribe for new shares in the issuer. It is undoubtedly true that warrants are a category of call options. However, it is distinctively characterised from stock options. Warrants involve a longer term as compared to equity options. It is potentially possible for the holder of the warrant to become an equity investor in the issuing company in future. The issuance of warrants is offered in terms of part of the overall financial package and not as a separate exercise. This is how investors are potentially capable of participating in the company's growth without having to be a shareholder. Issuing companies are attracted to warrants because by attaching the same as a part of the package, they would conveniently get a chance in issuing other forms of securities at a lower cost. The *NewHorizon* magazine published in London has put forth an example of the issue of warrants on new shares in Petronas Dagangan Berhad as a part of an Islamic financing package. Warrants are issued by the associated company as part of an underlying financing package. The underlying transaction of Petronas warrants was actually an Islamic finance contract, supporting the fact that warrants are a permissible form of security.

10.6 Conclusion

At present, the development of *Shari'ah*-compliant derivative instruments is limited to a very small number. If the universal acceptance of these *Shari'ah*-compliant derivative instruments is taken into consideration, the small number comes down to zero. Developing these instruments with complete adherence to *Shari'ah* laws is quite a complicated process in terms of intellect as well as finances owing to multiple *Shari'ah* prohibitions and the large-scale sceptical approaches of *Shari'ah* scholars and investors. However, a committee has been formed and established by the International Swaps and Derivatives Association (ISDA) for developing derivatives in harmony with *Shari'ah* principles. It has the potential of developing the same in the markets.

We have attempted to put forth a discussion in this chapter on the development of *Shari'ah*-compliant capital markets instruments, which started around 2002 and was followed by continuous evolution and expansion over the years. However, the absence of clarity on *Shari'ah* guidance regarding their acceptability is considered the most probable reason. It is thus required for Islamic financial institutions to adopt *Shari'ah*-compliant instruments as well as appropriate techniques that could possibly help in managing risks of various kinds with special reference to market and currency risk for being able to compete with their conventional counterparts. A well-defined analysis of stock index futures (financial futures), stock options and warrants has been done to understand when and where obstacles are created by these instruments while finding Islamic alternatives within Islamic capital market activities.

Speculations or contracts that potentially open doors for speculative trading lead to a wide variety of difficulties. Technical problems are equally raised corresponding to contracts which do not specify the purchase and sale of a stock at a clearly predetermined price. The issues discussed in this chapter make it quite evident that Islamic stock market as a part of Islamic capital market activity is a distinctively exclusive institution in comparison to conventional stock markets. Any form of development towards a separate market is most likely to incorporate a gradual introduction of Islamic contracts and practices. Speculation and activities associated with it need to be accepted but at the same time, it is possible to restructure stock index futures, stock options and warrants, and so forth for overcoming technical problems associated with their present form that have been limited their usage.

Review Questions

1. What is meant by futures, options, and warrants?
2. Discuss the difference between *Shari'ah*-compliant futures, options and warrants, and their conventional counterparts.
3. Why do we need *Shari'ah*-compliant futures, options, and warrants despite different opinions of *Shari'ah* scholars?
4. What hindrances come into play during the practice of derivatives in Islamic financial markets?

References

Al-Amine, Muhammad al-Bashir Muhammad (2005), Financial Engineering and Islamic Contacts, in *Commodity Derivatives: An Islamic Analysis*, edited by M Iqbal and Tariqullah Khan, Hampshire: Palgrave MacMillan

Al-Suwailem, S (2006), *Hedging in Islamic Finance*, Occasional Paper No. 10, Jeddah: IRTI-IDB

Chapra, MU (1985, Winter), Commentary on M. M. Metwally: Role of the Stock Exchange in an Islamic Economy, *Journal of Research in Islamic Economics*, 75–81

Elgari, M (1994), Towards an Islamic Stock Market, *New Horizon*, 32, 4–7

Hull, JC (1995), *Introduction to Futures and Options Markets*, Hertfordshire: Prentice Hall International

JIBF (1994), Editorial: Latest Islamic Fiqh Academy Rulings on Finance, *Journal of Islamic Banking and Finance*, 11(2), 58–61

Jobst, AA (2007), Derivative in Islamic Finance, *Islamic Economic Studies*, 15(1), 42–51

Jones, CP (1996), *Investments: Analysis and Management*, 5th ed, New York: John Wiley & Sons

Kamali, M (1999), Permissibility and Potential of Development of Islamic Derivatives as Financial Instruments, *IIUPM Journal of Economics and Management*, 7(2), 73–86

Kamali, M (2005), Financial Engineering and Islamic Contacts, in *Fiqhi Issue in Commodity Futures*, edited by M. Iqbal and Tariqullah Khan, Hampshire: Palgrave Macmillan

Khan, M (1988), Commodity Exchange and Stock Exchange in Islamic Economy, *American Journal of Islamic Social Science*, 5(1), 91–114

Robertson, H (1933), *Aspects of the Rise of Economic Individualism*, Cambridge: Cambridge University Press

11

THE ISLAMIC MONEY MARKET VIS-À-VIS THE CONVENTIONAL MONEY MARKET

Learning Objectives

On completing this chapter, learners will be able to:

- Compare the functionality of conventional money markets and Islamic markets
- Understand the process through which surplus funds are invested by Islamic banks and how they obtain funding for deficits
- Comprehend the characteristics of Islamic money markets and the instruments that they use in the different Muslim countries, especially Malaysia
- Know and define the role that central banks play in Islamic money market operations
- Understand how the Islamic money market provides opportunities to market players to be able to execute similar functions as that of the conventional markets, the only difference being their complete adherence to the *Shari'ah* law.

11.1 Introduction

The vertical of the financial market where trading is being subjected to financial instruments having high liquidity and short-term maturities can be essentially summed up as the money market. As a component of the financial market, it involves purchasing and selling securities, particularly short-term maturities, of a year or less. This includes treasury bills and commercial papers. Trading here is mostly over-the-counter, done through a wholesale process. Participants use it as a way of borrowing and lending for a shorter period of time.

Different kinds of negotiable instruments such as treasury bills, commercial paper and certificates of deposit are included in the money market. Multiple participants and even companies sell commercial paper in the market to be able to raise funds. Owing to its high liquidity of securities, the money market is considered

DOI: 10.4324/9780429321207-11

a safe place for making investments. Certain risks are equally associated with the money market, one being that investors need to be cautious of defaulting on securities such as commercial paper. The money market comprises several financial institutions and dealers seeking to borrow or loan securities. It is undoubtedly the best source for making investments in liquid assets. Unlike a capital market, where things are formally organised, the money market is unstructured, unregulated and informal. Individuals investing in these markets get to choose from a variety of options. However, the returns provided are lower.

The chief difference between money markets and capital markets is how the former is used for considerably a shorter period of time while the latter is used for a longer period of time. The Islamic money market is a mechanism through which an Islamic banking institution having a deficit (investee bank) can procure investments from an Islamic banking institution having a surplus (investor bank) on the basis of *Mudharabah* (profit sharing). This stands as an implication of Islamic money market covering the *Mudharabah* interbank investment and interbank trading of Islamic financial instruments. The three major components of Islamic money market are the interbank deposit facility, the trading platform for Islamic money market instruments and the Islamic check-clearing system. A lot of the conventional instruments have been adapted and recreated into *Shari'ah*-compliant ones. The Islamic money market is responsible for carrying out important functions in the financial system and is thus considered to be a determining factor for the proper functioning of the Islamic banking system. Through the money market, Islamic financial institutions are facilitated with the opportunity of being able to raise funds and adjust portfolios over a short-term. When a surplus liquidity environment emerges, the Islamic bank ensures liquidity management by accepting *Qard* (loans). This is generally done by inviting Islamic banking institutions to place their surplus funds with the Islamic banks. The Commodity *Murabahah* Programme (CMP) is equally used by multiple Islamic banks for managing liquidity. The Islamic money market is discussed in details later in this chapter.

11.2 Conventional Money Market Yields

The major function of conventional money market instruments is to help businesses maintain liquidity. In the mainstream (conventional) money market, there exist four different kinds of money market yields:

1. The bank discount yield
2. The holding period yield
3. The effective annual yield
4. The money market yield.

The financial instruments which mature in less than a year are referred to as money market instruments. Some examples include treasury bills, commercial paper, or municipal notes. The maturity period of T-bills is generally 91 days or 180 days.

Bank discount yield	Money market yield (or CD equivalent yield)
$r_{BD} = \frac{D}{F} \times \frac{360}{t}$	$r_{MM} = \left(\frac{D}{F-D}\right) \times \frac{360}{t}$
Holding period yield (HPY)	**Effective annual yield (EAY)**
$HPY = \frac{P_1 - P_0 + D_1}{P_0}$	$EAY = (1 + HPY)^{\frac{365}{t}} - 1EAY = (1 + HPY)^{\frac{365}{t}} - 1$

FIGURE 11.1 Money market yields.

The distinguishing characteristics of the yield measures of money market instruments and longer-term fixed-rate bonds can be understood through the key points, as given below:

- In both cases, yield measures are annualised. However, bond yields to maturity are compounded while yield measures in money markets are not. The rate of return is decided on the basis of a simple interest.
- Contrary to the bond yields to maturity being calculated using the standard time value of money, money market instruments are mostly quoted using non-standard interest rates (e.g. discount rates or add-on rates).
- Money market instruments subjecting to different times to maturity have different periodicities. Bond yields to maturity, on the other hand, are given a common periodicity for all times to maturity.

11.3 Conventional Money Market Rates

Money market rates are quoted as discount rates or add-on rates.

11.3-1 Discount Rates

The rate of interest used for the computation of the present value of payment(s) is conventionally termed the discount rate. In the context of the money market, the discount rate corresponds to the type of rate with which short-term money market instruments are valued.

11.3-1-1 Pricing Money Market Instruments Using Discount Rates

The pricing of the money market instrument is obtained through the formula

$$PV = FV \times \left[\left(1 - Days / Year\right) \times DR\right)]$$

where
PV = the price of the money market instrument (present value)
FV = face value of the money market instrument (future value paid at maturity)
Days = count of days between settlement and maturity
Year = number of days in a year
DR = annualised discount rate.

A problem can be taken as an example to understand the concept with clarity. Let us consider that we have to calculate the price of the money market instrument using discount rates.

A 91-day UK T-bill (treasury bill) has a face value of 20 million euros at a discount rate of 2.5%. Based on an assumption of a year having 360 days, the price of the T-bill can be calculated as follows.

As per the information stated above:

$$PV = ?$$

$$FV = 20{,}000{,}000$$

$$Days = 91$$

$$Year = 360$$

$$DR = 2.5\%$$

On using the formula provided earlier:

$$PV = 20{,}000{,}000 \times \left[\left(1 - 91/360\right) \times 0.25\right)] = 19{,}873{,}611.11$$

The formula used above can be simultaneously transformed so as to ensure the discount rate becomes the subject:

$$DR = \left(Year / Days\right) \times \left[\left(FV - PV / FV\right)\right]$$

The definition of the variables are similar to that of the ones mentioned earlier. It must be carefully observed that Year/Days is associated with the periodicity of the annual rate, $\left(FV - PV\right)$ becomes the interest earned on the money market instrument.

In this regard, let us take another example to calculate the money market discount rate.

Let us consider a 91-day US T-bill (treasury bill) having a face value worth US\$5 million at a discount rate of 2.5% and a price of US\$4.9 million. Based on an assumption of a year having 360 days, the discount rate as per assumed by the T-bill can be calculated as follows.

As per the information stated above:

$$PV = 1{,}500{,}000$$

$$FV = 5{,}000{,}000$$

$$Days = 91$$

$$Year = 360$$

$$DR = ?$$

On using the formula provided:

$$\begin{aligned} DR &= (Year / Days) \times [(FV - PV / FV) \\ &= (360 / 91) \times [(5{,}000{,}000 - 4{,}900{,}000 / 5{,}000{,}000)] \\ &= 0.07912 = 7.912\% \end{aligned}$$

11.3–2 Add-on Rates

The computation of the money market instrument occurs on the basis of the add-on rate. This implies that the interest rate is added to the principal to be able to calculate the future value of the money market instrument.

11.3–2-1 Pricing Money Market Instruments Using Add-On Rates

The pricing subjected to the money market instruments depending on the add-on rate basis is obtained through the formula given below:

$$PV = FV / \left[1 + Days / Year\right) \times AOR$$

where
PV = the price of the money market instrument (principal amount or the present value)
FV = the redemption amount paid at maturity, including interest (future value)
Days = number of days between settlement and maturity
Year = number of days in the year
AOR = annualised add-on rate.

An example can be taken to understand the process of calculation through which the price of a money market instrument quoted on an add-on rate basis is obtained.

Let us consider that a US-based insurance company buys a 90-day banker's acceptance (BA) with a quoted add-on rate of 5% and a redemption value of US$10 million. Based on the assumption of a year having 365 days, the price of the BA can be calculated easily as follows.

As per the information stated above:

$$PV = ?$$

$$FV = 5{,}000{,}000$$

$$Days = 90$$

$$Year = 365$$

$$AOR = 5\%$$

On applying the formula provided earlier, the price of the BA is obtained by:

$$PV = \left[5{,}000{,}000 / \left(1 + 90 / 365\right) \times 0.05\right)] = 4{,}939{,}106.90$$

The redemption value of the money market instrument can be simultaneously calculated when the price (initial principal) and the variables are provided.

If FV is considered as the subject in the formula stated above,

$$FV = PV + \left[PV / \left(Days / Year \times AOR\right)\right]$$

The resulting formula (for FV) evidently projects that the redemption value is an initial principal (PV) plus the interest $PV\left[\left(Days / Year \times AOR\right)\right]$.

The interest is the principal times the product of the fraction of the year and the add-on rate.

Let us make an assumption that we are not aware of the redemption value in our example above. In this context,

$$\text{FV} = [4{,}939{,}106.90 + 4{,}939{,}106.90(90/365 \times 0.05)] = 5{,}000{,}000$$

The interest, thereby, earned on the BA, is

$$4{,}939{,}106.90\left[\left(90 / 365 \times 0.05\right)\right] = 60{,}893.09877$$

At the same time, the AOR can be equally made the subject of the formula. In this context,

$$AOR = \left(Year / Days\right) \times \left[\left(FV - PV\right) / PV\right]$$

Careful observation of the formula can clearly tell one that the add-on rate is a more effective and logical yield measure for the money market instrument in comparison to the discount rate since the Year/Days is the periodicity, and the $\left[\left(FV - PV\right) / PV\right]$ is the interest rate earned divided by the initial principal (PV). The interest earned in the discount rate is divided by the reaction value (FV), which understates the rate of return to the investor and the cost of borrowed funds to the investor since $PV < FV$ provided that $DR \geq 0$.

An example can be taken in this regard as well to understand the real-time implication of the formula for the calculation of the add-on Rate.

Let us consider a US-based insurance company buys a 135-day banker's acceptance (BA) with a redemption value worth US$20 million and a price of

US$19,951,106.90. On the basis of an assumption of the year having 365 days, the rate of the BA can be calculated through the mentioned formula.

As per the information stated above:

$$PV = 19{,}951{,}106.90$$

$$FV = 20{,}000{,}000$$

$$Days = 90$$

$$Year = 365$$

$$AOR = ?$$

The calculation of the rate of return (AOR) from the BA is obtained by:

$$AOR = (Year / Days) \times \left[(FV - PV / PV) \right]$$

$$PV = (365 / 135) \times \left[(20{,}000{,}000 - 19{,}951{,}106.90) / 19{,}951{,}106.90 \right]$$

$$= 0.01328 = 1.328\%$$

11.4 Comparison of Money Market Instruments Using Bond Equivalent Yield

The analysis of money market investment can be a tad bit challenging for the following reasons:

- The quotation of some of the money market instruments is done using discount rates while add-on rates are used for others.
- The number of days in a year is assumed as 360 by some and 365 by others.
- The quoted amount for the face value of the discount rates is paid at maturity. In the case of the add-on rate, it is the principal (price at the issue date).

Therefore, it becomes quite important to compare the discount and add-on rates of the money market instruments on a uniform basis. This can be done when one rate is converted into another to obtain the bond equivalent yield, more often than not, quoted on a 365-day add-on rate basis.

An example can be taken to understand the calculation of the bond equivalent yield.

Let us consider that a 91-day commercial paper is quoted at a discount rate of 5.5% for a year based on the assumption that it has 360 days. Owing to the face value of the price of instrument being 100, the bond equivalent yield rate can be calculated as shown below.

The price of the commercial paper is calculated using the discount rate:

$$PV = FV \times (1 - Days / Year \times DR) = 100 \times \left[(1 - 91 / 360 \times 0.055) \right] = 98.610$$

As per the formula provided earlier,

$$\begin{aligned} AOR &= Year / Days \times \left[(FV - PV) / PV \right] \\ &= (365 / 91) \times \left[(100 - 98.610) / 98.610 \right] \\ &= 5.655\% \end{aligned}$$

Thus, the obtained bond equivalent yield is 5.655%.

11.5 Islamic Money Markets

By virtue of the profit-and-loss sharing (PLS) paradigm as the foundational morale of Islamic financial products, Islamic financial institutions are supposed to share the profit and loss together. The same does not hold true for conventional financial products since the interest rate is fixed in this case. Thus, these financial institutions do not have to bear any kind of risk. This is equally applicable in the conventional money markets. In regard to Islamic money markets, banks use short-term financial instruments such as the negotiable Islamic certificate of deposit (NICD), Islamic accepted bills (IABs) and Islamic treasury bills (ITBs) to be able to lend or/and borrow from other banks. The liquidity provided by the Islamic money market in the global financial system ranges from the short term to the middle term. One of the most crucial roles that the Islamic money market plays in the larger economy is how it provides an efficient means so that the economic units can adjust their liquidity positions. The nature of funding offered by the Islamic money market to individuals, businesses and the government is primarily short-term. Table 11.1 is a representation of the comparative differences between the Islamic money market and the conventional money market. The table is indicative of the fact that the Islamic money market uses a host of *Shari'ah* contracts with particular reference

TABLE 11.1 Comparison Between Islamic and Conventional Money Markets

	Islamic Money Market	*Conventional Money Market*
Interbank market	*Shari'ah*-compliant contracts are used. This includes *mudarabah*, *murabaha* and *wakalah*.	Debt contract is used for placement of funds.
Money market instruments	Negotiable Islamic certificate of deposit (NICD), Islamic accepted bills (IABs) and Islamic treasury bills (ITBs).	Treasury bills, commercial paper, certificates of deposit, etc.
Issuance process	Must be *Shari'ah*-compliant and approved by Shari'ah Council/Board and Central Bank.	Approved by regulatory authorities only.
Types of structure	Structured based on assets, equity and debt.	Structured based on debt only.
Investors	Both Islamic and conventional investors.	Conventional investors only.

Sources: Omar et al. (2015); Bank Negara Malaysia.

to the issuance and trading of Islamic money market instruments. On the other hand, the conventional money market is dependent on debt-based contract only. Returns in the *Mudarabah* interbank investment as well as *wakalah* investment are also not predetermined when placed. Instead, they are fixed only upon maturity of investment. On the other hand, returns from commodity *Murabaha* are fixed. Information about the return is provided to the investor at the beginning of the placement of funds itself.

11.5–1 Functions of the Islamic Money Market

According to Omar et al., (2015), there are three major categories that the functions of an Islamic money market can be classified into. The first and the most important function is that of liquidity management. To be able to source daily funding or make short-term investments, Islamic banks can utilise the money market as a major pathway. Islamic banks maintain optimal liquidity by being able to access the money market. This in turn helps them in fulfilling the demands of their customers at any time, further enabling Islamic banks to cope up with short-term pressures if and when they arise. Islamic banks, therefore, acquire the flexibility for facing every liquidity situation which is likely to emerge as a result of varied timings of cash inflows and outflows. The money market comes to the rescue of non-financial institutions in managing the fluctuations in their working capital needs. This is done by obtaining either short-term funding or placement following which they get to enjoy low-cost funding or investment returns with lower risk.

The second function that forms the characteristic of the money market is how it acts as the avenue for secondary trading of money market instruments. On the basis of the perspective that money market participants have on return rates, they are likely to sell or purchase money market instruments with the expectation to be able to obtain investment returns. The money market instruments bring forth different levels of risks, returns and maturity to investors.

The third functionality of the money market is associated with how the central bank utilises it in channelling and conducting its monetary policies. Open market operations are used by the central bank. In order to do so, they undertake repos and reverse repos, buy and sell eligible securities, and provide short-term financing directly to Islamic banks which are under a deficit situation. This is how liquidity is managed and the benchmark rates are influenced in the money market by the central bank. Any change in the liquidity and benchmark rates in the money market is undeniably going to influence liquidity and return rates in other markets. For instance, the effect of a monetary policy change initially gets reflected in the money market thereby leading to further adjustments in other markets comprising *Sukuk* and bond, equity, and Islamic banking systems.

The money market acts as the mechanism for managing the liquid asset in the banking system in a country. Accordingly, the market is stringently regulated. Thus, the Islamic money market serves the purpose of the maintenance of the minimum liquidity ratio and statutory reserve. It is also the connection point between the central bank and the entire banking industry as a whole. On the other hand, the central bank uses it as the means and medium for passing monetary policies to the subordinate banks. In essence of the banking system, the Islamic money market serves as the keeper of liquid assets, rating it higher than any other branches of the financial market. Based on the available regulatory framework in different countries, the functions are hereby elaborated.

11.5-2 Safeguard of Liquid Assets

The term 'liquid assets' corresponds to the idea of assets in the direct form of money itself or any asset that has the potential to be converted into money subjected to minimum delay and risk of loss (Olayemi et al., 2015). In the banking sector, liquid assets necessarily comprise the 'minimum liquidity ratio', which is the proportion between a bank or other financial institution's holdings of liquid assets and its total liabilities. The imposition of a minimum liquidity ratio is generally done by law. However, it can be voluntarily adopted subjecting to commercial prudence. The minimum liquidity ratio acts as a major instrument for the monetary control of central banks globally. The instrument is used for the purpose of general credit and selective control purposes (Majid, 2003).

This liquidity ratio acts as a successful measure of understanding a firm's ability to meet its current liabilities. With regard to banks, the demand deposits are their current liabilities. Thus, in a financial statement analysis of a bank, the 'current ratio' would be the ratio of liquid assets to demand deposits (current ratio = current assets/current liabilities). One of the three functions of the Islamic interbank money market in the Islamic banking sector as well as the window system of the conventional banks is the maintenance of the liquidity assets, otherwise known as the minimum liquidity ratio (Iqbal, 2001). That is, the asset which is itself money, or the conversion of it into money is easily possible without the risk of loss and other short-dated marketable securities such as treasury bills (Olayemi et al., 2015).

When a bank suffers from a liquidity problem referring to its issue of liquidity portfolio, either being in surplus or deficit, the bank can access the interbank money market for short-term instruments to cover its liquidity mismatch. In situations of not being able to cover an unexpected shortage of cash flow in the banking system, the market acts as a form of insurance measure where a bank could use its portfolio of marketable securities and quickly liquidate them to be able to meet the sudden need (Olayemi et al., 2015). The requirement for the maintenance of a minimum liquidity ratio or reserve is not peculiar to the conventional bank alone. It also applies to the Islamic bank with some modifications. The primary reason of this is associated with the liquidity risk's conceptual focus on the ability of a bank to maintain sufficient funds in order to meet its commitments, which in turn is likely to be related to its ability to attract deposits. All in all, it is associated with the ability to mature assets and liabilities daily and simultaneously cope with short-term pressures, if and when they emerge while in the process of ensuring fully funded assets (Hudson et al., 1998).

11.5-2-1 Maintenance of Statutory Reserve Requirement

The second objective of establishing the Islamic interbank money market is to serve the purpose of maintaining the statutory liquid reserve requirement in the Islamic banking industry. The statutory liquid reserve requirement can be defined as the minimum percentage of the total assets of a bank or any other financial institution which is a mandate to be held in the form of money balance, or in some form of assets that are highly liquid in their nature. Central banks utilise the minimum reserve requirement as an instrument to enforce monetary policies. It is also employed to ensure that the banks and other financial institutions maintain the principles of solvency. The financial institution in which the asset depreciates to the level of being worthless against its debts will be insolvent even if its remaining assets are highly liquid in nature. Thus, the statutory reserve requirement is a crucial measure for the subjecting banks and other financial institutions to the policy of the central bank in observing strong reserve positions. The measures that are adopted for the policy execution include the transfer of assets such as cash to the position of immediate control of the central bank for the purpose of effective management of money supply and credit (Black, 2002). The adequate reserve requirement does not require the central bank to employ any major credit control instrument such as the open market operation. Conversely, the statutory reserve requirement is generally important since the instrument is eminently useful for situations that require large changes, such as substantial inflow of foreign exchange or when the economy is under the threat of inflation. The instrument is also helpful for the operation of other credit control instruments in terms of upward or downward changes in the direction of monetary policies to produce or evoke remedy for the situation (Black, 2002).

11.5-2-2 Monetary Policy Implementation

Islamic central banking has a parallel function with conventional central banking given that its primary responsibility is formulating and conducting monetary policy through the Islamic money market. Monetary policy is defined in s. 25(1) of the CBMA 2009 as 'any transaction undertaken by the Bank' (Choudhury and Mirakhor, 1997). Central banks are to manage liquidity in the financial system. Therefore, monetary policy is part of the regulated economic policy of a country. Its objective is expected to reinforce the positions of the macro-economic variables, which are rapid growth of the total production, full employment and price stability, among other things. Monetary policy also plays a significant role in the achievement of three other goals involving domestic financial stability, external balance and economic development (Olayemi et al., 2015). The role that is played by monetary policy is carried out by implementing some specific short liquidity management instruments of the money market. In light of the above, the central bank has the power of discharging the monetary policy in the country. To be able to provide and promote monetary stability, the central bank of a country should pursue a monetary policy in a way which is aimed at serving the interests of the country; the fundamental objective of which is to maintain price stability by properly acknowledging the developments in the economy. It must be carefully noted that the central bank is in charge to formulate and implement the monetary policy of the bank without the influence of any external effect (Choudhry and Mirakhor, 1997).

11.6 Islamic Money Market Instruments Experienced in Some Muslim Countries

There are Islamic money markets existing in many Muslim countries. A concise comparison has been made about the instruments of the Islamic money market in some selected prominent Muslim countries in various jurisdictions of Islamic banking. These countries include Malaysia, Bahrain, and Pakistan and are discussed in detail here.

11.6-1 Islamic Interbank Money Market in Malaysia

The financial instruments available in the Malaysian Islamic interbank money market in the form of government securities are given below. The government of Malaysia issues these securities as marketable debt instruments to be able to raise funds from the domestic capital market so as to finance the expenses and working capital for the development of the government itself.

The Central Bank of Malaysia (Bank Negara Malaysia) plays the role of both the banker and the adviser to the government. It primarily advises on the details of government securities issuance and facilities such issuance through various market infrastructures that it owns and operates (BNM, 2007). Broadly, the main three types of government securities are as follows:

1. Malaysian government securities (MGS) are bonds that bear interest on a long-term basis. In order to be able to cater to the development expenditure, funds are raised by the Malaysian government from the domestic capital market.
2. Malaysian treasury bills are interest based with short-term maturity. However, these two branches of the government securities are not relevant here owing to their conventional interest-based nature.
3. The Government Investment Issues (GIIs) are government securities which mature on a short-term basis, and the Malaysian Islamic Treasury Bills (MITB) are government securities that do not bear any interest. Both of these securities are issued by the Malaysian government with strict adherence to *Shari'ah* laws.

11.6-1-1 Malaysian Islamic Treasury Bills (MITB)

As an alternative to the conventional treasury bills, the Malaysian government has introduced MITB in the country. The government issues these short-term securities for financing its operational expenditure. The *bai' al-inah* principle forms the foundational concept for structuring the MITB under which the government's assets would get identified and sold by Bank Negara Malaysia (BNM) on behalf of the Malaysian government. The selling of the assets will be on a competitive tender basis, to form the underlying transaction of the deal. The highest price tendered (or lowest yield) gets the allotment. After the profit element has been imputed so as to see where discounts can be offered, the ultimate price is determined. The bidders who get to have a successful deal will then pay the government in cash (Omar et al., 2015).

The governments will be sold back the assets by the bidders. The price is supposed to be at par depending on the credit team. The bidders get the MITB issued to them by the government in order to represent the debt created. More often than not, the issuance of MITB occurs on a weekly basis subject to the original maturities of one year and is priced on the basis of discounts. The conventional institutions as well as the Islamic institutions can purchase and trade on MITB.

To be able to find out the MITB proceeds, the discounting formula as depicted below is generally used:

$$\text{Proceed} = FV\left(1 - \frac{r \times t}{365}\right)$$

where
FV = face value
r = discounting rate
t = number of days remaining to maturity.

11.6-1-2 Government Investment Issue (GII)

In an alliance formed with the Bank Islam Malaysia Berhad, which is the first Malaysian Islamic bank, the introduction of Government Investment Issues (GIIs) occurred in July 1983. On behalf of the government of Malaysia, the BNM issued GII for the first time. GIIs bear no interest and were mainly issued for being able to meet the exclusive requirements of the banks and other corporations who are sincerely keen in these securities. Certifications are done and provided under the Government Investment Act 1983. The certificates are issued and provided with maturities of one year or more. As for dividends, instead of interest, it is supposed to be paid on the certificates. The original GIC was issued under the principle of *qard al-hasan* (benevolent loan), making its trading in the secondary market completely restricted. Dividends will be paid to the financial institutions who require liquidity only when and after they are done selling or surrendering their GICs back to BNM. The determination of the dividend is generally ex-post and not ex-ante (Omar et al., 2015).

The constraints as briefly described above eventually led BNM to come up with GII by replacing in 2001. The structuring of GII is based on the contract of *bai' al inah* (sale and buyback). This can be illustrated with an example. After identifying a *Shari'ah*-compliant asset, BNM would invite tenders from Islamic financial institutions for the asset. Islamic financial institutions (IFIs), which generally offer the most competitive price, are most likely to be selected as buyers as well as investors. This entitles IFIs to have the opportunity of buying the asset on spot sale. The asset will be sold back to BNM by the investing bank based on the principle of *bai bithaman ajil* (deferred sale) if the coupon is to be paid periodically. Otherwise, the principle of *murabaha* (cost plus) is used if the GII is a zero coupon instrument. The debt incurred by BNM through the deferred buyback is securitised in the form of GII. As a result of this process, the investing bank's spot price will be at face value owing to the GII being issued on the principle of *bai bithaman ajil* or discounted value if the GII is issued under *murabaha*. The investing bank can choose to hold the GII until it matures, else the GII can be sold in the secondary market. During the time of maturity, BNM pays the complete purchase price of the assets for successfully redeeming the security.

The formula to obtain the GII price is shown below.

$$Price = \{Discounted\ Value\ of\ Redemption\ Value\ at\ Maturity\} + \{Discounted\ Value\ of\ Stream\ of\ Coupon\ Payments\}$$

$$\text{Price} = \left\{ \frac{RV}{\left[1 + \frac{r}{200}\right]^{N-1+\frac{T}{E}}} \right\} + \left\{ \sum_{K=1}^{N} \frac{\frac{C}{2}}{\left[1 + \frac{r}{200}\right]^{K-1+\frac{T}{E}}} \right\}$$

where

FV = face value

RV = redemption value (= FV, if redemption is at par)

C = coupon rate

r = market yield for a similar maturity period

N = number of semi-annual coupon payments between the value date and the maturity date

T = number of days from the value date to the next coupon payment date

E = number of days in the coupon period in which settlement takes place

K = time period in which the coupon or principal payment occurs.

Let us consider an example to understand the price calculation of GII.

Let us say BMMB purchased a GII. The details of the purchase are given below:

Issuance date: 7 April 2006

Maturity date: 7 April 2009

Transaction date: 15 October 2007

Coupon: 6% p.a., paid semi-annually

Maturity value: RM100

Yield: 7% p.a.

To find out the answer, we need to apply the formula stated earlier.

Therefore,

$$\text{Price} = \left\{ \frac{100}{\left[1+\dfrac{7}{200}\right]^{3-1+\frac{175}{183}}} \right\} + \left\{ \sum_{K=1}^{N} \frac{3}{\left[1+\dfrac{7}{200}\right]^{3-1+\frac{175}{183}}} \right\}$$

$$= RM98.75$$

(*Source*: Omar et al., 2015).

11.6-1-3 Islamic Accepted Bill (IAB)

According to Omar et al., (2015), an Islamic accepted bill (IAB) is the *Shari'ah* equivalent to the acceptance of the conventional banker. IAB can be defined as an exchange bill drawn on or drawn by a bank. A specified date subjected to a future timeline is scheduled for the bill to be paid which acts as an evident that trade transactions give rise to debts. Importers might utilise these IABs for financing their imports or purchases. Similarly, exporters are likely to utilise the IABs for financing their exports or sales. The BNM has set certain conditions for the issuance of IAB. These include:

- The facility provided for financing must be utilised for a genuine trade.
- The goods involved must be tangible in form and must necessarily be in harmony with *Shari'ah* laws.
- The selling or purchasing of services cannot be involved here.
- The parties involved in this process should not be a single entity.

The latest BNM rules have made it a mandate that the minimum denomination for an IAB is RM50,000 and in multiples of RM1,000.

11.6–1–3–1 Import

The process of import IAB begins with the Islamic bank appointing the customer as its agent. The agent then goes on to purchase the needed asset from the exporter or seller on behalf of the bank following which the asset is consequently resold to the customer/agent. The re-selling is done on the basis of *murabaha* principle at a marked-up price and an agreement to make a deferred repayment, which might go up to 365 days. Once it matures, the customer pays not only the cost of the goods to the bank but also its profit margin. Debt is represented through the deferred sale of goods to the customer by the bank which is then securitised in the form of an exchange bill. This bill of exchange is drawn on by the bank and accepted by the customer for the full amount of the selling price that will be paid at maturity. As the drawer of the IAB, the Islamic bank can opt for holding the IAB until it completely matures to be able to receive its full selling price. As an alternative, it can even choose to sell the IAB, before it matures, to investors at a discount. However, the selling can be done only using the *bai' al-dayn* (a contract of the sale of debt) principle.

11.6–1–3–2 Export

In this process, the exporter has to acquire the bank's approval for export trade finance facilities. This will entail the exporter fulfilling certain export documentations required under the export or sales contract. Once the documentation is successful and the approval is obtained, the documents are sent to the importer's bank. Later, the exporter draws a new exchange bill from his bank as a substitution bill representative of the IAB. The bank's acceptance is an implication of the assurance that it will pay the full value of the bill to the bearer once it completely matures. The bank then goes on to buy the IAB from the exporter at a discount as per the Islamic principle of *bay' al-dayn*. The bank can choose to hold the IAB until it matures so as to receive the full selling price. Again, it can alternatively seek to sell the bill to a third party prior to its maturity at a discount.

The price of IAB following the principle of *bay' al-dayn* can be calculated based on a discounting formula:

$$\text{Proceed} = FV\left[1 - \frac{r \times t}{365}\right]$$

where
FV = face value
r = discounting rate
t = number of days remaining to maturity.

Let us take an example to understand how the calculation of the price of IAB is done under the principle of *bai al-dayn*.

Considering an IAB with a face value of RM3,000,000 is sold at a discount rate of 5% and has 42 days remaining to maturity.

The price of the IAB can be easily calculated using the formula as stated earlier, which is:

$$\begin{aligned}\text{Proceed} &= RM3{,}000{,}000\left[1 - \frac{5\% \times 42}{365}\right]\\ &= RM3{,}000{,}000(1 - 0.005753)\\ &= RM2{,}982{,}741\end{aligned}$$

11.6-1-4 Bond Mudarabah *Cagamas*

The Bond *Mudarabah* Cagamas is another instrument of the Malaysian Islamic interbank money market issued by Cagamas Berhad. Cagamas Mudarabah bonds were the instruments that were introduced to the Islamic interbank money market. The financial institutions have the provision of providing Islamic housing finance to their clients and employees. Islamic housing debts are being purchased from these institutions through the help of these bonds. The bonds are packaged under the *Shari'ah* based contract of *al-mudarabah* (that is, profit sharing and loss bearing by the investor) by Cagamas.

The Bond Mudarabah Cagamas is purposely issued for the financing of the purchases. Let us consider the purchase of housing debt based on *Shari'ah* principles by Cagamas which is thereafter managed on the basis of *bay' al-dayn* contract. However, the issuing of the Cagamas Mudarabah Bonds is based on the contract of *al-mudarabah*, which claims that the bondholder and Cagamas share profits accruing to certain agreed profit ratios or percentage.

The agreements which are likely to be applicable on the purchase of housing debt following the *Shari'ah* contract will be sealed between Cagamas Berhad and Bank Islam Malaysia Berhad. Let us consider an example. On purchasing debts of housing estate worth RM30 billion from Bank Islam Bhd by Cagamas, a total of RM30 billion of Cagamas *Mudarabah* bonds gets created based on the agreements.

The Bond *Mudarabah* Cagamas can be redeemed at par on the maturity date except when there is principal diminution. The maturity of Bond *Mudarabah* Cagamas can run up 10 years.

The price and proceeds of Bond *Mudarabah* Cagamas can be calculated as per the formula:

$$P = \left[\frac{100\left(100 + \left(\frac{C+E}{365}\right)\right)}{100 + \left(\frac{r \times T}{365}\right)} \right] - FV\left(\frac{C \times t}{36{,}500}\right)$$

$$\text{Proceed} = \frac{NV \times P}{100} + NV \times \left(\frac{C \times t}{36{,}500}\right)$$

where
P = price per RM100 face value
C = indicative coupon for the current coupon period
E = number of days in the current coupon period
T = number of days from the transaction date to next coupon payment day
r = yield to maturity
t = number of days from the last coupon payment date to the value date
NV = nominal value of Bond *Mudarabah* Cagamas transaction.

Let us take an example to understand the calculation of the Bond *Mudarabah* Cagamas.

Let us consider that the Islamic Bank Berhad bought a RM25 million Bond *Mudarabah* Cagamas, the details of which are:

Issuance date: 7/04/2017
Maturity: 7/04/2019
Transaction date: 20/08/2017
Next coupon date: 7/10/2017
Indicative coupon: 5.47%
Yield to maturity: 5.57%

The price of the instrument can be easily obtained using the formula stated earlier. Therefore,

$$P = \left[\frac{100\left(100 + \left(\frac{5.47 + 184}{365}\right)\right)}{100 + \left(\frac{5.57 \times 48}{365}\right)} \right] - 100\left(\frac{5.47 \times 74}{36,500}\right)$$

$$= 100.90$$

$$\text{Proceed} = \frac{RM25,000,000 \times 100.90}{100} + RM25,000,000 \times \left(\frac{5.47 \times 74}{36,500}\right)$$

$$= RM25,502,246,58$$

(*Source:* Omar et al., 2015).

11.6-1-5 Islamic Negotiable Instruments (INI)

The Malaysian Islamic banking system which started in 1993 began to develop at a rapid pace as a result of which Islamic negotiable instruments (INIs) were introduced. In order to be able to accelerate the system by creating more marketable deposit instruments that are similar to the conventional negotiable instrument of deposit (NID), the need for creating an Islamic money market emerged. Introduced in 1973, the NID was designed as an instrument for commercial banks, merchant banks and other eligible finance companies. The motive behind its creation was to be able to mobilise domestic savings for the banks and financial institutions from the public. However, the conventional nature of negotiable instruments necessitates the creation of another similar instrument ensuring its adherence to the *Shari'ah* principle, which is why and how INI got created.

The INI can be broadly classified into two types, namely, the Islamic negotiable instruments of deposit (INID) and the negotiable Islamic debt certificate (NIDC). These instruments are discussed below.

11.6–1–5–1 Negotiable Islamic Debt Certificate (NIDC)

Under this transaction, the assets of the banking institution are sold to the customer in cash. The price on which the asset is sold is based on an agreement set beforehand. As the next part of the process, the assets are bought back from the customer at principal value plus profit and are scheduled to be settled at an agreed future date. The INI includes the Islamic negotiable instruments of deposit (INID) and negotiable Islamic debt certificate (NIDC), both of which are being governed, regulated, and issued by the government of Malaysia.

11.6–1–5–2 Islamic Negotiable Instruments of Deposit (INID)

The concept applied in this context is the *Mudarabah*, which means a sum of money deposited with the Islamic banking institutions that can be repaid to the bearer on a particular date in the future at the nominal value of INID plus the declared dividend. The approval is done by the Central Bank of Malaysia (BNM) after the approval and the endorsement of the National *Shari'ah* Advisory Council. Islamic negotiable instruments of deposit (INID) are bearer instruments. This implies that they are being traded on the basis of price, meaning that the principal value is quoted in terms of price per RM100 nominal value. The price of INID can be computed as per the formula:

$$\text{Price} = FV\left[\frac{(a+b)}{36{,}500}+1\right] \star 100$$

where
a = expected dividend rate
b = number of days from the issue date or last dividend date to the value date of the transaction.

Let us take an example to understand the calculation of proceeds for an INID.
In consideration of the details given below:

Issue date: 13 December 2008
Maturity: 13 December 2009
Nominal value: RM5,000,000
Profit sharing ratio: 75:25
Expected dividend rate: 11.5%
Profit date: Quarterly with the first dividend date on 31 March.

The price:

$$\text{Price} = \left[\frac{(8.625 \times 90)}{36{,}500}+1\right] \star 100$$

$$= 102.1267$$

The proceeds that the buyer needs to pay is computed as:

$$\text{Proceed} = \frac{RM5{,}000{,}000 \times 102.1267}{100}$$
$$= RM5{,}106{,}355$$

(*Source*: Omar et al., 2015).

11.6-2 Islamic Interbank Money Market in Bahrain

The money market in Bahrain includes two instruments. These are the interbank money market and the central bank standing facilities. The instruments of the interbank money market are described below.

11.6-2-1 Murabaha *Deposits and the Reverse* Murabaha

The *Murabaha* deposits and the reverse *Murabaha* as the instruments of the interbank money market are already quite prevalent in the market. The underlying asset of the instruments is metals. The participants in the *Murabaha* deposits are both the Islamic and conventional institutions. These are the Islamic bank, conventional bank, a selling broker and a buying broker. The tenure of the instrument ranges from one week to one year. In general, however, the tenure is three months. The benchmark is determined by the London Interbank Offered Rate (LIBOR). The Islamic banks are free to design the instrument based on the standards that is put in place by the Central Bank of Bahrain (CBB). However, the transaction in the reverse *murabaha* can be done among the Islamic financial institutions only. The Islamic banks in Bahrain are considering moving from the commodity *murabaha* to *wakalah*-based interbank transaction, which will allow an Islamic bank to assign its liquidity management to another Islamic bank within. This is due to the fact that the commodity *murabaha* is not interchangeable and it requires a lot of documentation.

11.6-2-2 Sukuk

The second instrument is the *Sukuk*. It is the instrument that is used by the CBB to control monetary stability and liquidity mismatch in the banking system. Although the *Sukuk* is characterised by its short maturity period, it still remains unable to meet the needs of the financial system, given the fact that the banks hold them until maturity since they are not tradable. Thus, the *Sukuk* cannot be used for liquidity management. It can only be used for investments.

11.6-2-3 The Central Bank Standing Facilities

The Bahrain Central Bank provides 'special lending of last resort' to the Islamic banks. However, the Islamic banks hold excess liquidity in their reserve. This is due to the fact that the available short-term deposit facility is only for the conventional banks and not for the Islamic banks. Likewise, the Islamic banks cannot participate in the repo transaction due to the *Shari'ah* restriction. Thus, there is no 'special lending of last resort' actually applicable to the Islamic banks.

11.6-2-4 The Market-Based Instrument

The government of Bahrain and its Central Bank (CBB) instruments which are considered as market based are managed by the CBB which acts as an agent of the government in issuing *Sukuk*. The instruments are backed by the government assets and are guaranteed by the government of Bahrain via its binding promise to purchase it at maturity and at its original par value. However, the short-term *Sukuk* are not tradable because there is no active secondary market for the Bahraini *Sukuk*, given the fact that the volume of issue is very low. Furthermore, there is a National *Shari'ah* Committee whose ruling is binding on the players in the *Sukuk* market (Olayemi et al., 2015).

11.6-3 Islamic Interbank Money Market in Pakistan

The Islamic money market in Pakistan includes the interbank money market and Islamic placement funds system as explained below.

11.6-3-1 Interbank Money Market

The instruments of the interbank money market that are available in Pakistan are the *Sukuk al-ijarah*, *Sukuk al-musharaka* and *Sukuk al-murabaha*. The tenure of the *Sukuk* are three months, six months and 12 months. The available instruments to the conventional banks, which are the repos, reverse repos and the outright sale of market treasury bills (MTB) and Pakistan investment bonds (PIBs), are not *Shari'ah* compliant and thus cannot be used by the Islamic banks. However, there is a secondary market for the *Shari'ah*-based instruments. The primary dealers in the market are the Islamic bank branches of the conventional banks. The purchase of the instruments is at a discount which will be treated at face value as opposed to the transaction in the market treasury bills (MTBs), where the discounting is at par value. This indicates that the Pakistani Islamic banking market is lacking an appropriate liquidity management instrument. Thus, the Islamic banks in Pakistan normally rely on the placement of funds in the form of pools of investment for their liquidity management. The pool of investment is a hybrid investment pool comprising different investment assets such as *ijarah, murabaha* and other tangible assets. The pool of investments gets dissolved at maturity and transferred to other investment pools. The tenure of the pool must be equal to the tenure of the financing of the asset or less than it. The pool of investments is of various types. It might either be a *musharaka*-based pool of investment, whereby the conventional financial institution will participate in the pool as a sleeping partner with an Islamic financial institution, which will be the working partner. The profits and the losses of the pool will then be shared on the basis of a *musharaka* contract. The other type is that of the *mudarabah* based pool of investments, whereby a financial institution will participate as the investor (*rabb al-mal*), while the Islamic financial institutions will be the entrepreneur (*mudarib*). Thus, the profit and loss of the transaction will be shared on the basis of *mudarabah* transaction.

11.6-3-2 Islamic Placement Funds

Islamic banks in Pakistan also use Islamic placement funds as a mechanism for liquidity management. In this context, the Islamic financial institution (Islamic bank) will place a fund with another Islamic bank or Islamic conventional window for the purpose of liquidity management. The agreement on the deposit will be based on the *mudarabah* contract. Moreover, commodity *murabaha* is also available with a maturity ranging from overnight to one year. The commodity will be purchased by the Islamic bank on a spot basis from a commodity broker. Then, the bank will sell the commodity through its commodity broker on a deferred payment basis. Local commodities such as fertilisers, pulses and sugar are utilised for sale after they have been identified.

In addition to the ones mentioned above, other similar liquidity management mechanisms in the country are *wakalah* and *tawarruq* managements. In the *wakalah* arrangement, the agent bank will receive funds from the principal bank for the purpose of financing. The rule of agency is where the principal is entitled to the total profit will simultaneously bear the loss if applied. However, in the *tawarruq* arrangement, the bank will buy a liquid commodity or stock from the market from any institution on deferred payment basis. The purchaser will then sell the commodity after its deliverability to it, at market price. Thus, it will acquire the required liquidity: the cash. This is also referred to as commodity *murabaha* or reserve *Murabaha*. The central bank (State Bank of Pakistan) standing facilities in Pakistan are only available to the conventional banks (Olayemi et al., 2015).

11.7 Conclusion

The role of the Islamic money market is crucial to the operation of the Islamic banks as well as non-banking financial institutions such as *Takaful* and insurance companies, business corporations, government treasuries, and the central bank. The money market serves as the ultimate mechanism for maintaining the liquid ratio, reserve ratio and monetary policy. It equally caters to liquidity management in the banking system. The Islamic money market takes care of three essential functions: liquidity management, avenue for trading of Islamic money market instruments, and acts as the channel the central bank uses to transmit its monetary policy. Some of the Islamic money market instruments are Islamic treasury bills, Islamic accepted bills, *mudarabah* bonds, *Sukuk* reverse *mudarabah*, Islamic negotiable instruments and so forth, as discussed in this chapter.

Through the Islamic money market, market players are given the scope and opportunity to be able to perform similar functions like that of the conventional market; the only exception being the mandate of the instruments used in performing these functions to be in full compliance with *Shari'ah* laws and principles. If the Islamic money market is to fulfil its multiple functions, it must necessarily have several different types of participants, varieties of Islamic securities based on different risks, yields, and tenure, and various interbank investment markets. A number of Muslim countries have launched Islamic money markets. However, Malaysia remains the leading country subjected to the market. The country has developed the instruments which grant the Islamic banks to get engaged in all aspects of the economy. It is therefore suggested that other jurisdictions borrow from the Malaysian approach.

Review Questions

1. Compare and contrast between Islamic and conventional money markets.
2. Why is there a need for an Islamic money market?
3. List and explain the three major functions of the Islamic money market.
4. Explain the concepts of commodity *murabaha* and Islamic accepted bills.
5. Briefly explain the Islamic negotiable instrument of deposit (INID) and the negotiable Islamic debt certificate (NIDC), and make a comparative analysis between them.
6. What do you understand by the *wakalah* concept? How can *wakalah* be used as a liquidity management tool?
7. Explain the mechanism of an Islamic accepted bill and show how it facilitates trade (export/import).
8. Find out the price of an Islamic treasury bill having a face value of US$5,000,000 and sold at a discount rate of 4.8%, considering that there are 30 days to maturity.

References

Black, J (2002), *Oxford Dictionary of Economics*, 2nd ed, New York: Oxford University Press

BNM (2007), *A Guide to Malaysian Government Securities*, 2nd ed, London: Monetary Policy Implementation Section, Investment Operations and Financial Market Department

Choudhry, N and Mirakhor, A (1997), Indirect Instruments of Monetary Control in an Islamic Financial System, *Islamic Economic Studies*, 4(2), 29–40

Hudson, R, Colley, A and Largan, M (1998), *Treasury Management*, 3rd ed, London: The Chartered Institute of Bankers, p. 37.

Iqbal, M (2001, April), Islamic and Conventional Banking in the Nineties: A Comparative Study, *Islamic Economic Studies*, 8(2), 14.

Majid, A (2003, September 30–October 3), *Development of Liquidity Management Institutions: Challenges and Opportunities*, International Conference on Islamic Banking: Risk Management, Regulation and Supervision, Jakarta, pp. 5–12

Olayemi, A, Hassan, A, Ibrahim, U, Yasin, N and Buang, A (2015), *Islamic Interbank Money Market: A Comparative Legal Study Between Malaysia and Some Notable Jurisdictions, Shari'ah* Report, Kuala Lumpur: IPPP/Department of Syariah and Law, API, University of Malaya

Omar, A, Abduh, M and Sukmana, R (2015), *Fundamentals of Islamic Money and Capital Markets*, Singapore: Wiley

12

SUKUK SECURITIES

New Ways of Debt Contracting

Learning Objectives

On completing this chapter, learners will be able to:

- Have a thorough understanding of *Sukuk*
- Use financial tools and techniques to create value through *Sukuk* bonds
- Foresee and identify challenges to the model of *Sukuk* funds
- Innovate to offer better, more relative solutions related to *Sukuk*
- Gain exposure and broaden the scope of *Sukuk* growth.

12.1 Introduction

The classical Islamic period (700–1300) is considered to have witnessed the origin and practice of *Sukuk*. It was during this period where any form of financial obligation arising as a result of activities subjected to trade and commerce were represented officially on paper. The issuance of these obligations on paper would always be done in conformity with the Holy Qur'an where 'writing' has been encouraged for fixing contracts. The verse, 'When ye deal with each other, in transactions involving future obligations in a fixed period of time, reduce them to writing . . . It is more just in the sight of God, more suitable as evidence and more convenient to prevent doubts among yourselves' (2:282), is evident of the same. A document that represented financial liability was termed as *sakk* during that time. Used as a singular of *Sukuk, sakk* can be literally understood as a 'deed' or 'instrument'.

The International Islamic *Fiqh* Academy, Jeddah, is an academy for the advanced study of Islamic laws. In 1988, to be able to initiate the development of the *Sukuk* market, this organisation opted for a fundamental approach of issuing a statement through an Islamic conference. The statement describes how representation of any

DOI: 10.4324/9780429321207-12

combination of assets (or the usufruct of such assets) can be done in the form of written financial instruments. These can be then sold at a market price only when the composition of the groups of assets represented by *Sukuk* is largely inclusive of more tangible assets (Adam and Thomas, 2004).

The terms and structures of these Islamic bonds (*Sukuk*) must necessarily be in full compliance with *Shari'ah*. The Accounting and Auditing Organization for Islamic Financial Institutions (AAOIFI) defines *Sukuk* as 'Certificates of equal volume representing, after closing subscription, the receipt of the value of the certificates and putting it to use as planned, common title in shares and rights in tangible assets, usufructs and services or equity of a given project or equity of a special investment activity' (AAOIFI Standard 17, 2008). In the general context, *Sukuk* can be understood in the form of transferrable certificates. These certificates are representative of a share in the ownership of assets or business ventures. When the *Sukuk* matures, *Sukuk* holders are entitled to receive periodic fixed returns and full redemption via the authorisation of the certificates. The structuring of *Sukuk* is primarily done on the basis of two principal contracts:

- Contracts of exchange, such as *ijarah, murabaha* and *istina*
- Contracts of participation, such as *musharaka* and *mudarabah*.

A conventional bond (secured or unsecured) is representative of the debt obligation of the issuer. However, a *Sukuk* is an implication of the concentration in an underlying funding arrangement designed on the principles of *Shari'ah*. The arrangement enables the holder to receive a proportionate share of the returns generated at a set future date. The whole idea of *Sukuk* to be *Shari'ah* compliant has to have the following points mandatorily fulfilled:

1. These funding arrangements generate profits which can be only derived through trading from commercial risk-taking.
2. Any form of income generated via conventional interest is not allowed.
3. Assets subjected to the funding arrangement must be permissible (*halal*).
4. In an underlying asset, *Sukuk* holders are basically considered as equity holders. However, in comparison to common shareholders in any entity, the claim of *Sukuk* holders is asset specific as well as specific about the maturity.

Investments in Islamic instruments are not bounded by any such restriction. On top of that, Islamic instruments provide several unique offers, thereby widening the scope for new investment opportunities. This enables different kinds of investors for purchasing *Shari'ah*-compliant products. The ownership of the underlying asset and cash flow strengthens the position of the *Sukuk* holders in comparison to the otherwise conventional debt instruments. It must be remembered that the structure of the *Sukuk* will ultimately determine whether the issuer should have recourse. There has been a continuous rise in the market demand for Islamic finance as a result of which the liquidity risk of *Sukuk* has relatively improved. Owing to this, investors have been largely considering to invest and explore more via these tradable instruments (*Sukuk*). Generally, any change in market interest rates does not influence *Sukuk*. However, some sort of uncertainty about the return rate would always prevail with respect to the concept of sharing profits and losses.

The growth of the *Sukuk* market is being largely driven by the accelerated growth in urbanisation in the countries of the Middle East. At the same time, the emerging countries experience diversification of investment patterns and increasing cross-border transactions which simultaneously helps in amplifying the *Sukuk* market. On the other hand, Islamic banking institutions are attempting to strategically build partnerships with foreign institutions to be able to facilitate trade with other countries. This is why governments of multiple countries are taking steps ahead to develop *Shari'ah*-compliant financial institutions which are more sophisticated and offer products and services which are more innovative, thereby, enhancing the overall outlook of the *Sukuk* market. Since the inception of the online mode for making transactions, financial institutions have been encouraged to take the plunge in investing into analytics to be able to curate a better user experience and customise *Sukuk* products as per the need and demand of their customers. The governments of Muslim countries are increasingly investing in sovereign *Sukuk* to not only cater for the infrastructural development of their financial service but also equally strengthen the digitisation of these services. All of these factors have the full potential to extraordinarily expand the growth of the *Sukuk* market.

12.2 *Sukuk* Structuring

The transaction of a *Sukuk* is structured on the basis of 14 approved categories and several techniques as prescribed by the AAOIFI. Prior to the selection of the type of structure, certain factors need to be taken into consideration, some of which are the character of the underlying assets, taxation and regulatory norms, the targeted investor base and most importantly, the opinions of the *Shari'ah* scholars ensuring the approval of the *Sukuk* issuance. In the present day, the *Sukuk* structures that are mostly opted for are *ijara, murabaha* and *mudarabah-wakala*. This is primarily because of the statement given by the AAOIFI where restrictions had been put forth on the requirement that *Sukuk* issuers buy back the *Sukuk* at their face value. To add to this, loans having free interest or liquidity facilities that were once operational and utilised to overcome the income-deficit emerging from underlying assets were prohibited. As a matter of fact, following the AAOIFI statement, the popularity of the *musharaka* and the *mudarabah Sukuk* structures dropped massively (Salah, 2010).

Irrespective of the type of structure opted; an entirely owned financial intermediary (in the form of a special-purpose vehicle [SPV]) will be incorporated by the entity trying to raise finance (the originator). The title will then be transferred to the SPV's underlying assets followed by the SPV issuing the *Sukuk* and utilising the funds raised to pay the originator for those assets. Theoretically speaking, the *Sukuk* assets and the originator's remaining assets are considered separate entities. In practical usage, the originator remains involved in using or/and managing the assets. Examples can be considered of continuing to use it under a lease in the *ijara* or managing the same under a *musharaka* or *mudarabah*. In the general context, the structuring of *Sukuk* issuance occurs as corporate credit-risk instruments. In context of a default and redemption scenario, the *Sukuk* holders would not have recourse to the assets themselves. While undertaking a purchase, if the *Sukuk* holder exercises the right against the originator, redemption gets affected. It is true that as per the norms of *Shari'ah*, *Sukuk* certificates are indicative of the underlying ownership in an asset. However, a realistic point of view from the commercial and economical perspective would tell that a large proportion of the *Sukuk* issued is not secured, thereby making them equivalent to other conventional bonds, like credit-risk instruments (Latham & Watkins, 2018).

To be able to successfully select an appropriate *Sukuk* structure, several issues need to be considered beforehand. These issues are discussed below.

1. Transfer of title: The local legal framework has to be considered by the issuer prior to the transfer of title to the assets underlying a *Sukuk*. This has to be done subjected to the respective jurisdiction, the nature of assets to be transferred and the particular *Shari'ah* structure used. In order for this process to become fully functional, certain formal procedures can become important mandates. This might include registration and the payment of any associated fees and taxes.
2. Nature of the assets: The assets employed for underpinning the *Sukuk* structure by the issuer must be used by the obligor for purposes that are necessarily *Shari'ah* compliant. Any kind of activity or business dealing with products such as pork, gambling, alcohol or conventional finance is strictly forbidden. On the date of the *Sukuk* being issued, the relevant assets should be completely free from encumbrances. At the same time, their market must either be equivalent or exceed the principal amount of the *Sukuk* being issued. More often than not, there is no other requirement of a third-party valuation but in case it is sought, one needs to properly consider the methodology used for valuation as well as the timing.
3. Tax and *Zakah*: When assets are being acquisitioned or purchased as per the norms of *Shari'ah*, multiple types of taxes might be imposed. This includes may create exposure to value added tax (VAT), income tax, capital gains tax, stamp duties, and so forth. An asset after it is being owned can also lead to the creation of tax residency issues. Certain jurisdictions such as Saudi Arabia practice *Zakah*. Under *Zakah*, a Muslim person needs to donate a fixed portion of their wealth to charity as per the Islamic law. All in all, any kind or form of taxation should be taken into consideration during the phase when *Sukuk* is structured and tax advices are attained.
4. Tradability of *Sukuk*: To be able to trade *Sukuk* in the secondary market in sync with the *Shari'ah* law, *Sukuk* must represent an interest in physical assets rather than simply representing debts or obligations. A section of the *Shari'ah* scholars are fine with physical assets underlying *Sukuk* structures representing at least

33% of the *Sukuk*'s face value. On the other hand, a section of the *Shari'ah* scholars demand the representation of physical assets underlying *Sukuk* structures to be in the range of 51% and 70%.

5. Regional differences: Region plays a characteristic role in determining the nature of *Shari'ah*-compliant financing structures. The ones adopted in the Middle East are largely different from those adopted in Asia. The prevailing differences occur due to several reasons; the primary one being the distinctive interpretation of *Shari'ah* by the scholars of the Middle East and Asia. Earlier, Middle Eastern scholars were of the opinion that the Asian way of interpreting the *Shari'ah* law was less conservative than that in the Middle East. As a result of the increasing number of cross-border transactions between these two regions, greater convergence between the *Sukuk* markets in the Middle East and Asia is looked forward as a possibility. This might even help in building a more consistent approach among all the scholars subjecting to the acceptability of certain *Sukuk* structures. The regional divergence is equally shaped by the difference in a local legal framework and the difference in approaches adopted for tax treatments. In this regard, let us consider the example of VAT or income tax, which hardly exists in the Gulf countries. Hence, here *Sukuk* structures are generally not driven by taxes. Meanwhile, certain countries in Asia incorporate several kinds of taxes such as VAT, income tax, capital gains tax, stamp duties and others, thereby significantly impacting the *Sukuk* structure (Latham & Watkins, 2018).

12.2-1 Popular Types of Structured Sukuk

Under the governance of English law, the issuance of *Sukuk* in global capital markets occurs in the form of trust certificates. The structuring of *Sukuk* issuance is at times done in the form of participating notes under legislation. This process of structuring is quite similar to the method used for asset-backed securities and is mostly applied by certain civil law jurisdictions that do not recognise the concept of trust. The *Shari'ah* standards for issuing *Sukuk* is set by the Accounting and Auditing Organization for Islamic Financial Institutions (AAOIFI). At present, the organisation has set up 14 varieties of *Sukuk* structures which aim to provide an in-depth explanation of the entire *Sukuk* market. Some of the *Sukuk* are briefed below.

12.2-1-1 Trust Certificates

When a transaction involves issuing trust certificates, an SPV is being established by the obligor (i.e. the entity aiming at fundraising). The SPV is established considering the particular jurisdiction. The trust certificates are issued to the investors. In doing so, the SPV utilises the proceeds to be able to accomplish a funding arrangement with the obligor. In this context, the guidelines of the English law come into action, which ensures that the SPV's rights as financier are held in favour of the certificate holders. Some of the most popular funding structures which operate in the Islamic capital market include *Mudarabah* (trust financing) *Sukuk, Musharaka* (a joint-venture equity investment), sale and leaseback (*ijarah*) structure and a form of trade finance (*murabaha*).

12.2-1-2 Mudarabah Sukuk

For an entrepreneur to be able to run his business venture, an investor will supply funds in exchange of which, the latter would be getting a return on the funds provided. The amount of return will be determined on the basis of a profit-sharing ratio. The structure of *Sukuk Mudharabah* is based on the principle that investors serve as dormant business partners (Figure 12.1). At the same time, investors are not supposed to act as the responsible body or agency to be managing the underlying asset, business or project. This structure clearly claims that the working partner is the issuer (i.e. the party utilising the funds).

It must be remembered that the profit generated out of the investment activity is shared between the parties, while if losses are incurred, they will be borne by the investor alone. The ratio of profit sharing is generally pre-agreed. The ratio is largely determined on the basis of the performance of the asset or project. At the same time, *mudharabah Sukuk* should not operate on the basis of the issuer's guarantee for the capital or a fixed profit, or a profit based on any percentage of the capital.

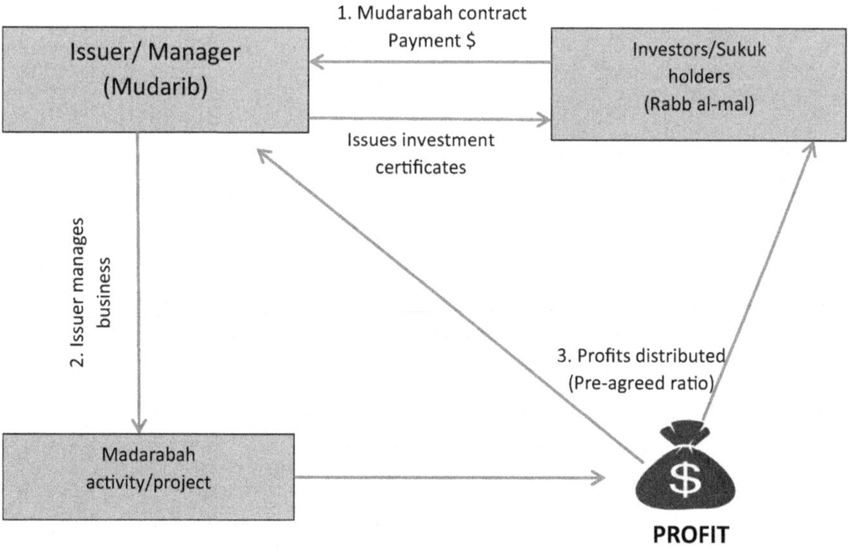

FIGURE 12.1 Structure of *Mudarabah Sukuk.*

12.2-1-3 Musharaka Sukuk

Under the funding structure of *Musharaka Sukuk*, a partnership is formed between two or more parties for financing a business venture; where capital is being contributed by all the parties involved in terms of cash or kind. A pre-agreed profit sharing ratio drives the eventual distribution of profits generated as an outcome of the venture (Figure 12.2). Here, losses are simultaneously shared based on the contribution of capital. The funding as per the *musharaka* contract is generally used for a joint business venture. The parties contributing capital for financing a project under this contract must be doing so in full compliance with *Shari'ah* laws.

A *musharaka* contract is set as a funding contract between partners. The partnership can be between the issuer and the *Sukuk* holders or just among the *Sukuk* holders. The signature of the obligor (or issuer) is a crucial step in the beginning of setting the *musharaka* contract.

A ratio on the basis of which profits will be shared later has to be specified early on, in the contract itself. At the same time, the contract must necessarily contain information on the contribution of assets by the obligor. The contribution aimed for the joint venture can be in terms of cash or kind which has to be equally mentioned in the contract. As already discussed, profits will be shared on the basis of a predetermined ratio while sharing of losses will be determined on the basis of

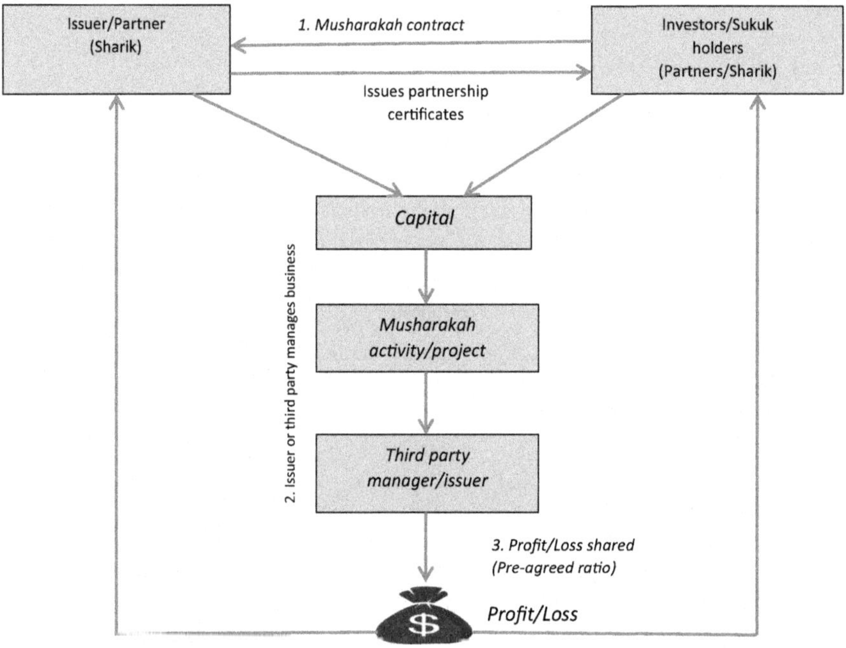

FIGURE 12.2 Structure of *Musharaka Sukuk*.

capital contribution. The *Musharaka* contract gives the ownership of the joint venture, asset or business activity to the *Sukuk* holders (investors).

12.2-1-4 Murabaha Sukuk

Under a *Murabaha* contract, assets are being sold or purchased and all the parties involved have full knowledge about the cost and the profit margin (the marked up price). The contract can be also seen as an agreement between a buyer and seller for delivering an asset (Figure 12.3). An example can be taken of the *Sukuk* holder purchasing an asset to be able to supply it to the *Sukuk* issuer since the latter does not have the capacity to purchase the asset directly. The asset gets sold to the issuer by the holder at a mark-up price which includes cost-plus profit. This is generally agreed upon by both the issuer and the holder. Later, the *Sukuk* holder is paid in terms of instalments by the issuer.

12.2-1-5 Ijarah Sukuk

Among all the other types of investment *Sukuk*, *Ijarah Sukuk* constitutes to be the most widely used one. It comprises certificates carrying equal value. The issuance of *Ijarah Sukuk* is either done by the owner of an underlying leased or leasable asset or by the owner's agent (Figure 12.4). The aim is to sell the leased/leasable asset to be able to recover its value through subscription as a result of which *Sukuk* holders can attain the ownership of the leased/leasable assets. The rights and obligations of the owner/lessor will have to be considered by the *Sukuk* holder in proportion to its holdings of *Sukuk*. The structuring of *Ijarah Sukuk* happens in two different ways: asset backed and asset based.

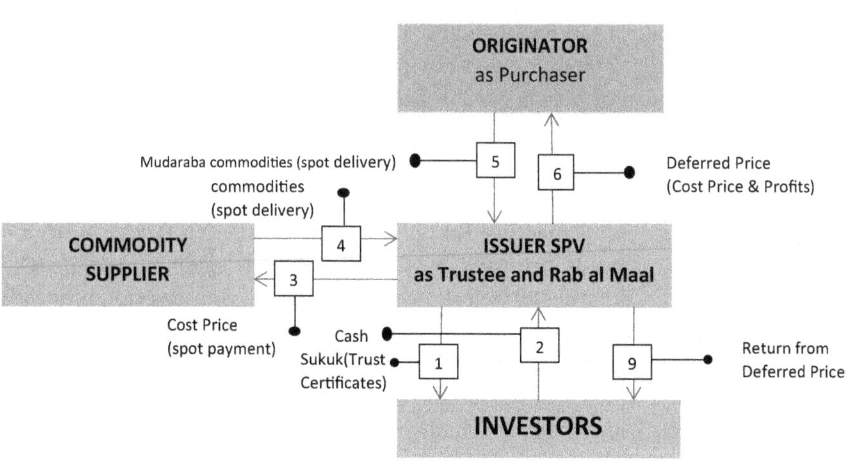

FIGURE 12.3 Structure of *Murabaha Sukuk*.

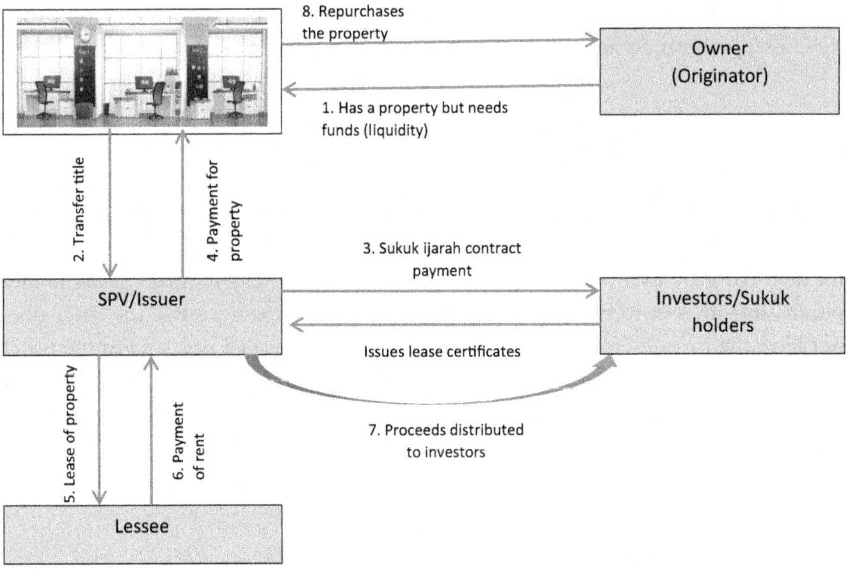

FIGURE 12.4 Structure of *Ijarah Sukuk*.

12.2-1-6 *Asset-Backed* Ijarah Sukuk

The fact that it is structured through an asset-backed securitisation and not as a debt obligation accounts for its wide acceptance and popularity among other types of *Sukuk*. To make the concept clearer, this type of *Sukuk* is backed by tangible assets where certain tangible and leasable assets are sold to a special purpose vehicle (SPV) by the originator company. The assets are sold subjected to the principal amount need for financing. It must be carefully noted that the SPV pays the price of the underlying assets by raising funds through *Sukuk* issuance to the investors. Instead of paying for the assets directly, the SPV uses the proceeds of the funds raised to be able to make the purchase of the assets. The investor attains a proportionate ownership in the assets and the lease under the terms of the contract.

As per the agreement made in this *Ijarah* contract, the assets will be leased back to the originator or company by the SPV. This is again subjected for a specific amount fixed earlier as well as a certain maturity. Subscription proceeds are paid by the *Sukuk* holders to the SPV for their *Sukuk*, which is likely to make period distributions. These distributions will be made out of the rental payments over the *Sukuk* term held concurrent with the lease term. The originator can opt for normal *Ijarah* which involves in paying rentals periodically with a repayment of the principal at maturity. Alternatively, the originator can choose to repay the principal along with the rental payments periodically. The *Sukuk* has the right to receive a portion of the rent in light of the proportional ownership, agreed in the leased asset even if they bear losses to the extent of their ownership.

12.3 Global Sukuk Market Performance

Earlier in this chapter, we have already discussed the types of *Sukuk*. However, to gain clarity on the types of *Sukuk* in terms of market segmentation, *Sukuk* can be categorised in the market depending on *Sukuk* type, currency, issuer type, and region.

Categories of *Sukuk* based on *Sukuk* type include:

- *Murabaha Sukuk*
- *Salam Sukuk*
- *Istisna Sukuk*
- *Ijarah Sukuk*
- *Musharaka Sukuk*
- *Mudarabah Sukuk*
- Hybrid *Sukuk*
- Others.

Categories of *Sukuk* based on currency include:

- Turkish lira
- Indonesian rupiah
- Saudi riyal
- Kuwaiti dinar
- Malaysian ringgit
- US dollar
- Others.

Categories of *Sukuk* based on issuer type include:

- Sovereign
- Corporate
- Financial institutions
- Quasi-sovereign
- Others.

Categories of *Sukuk* based on region include:

- Gulf Cooperation Council (GCC)
- Southeast Asia
- Middle East and Africa (excluding GCC countries)
- Others.

12.3–1 Short-Term Sukuk

To be able to fulfil the required liquidity management of Islamic financial institutions, a short-term *Sukuk* has absolutely have the maturity of one year or lesser. Table 12.1 shows that the 'total global short term *Sukuk* issuance' of the *Sukuk* market since it came into action stands today at US$502.05 billion. In 2020, the short-term *Sukuk* issuance accounted for US$56.741 billion, which is indicative of an increase of US$16.738 billion from 2019 when the issuance accounted for $40 billion. This can be also observed in the form of rise in 41.84% p.a. of short-term *Sukuk* issuances (IIFM Sukuk Report, 2020).

Table 12.1 shows that Malaysia leads the short-term *Sukuk* market. However, there has been a trivial reduction in the country's market share of the total global short-term *Sukuk* issuances. The market share of 83.30% (US$370.755 billion) during

TABLE 12.1 Total Global Short-Term *Sukuk* Issuances: All Currencies 12 Months or Less (January 2001–December 2020)

Asia and Far East	*Number of Issues*	*Amount (Million US$)*	*% of Total Value*
Bangladesh	29	790	0.16
Brunei Darussalam	195	11,830	2.36
Indonesia	112	12,465	2.48
Malaysia	3,643	400,797	79.83
Maldives	2	21	0.00
Pakistan	16	399	0.08
Singapore	3	221	0.04
Total	4,000	426,522	85.0
GCC and Middle East	*Number of Issues*	*Amount (Million US$)*	*% of Total Value*
Bahrain	384	20,018	3.99
Oman	1	130	0.03
Saudi Arabia	6	1,301	0.26
United Arab Emirates	1	100	0.02
Yemen	1	234	0.05
Total	393	21,782	4.3
Africa	*Number of Issues*	*Amount (Million US$)*	*% of Total Value*
Gambia	490	413	0.08
Sudan	26	17,419	3.47
Total	516	17,832	3.6
Europe and Others	*Number of Issuers*	*Amount (Million US$)*	*% of Total Value*
Turkey	578	35,916	7.15
Total	578	35,916	7.15
Grand Total	5,487	502,053	100

Source: IIFM *Sukuk* Report (2020).

the 2001–2019 period was reduced to 79.83% (US$400.797 billion) during 2001–2020. There are other issuers who remain involved in the short-term *Sukuk* market quite regularly. Some of these issuer countries are Bahrain, Brunei, Indonesia, Gambia, Sudan and UAE. In Turkey, the short-term issuances have doubled in comparison to the previous year of 2019.

Interestingly, this group of issuers have formed around 20.17% of the total short-term market since the inception. Malaysia's International Islamic Liquidity Management (IILM) simultaneously began its short-term issuances in the year 2013. Eventually, it went on to issue the highest number of *Sukuk* in 2020. The Indonesian government has increased the number of its *Sukuk* issuance, while the Turkish government and IFIs have been working on increasing their pace in issuing short-term *Sukuk* (IIFM *Sukuk* Report, 2020). The table shown below presents the evaluation of the key trends in each sub-segment of the global *Sukuk* market. The global and regional forecasts from 2001–2020 with special emphasis on the regional break-up of total short-term *Sukuk* have been portrayed through the table.

Considering the fact that several new issuers came into the global scenario in 2020, Malaysia still continues to dominate the short-term *Sukuk* market including IILM with its market share worth US$29.84 billion accounting for 52.60% of the global market (IIFM *Sukuk* Report, 2020).

12.3-2 Composition of International Long-Term Sukuk *Issuance*

The international *Sukuk* market accounts for 24% of the *Sukuk* issuances globally. Right from its inception, it has served to be the driving force of the *Sukuk* market from a global point of view. The denominations used as exchanges in issuing *Sukuk* in the international market are either in the form of US dollars or any other stable currency. The international *Sukuk* is issued subject to a longer time frame that might go up to 30 years which is even anticipated to grow into the possibility of 50 years considering the consistent growth of this industry. The perpetual call option is generally seen to be of 5 years.

The international *Sukuk* having a time frame ranging from medium to long along with perpetual *Sukuk* managed to maintain its volume growth during 2020. At the same time, with the increase in demand for high-quality liquid assets (HQLAs), it has been recorded that the size of international short-term *Sukuk* particularly from the International Islamic Liquidity Management (IILM) Centre has simultaneously grown to a large extent. In recent times, there has been quite an increase in the numbers of sovereign and quasi-sovereign issuances, thereby constituting a large chunk of the *Sukuk* market during 2020. The same year witnessed Islamic financial institutions (IFIs) issuers to have had a record year while corporate issuances such as Malaysia remained subdued.

Table 12.2 shows that UAE has led in terms of its value and volume, with a whopping 27.01% in the international *Sukuk* market. Malaysia followed with 25.77%, Saudi Arabia with 19.67%, Indonesia with 6.38%, Bahrain with 4.69%,

TABLE 12.2 Regional Breakup of International *Sukuk* Issuance (January 2001–December 2020)

Asia and Far East	*Number of Issues*	*Amount (Million US$)*	*% of Total Value*
China	1	97	0.03
Hong Kong	5	3,195	0.96
Indonesia	24	21,203	6.38
Japan	3	190	0.06
Malaysia	174	85,633	25.77
Pakistan	4	3,600	1.08
Singapore	4	711	0.21
Total	215	114,630	34.49
GCC and Middle East	*Number of Issues*	*Amount (Million US$)*	*% of Total Value*
Bahrain	109	15,589	4.69
Kuwait	21	5,177	1.56
Oman	5	4,219	1.27
Qatar	25	16,195	4.87
Saudi Arabia	78	65,353	19.67
UAE	138	89,764	27.01
Total	376	196,297	59.07
Africa	*Number of Issues*	*Amount (Million US$)*	*% of Total Value*
Nigeria	1	150	0.05
South Africa	1	500	0.15
Sudan	1	130	0.04
Total	3	780	0.23
Europe and others	*Number of Issues*	*Amount (Million US$)*	*% of Total Value*
France	1	1	0.0003
Germany	3	206	0.06
Luxembourg	3	280	0.08
Turkey	33	16,917	5.09
United Kingdom	11	1,769	0.53
United States	5	1,367	0.41
Tajikistan	1	77	0.02
Total	57	20,617	6.20
Grand total	651	332,325	100%

Source: IIFM Sukuk database.

and Turkey with 5.09%. The five GCC countries (Saudi Arabia, Qatar, UAE, Oman, and Bahrain) collectively account for more than 59.07% of the overall *Sukuk* issued internationally since 2001.

Some of the Islamic jurisdictions have been issuing benchmark *Sukuk* at various times in both domestic and international markets. In 2001, Bahrain initiated a strategy that went on to be adopted by Africa and several other jurisdictions.

The strategy is aimed to ensure the regular floating of short- to medium-term *Sukuk* for being able to support the requirements of Islamic institutions within the jurisdiction subjecting to their liquidity and investment. The IIFM Sukuk Report (2020) claims that *Sukuk* is firmly emerging as a major alternative source of funding which is not only limited to the Islamic markets but also in markets around Europe, Africa, Asia and the countries of the Commonwealth of Independent States (CIS), which have shown a keen interest. In the context of issuing benchmark *Sukuk*, certain milestones which are worth mentioning are that of *Sukuk* issued by Emaar Malls, Sadara Chemical, Saudi Electric company, the government of Turkey, *Sukuk* issuances from Saudi Arabia, Qatar, and the UAE, debut domestic *Sukuk* by Senegal, debut international issuances by Europe and Asian countries, Tier 1 Perpetual Sukuk by Al Hilal Bank, GEMs School Perpetual Sukuk and so on.

12.3-2-1 Case Study: Dar Al-Arkan Real Estate Development Company

DAR AL-ARKAN SUKUK COMPANY LTD.
(Incorporated in the Cayman Islands)
US$1.8 Billion Trust Certificate issuance programme

The *Sukuk* Issuance Programme by Dar Al Arkan Sukuk amounts to a worth of US$1.8 billion. Under this programme, US$450 million was initially issued in May, 2013 followed by US$4.3 billion issued in November 2013; US$400 million issued in May 2014 and US$4.5 billion issued in April 2017. This *Sukuk* issuance structure has been inspired from the first transactional model of its type in 2010 when Dar Al Arkan successfully offered US$450 million. The reason that this transaction has been considered as the first high-yielding *Sukuk* is because it involved the combination of an innovative *wakalah* structure with a high-yield covenant package so that certain features, typical to the characteristic of otherwise conventional high-yield real estate transactions in emerging markets can be equally replicated via this particular transaction model.

After this mode of transaction witnessed enormous success, Dar Al Arkan was encouraged to apply the structure of the programme for its next series of issuances. Hence, repeat issuances with minimal cost got approved. An SPV was incorporated by Dar Al Arkan in harmony with the legal framework of the Cayman Islands. This SPV is known as Dar Al Arkan Sukuk Company Ltd., which acts as the nodal agency in issuing the *Sukuk* and serves as the trustee of the investor. Furthermore, Dar Al Arkan went on to incorporate an entirely owned subsidiary, known as the Dar Al Arkan *Sukuk* International Company. This company was incorporated in sync with the laws of Saudi Arabia and served the purpose of *wakil*, or investment manager associated with the *Sukuk*. This *Sukuk* issuance programme has certain arrangers and dealers, two of which are Alkhair Capital (Dubai) Limited and Deutsche Bank AG, London Branch.

The transactions involved in *wakalah* consist of the following:

1. Issuance of *Sukuk*: As an issuer, the SPV issue the *Sukuk*, thereby representing an ownership interest in the underlying *wakalah* assets or transactions. The ownership interest is undivided. At the same time, a right would be entailed against the issuer for paying the periodic distribution amount and the dissolution distribution amount.
2. Subscription to *Sukuk*: The subscriptions to *Sukuk* are made by the certificate holders who then follow up to pay the proceeds of the *Sukuk* to the issuer.
3. Investment management (*wakalah*) agreement: The issuer then provides the *Sukuk* proceeds to the investment manager for investing in a portfolio of investments which comprise of an *ijarah* agreement and a *murabaha* agreement. These agreements are set between the investment manager and particular restricted subsidiaries of Dar Al-Arkan. A minimum amount adhering to 51% of the face amount of the certificates outstanding, has to be always invested by the investment manager in tangible *ijara* agreements; the only exception being the time periods crucial for replacing any *ijara* agreement.
4. Investment plan: An agreement is made by the investment manager in ensuring the investment of the *Sukuk* proceeds into a portfolio of *Sukuk* contracts generating returns. The returns generated have to be equivalent to the periodic distribution amount for a certain time frame which is either equal or greater than the remaining time frame of the certificates outstanding. This would in turn preserve the value of the *Sukuk* portfolio. Here, the assets of the investment manager cannot be combined in the *Sukuk* portfolio. In an agreement made for managing an investment, it is equally imperative for the investment manager to be fully aware of certain investment conditions.
5. Profit collections and distribution to certificate holders: Before every periodic distribution date, the investment manager has to collect the entire amount which is due from the counterparties to the *ijara* agreements and *murabaha* agreements. On behalf of the issuer, the investment manager has to pay the collected amount to the principal paying agent on the same date. This is then followed by the principal paying agent, who uses the periodic distribution amount in paying the certificate holders on the periodic distribution date. As a guarantor, Dar Al-Arkan is obligated to pay a shortfall restoration amount in case there emerges any kind of shortfall between the profit collections and the periodic distribution amount due under the *Sukuk*.
6. Liquidation: Before the maturity date comes, the investment manager has to liquidate the *Sukuk* portfolio and ensure that the proceeds are being paid to the principal paying agent. This will be followed up by the principal paying agent, who has to ensure that the amount is used in paying the certificate holders their dissolution distribution amount. As a guarantor, Dar Al-Arkan is obligated to pay a shortfall restoration amount in case there emerges any kind of shortfall between the profit collections and the periodic distribution amount due under the *Sukuk*.

12.4 Challenges to the Development of the *Sukuk* Market

Despite its consistent developmental pace, the *Sukuk* market faces multiple challenges which have the potential to impede its growth and restrict further development. Some of the challenges that can be possibly encountered by the *Sukuk* market are discussed below (Latham & Watkins, 2018).

12.4–1 Legal Regime

The creation of a special purpose vehicle (SPV) is considered as a fundamental requirement in *Sukuk*. The originator who acts as the entity raising funds transfers the assets underlying the *Sukuk* to the relevant SPV. As a result, additional taxes and stamp duties could emerge on the surface. This might put *Sukuk* in a disadvantageous position in comparison to other conventional bonds. Malaysia continue to account for a whopping 60% of the global *Sukuk* issuances is backed by its government which has not only enacted tax but also regulated land transfer and registration laws so as to not penalise *Sukuk* issuances when compared with conventional bond issuances. Several countries have been desiring to develop an Islamic finance market which is why they are taking steps to enact legislation to make *Sukuk* issuances a possibility. In this context, let us take the example of UK's Finance Act, 2009. On receiving the royal assent on 21 July 2009, certain tax barriers were removed, thereby making *Shari'ah*-compliant financial products less tax efficient as compared to their conventional counterparts. This particular legislative enactment has catalysed UK's ambition in wanting to lead the international centre for Islamic finance. In July 2014, the UK government issued a £200 million sovereign *Sukuk*. This was witnessed as the first of its kind by a European sovereign state. After making changes in their legal framework in July 2013, the government of the Hong Kong Special Administrative Region of the People's Republic of China followed suit and issued a $16 billion *Sukuk* in September 2014. Among other countries, Japan and Singapore have simultaneously enacted similar reforms in their legislative practices in an attempt to put an end to certain asymmetries subjected to the tax treatment of *Sukuk* and traditional bonds. Changes in legislation or the legal system would ensure a uniform level for the *Sukuk* to be able to compete with conventional debt products.

12.4–2 Standardisation

During a *Sukuk* transaction, issuers and investors are provided with a *fatwa*. The *fatwa* can be understood as a legal procurement which is aimed at comforting the issuers and investors with the assurance that the *Sukuk* is in full compliance with *Shari'ah* principles. It must be noted that these endorsements are interpreted differently thereby giving rise to different opinions which in turn could possibly make the market volatile as already observed with the impact of the statement given by AAOIFI. Any doubt associated with *Shari'ah*-compliance is possibly going to affect marketability, which is why developing a set of guidelines is crucial. The guidelines must have the majority consent of the *Shari'ah* advisors. This problem has been nationally addressed by the government of Malaysia by establishing a centralised *Shari'ah* supervisory board so as to provide full assurance of every *Sukuk* that gets issued in Malaysia is in full compliance with nationally accepted *Shari'ah* principles. The countries in the GCC region are yet to come up with a similar regional supervisory body or any such uniformly agreed set of *Shari'ah* principles, the establishment of which can largely benefit them in the future.

12.4–3 Mechanics for Default

For a mature market to be developed, *Sukuk* investors must be able to comprehend and be aware of their rights and remedies in case of default scenarios. Earlier, many investors considered *Sukuk* as secured instruments which would benefit from security in the underlying *Sukuk* assets. Eventually, as a result of some notable high-profile *Sukuk* defaults, investors got to learn that most *Sukuk* instruments do not ensure security in the conventional sense. In light of the *Shari'ah* perspective, *Sukuk* represent an undivided share in the ownership of a pool of tangible assets, usufructs and/or services. The structuring of the *Sukuk* would determine if investors are eligible to put forth a claim against these assets upon a default under *Sukuk* terms. The structuring of *Sukuk* is done for the asset originator to be able to conduct a nominal sale of the underlying assets to the SPV. It is not really a true sale. Accomplishment of the sale might be done by assigning rights without completing the required formal procedures associated with the registration of the asset. The absence of a true sale makes *Sukuk* holders to be treated as unsecured creditors of the SPV. In consideration of a true sale of asset ownership to the SPV, there still might be contractual arrangements for ensuring that *Sukuk* holders do not hold any legitimate claim on the underlying assets. A purchase undertaking is generally provided by the originator. The undertaking is aimed to ensure that the SPV must have to transfer the assets back to that originator upon the redemption of the *Sukuk* or in case of a default. This purchase undertaking equally serves as the contractual claim for the SPV against the originator for non-payment of the purchase price for the assets. When this purchase price is equivalent to the face amount of the *Sukuk* having no claim against the assets, the *Sukuk* holders are placed in a position similar to that of bond holders under a conventional unsecured bond. The level of protection provided to investors largely depends on the structure of a certain *Sukuk*. The AAOIFI is seen to be supportive of a switch in the direction of asset-backed structures where investors have actual recourse to the assets in case a default event arises. A majority of the *Sukuk* in the existing market are designed to treat *Sukuk* holders in similar notions as that of the conventional unsecured bond holders would be treated in a restructuring or an insolvency. It is undeniably true that the occurrence of asset-backed *Sukuk* structures is quite rare (Latham & Watkins, 2018).

12.5 AAOIFI's Concern on *Shari'ah* Compliance of *Sukuk*

In 2007, the Accounting and Auditing Organization of Islamic Financial Institutions (AAOIFI) in Bahrain raised three major criticisms against *Sukuk* corresponding to the issues as discussed below:

1. The absence of real ownership interest among *Sukuk* holders in the underlying assets.
2. The actual performance does not serve as a determining factor for the regular distributions to *Sukuk* holders.
3. Purchase undertakings are used to ensure a guarantee of the return on capital.

In the first criticism corresponding to asset-based *Sukuk*, no legal sale of the underlying assets is involved. This implies that no real transfer of ownership of the assets occurs from the originating company to *Sukuk* holders. The legal documentation in asset-based *Sukuk* projects the idea that the *Sukuk* holders do not possess an interest in the underlying asset. This conflicts with *Shari'ah* ideology which requires the *Sukuk* investors to have rights over the *Sukuk* assets.

In the rest of the criticisms, emphasis was given to the structural features of the equity based *Sukuk* including the *Sukuk al musharaka, Sukuk al murabaha* and *Sukuk al wakalah* structures. The criticisms talked about how *Shari'ah*-compliant funding would be immediately used for compensating any shortfalls arising in different scenarios. This might occur when the original profit is below the stipulated percentage to *Sukuk* holders or the payment of any excess profit realised beyond the expected profit percentage has to be paid in the form of incentive fees to the manager. It is also applicable during the use of purchase undertakings to guarantee the *Sukuk* holders' principal as an anticipation of the issuer buying back the underlying asset at the expiration date of the *Sukuk* or in the event of default at face value regardless of their true value on that very day. The prevalence of these practices results in converting equity-based *Sukuk* to debt-based structures. Here, the *Sukuk* gets redeemed at par value at the maturity date. At the same time, during the entire course of the *Sukuk*, the *Sukuk* holders are paid a guaranteed periodic return on capital.

In February 2008, the AAOIFI issued additional guidelines associated with the structuring of *Sukuk*. These guidelines serve as a response in light of all the *Shari'ah* concerns. The key points discussed below are forbidden in equity based *Sukuk*:

1. Usage of *Shari'ah*-compliant financing to resolve periodic income distribution amounts to *Sukuk* holders.
2. Usage of purchase undertakings for ensuring the return of the principal amount to *Sukuk* holders at its par value. It must be noted that the AAOIFI Resolution does not prohibit the use of purchase undertakings in *Sukuk al ijarah* when the lessee is not an investment partner, *mudarib* or agent.

According to the norms under the AAOIFI Resolution, a reserve account is allowed to be used for covering shortfalls as well as distribution on the account provided that the latter is subjected to reconciliation before the final distribution. In its 20th session in 2012, the resolution of the International Islamic *Fiqh* Academy (IFA; a branch of the Organization of Islamic Cooperation [OIC]), declared a similar statement to the resolution of the AAOIFI made in 2008 about the disapproval of purchasing equity-based *Sukuk* at their nominal value or at a predetermined price which would typically lead to the capital of *Sukuk* holders being ensured. At the same time, the provision of loans to *Sukuk* holders when actual *Sukuk* revenue is less than expected is banned. However, approval is made for the recourse to reserve accounts to redress potential shortfalls. In the context of the *Sukuk al ijarah*, the Islamic *Fiqh* Academy in Jeddah has banned the usage of the present structure of asset-based *Sukuk al ijarah* since it falls under *inah* (an arrangement where assets are sold and bought back).

The Islamic *Fiqh* Academy also claimed the disapproval of selling an asset on a cash basis if the seller leases the asset in terms of a lease ending in ownership. Here, the total rental payments and repurchase price (paid by the *Sukuk* issuer) would be greater than the cash price (paid by the *Sukuk* holders) and thus stands to be prohibited irrespective of being mentioned explicitly or implicitly. Anything taking the shape of the prohibited *inah* cannot be allowed since *Sukuk* will not be issued using this structure. The Islamic *Fiqh* Academy put forth an enormous emphasis on the fact that *Sukuk* should ensure in establishing authentic ownership of the underlying assets, keeping in sync with both the *Shari'ah* and conventional law. The legal effects must be simultaneously attended and enabled. For instance, the power of disposing assets and bearing the liability associated with its ownership.

12.6 Conclusion

The idea of developing *Sukuk* emerged from the quest of an alternative to interest-bearing bonds. The current concerns of *Shari'ah* alignment associated with *Sukuk* structures has made the *fiqh* councils focus on the assurance that the structuring of *Sukuk* is done in absolute adherence to the principles of *Shari'ah*. The ultimate goal is distinctively segregate *Sukuk* and conventional bonds in light of the structure, design, utilisation of proceeds and overall objective of supporting genuine activities and economic development.

Sukuk has been continuously serving as the vehicle carrying the opportunity to provide resources that are in conformity with *Shari'ah* principles. It simultaneously contributes to the future economic aspect. The dramatic growth of the *Sukuk* market is witnessed as one of the fastest emerging alternative instruments. *Sukuk* acts as a significant tool in the capital markets, increasingly used globally by governments, government-held entities, financial institutions, corporations and so forth. In 2020, the International Islamic Financial Market (IIFM) published two important *Sukuk* standard documents for the market: Template *Sukuk Al Ijarah* Standard Documents and Template *Sukuk Al Mudarabah* Tier 1 Standard Documents. The documentation can further help in contributing towards sustainable progress in this crucial sector of this Islamic financial industry (IIFM, 2020). The Council of the Islamic *Fiqh* Academy of the OIC and other relevant Islamic institutions have legitimised *Sukuk* issuance and its concept, thereby paving an alternative way of financing to be able to meet the needs of Islamic issuers and investors who in adherence to *Shari'ah* rules and principles, aren't otherwise allowed to invest in the *Riba* (interest) based conventional bonds.

Through a basic point of view, the participation in the underlying asset is reflected via *Sukuk*. It is because each certificate is representative of an undivided interest in the asset and thus, trade does not occur in terms of a mere debt. This is again in conformity with *Shari'ah* guidelines, which prohibit *Riba* as a result of which any kind of trading in a pure debt instrument is not permitted. Hence, the structuring of *Sukuk* in order to achieve a desired economic objective has to mandatorily be in conformity with the rules, principles and spirit of *Shari'ah*. Investment in tangible assets, used for productive purposes and obtaining the rewards as a result of investing in those assets are imperative to Islamic finance.

The years have witnessed the emergence of a variety of *Sukuk*, but the most widely used structure of the *Sukuk* issuance till date has been *ijara Sukuk* since it is based on the undivided pro rata ownership of the underlying leased asset and can be traded freely at par, premium or discount. The fact that *Sukuk* is more tradable in the secondary market makes them more attractive. Apart from *ijarah Sukuk*, multiple types of *Sukuk* are equally operational and opted in emerging markets to help issuers and investors for participating in major projects, including airports, bridges, power plants and so forth. Malaysia as the lead followed by GCC and other sovereign *Sukuk* are equally enjoying the extensive positive acclaim among Islamic investors as well as international institutional investors.

The progress of the *Sukuk* market is undeniably impressive. However, it must be remembered that to ensure the sustainability of its consistent growth, and facilitate a robust and transparent *Sukuk* market, a set of challenges that might emerge need to be addressed. In catering to and resolving these challenges, the role of standard setting bodies is imperative since the issues arising in the primary and secondary market need to be addressed in absolute harmony with *Shari'ah* principles.

Review Questions

1. What is *Sukuk*?
2. Discuss the popular types of *Sukuk*.
3. What are the reasons that are leading to make *Sukuk* popular products in Islamic finance?
4. How does *Sukuk* help in liquidity management for Islamic banks and Islamic financial institutions?
5. Demonstrate the process of flow and steps for obtaining industrial machinery on a long term financing basis through *Ijarah Sukuk* in financial markets.
6. Explain the process for structuring *Mudarabah* and *Musharaka Sukuk*.
7. What are the challenges that come in the way of developing the *Sukuk* market?
8. Discuss a case study on *Sukuk*.

References

AAOIFI (2008), *AAOIFI Sharia Standard*, Bahrain: AAOIFI

Adam, NJ and Thomas, A (2004), *Islamic Bonds: Your Guide to Issuing, Structuring and Investing in Sukuk*, London: Euromoney Books

IIFM (2020), *Sukuk Report, a Comprehensive Study of the Global Sukuk Market*, Kuala Lumpur: IIFM, retrieved from www.iifm.net/wp-content/uploads/2021/08/IIFM-Sukuk-Report-10th-Edition.pdf (Access date May 2021)

Latham & Watkins (2018), *The Sukuk Handbook: A Guide to Structuring Sukuk*, retrieved from www.lw.com/thoughtLeadership/guide-to-structurings-sukuk (Access date May 23, 2020)

Salah, O (2010), Islamic Finance: The Impact of the AAOIFI Resolution on Equity-Based Sukuk Structures, *Law and Financial Market Review*, 4(5), 7–17

13

GREEN *SUKUK* VIS-À-VIS GREEN BONDS

Learning Objectives

On completing this chapter, learners will be able to:

- Determine the strategies for green investments that are in sync with sustainable development goals
- Discuss why green *Sukuk* market matters and how it works
- Identify recent trends and potential future developments of green *Sukuk*
- Develop an understanding of how green *Sukuk* can be renovated to positively impact environmental and sustainable development in the society and enhance organisation's long-term ethical financial values
- Enhance the knowledge framework on green *Sukuk* in responding to financial risk posed by social and sustainability issues including green investing, environmental, social and governance (ESG) investing.

13.1 Introduction

The projects that are financed using green bonds primarily revolve around energy efficiency, pollution prevention, sustainable agriculture, fishery and forestry, the protection of aquatic and terrestrial ecosystems, clean transportation, clean water, and sustainable water management. Buyers investing in green bonds are asked for their capital to be directed towards projects that correspond with the values of these bonds. Buyers wanting to invest in green bonds with clean and purposeful intent are often issued bonds with lower yields as compared to non-green bonds. This will thereby save interest expenses for the buyers. In the present day, the idea of investing in green bonds has quite captivated new investors and has eventually resulted in the formation of a large investor community. Green bonds also serve to be beneficial for firms from the perspective of public relations where making investments

DOI: 10.4324/9780429321207-13

in these bonds would subtly shape up their identities based on righteousness. This would imply that these firms are actively working to fight climate change through investments in green bonds.

Green bonds are of two broad varieties:

1. Labelled: Certified as green, these bonds imply that the issuer has ensured that the proceeds emerging as a result of the issuance will be projected in financing green projects which more often than not have lower yields.
2. Unlabelled: This implies that the issuer has not pledged for the proceeds of the issuance to be directed specifically in favour of green projects as a result of which the yields are comparatively higher.

In 2007, the very first issuance of green bonds was made, and since then these bonds have been issued globally. However, their success rate has been a lot lower in North America as compared to other markets, like China. In 2018, Apple issued a green bond worth US$1.5 billion with a maturity of seven years. This was the largest green bond ever issued.

13.1–1 Types of Green Bonds

As the markets will keep evolving, several types of green bonds might emerge. However, at present, there are four different types of green bonds:

1. Green revenue bond: A non-recourse-to-the-issuer bond where debt obligation is aligned with the global bond principles (GBPs). Here, the credit exposure in the bond is to the pledged cash flows of the revenue streams, fees, taxes, and so forth. The proceeds generated are directed towards related or unrelated green project(s).
2. Green project bond: A project bond for a single or multiple green project(s). Here, the investor is directly exposed to the project risks, with or without potential recourse to the issuer. This bond is aligned with the GBP.
3. Green securitised bond: A bond collateralised by one or more specific green project(s). This is inclusive of but not in any way restricted to covered bonds, Asset-Backed Securities (ABS), Mortgage-Backed Securities (MBS) and other structures. This bond remains aligned with the GBP. Mostly, the cash flows of the assets act as the first source of repayment.
4. Standard green use of proceeds bond: A standard recourse-to-the-issuer debt obligation.

13.1–2 Type of Projects of Green Bond Investment

According to ICMA (2021), the dimensions eligible to be categorised under green projects are as follows:

- Renewable energy: These constitute investments made in projects associated with non-fossil fuel energy sources. The energy sources are inclusive of solar, wind, hydro, biomass, geothermal, tidal, and so on.

- Energy efficiency: These constitute investments made in projects associated with equipment, systems, products, and services. The idea of these investments is aimed to ensure a reduction in the energy consumption per unit of output.
- Emissions reducers: These constitute investments made in projects that are associated with reducing greenhouse gas emissions.

Please note that this is not an exhaustive list of categories.

13.1–3 Green Bonds Issuers

As an issuer, one has to have a keen interest in green projects and at the same time must be equally inclined towards lowering the nominal rates of interest. Issuance of green bonds is done by governments as well as companies. Green bond issuers include the Chinese government, the City of Toronto, Banco Colombia, Toyota Financial Services, Fannie Mae, Bay Area Rapid Transit, and Apple.

13.1–4 Themes of Green Bond Investment

The ICMA (2021) has prescribed various themes upon which projects can be conceptualised and investments can be made. Some of these themes are:

- A major section of the top 10 GDP entities, such as the EU, China, and Japan experiencing the aging of their populations.
- Climate change and the consequences that it brings along. This includes the destruction or reduction of land and real estate, destruction or reduction of crop yields. Migration as a subsequent result of climate change is also included.
- Innovative green technologies that are ideally designed to mitigate the effects of climate change.
- Bonds aimed at addressing global income inequality.

It can be denied that green bonds constitute a relatively smaller proportion of total fixed-income issuance. However, it is simultaneously true that their share of total issuance is growing at an impeccable pace in comparison with the overall market. Governments and businesses are issuing green bonds at greater breadth and depth of the market. The emergence of the importance of investing that prioritises environmental, social and governance (ESG) issues is remodelling the financial landscape worldwide. As a result, corporations have been simultaneously incorporating ESG principles into their businesses and borrowings (Arab News, 2021).

It is evident that there exists a market of bonds that corresponds to sustainable themes. The market is aimed toward financing a combination of green and social projects which simultaneously includes projects that are associated with the United Nations Sustainable Development Goals (SDGs). In certain specific cases, the organisations that are primarily or entirely involved in sustainable activities might also issue these bonds.

13.2 Green *Sukuk*

Right from their inception in 2008, green bonds have actively advocated and shown how finance is imperative to the protection of the planet. It is through finance that investors can utilise newer opportunities and apply monetary resources to supporting environmental goals. According to a report by Moody's, it has been claimed that new sustainable bond issuances are likely to cross $650 billion in 2021, which in itself will be a 32% hike from that of the 2020 record. On the other hand, the World Bank has issued an approximate equivalent of US$16 billion in green bonds since their inception in 2008. Over 185 bonds have been issued in 23 currencies, which is still a lower percentage owing to the fact that a larger proportion of these bonds constitute investments that are *Riba* based (interest bearing). Hence, investors following Islamic finance do not find these conventional green bonds aligned with the morale of *Shari'ah*. Therefore, as an alternative, they opt for green *Sukuk*.

Sukuk, a term used for Islamic bonds refers to financial instruments that are designed in full compliance with the *Shari'ah* law. The Islamic doctrine is represented through a broad set of rules which collectively constitute the *Shari'ah* law. More often than not, *Sukuk* are referred to as *Shari'ah*-compliant bonds. In practical usage, their structuring resembles equity-based financial instruments more than fixed-income financial instruments because as per the norms of *Shari'ah*, any form of fixed income or risk-free return is forbidden. When making investments in a *Sukuk*, an investor buys a certificate from an issuer. The issuer, in turn, does not earn the interest but goes on to utilise the proceeds in buying an asset. Meanwhile, the investor gets to earn a share of the profits at periodic intervals. To be able to provide a product or service to the market, *Sukuk*-funded projects should anticipate some form of risk. As a partial owner, the *Sukuk* holder gets to have a share of the revenue generated but at the same time has to share the risk taken. It must be carefully ensured that the particular project should not generate profit by remaining linked in any kind of industries that are prohibited under *Shari'ah* law, such as gambling, tobacco or any other industry that is based on *riba*. The initial development of *Sukuk* has been observed in markets where Muslims constitute the majority of participants. However, in the present day, there has been an increasing demand for them globally (World Bank, 2020). Green *Sukuk* refer to Islamic bonds directed towards the financing of initiatives that are environmentally sustainable. For instance, green *Sukuk* can be used in funding renewable energy production, waste management, sustainable agriculture, construction of energy-efficient buildings, natural resource management, or other endeavours that are aimed at enriching the environment or mitigating risks that have emerged as a result of climate change.

13.2-1 Difference Between Green Islamic Bonds and Green Bonds

A green *Sukuk* (Islamic bonds) and a green bond can be distinctively differentiated on the basis of their underlying financing structure. This can be observed in

TABLE 13.1 Investors for Bond and *Sukuk*

	Non-green	*Green*
Bond	Conventional investors	Conventional investors and conventional green investors
Sukuk	Conventional investors and *Shari'ah*-compliant investors	All investors

a similar context to the difference between a *Sukuk* and a bond. Green *Sukuk* is a big approach that attempts to bridge the gap between conventional financing and Islamic financing. As a new financial product with multiple innovate uses, green *Sukuk* can be applied around the world. Apart from meeting sustainable requirements and ensuring that funds are channelled to environmentally sustainable projects, the ultimate advantage embedded in a green *Sukuk* is its wider appeal to a larger set of investors as compared to a general *Sukuk* or a green bond. To put it up simply, a green *Sukuk* is more likely to be attracting green investors, *Shari'ah*-compliant investors and conventional finance investors. Table 13.1 illustrates the investors subjected to bond and *Sukuk*.

The general *Sukuk* structure backed by assets is inherently suited to project financing. Simultaneously, the green *Sukuk* is inherently suited for green project financing. This includes renewable energy power plants, green buildings, mass transportation infrastructure which is environmentally friendly, and so forth. Similar to that of a green bond, the earnings of green *Sukuk* can be utilised for projects that are environmentally useful.

13.2–2 Method of Issuance of Green Sukuk

Issuance of a green *Sukuk* is a process which involves issuing a general *Sukuk* along with the integration of green elements. The procedure is similar to that of a green bond, which is nothing but an otherwise traditional bond which has successfully embraced green elements. The process of issuing traditional *Sukuk* requires overall structuring, timeline tagging, and deliverables. This remains similar for green *Sukuk* except for the differences as explained below (World Bank, 2020):

Pre-issuance Period

1. Use of proceeds: It is crucial to identify how the proceeds of a green *Sukuk* project will be utilised. Clarity regarding how the environment will be impacted and which aspect of the environment will the project be catering to is imperative before the issuance is done and the project officially begins. At the same time, the identification of the environmental benefit has to be simultaneously characterised by parameters that are either measurable or quantifiable so that the process of evaluating progress becomes convenient.

2. Project evaluation and selection: The issuer needs to explain how the proposed project will be identified, validated and approved in terms of its green strategy and commitment. If selected after the evaluation process, the project stands ready to be financed. The financing of the project is relatively simpler as the identification and selection of the proposed project has been already done.
3. External review: In order to analyse the authenticity of the green framework of the proposed *Sukuk*, an independent review of an external reviewer is required most of the time. Investors consider the report provided by the external quite crucial, as it enables them to decide on the qualitative factors of the investments. It seeks to find out how impactful the utilisation of the proceeds of the proposed project might turn out to be. Certain external review reports might specifically identify how each project is impactful to the environment in terms of its 'greenness'.

Post-issuance Period

1. Management of proceeds: Once the issuance of a green *Sukuk* is done, segregation of the bond proceeds is crucial. In order to be able to do so, a sub-account or sub-portfolio can be brought into effect to ensure appropriateness and transparency. At the same time, clarity must be provided on intended types of temporary placement for the balance of unallocated net proceeds. Besides the normal accounting audit process, a special audit can be facilitated through the verification of internal tracking methods and allocation of proceeds by a third party.
2. Reporting – impact reporting: Post-issuance reporting constitutes to be one of the major elements of green *Sukuk*. The progress of the underlying projects and assets are expected to be reported by the issuer issuing the green *Sukuk*. Referred to as the impact report, the post-issuance report can be merged with the progress report of the normal finances or reported separately. The quantitative as well as the qualitative elements are to be covered under this report. The report must focus on how the issuance proceeds are to be utilised and how the proceeds are going to be allocated among projects that are eligible. The impact of the projects on various stakeholders are assessed through quantitative as well as qualitative indicators. Quantitative indicators include metrics that determine the amount of carbon dioxide (CO_2) emissions avoided or clean energy generated. Qualitative indicators include elements that help in determining the sustainability objectives of the issuer and how the projects financed are likely to fulfil the same.

13.2–3 Eligible Projects Under the Green Sukuk *Framework*

To ensure their eligibility, green projects must cater to sectors that have adapted the actions plan of the United Nations Framework Convention on Climate Change (UNFCCC) and are thus contributing towards climate change mitigation. According to the green bond or the *Sukuk* framework, the projects that are deemed eligible should fall into one of the categories shown in Table 13.2.

TABLE 13.2 Eligible Projects Under the Green Bond/*Sukuk* Framework

Eligible Sectors	*Details of Eligible Green Sukuk Projects*
Renewable energy	• This entails the usage of renewable sources of for generating and transmitting energy. The renewable energy sources used include offshore and onshore wind, solar, tidal hydropower, biomass and geothermal. • Research and development (R&D) of products or technology for the generation of renewable energy which is inclusive of turbines and solar panels.
Energy efficiency	• The focus must be on improving the energy efficiency of infrastructure which could possibly result in an energy consumption of at least 10% lower than the average energy consumption of an equivalent infrastructure. • R&D of products or technology that could possibly reduce energy consumption of an underlying asset, technology, product or system(s). The implementation of the products developed is crucial to attain the benefit of the innovation. Products can include improved chillers, improved lighting technology, and manufacturing operations which run on less power.
Resilience to climate change for highly vulnerable areas and sectors / disaster risk reduction	• Research leading to technology innovation with sustainability benefits • Security of food • Mitigation of floods • Management of droughts • Management of public health
Sustainable Transport	• Development of transportation systems that are cleaner and more hygienic. • To be able to transport network upgrade to higher climate resilient design standards.
Waste to energy and waste management	• Ensuring improved waste management • Transformation of wastes into renewable sources of energy • Rehabilitating landfill areas
Sustainable management of natural resources	• Natural resources have to be managed sustainably. This implies that the management should be directed towards avoiding or reducing carbon dioxide and increasing carbon sequestration by planting new forest areas and/or replanting the areas that suffer from degradation. Use of drought/flood/temperature resistant species are also advocated. • Conservation of biodiversity and habitat through sustainable usage and management of land, sustainable management of agriculture/fisheries/forestry, protection of coastal and marine environments, management of pests and so forth.
Green tourism	• Development of new tourism areas in alignment with the principles of green tourism • Optimising supporting infrastructure as to be able to support sustainable tourism (such as water treatment, energy efficiency) • Development of tourism resiliency against risks associated with climate change

(*Continued*)

TABLE 13.2 (Continued)

Eligible Sectors	*Details of Eligible Green Sukuk Projects*
Green buildings	• Development of green buildings in compliance with green-ship developed by national-level green building organisations • Energy efficiency and conservation • Conservation of water • Cycling materials and resources • Concentrating on the quality of air as well as water; indoor health and comfort are to be considered as well • Management of buildings as well as the environment
Sustainable agriculture	• Development of agriculture management and methods which are sustainable. This can include organic farming, less pesticides, R&D on climate resilient seeds and energy-efficient agriculture. • Introducing subsidy mechanism for agriculture insurance.

Source: Climate Bonds Initiative (2020); World Bank (2020); ICMA (2021).

13.2-4 Demand for Green Sukuk

Green *Sukuk* is mostly demanded by investment advisors, banks, insurance companies and sovereign wealth funds. A list of countries that put forth high demand are the United States, Luxembourg, Ireland, Malaysia, Canada, Switzerland, Taipei, China, Japan, Germany, France, United Kingdom, Hong Kong, China, Australia, Singapore and Turkey (Azhgaliyeva, 2020). The countries listed here are in descending order. It has been evidently observed that green *Sukuk* country investors are most of time the same top country investors in *Sukuk*, implying that the countries with high demand for *Sukuk* are also the countries demanding green *Sukuk*. Thus, most of the investors in green *Sukuk* have remained top investors in *Sukuk*. All in all, it can be said that investors in *Sukuk* who are concerned about the environment are ultimately attracted to invest in green *Sukuk*. A larger section of green *Sukuk* issuers are dependent on the international demand, the only exception being the issuers from Malaysia because they denominate green *Sukuk* in domestic currency. A whopping 80% of overall green *Sukuk* issuances are in US dollars, followed by 11% in euros and 10% in Malaysian ringgit (10%). Green *Sukuk* issuances in US dollars and euros attracted investors globally. Meanwhile, green *Sukuk* issuances in Malaysian ringgit are aimed at attracting domestic investors.

13.2-5 External Reviewers

The role of external reviewers is quite crucial in providing an independent assessment of the green bond or green *Sukuk*. The external review would ultimately help potential investors to determine whether the particular issuance stands suitable for their portfolios. Often termed as a 'second opinion' review, it is similar to that

TABLE 13.3 CICERO's Shades of Green

Shades of Green	*Examples*
Dark green: This colour is allocated to projects and solutions which are conceptualised towards the long-term vision of a low carbon and climate resilient future.	Wind energy projects with a governance structure where environmental concerns are simultaneously integrated
Medium green: This colour is allocated to projects and solutions which are indicative of the steps towards the long-term vision but are not quite there yet.	Plug-in hybrid buses
Light green: This colour is allocated to projects and solutions which environment friendly in their nature but do not represent or contribute to the long-term vision of the same by themselves.	Efficiency in fossil fuel infrastructure which helps in decreasing cumulative emissions

of a credit rating provided by a rating agency with the difference being that the focus here is on the environmental aspects. External reviewers can grade or score green bond or *Sukuk* on the basis of a scale based developed as a result of their own proprietary methodology. Let us consider an example in this regard. CICERO uses the Shades of Green methodology that provides information on how well a green or sustainability bond is in alignment with a low-carbon resilient future. The transparency of the information provided is fully insured. The opinions are based on the basis of three grades: light, medium, and dark green. Table 13.3 gives a clearer insight into the methodology used (CICERO, 2021).

Reviewing green bond or green *Sukuk* externally provides assurance of the bond or *Sukuk* being in alignment with the expectations of the market and best practices of the industry. An external review definitely puts up a demonstration of the impact and credibility of the green bond or green *Sukuk* but more importantly, it inculcates confidence in investors to move ahead with green issuances.

13.2-6 Impact Reporting

Impact reports can be referred to as post-issuance reports. Issuers put out these reports annually based on how the issuance proceeds have been utilised as well as the environmental impact of the projects or investments, the proceeds have helped in financing. A project's impact report must necessarily show the amount of total investment cost, financed by the issuer through the green bond or *Sukuk* issuance. An impact report attempts to quantitatively assess the environmental benefits of the project. Investors opt for impact reporting so that the progress of the project can be monitored. At the same time, using an impact report can help in evaluating the positive and negative results of investments made. A guide has been published by the World Bank for public sector issuers. The guide is titled the *Green Bond Proceeds Management and Reporting* (World Bank, 2018).

13.3 Global Green *Sukuk* Market Trend

Table 13.4 shows how global green bond issuance has experienced a hike from US$182 billion in 2018 to US$271 billion in 2019 (Bloomberg NFE, 2019). The European market with 45% of global issuance largely dominated the 2019 global green bond (CBI, 2020). Asia Pacific with 25% and North America with 23% followed up. Fourteen percent of 1,788 green bonds issued, 250 were from new issuers, which amounted to US$67.8 billion and accounted for 26% of the total green bond issuances. Fifty-one jurisdictions had green bond issuances, out of which eight were new. In 2019, the global green *Sukuk* issuance amounted to US$3.5 billion.

As of 31 July 2020, US$6.1 billion of green *Sukuk* have been issued globally (Table 13.5). As a financial instrument, the green *Sukuk* has the full potential in channelling the Islamic finance market worth US$2 trillion towards the funding of investment projects that are green and sustainable (Arab News, 2021). Twelve distinct issuers in Indonesia, Malaysia, UAE, and one multilateral development bank were observed to issue green *Sukuk* so as to raise an approximate amount of US$6.1 billion in four currencies (euros, Indonesia rupiah, Malaysian ringgit, and US dollars) by the end of July 2020.

In the context of green *Sukuk* issuance, Indonesia's annual sovereign green *Sukuk* issuances exhibit leadership in the public sector, which also includes the first retail green *Sukuk*. On the other hand, corporates in Malaysia are making innovations by issuing multiple varied green *Sukuk* such as the Sustainable Development Goals *Sukuk* (SDG *Sukuk*) and the sustainability *Sukuk*. It must be simultaneously noted that the first multilateral development bank to not only issue a green *Sukuk* but also the first euro-denominated green *Sukuk* was the Islamic Development Bank (IsDB).

The severe impact caused due to COVID-19 in 2020 resulted in the issuances of green *Sukuk* going down 44.4% in the initial seven months of 2020 when compared with the equivalent period in 2019 (Climate Bonds Initiative, 2020). This is equally reflective of the global *Sukuk* market, which experienced a downfall of 9.1% in the first half of 2020 when compared to the same period in 2019. The issuance of global *Sukuk* issuance witnessed a major downfall during March and April in 2020 as the pandemic brought financial volatility in markets across the world. It was not until May and June 2020 that international *Sukuk* issuance bounced back. According to Fitch Wire (2020), global *Sukuk* issuers need to ensure the diversification of their funding bases so that innovation in sustainable, green and hybrid *Sukuk* can be continued (Fitch Wire, 2020). The Fitch Rating forecast claimed

TABLE 13.4 Global Green Bond/Green *Sukuk* in 2019

Total number of green bond/*Sukuk* issuers: 495
Total number of green bond/*Sukuk* issuance: 1,788
Amount of green bond/green *Sukuk* issuance: US$271 billion
Amount of green *Sukuk* issuance: US$3.5 billion

TABLE 13.5 List of the Issuances of Green *Sukuk*, as of July 2020

Issuer	*Amount Issued (Million USD)*	*Issue Date*	*No. of Tranches*	*Country of Domicile*	*First Maturity*	*Final Maturity*	*Sector*	*Structure*
Tadau Energy	58.4	27 July 2017	15	Malaysia	29 July 2019	27 July 2033	Renewable energy	*Istisna* and *Ijarah*
Quantum Solar Park	235.9	6 October 2017	33	Malaysia	6 Oct 2017	6 April 2035	Renewable energy	*Murabaha*
PNB Merdeka Ventures (Tranche 1)	169.9	29 December 2017	5	Malaysia	29 Dec 2017	29 December 2032	Renewable energy	*Murabaha Al Wakalah*
Sinar Kamiri	62.8	30 January 2018	17	Malaysia	30 Jan 2018	30 January 2036	Renewable energy	*Wakala Bi-Al Istithmar*
Indonesia (SBSN) INDO III)	1,250	1 March 2018	1	Indonesia	1 Mar 2018	1 March 2023	Sovereign	*Al Wakala Al Istithmar*
UITM Solar Power	56.6	27 April 2018	17	Malaysia	27 Apr 2018	25 April 2036	Renewable energy	*Murabaha*
Indonesia (SBSN) INDO III	750	20 February 2019	1	Indonesia	20 Feb 2019	20 August 2024	Sovereign	*Al Wakala Al Istithmar*
Pasukhas Green Assets	4.2	28 February 2019	10	Malaysia	28 Feb 2019	27 February 2029	Renewable energy	*Murabaha*
MAF Sukuk Ltd	600	14 May 2019	1	UAE	14 May 2019	14 May 2029	Real estate	*Al Wakala Al Istithmar*
PNB Merdeka Ventures (Tranche 2)	107.5	28 June 2019	5	Malaysia	28 June 2019	28 December 2032	Real estate	*Murabaha Al Wakalah*
Telekosangy Hydro	112.1	6 August 2019	15	Malaysia	6 Aug 2019	6 August 2037	Renewable energy	*Murabaha Al Wakalah*
MAF Sukuk Ltd	600	30 October 2019	1	UAE	30 Oct 2019	28 February 2030	Real estate	*Al Wakalah Murabaha*
Islamic Development Bank (IsDB)	1,100.6	27 November 2019	1	Saudi Arabia	27 Nov 2019	27 November 2024	Green projects	*Al Wakalah*
Indonesia (Sukuk Tabungan Seri)	86.2	28 November 2019	1	Indonesia	28 Nov 2019	10 November 2021	Sovereign (retail)	*Al Wakalah*
PNB Merdeka Ventures (Tranche 3)	105.3	27 December 2019	5	Malaysia	27 Dec 2019	27 December 2032	Real estate	*Al Wakalah Murabaha*
Republic of Indonesia	750	17 June 2020	1	Indonesia	17 June 2020	17 June 2025	Sovereign	*Wakalah Bi-Al Istithmar*
Leader Energy	62.7	16 July 2020	18	Malaysia	16 July 2020	16 July 2038	Renewable energy	*Murabaha Al Wakalah*
Saudi Electricity Company	4.8	November 2020	1	Saudi Arabia	October 2021	November 2024	Renewable energy	*Murabaha*
Kuveyt Türk Katilim Bankasi A.S	360	Sept ember 2021	1	Turkey	August 2022	August 2031	Pollution control and affordable housing	*Al akalah Murabaha*
Total	6,112.2		126					

Sources: Compiled by authors from World Bank (2020) and Azhgaliyeva et al. (2020).

there is a considerable need to put effort into being able to tackle climate change and achieve national sustainable development goals which are likely to be achieved through greater issuances of green *Sukuk* in terms of number as well as volume of issuances (Fitch Wire, 2020).

13.3–1 Case Study

Kuveyt Türk Katilim Bankasi A.S. Issues World's First Regulatory Capital Tier 2 Environmental, Social and Governance (ESG) and *Shari'ah*-Compliant Trust Certificates (Green *Sukuk*).

Primarily owned by Kuwait Finance House, one of the leading Turkish participation banks was listed on the Irish Stock Exchange plc (Euronext Dublin) in September 2021. With issuance of US$350 million fixed-rate resettable sustainability Tier 2 certificates due in 2031, the bank achieved a financial landmark. These trust certificates constitute to be the world's first regulatory capital Tier 2 ESG and Islamic compliant trust certificates (green *Sukuk*). An amount equivalent to the net proceeds of the issuance was applied for financing and/or refinancing projects that were deemed eligible in terms of their social and green appeal and in sync with Kuveyt Türk's Sustainable Finance Framework.

With an order book of $4 billion, the issuance was oversubscribed by 12 times, making it evident that there exists a strong demand for ESG and Islamic compliant trust certificates. When the issuance achieved 6.125%, which has indeed been the tightest pricing for any Tier 2 issuance out of Turkey since 2017, the strong fundamentals and positive sentiments of the market emerged with clarity.

The issuance of sustainable Tier 2 certificates worked wonders for Kuveyt Türk subjected to certain reasons as detailed next.

First, as a member of the Kuwait Finance House family, Kuveyt Türk had already conducted its operations without compromising the thought on the environmental impact of its actions. Thus, several sustainability efforts were undertaken and various sustainable project financings were supported in Turkey which also included multiple projects associated with renewable energy and social housing. Thus, the issuance of sustainability Tier 2 certificates was in full sync with its existing values and considerations.

Second, Kuveyt Türk had the ability to allocate the proceeds of a particular green, social or sustainable *Sukuk* issuance towards eligible green and/or social projects that had begun not more than three years before the issuance. This in turn allowed Kuveyt Türk to be reliant on some of its existing projects in the dimension of sustainability instead of having to ponder over and designate funds for new projects in the future which will possibly require the entire investment of *Sukuk* proceeds. This principle critically amounted to the success of the transaction, the absence of which could have led to issuers struggling to source new projects/allocate new purposes for the overall proceeds of an issuance.

Third, the absence of a market consensus of what is perfectly sustainable. In simpler words, the absence of a concrete, clear and uniform definition (legal, regulatory or otherwise) of what constitutes green, social, or sustainable projects, there is a large scope for issuers to borrow and use the understanding of the same from multiple international frameworks. For example, Kuveyt Türk's Sustainable Finance Framework was conceptualised in alignment with various international principles which includes the International Capital Market Association (ICMA) Green Bond Principles 2021, ICMA Sustainability Bond Guidelines 2021 and the Loan Market Association (LMA) Social Loan Principles. In the context of Kuveyt Türk's landmark issuance, the sustainable projects considered eligible included those that fell within specific categories. These categories were mostly inclusive of renewable energy, pollution prevention and control, energy efficiency, employment generation, affordable housing and access to essential services.

Fourth, the emergence of a shift towards corporate reporting on sustainability happening globally. The primary reason being that of the entities increasingly acknowledging and recognising the impact of their operations on the environment and society at large. Besides the publication of Kuveyt Türk's Sustainable Finance Framework, an allocation report and an impact report are supposed to be published by Kuveyt Türk within a time period of 12 months from the date of the issuance. Such reporting builds the confidence of investors in the sustainable value of their investments. Kuveyt Türk was of the opinion that this should not become burdensome.

Last, Kuveyt Türk was able to generate an appeal to a broad range of investors through the assurance of Tier 2 certificates which were ultimately sustainability trust certificates. It is in this way that a diversified investor base was simultaneously achieved.

The process of green or sustainable *Sukuk* issuance entails a combined process of traditional *Sukuk* issuance as well as the incorporation of ESG-specific elements (in association with the management of the use of proceeds, independent third-party reviewers and ongoing sustainability reporting). Out of all other things required, innovative structuring is one of the most important components. At the same time, advice of experienced legal counsel should be sought by transaction parties for navigating such issues (extracted from Akin Gump, 2021).

13.4 Challenges and Opportunities

The green *Sukuk* market is at a relatively smaller size because of a combination of challenges as discussed below.

13.4-1 Marginal Market

It is undeniably true that there are multiple reasons to be optimistic about the green *Sukuk* market but at the same time, a few challenges persist. Requirements of clear uniform standards particularly subjected to taxonomy, certification and regulation remain missing. The justification as to why there exists an insufficient share of the green *Sukuk* market can be understood through the following explanations:

- Green *Sukuk* issuance is perceived to generate benefits that remain uncertain.
- The issuance of green *Sukuk* issuance corresponds to higher costs and complex processes.
- Irrespective of substantial improvements, there still remains a lack in the standardisation procedure thereby, making it difficult for market participants.
- Being relatively young in the overall *Sukuk* market, it is not possible for green *Sukuk* to offer the level of credentials or the amount of supply that investors are expecting.
- Stakeholders continue to remain threatened by the risk of being greenwashed.

All market participants experience these challenges. The significance of the challenges for different participants are likely to vary:

- Issuers are apprehensive towards green *Sukuk* issuance because of the process being complex without a clear financial incentive. There is also a lack of identifiable projects to finance as well as the existence of high risks of greenwashing.
- Investors remain reluctant about the same owing to the key issues associated with the lack of standardised frameworks, the demanding level of requirements, and the liquidity problem.

When Islamic financial institutions deal with their clients on the issuance of green *Sukuk*, they have to simultaneously cater to the concerns associated with operations and management.

There are also several other challenges, some of which are discussed below.

13.4–2 Unclear Benefit

Green *Sukuk* issuance does generate benefit but there exists an uncertain idea around the benefit. It therefore emphasises on the essential role that intermediaries play in issuing companies. In the initial days, qualified teams were put up by Islamic financial institutions for green *Sukuk* issuances. These teams played the role of an advisory and dedicated greater proportion of resources for originating a green *Sukuk* issuance. This might include the identification of strategic proceeds, development and review of a green *Sukuk* framework, liaison with second-party opinions and so forth. In this context, Islamic financial institutions are not likely to charge an extra penny to issuers owing to the fact that it can possibly weaken the perception of a green issuance and result in making it less competitive than traditional bonds. It will sound sensible to employ and widen a dedicated coverage team when the market matures and attains a critical size. Furthermore, their summary report on green finance published in 2016 put into focus that G20 members explicitly mentioned the lack of clarity of green activities and products as an investment hurdle (Climate Bonds Initiative, 2020). Besides this, other financial obstacles comprised of existing high subsidy levels for the production and consumption of fossil fuels, green bond market still maturing, and the absence of a single carbon price which discourages companies to offer low-carbon solutions to the market; the structural obstacles included transaction costs. A lack of standardised frameworks has also been mentioned for green *Sukuk* to get mispriced often. As a matter of fact, green *Sukuk* would ultimately end up remaining less attractive as compared to brown projects.

13.4–3 Lack of Supply

The development of green assets is taking place at a rapid speed, but they still constitute a relatively limited asset class. In simple words, the taxonomy of what shapes up the definition of a green asset is still at an infant stage. The current focus on green *Sukuk* revolves around adaptation and mitigation related projects which can act as a limitation for companies which are more familiar with socially responsible investments. Green *Sukuk* are not opted adequately by companies willing to develop socially oriented projects (e.g. affordable housing, education, sustainable sourcing). Thus, the combination of green and social projects in sustainable bonds/*Sukuk* offer a wider array of approaches and ensure more flexibility. However, there is a requirement for the proceeds of green, social, and sustainable bonds/*Sukuk* to be segregated into specific projects, thereby remaining to be a limit for green investments to be expanded. In addition to this, there exists a risk in terms of cannibalisation. With entities issuing sustainability bonds and not green, the supply of green projects can become significantly restricted.

13.4–4 Costly in the Process of Issuance

Certain requirements post the issuance of a green *Sukuk* are required for its management in the long run. This includes monitoring, disclosure and impact reporting in adherence with the global bond principles (GBPs) and can possibly end up acting as a major deterring factor. Issuers must be prepared before a green *Sukuk* issuance itself. Staff aware about environmental, social and governance (ESG) issues need to be hired and trained; environmental accounting must be developed. Emphasis must be laid on environmental, social and governance communication, like that of sustainability reports for investors, shareholders and customers. A framework must be developed in alignment with the GBP prior to the issuance; a second-party opinion has to be obtained for analysing the strategies designed by the issuer for ESG risks and mitigation; the project selected, the funds allocated and the reporting process have to be reviewed; and opinions have to be obtained subjected to the social and environmental impact of the projects.

13.4–5 Opportunities

Green *Sukuk* ultimately constitute *Shari'ah*-compliant investments with regard to renewable energy and other environmental assets. *Shari'ah* concerns are being addressed to ensure the protection of the environment. Proceeds generated are used in financing construction, refinancing construction debt, or for financing the payment of a government-granted green subsidy. Green *Sukuk* might involve ensuring security to future income cash flows from ring-fenced projects or assets based on certain criteria. There exist multiple opportunities for green *Sukuk* in the solar energy plans of Gulf countries. There exists a simultaneous potential to be used as renewable sources of energy in facilitating sustainable development. Moreover, significant investments are required for protecting themselves from climate change and its consequences.

13.5 Conclusion

A *Sukuk* is referred to as an interest-free Islamic bond generating returns to investors in complete compliance with the principles of Islamic law (*Shari'ah*). Certain common grounds that are familiar to both green *Sukuk* and green bonds can be used to channelise the Islamic capital markets and maximise private sector financing for environmental projects:

1. In both these cases, funds are raised for a particular purpose. The asset-based structure of a *Sukuk* complements the green bond structure because investors get to be ensured with a higher degree of certainty that the funds raised are used for the designated purpose only.
2. Both of these are based on values that are deeply associated with ethically and socially responsible principles. It must be remembered that the assets financed by *Sukuk* do not include investments made in gambling, weapons, pork and alcohol and other forbidden sectors.
3. The ideas of catering to the protection of the environment, the protection of air, water and land, and the ecosystems that depend on them constitute as the intrinsic crux of *Shari'ah* principles. Irrespective of having absolute potential, the green *Sukuk* market didn't grow relatively well because of the lack of knowledge at the issuer and investor levels regarding the process and benefits of such issuances; perceptions about complexity and pricing; absence of a uniform and standardised framework, lack of consensus for coordinating policies among government agencies, lack of bankable green projects and so forth.

The investors, issuers and enabling Islamic financial institutions have been experiencing multiple challenges across their investment, underwriting and group-wide risk management practices with respect to green *Sukuk*. These hurdles are preventing green *Sukuk* from being leveraged as an essential instrument in addressing challenges related to climate change. Expansion of the green *Sukuk* market is hindered by certain factors, some of which are lack of clarity in perceptions around financial benefits from issuers, limited benchmarks, scarcity of supply diversity and liquidity, a deficit of standard approaches for the management of proceeds, and difficulties associated with impact reporting which ultimately possesses the risks of greenwashing.

To be able to ensure the expansion of the green *Sukuk* market, certain steps need to the initiated. First and foremost, it is imperative to put in effort for shaping up a standardisation of issuance through the development of a uniform green bond/*Sukuk* framework. A common standard that can be applied to a greater section will undoubtedly attract more issuers and investors. As the next step, transparency and disclosure need to be improved by facilitating the sharing of knowledge sharing and bringing impact measurement and reporting procedures into effect with the promotion of the Taskforce for Climate-Related Financial Disclosures Framework (Climate Bonds Initiate, 2020). Third, it is essential for the green *Sukuk* market to be distinguished from other instruments, like transition bonds and sustainability-linked instruments which can further help in reducing the risk of greenwashing. Fourth, a mechanism needs to be incorporated which would facilitate investments in emerging economies and can serve as a relevant source of issuance.

The scalability of the green *Sukuk* market will eventually depend on a paradigm shift. At present, stakeholders consider the green *Sukuk* market as a communication tool and perceive the economic benefit generating out of it to be mostly unclear or relatively limited. However, the green *Sukuk* market can obtain a data-driven legitimacy in terms of sustainability as well as financial returns. That shift has the potential to eventually lower transaction costs and bring in more issuers, particularly the smaller ones. On a wider investor base being generated, the scope of green *Sukuk* can get considerably expanded to more corporate sectors and geographies.

Review Questions

1. What is green *Sukuk*?
2. What are the similarities and differences between green bonds and green *Sukuk*?
3. Why conventional green *Sukuk* might not meet the needs of investors who adhere to the principles of Islamic finance?
4. What are the challenges in green *Sukuk* issuance?
5. Discuss the eligibility of the types of projects under green *Sukuk* schemes.

References

Akin Gump (2021), *ESG Sukuk: A Next Step in the Evolution of the Global Sukuk Market*, retrieved from www.akingump.com/en/news-insights/esg-and-sukuk-in-the-middle-east.html (Access date October 15, 2021)

Arab News (2021, July 18), ESG to Spur Demand for Green Sukuk as Sustainable Assets top $40 Trillion, *Arab News*, retrieved from www.arabnews.com/node/1896151/business-economy (Access date October 15, 2021)

Azhgaliyeva, D, Kapoor, A and Liu, Y (2020), Green Bonds for Financing Renewable Energy and Energy Efficiency in South-East Asia: A Review of Policies, *Journal of Sustainable Finance & Investment*, 10(2), 113–140.

Bloomberg NFE (2019), *Clean Energy Investment Trends*, retrieved from https://www.gihub.org/resources/publications/bnef-new-energy-outlook-2019/ (Access date October 23, 2021)

Climate Bonds Initiative (2020), *Green Sukuk*, retrieved from www.climatebonds.net/projects/facilitation/green-sukuk (Access date January 31, 2021)

CICERO (2021), *CICERO Shades of Green 2021-Best Green Practices*, retrieved from https://cicero.green/ (Access date July 6, 2021)

Fitch Wire (2020), *Sukuk Issuance Picking Up After Coronavirus Slowdown*, retrieved from www.fitchratings.com/research/islamic-finance/sukuk-issuance-picking-up-after-coronavirus-slowdown-20-07-2020 (Access date May 6, 2021)

ICMA (2021, June), *Green Bond Principles Voluntary Process Guidelines for Issuing Green Bonds*, retrieved from www.icmagroup.org/assets/documents/Sustainable-finance/2021-updates/Green-Bond-Principles-June-2021-100621.pdf (Access date June 2, 2021)

World Bank (2018), *Green Bonds Proceeds Management and Reporting*, retrieved from https://documents1.worldbank.org/curated/en/246031536956395600/pdf/129937-WP-Green-Bond-Proceeds-Management-and-Reporting.pdf (Access date May 4, 2020)

World Bank (2020, October), *Pioneering the Green Sukuk: Three Years on*, Washington, DC: World Bank

14

THE BASEL STANDARDS IN RELATION TO ISLAMIC FINANCE AS AN INTERNATIONAL REGULATORY FRAMEWORK

Learning Objectives

On completing this chapter, learners will be able to:

- Comprehend Basel norms and accords in the form of international standards for financial institutions issued by the Basel Committee on Banking Supervision (BCBS)
- Describe the setting of arrangements by the BCBS which highlights the risks corresponding to banks and financial systems
- Become familiar with the Basel Accords/standards applicable in the Islamic financial system.

14.1 Introduction

Traditional perspective, banks have been playing the role of being the financial intermediaries, wherein they would serve to fulfil the demands of funding required. It is because of banks that people are able to purchase homes. With the facilitation of spending and investment, banks help in fuelling growth in the economy. The vital roles played by the bank in the economy do not necessarily signify that they get to be absolutely free from encountering failure. Just like any other business, banks can go bankrupt as well. However, bank failures, particularly large-scale ones, can have consequential impacts. Examples can be taken of the well-known Great Depression and the last global financial crisis during 2007–2008 and its ensuing recession. An unhealthy bank is most likely to trigger economic calamities that can affect people in multitudes. Thus, it is imperative for banks to remain operational in a safe and sound manner so that failure can be avoided. If governments provide diligent regulation of banks, the same can be ensured. With the onset and

DOI: 10.4324/9780429321207-14

rapid growth of globalisation, banking activities are no longer restricted to the borders of a particular country or jurisdiction. The rapid increase of cross-border banking activities, the need for international cooperation in bank regulation has simultaneously risen. The Basel Committee on Bank Supervision (BCBS) has been brought into effect with the vision of being able to meet this need.

As the international advisory authority on bank regulation, the BCBS has successfully put forth guidance on issues critical to ensuring health in the banking systems across the world. One of the most important issues which also happens to be of vital importance in the recent global financial crisis is the regulation of bank capital. The BCBS has been addressing this issue consistently over the last two decades, as a result of which capital adequacy standards have been promulgated in a way that can be implemented by national regulators. These standards are collectively known as the Basel Accords, which were named after the city in Switzerland where the BCBS resides. There have been times when the Basel Accords did stir up disagreements, but they are undoubtedly very important to the formulation of regulatory policies subjected to bank capital. Up until now, three such accords have been produced by the BCBS.

The finalisation and approval of Basel I by the BCBS happened in 1988. Owing to the fact that the BCBS does not consist of any binding legal authority, countries could choose to refrain from adopting Basel I's standards. Interestingly, a lot of the BCBS member countries as well as several non-member countries adopted Basel I, but they did so by incorporating its features into their own domestic regulatory law. The work of BCBS emphasised banking at the international level. It was thereby perceived that the applicability of Basel I was intended for internationally active banks. However, over time, multiple countries happened to apply Basel I's requirements to all of their respective banks.

BCBS organised Basel II on the basis of the 'Three Pillar' approach. Our discussion will be primarily centred on Pillar I, which directly addresses the issue of calculating capital adequacy. Pillar I particularly attempts to rectify the deficiencies that are identified in Basel I. Supervisory review standards are being dealt with by Pillar II (of Basel II), while market discipline is taken care of by Pillar III (of Basel II). It must be noted that important aspects of capital regulation do not have a direct bearing on the calculation of bank capital adequacy.

The month of September 2010 saw the promulgation of Basel III by BCBS. The formal title of Basel III is 'A Global Regulatory Framework for More Resilient Banks and Banking Systems'. The title itself is a reflection of the attempts taken by BCBS to utilise the lessons learned during the financial crisis and subsequently apply them to the existing framework of banking regulation. Therefore, Basel III is not in any way a replacement for Basel II but serves as a counterpart. The major purpose of Basel III is to facilitate banks and financial institutions by improving their abilities to absorb asset losses without any adverse impact on the economy at large. The BCBS developed Basel III in the form of a set of measures that have been agreed upon internationally. Basel III came about in response to the financial crisis of 2007–2009. These measures are aimed at strengthening the regulation, supervision, and risk management of banks. The ultimate intent of bringing the Basel III package into effect as an agreed standard was to make sure that the financial system does not suffer the kind of crisis and collapse it did during the economic slowdown between 2007 and 2009. On 7 December 2017, the Group of Central Bank Governors and Heads of Supervision (GHOS), the Basel Committee's oversight body, endorsed the reforms that were brought into regulation after the crisis. On 14 January 2019, the GHOS endorsed the adjustments to the market risk framework. The revised standards are expected to bring resilience to financial systems and simultaneously restore faith and confidence in banking and other financial systems. They encompass the following:

- An unweighted leverage ratio
- Two new capital buffers: a conservation buffer and a countercyclical buffer
- New and substantial capital charges for cleared derivatives that have not been cleared and other financial market transactions
- Significant revisions to the rules applied on the types of instruments that are considered as bank capital
- Minimum capital requirements for market risk.

The three sets of regulations (Accord), particularly Basel I, Basel II, and Basel III (BIS, 2017) are outlined below.

Basel I

- The introduction of Basel I occurred in 1988.
- Most of the focus centred on credit risk.
- When a borrower fails to repay a loan or meet the obligations of the contract as specified, the lender is likely to incur a loss, or what is termed 'credit risk'. From a traditional lens, credit risk is characterised by the lender possibly not receiving the owed principal and interest.
- It highlighted the capital and structure of risk weights for banks.
- The minimum required capital was kept at 8% of risk-weighted assets (RWA).
- RWA refers to assets having different risk profiles.

Let us take an example in this regard. An asset that has collateral in terms of backing is most likely to have lower risks in comparison to personal loans, where the collateral is absent.

Basel II

- The BCBS published the guidelines of Basel II in 2004.
- Basel II was the refined and reformed version of Basel I.

- Three parameters, or what the committee refers as 'pillars', have been used in determining the guidelines:
    - Capital adequacy requirements: A minimum capital adequacy requirement of 8% of risk assets has to be maintained by the banks.
    - Supervisory review: This entailed banks developing and using better risk management techniques for monitoring and managing the three types of risks that a bank faces, namely credit, market and operational risks.
    - Market discipline: As per this guideline, disclosure requirements are to be increased. The mandate compels banks to the disclosure of their CAR, risk exposure, and so forth to the central bank.

Basel III

- The guidelines on Basel III were released in 2010.
- These guidelines were developed as a response to the economic crisis of 2008.
- Pertaining to banks in the developed economies being under-capitalised, over-leveraged and being largely reliable on short-term funding, the importance of strengthening the system became a necessity.
- The capital under Basel II, in terms of quality as well as quantity, was observed to be insufficient for handling any further risk.
- The guidelines are aimed to bring stronger resilience to the banking system by putting emphasis on four important parameters of banking, namely capital, leverage, funding, and liquidity.
    - Capital: The maintenance of the capital adequacy ratio has to be done at 12.9%. The minimum Tier 1 capital ratio has to be maintained at 10.5%, and the minimum Tier 2 capital ratio has to be maintained at 2% of RWA. Moreover, banks are essentially required to maintain 2.5% of a capital conservation buffer as well as 0%–2.5% of countercyclical buffer.
    - Leverage: The leverage rate has to be a minimum of 3%. The leverage rate can be understood as the ratio of Tier 1 capital of the bank to its average total consolidated assets.
    - Funding and liquidity: Two liquidity ratios have been created by Basel III, namely LCR (liquidity coverage ratio) and NSFR (net stable funds rate).
- The LCR makes it a mandate for banks to hold a considerable quantity of a buffer of high-quality liquid assets. This is aimed to be used in dealing with the cash outflows encountered in an acute short-term stress scenario as specified by supervisors.
    - Prevention of situations like bank runs becomes possible with LCR. The goal is to make sure that the liquidity possessed by banks is at least enough for a 30-days stress period, in case such a scenario happens.
- As per the NSFR, a stable funding profile has to be necessarily maintained by banks corresponding to their off-balance-sheet assets and activities. As per

NSFR, banks need to fund their activities through stable sources of finance (reliable over a time period of a year.)

- The minimum NSFR requirement is 100%.

Hence, LCR attempts to measure resilience of banks for a shorter duration (30 days), while NSFR does the same for a medium term (1 year).

14.2 Basel Accord Application in Islamic Banks and Financial Institutions

Islamic banks are believed to be one of the best capitalised banks in the world. Their historical compliance with inflexible capitalisation standards for capital requirements imply that local banks already surpass the norms as fixed by the Bank for International Settlements (BIS) as part of the Basel I, II and III Accords. The capital requirements of a majority proportion of banks as prescribed in Basel III are far stricter than before. The fact that Islamic banks are among the best capitalised banking sectors globally puts them on the safer spectrum in comparison to their European or US counterparts. At present, the Tier 1 and total capital requirements of Islamic bank stand at 8% and 12%, respectively. The percentage proportion is already at a higher place, comparing to the target 2019 ratios put forth by Basel III.

It is true that the balance sheet underlying the rules of the Basel Accords pertains to the conventional banking system, the structural composition of which is largely different from that of Islamic banking system, not only in terms of liability but also assets. The Islamic banks had to adhere to the international standard of Basel Accords owing to capital adequacy becoming the major check for safety which is again a reflection of supervisory concerns. The credibility of Islamic banks has been undoubtedly enhanced with the adoption of Basel Accords. At the same time, growth of Islamic banks across the world got boosted with the adoption of the Accords irrespective of no such specific requirement addressing the particularity of Islamic banks' balance sheet structure was put forth as a mandate under these Accords.

The Islamic banking system has emerged as a financial system of global recognition. Basel II and Basel III do not view conventional banks and Islamic banks through different lenses. Irrespective of the limitations of the Basel standards on being applied to Islamic banks, the Islamic Financial Service Board (IFSB) has put in a lot of effort in developing standards or guidelines that tend to specify risk issues, particular to Islamic financing. Efforts have been simultaneously made in the adaption of certain elements from the Basel standards in such a way that their implications to Islamic banks and Islamic financial institutions (IFIs) become more relevant. The IFSB's Capital Adequacy Standard which was issued in 2005 formed the basis of the Capital Adequacy Framework for Islamic banks and eventually went on to make an issuance of a revised framework in 2007 subject to the Basel II revised accord. Moreover, keeping the Basel III guidelines in view, the IFSB published a risk management and capital adequacy guidance note for commodity *murabaha* (trade related cost plus mode of finance) transactions in December 2011. The previous work done by the IFSB, especially in those areas, is being complemented by the guidance note (IFSB, 2011).

In 2007, the Capital Adequacy Framework for Islamic banks was issued, which addresses potential risks to be encountered by Islamic banks in terms of credit, market, operational and liquidity. Risks typical to the transactions associated with Islamic banking like that of *Shari'ah* non-compliance risk, rate-of-return risk, displaced commercial risk, and inventory and equity investment risks have been simultaneously addressed. However, the concern is whether individual regulators of Islamic financial institutions are permitted exemptions to follow the IFSB standards within their jurisdictions or are given uniform treatment like that of other institutions which follow the Basel II standard. A majority of Muslim countries adopted the Basel II standards, especially making adherence to the standardised approach to risk measurement. However, several opinions and questions exist regarding how the new set of international capital adequacy standards in the Basel III proposals would get adapted so that they can fit into the market dynamics of those jurisdictions where Islamic finance is actively operational.

Due to their activities being very specific in nature, IFIs bear different risks from those outlined in Basel II. The difference in the risks can vary, nonetheless they are distinctively different. The IFSB, to the best of its ability, has attempted to develop a better capital adequacy framework that addressed the risk profile of IFIs. However, it also holds true that a larger segment of IFSB's efforts in developing a regulatory framework for Islamic banks already exist as guidelines for conventional banks. It must be clearly understood that Basel III is not symbolic of a third version of capital requirement for banks but rather represents reinforcement of Basel II framework. To put it more simply, the Basel III must be perceived as a response to systemic failures that occurred in the conventional banking system, which is why attempts are made to prevent the occurrence of similar problems in the future that Islamic financing might get trapped into.

Numerous issues are yet to be clarified and addressed owing to the particular nature of financing techniques that have been developed by Islamic banks.

14.2-1 Capital Adequacy Framework Under the Basel Accord

Capital adequacy ratios can be defined as a measure of the amount of capital that should be held by a bank. It is expressed in terms of the percentage of the bank's total risk-weighted assets. Under the agreements of Basel I and Basel II, for classification to be done for the banks as 'adequate capitalised', a minimum of 8% capital to assets rations is to be held (Tier 1 representing at least 4% in Basel I). The division of total capital by total risk-weighted assets is done for computing the capital adequacy ratio. On the basis of credit and counterparty risk, Basel I assets can be classified into five risk groups: 0%, 10%, 20%, 50%, and 100%. The Basel I Accord was found to have several loopholes, which is why it became subject to further review. For instance, short-term funding was considered less risky than long-term financing, as a result of which a weight of 20% was received. On the other hand, anything with a maturity greater than one year was risk-weighted 100%. This risk-weighting system most likely stirred up financial instability by promoting short-term lending at the expense of longer term stable credit.

14.2-1-1 New Basel II

A consultative document has been released by the BCBS subjecting to the confirmation of its proposal for the Basel Accord in 2001. The document covers three areas that happen to be mutually reinforcing areas. These areas are also termed as 'pillars', which include:

- Minimum capital requirements
- The supervisory review process
- Market discipline.

The first pillar is involved in reviewing the calculation of minimum capital requirements and technical issues paving the way for capital adequacy requirements. With the second pillar, major principles have been established. These principles were developed and designed for ensuring an efficient supervisory process. The third pillar is involved in reviewing minimum disclosure requirements necessary for strengthening market discipline (Basel Committee on Bank Supervision, 2011; Muljawan et al., 2004). The Basel II Accord does not make an attempt to change the conceptual understanding of capital but rather modifies the process of computing risk-weighted assets with the incorporation of two additional types of risk: market risk and operational risk. Market risk is generated from the risk of losses in on- and off-balance-sheet positions arising from the fluctuations in market prices. As per the innovations under Basel II, classifications of bank activities are done either into banking or trading books for the purpose of calculating the capital adequacy ratio. The banking book is inclusive of all the activities related to banking, like transformation of the depositors' funds. The trading book, on the other hand, consists of the activities that involve buying and selling of securities. The exposure to market risk as gained by the bank is easily reflected in their portfolio of securities, which is why the estimation is made on the basis of its trading book.

Operational risk can be understood as the risk of less resulting from inadequate internal processes. The capital adequacy ratio for conventional banks as per the specifications of Pillar 1 of Basel II is expressed in the form of the capital adequacy ratio. Thus:

$$(\mathrm{CAR}) = \frac{Tier1\ Capital + Tier2\ Capital}{Risk\ Weighted\ Assets}$$

(Note that Tier 1 capital consists of current accounts, savings accounts, time deposits, certificates of deposit and share capital plus reserves. Tier 2 capital consists of cumulative preferred shares plus subordinated debt.) The methodology opted for the calculation of risk-weighting assets is crucial because this is an implication that with assets getting riskier, banks will simultaneously need to increase its capital base to be able to remain adequately capitalised. Pillar 1 of Basel II has put forth a detailed framework for the calculation of risk-weighted assets to be able to face risks at different levels that otherwise are faced by conventional banks in most of their regular activities.

14.2-1-2 Basel III: Higher Capital Requirements and Liquidity Rules

In December 2010, two documents including a reform to the minimum capital requirements of banks were issued by the BCBS. The committee developed the framework, Basel III, as a response to the last financial crisis. One must understand that Basel III is not symbolic of a third version of capital requirement for banks but rather represents reinforcement of the Basel II framework. The latest curation of rules in the form of Basel III (BCBS, 2011) along with the transitional arrangements are briefly discussed below.

14.2–1–2–1 New Capital Requirements

1. Capital ratios and deductions (Core Tier 1/common equity): The rules under Basel II have put forth the mandate that a bank must hold 2% of Core Tier 1 capital to risk-weighted assets. Core Tier 1 comprises ordinary shares, retained earnings and profits. With Basel III, the existing rules are replaced with a stricter categorisation of 'common equity', which is the total of common shares and retained income. As per these rules, banks are mandated to hold 4.5% of common equity.
2. Total Tier 1: The requirement of total Tier 1 escalates from 4% to 6% under Basel III. This is an implication of the fact that other types of Tier 1 instrument, referred as additional going concern capital, can add up to 1.5% of Tier 1 capital.
3. Total capital: With reference to a new capital buffer, the total minimum capital requirement is set at 8%. It must be taken care that Tier 1 should hold 6% of capital. This implies that not more than 2% of capital can be held by Tier 2. There will be no divisions of Tier 2 into upper and lower tiers. Tier 3, used solely for the purpose of market risk, will be entirely removed.
4. Deductions from capital: Generally, under Basel III, capital is deducted from common equity Tier 1. This is quite a strict rule as compared to the current one, where considerable deductions are made from total capital. However, amendments made to Basel III and brought into effect in July 2010 relaxed some of the proposed deductions. This led to the allowance of partial inclusion of minority interests, some of the deferred tax assets as well as

mortgage-servicing rights instead of completely deducting them as per the proposal made in December 2009.

14.2–1–2–2 New Capital Buffer

1. Capital conservation buffer: Banks are mandated to hold enough capital for being able to meet the minimum capital ratios. The mandate also extends for banks to have a capital conservation buffer above the minimum 8% total capital. This buffer is set at 2.5%. After all the necessary deductions, the buffer must only hold common equity. For their practical usage, common equity capital should be equivalent to 7% of risk-weighted assets. The exception is the stress period, when the buffer is allowed to be drawn down. This evidently portrays more than a threefold increase in the present 2% Core Tier 1 requirement. The buffer is designed in order to ensure that capital levels are maintained in banks throughout a significant downturn. The buffer also aims to ensure that banks do not discretely deplete their capital buffers by giving dividend payments. Banks not qualifying the requirement of this buffer will not be allowed to pay dividends, buy shares back and pay discretionary employee bonuses.
2. Countercyclical buffer: Adding to the conservation buffer is the countercyclical buffer, under which banks might sometimes need to hold a buffer of up to 2.5% of capital in terms of common equity or other fully loss-absorbing capital. This buffer serves as a macro-prudential tool for protecting banks from extremely high credit growth periods. The buffer is regulated at the discretion of the national regulators. Thus, the application of this buffer is done when a national regulator thinks that there is excessive credit growth in the national economy, as a result of which the countercyclical buffer is brought into effect as an extension of the capital conservation buffer.

14.2–1–2–3 Leverage Ratio

It is already known that banks in the United States have been subject to a leverage ratio for a considerable amount of time. However, the leverage ratio was not an initial component of the Basel regulatory framework. As per the agreement of the committee, an unweighted ratio of 3% was analysed over a transition period. Several changes occurred in features of the ratio owing to them being set out in its July 2010 revisions. Among multiple changes, allowance is made for netting on the basis of Basel II rules.

14.2–1–2–4 Systemically Important Banks

As per the statement provided by the committee, systemically important banks must be subjected to higher capital requirements compared to those in the Basel III package. However, work is in progress on the proposals. Options consist of capital surcharges, contingent capital and bail-in-debt.

14.2–1–2–5 Liquidity Rules

The latest liquidity coverage ratio and net stable funding ratio are likely to be brought into effect according to the timing as discussed below.

- Common equity, Tier 1, total capital and national implementation: New capital ratios were put into effect through national implementation on 1 January 2013. As per the new mandate, banks are required to have 3.5% common equity, 4.5% Tier 1 capital and 8% total capital. In 2014, the minimum requirement was increased to 4% for common equity and 5.5% for Tier 1 capital followed by a further increase in full ratios in 2015, where 4.5% was meant to be for common equity and 6% was meant to be for Tier 1 capital.
- Grandfathering of existing capital instruments: Capital instruments that do not sync with the mandates in order to be included in the common equity element of Tier 1 ceased to be counted as common equity from 1 January 2013. In case of particular instruments, the issuance of which is done by non-joint stock companies which have been Core Tier 1 at that present time, the grandfathering was done on a declining basis over a longer span of time. A set of conditions was applied including the provision of treating the instruments as equity under prevailing accounting standards. Capital instruments no longer qualifying as non-common equity Tier 1 capital or Tier 2 capital got phased out during the course of a 10-year period from 1 January 2013. Initially capped at 90%, a decrease by 10% each year was identified. Instruments having an incentive to be redeemed were phased out at their effective maturity date. The instruments whose issuance was made prior to 12 September 2010 qualified for the transitional arrangements. Existing public-sector capital injections had been exempted until 1 January 2018.
- Regulatory deductions: Several deductions were integrated. At the initial start, 20% of the required deductions from common equity were applicable by 1 January 2014, which went on to be hiked by 20% the following year until 100% of the deductions were made from common equity by 1 January 2018.
- Capital buffers: On 1 January 2016, the capital conservation buffer was brought into effect at 0.625%, which was supposed to reach 2.5% by 1 January 2019. As per the committee's statements, banks which fulfil their general ratios but still happen to stay below the 7% common equity target during the transition period must 'maintain prudent earnings' to be able to meet the buffer at earliest. This mandate lacked a bit of clarity in terms of whether the requirement would hold banks adhering to transitional capital buffer phase in

requirements over the period until 1 January 2019 but happened to not meet the 7% requirement until that date.

- Leverage ratio: The ratio requirement of 3% was supposed to run parallel starting from 1 January 2013 to 2017. The committee was in charge of tracking the ratio, its component factors and impact over this time span and required bank-level disclosure of the ratio and its factors from 1 January 2015. The results determined the final adjustments to be made to the ratio in the first half of 2017 so that effective implementation could be done from 1 January 2018.
- Liquidity ratios: The liquidity coverage ratio was brought into effect on 1 January 2015. The application of the net stable funding ratio as a minimum standard started from 1 January 2018.

14.3 Basel Methodology to Islamic Banking and Finance

It must be notably mentioned that the Basel II standards do not account for particular risks associated with the nature of the activities of Islamic banks. Islamic finance is fundamentally built on the principle of fairness, which is why the primary structural format of any Islamic financial institution starts with fee-based revenues for services offered along with the sharing of profits and losses. Therefore, talking from the spiritual perspective, it can be said that Islamic financial institutions are closer to asset management companies in comparison to conventional banking institutions. Also, their operations happen to have a unique impact on the balance sheets. The key distinction of Islamic banks from conventional banks can be traced that their activities are not confined to financial intermediation only. An Islamic bank plays multiple roles: an investor, a trader, a financial advisor, a consultant and a financing house. This leads to the occurrence of several Islamic modes of financing, each one being characteristically different from the other and equally affecting both sides of the bank's balance sheet in its own way. The unique characteristics of Islamic banks are put into the limelight through these specifications. At the same time, concern is being raised subjected to the applicability of the Basel methodology to Islamic banks.

The risks emerging out of the operational structures of Islamic banks differ from the conventional risks backed by their peers. These risks are not accounted for in Basel II. For being able to apply the Basel Capital Accord guidelines within the Islamic banking system, prior to the IFSB guidelines, the proposals of Accounting and Auditing Organisation for Islamic Financial Institutions (AAOIFI) capital adequacy framework was put forth before Islamic banks for consideration.

14.3-1 AAOIFI Capital Adequacy Framework

The AAOIFI attempted to develop a better capital adequacy framework in 1999. The framework was designed with the purpose of addressing the risk profile of Islamic banks. A method was proposed by the AAOIFI for the calculation of the capital adequacy ratio for Islamic banks. A larger portion of the methodology used is based on Basel II standards; the primary difference relates to the liabilities side of Islamic banks' balance sheets.

To speak from a factual perspective, sources of funds of Islamic banks are different from those of conventional banks. When the capital adequate ratio of Islamic banks is evaluated as per equation (14.1), the calculation of capital is not complex or difficult because there are neither preferred shares nor subordinated debt. This implies that the capital sources of the Islamic banks are current accounts and savings accounts. The equity capital and reserves of the shareholders are also included. Investment accounts are of two major types: restricted and unrestricted. The funds collected under restricted investment accounts are representative of fiduciary services because investment decisions are being made by depositors while the Islamic bank, in terms of an agent, just collects the respective fee. Those funds are invested as per the directives of the clients and are not at the discretion of the banks; they cannot be included in a bank's source of funds. As per the recommendations given by the AAOIFI, restricted investment accounts can be included as off-balance-sheet items provided that such investment funds should not be included when calculating the capital adequacy ratio.

The inclusion of unrestricted investment accounts must be done in the balance sheet of Islamic banks and have to be subsequently considered in the capital adequacy ratio. An important aspect that is worth mentioning here is the characteristic liability of Islamic banks, wherein unrestricted investment account holders agree to share profit and loss with the bank. This is an implication of the fact that these funds cannot be guaranteed by assigning them 100% weight in calculating the capital adequacy ratio. This will then be in contradictory terms to the *Shari'ah* principle of participation. The AAOIFI document on capital adequacy is aimed at addressing this issue so that appropriate risk weights to unrestricted investments can be determined. In the risk-sharing scheme proposed by AAOIFI, investment account holders share a section of the risk with shareholders.

The capital adequacy ratio (CAR) for an Islamic bank is calculated as:

$$\text{CAR} = \frac{\textit{Total Capital}}{RWA_{K\delta CA} + 50\%\left(RWA_{UIA}\right)}$$

Here $RWA_{K\delta CA}$ symbolises the average risk-weighted assets which have been financed by the bank's capital and depositors' current accounts, while RWA_{UIA} symbolises the average risk-weighted assets which have been financed by the investment accounts of the unrestricted depositors.

The proposal put forth by AAOIFI undoubtedly serves as an important contribution in the unexplored topic of how the risk exposure of Islamic banks is accounted following which the development of a reliable capital adequacy framework is done. At the same time, one needs to understand that these AAOIFI proposals do not necessarily deal with the characteristic specifications of Islamic banks assets and the specific risks associated with them most likely because of the lack of implementation of standards accepted uniformly throughout the industry for Islamic banking practices.

14.3-2 The IFSB Capital Adequacy Framework

As an international entity, the Islamic Financial Services Board (IFSB) plays the role in setting regulatory and supervisory agencies whose main domain of work entails ensuring the reliability and stability of the Islamic financial services industry. IFSB functions around the key objective of 'promoting, spreading and harmonizing best practices in the regulation and supervision of the Islamic financial services industry'. To be more specific, the standardisation of *Shari'ah* committee rulings on Islamic banking practices is dealt with by the IFSB. At the same time, it makes attempts to standardise the approach, the application of which can help in identifying risks in *Shari'ah*-compliant products and services. The IFSB also assigns risk weights that are in sync with internationally acceptable prudential standards.

14.3-2-1 The IFSB Proposal

Similar to that of the AAOIFI proposal, the IFSB capital adequacy framework simultaneously plays the role of complementing guidelines on banking supervision by the Basel Committee to be able to meet the specific requirements of Islamic financial institutions. The emphasis of AAOIFI is on the sources of funds of an Islamic bank. Meanwhile, the IFSB does not only consider the uses of funds but also assigns appropriate risk weights to each asset item. IFSB's acknowledgement that the uses of funds for Islamic banks that are characteristically *Shari'ah* compliant are different from the typical asset side of the balance sheet for a conventional bank serves as a big-time contribution.

The IFSB framework is aimed at:

- The identification of the specificities in the structural format and contents of the *Shari'ah*-compliant products and services offered by Islamic banks that are not taken into consideration under Basel II or by the AAOIFI.
- The standardisation of *Shari'ah*-compliant products and services by assigning risk weights to those that fulfil the requirements to sync with internationally acceptable prudential standards.
- Developing a uniform format for the assessment of capital adequacy requirements of Islamic financial institutions.
- Incorporating market risk in the trading book as well in the banking book of Islamic banks owing to the nature of the banks' assets, such as *Murabaha, Ijara, Salam, Musharaka,* and *Mudarabah.*

In December 2005, the issuance of the 'Capital Adequacy Standard for Institutions (other than Insurance Institutions) Offering Only Islamic Financial Services' (IFSB, 2005a) took place by the IFSB. The specificity of investment account holders who share part of the risk with shareholders is being considered by the latest standard.

$$\text{Capital Adequacy Ratio } (\text{CAR}) = \frac{Tier1 + Tier2}{RWA_{(\textit{Credit Risk} + \textit{Market Risk} + \textit{Operational Risk})} \quad RWA \textit{ funded by Profit Sharing Investment Account}\,(PSIA)_{(\textit{credit risk} + \textit{market risk})}}$$

In this equation, $\text{RWA}_{(\text{Credit risk + Market risk + Operational risk})}$ includes those financed by both restricted profit sharing investment accounts (PSIA). Islamic financial institutions do not guarantee the capital amount of PSIA. Investment account holders have to bear the losses incurred as a result of investments or assets financed by PSIA. Therefore, a regulatory capital requirement is not commanded. This clearly indicates that assets funded by unrestricted or restricted PSIA should be excluded from the calculation of the denominator of the capital ratio.

14.3-2-2 Higher Capital Requirements and Liquidity Under Basel III and IFSB's Revised Proposal (Capital Conservation Buffer)

In accordance with the standards of Basel III, banks are mandatorily required to hold sufficient capital so as to fulfil the minimum capital ratios (at least 6% of RWA). Banks must also hold a capital conservation buffer above the minimum 8% total capital. Fixed at 2.5%, this buffer should be in common equity, after deductions. From its effective implication, common equity capital should be equivalent to 7% of risk-weighted assets (RWA). The exception is during time periods of financial distress when allowance is made for the buffer to be brought down. Hence, this is indicative of more than a threefold increase in the present 2% common equity Tier 1 (CET1) requirement.

Speaking from the context of Islamic banks, RWAs have to be defined in a different way. A typical Islamic bank generally consists of three fund resources: the respective bank's own capital, demand deposits and PSIA. This PSIA consists of further subdivisions: unrestricted investment accounts (UIA) and restricted investment accounts (RIA). In the UIA, the bank is entitled to discretely choose in making investments according to its will. The RIA account holders put forth to the bank the way it invests their funds in terms of contracts (IFSB, 2011). An Islamic bank plays the role of *mudarib* for these two types of accounts, which implies that neither profits nor the capital is guaranteed, which are both contingent on the success of the investment. As per the revised regulations, the Islamic banks simultaneously play the role in managing them on a *Wakalah* basis (agency contract) for which it does not earn from profit shares but earns only a fee (IFSB, 2011). However, the role observed to be in practice more often is that of being the *Mudarabah* between PSIA holders and an Islamic bank. Notably, certain market forces exist which prevent the mechanism of management of investment accounts (i.e. sharing of profit). They even do not guarantee the capital to work freely. Profits distributed to unrestricted investment account holders (UIAHs) are no longer attached to the performance of the underlying assets on a yearly basis.

It must be equally noted that certain Islamic banks, in dual as well as full-fledged Islamic banking systems, in numerous markets, are involved in implementing multiple practices so as to be able to give UIAHs an equivalent rate of return as compared to the respective market benchmark (IFSB, 2011). These technical implications make an Islamic bank have two reserves: profit equalisation reserve (PER) and investment risk reserve (IRR). The constitution of PER occurs prior to the allocation of profit which is available for distribution between shareholders and UIAHs. The constitution of IRR occurs after the bank takes its part of the profit as *mudarib*. In this context, PER is used in reducing the volatile effect of the return rate of the underlying assets in the distributed profit. The IRR, on the other hand, is used in compensating for the loss of capital for UIAHs (IFSB, 2005a). In both of these practices, part of the commercial risk (credit and market risk) initially supported by UIAHs is being borne by the shareholders. This transfer of risk from UIAHs to shareholders is termed 'displaced commercial risk' (DCR). To describe it with more accuracy, DCR is present only in the two former practices of 'smoothing' profit. If the bank is able to manage the volatility corresponding to the return rate of the assets by using PER and IRR, the DCR then will be nil (Sundarajan, 2008). As per the revised norms of the IFSB (2011), Islamic banks are compelled to manage the UIA as stated above owing to two reasons: the underlying assets do not meet a targeted return rate (temporarily or at all) and/or the supervisory authority from banks requires to give UIAHs a return rate as per a respective benchmark in order to ensure prevention of these banks from withdrawal risk which might lead to systemic risk.

In light of the above, the IFSB has taken the effect of DCR on capital requirement into consideration and modified the denominator of the capital adequacy ratio (CAR). The denominator of CAR, in the presence of DCR, is calculated as:

$$RWA_{DCR} = \left\{ \begin{array}{c} \textit{Total Risk Weighted Assets} \\ \textit{less} \\ \textit{Risk Weighted Assets by Restricted PSIA} \\ \textit{less} \\ (1-\alpha)\times(\textit{Risk Weighted Assets Funded by Unrestricted PSIA}) \\ \alpha\ (\textit{Risk Weighted Assets Funded by PER and IRR of Unrestricted} \\ \textit{PSIA} \end{array} \right\}$$

where α is symbolic of the part of profit added to the actual profit generated by assets funded by UIAH funds. When there is smoothing of profit to UIAHs, the distribution of profit to them will be the sum of:

- Actual profit generated during a year
- Profit transferred (share of *mudarib* and/or profit given as *Hibah* from shareholders)
- Part of profit taken from PER and IRR.

In terms of a conceptual take, α can be interpreted in correspondence with the part of assets funded by UIAs and generating the sum of profits in the second and third cases. In the case of not having DCR practiced by a given Islamic bank, α = 0, the value of the denominator will become:

$$\mathrm{RWA}_{\overline{\mathrm{DCR}}} = \left\{ \begin{array}{c} \textit{Total Risk Weighted Assets} \\ \textit{less} \\ \textit{Risk Weighted Assets Restricted PSIA} \\ \textit{less} \\ \textit{Risk Weighted Assets Funded by Unrestricted PSIA} \end{array} \right\}$$

The capital adequacy standard set by the IFSB (2005a) discretely gave the authority to supervisory bodies for defining the value of α on a case-by-case basis or to their jurisdiction as a whole. It was obvious for the amount of α to be arbitrary owing to the wide variation of smoothing mechanisms between Islamic financial entities, even if they were in the same jurisdiction. It was the guidelines of the IFSB in 2011 which talked about the methodology in calculating α for each Islamic bank. The methodology is quite an easy one and treats Islamic banks and financial institutions on an equal footing.

One has to carefully note that in addition to the minimum required regulatory capital, Islamic banks must retain at least 2.5% of RWA constituted from CET1 only in terms of capital conservation buffer. As CET1 is available to draw near the minimum 4.5% (75% of Tier1), an Islamic bank might be given two alternatives: its earnings can be retained by limiting the distribution of dividends, sharing buybacks and staff bonuses, and so forth. Otherwise, new capital can be raised from the private sector until the mandate of 7% of CET1 (4.5% + 2.5%) is attained. The part of profits belonging to PSIA in an Islamic bank must not be concerned with this restriction (retention of earnings). The point of view behind this is that assets financed by these accounts have been deducted from the calculation of risk weighted assets ($\mathrm{RWA}_{\overline{DCR}}$). But when DCR is present, smoothing part of the profits must be retained in the building of the buffer. For example, if P_{UIAH} symbolises the profit distributed to UIAHs and α is calculated for the given Islamic bank, we get:

$$P_{UIAH} + P_R + P_{per/irr} + P_{smooth}$$

where

P_R = actual profit generated by the assets funded by UIA during a year

$P_{per/irr}$ = profit taken from PER and IRR

P_{smooth} = profit transferred from shareholders' shares

In order for the buffer to be constituted, retaining the profit available for distribution to UIAHs will give us:

$$P_{smooth} = \alpha \; P_{UIAH} - + P_{per/irr}$$

Then the capital conservation buffer (*Ccb*) will be calculated as follows:

$$Ccb = 2.5\% \times RWA_{DCR}$$

The excessive on- and off-balance-sheet leverage that was developed in the conventional banking system has become a major factor in spreading the magnitude of the subprime crisis. This additional requirement was brought into effect by the Basel Committee on Bank Supervision (BCBS) owing to its quality to be a simple, transparent and non-risk-based 'backstop' measure. It can simultaneously serve as a credible supplementary measure to other risk-based capital measures (BCBS, 2010a). Two components are used in measuring the leverage ratio (LR): capital measure and exposure measure.

$$\text{LR} = \frac{Capital\ Measure}{Exposure\ Measure} \geq 3$$

The minimum value of 3% is still in the process of analysis and is likely to vary. The leverage ratio (LR) can be perceived as the average of the monthly LR over the quarter. As per the definitions prescribed in Basel III framework, capital measure refers to the amount of Tier 1 capital (Common Equity Tier 1 plus Additional Tier 1). One must note that the inclusion of PSIAs will be not done in additional Tier 1 capital owing to them not fulfilling certain criteria. Some of these criteria include that they must be held in the bank for a minimum of five years and their repayment of principal will need supervisory approval. The fact that PSIAs can be withdrawn before five years without notification to the supervisory authority accounts for the reasons of not integrating them.

In Basel III, the exposure measure is representative of the specific provisions and valuation adjustments of the accounting value of on-balance-sheet items. The components not taken into consideration for reducing the value of on-balance-sheet items are physical or financial collateral, guarantees and other credit risk mitigation. Allowance is equally not made for the netting of items in the assets and deposits. Assets financed by PSIAs are generally not included in the exposure measure because Tier 1 capital does not include PSIAs. However, on DCR being present, a proportion α of these assets should be included in the exposure measure, because then the financing is considered to have been done by shareholders' own capital. Similar to derivatives, repurchase agreements and securities finance do not find relevance for Islamic banks owing to the fact that they do not meet most of the *Shari'ah* requirements. To be able to incorporate in the exposure measure, off-balance-sheet items are converted into credit exposure equivalents by using a credit conversion factor (CCF) of 100% provided that a commitment is unconditionally cancellable by an Islamic bank at any given time without prior notice. In that case, a CCF of 10% will be applicable.

14.4 Risk Specification of IFIs

We are now well aware of the fact that the activities of Islamic banks differ in substance as well as in form from the operational format of conventional banks, which is why

TABLE 14.1 Difference of Risk Implications Between Conventional and Islamic Banks

Conventional Bank	*Islamic Bank*
Credit Risk	Credit Risk
Market Risk	Market Risk
➢ Equity risk	➢ Equity risk
➢ Commodity risk	➢ Commodity risk
➢ Interest rate risk	➢ Rate of return risk
➢ Foreign exchange risk	➢ Foreign exchange risk
Operational Risk	Operational Risk
	➢ Price risk
	➢ Fiduciary risk
	➢ Displace commercial risk

the risk profile faced by them is also very different. As per Basel II, three types of risk exposures have been identified for conventional banks: credit risk, market risk, and operational risk. Table 14.1 puts forth a comparative risk profile for conventional and Islamic banks. Credit risk is the default payment risk, and the allotment risk weights are done on the basis of counterparty risk. Market risk occurs as a result of the risk of losses in on- and off-balance-sheet positions emerging from shifts in market prices. It is applicable to the portfolio of financial instruments held by the bank and comprises four elements: interest rate risk (further divided into specific and general market risk), equity position risk, foreign exchange risk, and commodity risk. Operational risk is symbolic of the risk of loss that emerges as an outcome of inadequate internal processes.

Shari'ah scholars had identified a minimum of four risks during their initial attempts in catering to the specificities and characteristics of *Shari'ah*-compliant products and services. These risks have not been addressed under Basel II. In this particular section, the implication of risk on the trading and banking book of Islamic banks has been discussed. It is often argued that credit and operational risks can be accounted for in a similar way for both Islamic and conventional banks, but one must know that market risk needs special attention.

The operational pattern of Islamic banks is generally free of interest. However, there is a certain degree of interest rate risk owing to the fact that the London Interbank Offering Rate (LIBOR) is used as a benchmark in pricing. Hence, any change in the reference rate will most likely affect the return rate that the bank expects to collect on its use of funds and payments to its depositors. This is what the rate of return risk is. The risks identified for Islamic banks other than the ones as mentioned earlier are price, fiduciary and displaced commercial risks. Price risk can be defined as the risk that the price of the underlying asset might change during the transactional course.

When a commodity is acquired by a conventional bank for the purpose of trading, it is simultaneously exposed to a form of price risk, or market risk. To ensure absolute adherence to the *Shari'ah* rule pertaining to 'one cannot sell what one does not own', Islamic banks need to own different assets prior to them selling the same to clients in need of financing. This exposes a large section of transactions of the Islamic banks to price risk that gets generated as a result from the acquisition of numerous assets, which on the other hand calls in a new dimension of risk to the banking book of Islamic banks (Table 14.1).

14.4-1 Risk Specification in IFSB Guidelines

The recommendations in Basel II are suggestive of banks keeping track of their activities based on either the banking book or the trading book of the institution. Tables 14.2 and 14.3 show the possible implications of different risk exposure of conventional and Islamic banks on their banking book and trading book. As per the tables, market risk exposure for both conventional and Islamic banks is calculated in a similar way on the basis of their trading book. The interest rate risk is excluded from the calculation. The computation of their credit risk is also done on the basis their banking book. Table 14.3 shows that commodity price risk exposure of Islamic banks as a result from the acquisition of various physical assets gets reflected in the banking book of the Islamic bank. A new specificity gets introduced here which has not been addressed by Basel II. This latest specificity is that the calculation of market risk exposure has to be done not only on the basis of the trading book of the financial institution but also on the basis of the banking book.

On the parallel side, it must be noted that Islamic banks also encounter unique risks that emerge from the management of investment accounts. Fiduciary risk can be understood as the likeness of the bank being guilty of negligence or misconduct in implementing the deposit (*mudarabah*) contract, as a result of which depositors

TABLE 14.2 Difference of Trading Book Between Conventional and Islamic Banks

Conventional Bank	*Islamic Bank*
Market risk	Market risk
➢ Interest rate risk	➢ Commodity risk
➢ Commodity risk	➢ Equity risk
➢ Equity risk	➢ Currency risk
➢ Currency risk	

TABLE 14.3 Difference of Banking Book Between Conventional and Islamic Banks

Conventional Bank	*Islamic Bank*
Credit risk	Credit risk
➢ Portfolio risk	➢ Portfolio risk
➢ Transaction risk	➢ Transaction risk
	➢ Market risk
	➢ Commodity price risk

might end up losing confidence in the respective bank and withdraw their entire deposits. Displaced commercial risk emerges when the bank is likely to be unable in competing with other Islamic or conventional banks. For such risk to be countered, it is advisable for Islamic banks to hold a profit equalisation reserve account. A provision is deducted from the earnings of the investment account holder and is kept apart for distribution later. Therefore, it is quite evident that Islamic banks will be able to pay a competitive return on these accounts even if a lower rate of profits is earned them in comparison to market interest rates. The concern however is centred on the extent of *Shari'ah* compliance of this practice. In this context, the guidelines of IFSB in 2005 have set a mark in bringing harmony and standardisation of the risk exposure of Islamic financial institutions with the identification of the six risk categories: credit risk, equity investment risk, market risk, liquidity risk, rate of return risk and operational risk (IFSB, 2005a, 2005b). However, more effort must be incorporated in providing guidelines that account for some of these risk exposures, with focused reference to liquidity risk and operational risk.

14.4–2 Liquidity Risk in Basel III Framework

Introducing liquidity risk in the field of international harmonisation and regulation is credited to be Basel III's most original contribution reform. One of the two documents constituting the Basel III framework is devoted to liquidity risk in full exclusivity. Standards and monitoring tools have been introduced for successfully managing this risk. Monitoring tools have been proposed to supervisory authorities. The compliance with two ratios has to be made by the banks. These ratios are liquidity coverage ratio (LCR) and net stable funding ratio.

$$\text{LCR} = \frac{\textit{Stock Of High Quality Liquid Assets}}{\textit{Total Net Cash Outflows Over the Next 30 Calendar days}} \geq 100\%$$

This standard is aimed at ensuring that a bank can survive a stress scenario for a minimum of 30 days prior to other dispositions being taken. The calculation of the two components of the ratio is done under a stress scenario, the description of which is given in the document of BCBS where a typical scenario of the subprime crisis has been shown as an example (BCBS, 2010b). This situation is symbolic of a very minimum level of stress. Banks are entitled to discretionarily construct their own scenario and hold high-quality liquid assets.

14.4–2-1 Stock of High-Quality Liquid Assets

In this context, the stock of high-quality liquid assets symbolises the assets, the conversion of which is easily possible into cash provided that no value or very little of it is lost in the process. No compulsion, either explicitly or implicitly, can be made on them to secure, collateralise or credit-enhance in any transaction. The BCBS has put forth two categories of high-quality liquid assets: Level 1 and

Level 2. The maximum amount of adjusted Level 2 assets in the stock of high-quality liquid assets is equivalent to two-thirds of the adjusted amount of Level 1 assets after the application of the required haircuts (2010b). Here, Level 1 assets consist of cash, central bank reserves, and marketable securities (including *Sukuk*) issued by entities assigned a 0% risk weight as per the standard approach under Basel II. This category does not include financial institutions and their affiliated entities. Inclusion is made of non 0% risk-weight sovereigns and central banks if the issuance of securities is done in the currency where liquidity risk is incurred by the bank. The criteria of high quality liquid assets must be met by marketable securities as prescribed in the BCBS document (2010b). In compliance to this criteria, *Sukuk* or Islamic securities must be listed on a developed and recognised exchange market.

At Level 2, the inclusion of assets in the high quality liquid assets is done up to two-thirds of the total amount of stocks (securities). At least 15% of these assets must be additionally applied to the current market value of the securities that exist in this category. It can be incorporated during the issuance of marketable securities by an entity that was assigned a 20% risk weight under Basel II, with the only condition being the price of these securities must not have declined more than 10% over 30 days during a liquidity stress period. The inclusion of additional marketable securities can be done if their issuance is done by an entity rated at least AA− and not issued by a financial institution (including the bank itself) or one of its affiliates. In this context, the price remains stable during liquidity stress.

14.4-2-2 Total Net Cash Flow

Total net cash flow is equivalent to total cash outflows during the subsequent 30 days under the stress scenario, as above, deducting total cash inflows or 75% of cash outflows. The deduction is made with the smaller value. Thus,

> Total net cash outflows over the next 30 calendar days = Outflows − Minimum [inflows; 75% of outflows]

One must note that the inclusion of items in the stock of high-quality liquid assets will not be used in calculating the amount of cash inflows because of double counting.

14.4–2–2–1 Cash Outflows

According to the IFSB guidelines of 2001, in retail deposits for Islamic banks the demand deposits are likely to be treated as stable deposits and an application of a run-off rate of 5% is made to their value. When the profit sharing investment accounts (PSIAs) scheme is associated to time withdrawal account, then they can be approved for entering the category of lesser stable deposits where an application of a 10% run-off rate can be made to their value. On account of them not being under any time withdrawal scheme (until a future date, beyond the 30 days), they cannot be included in the liquidity coverage ratio (LCR).

Islamic banks are also entitled to hold an account for wholesale financial institutional customers provided that the relationship shared is that of an operational one (clearing, custody or cash management). In that context, a 25% run-off rate is received in the account. For being able to manage their liquidity risk, a given Islamic bank has to establish recourse with other Islamic banks corresponding to a technique called compensating mutual balances (CMB). It is the only form of exchange of interest-free deposit. This arrangement equally ensures that net balances are averaged to zero in a defined period (IFSB, 2008). Another liquidity risk management tool worth mentioning is that of the commodity *Murabaha*, where another bank can be appointed by an Islamic bank as its agent to perform certain tasks. Here, interbank funds are used for executing a *Murabaha* transaction in a commodity following which the proceeds (net of commissions) are passed on to the bank providing the fund.

A run-off factor equivalent to 75% is received from the deposits from other non-financial corporate entities, sovereigns, central banks, public sector entities and multilateral development banks. A run-off factor equivalent to 100% will be received from deposits from other legal entities (including other banks and *Takaful* companies). This implies that in the case of CMB, the run-off factor is 100%. According to the Basel accord, the integration of the conventional bonds issued by the bank is done in the latter category. As far as the Islamic banking system is concerned, assumption is made of *Sukuk* to be considered as the equivalent of conventional bonds. It goes without mentioning that the two are largely different. Direct ownership of the underlying asset is given to *Sukuk* holders under *Sukuk*, as a result of which no percentage of any run-off factor is received by *Sukuk*.

Islamic banks might opt for another liquidity management tool known as the interbank *Mudarabah* investment (IMI). It is an investment process where the interbank placement of funds for a certain generates returns on the basis of an agreed profit ratio. The time period can range from overnight to 12 months. Here, the formula for computing profit corresponds to *Mudarabah* investments of one year, or *Mudarabah* investments of comparable maturity based on receiving the interbank funds (IFSB, 2008). This is considered as a secured funding under Basel III. In this case, the application of a 100% run-off factor is done except when the investing entity is the domestic sovereign, central bank or a domestic public sector entity (risk-weighted 20% or lower under Basel II) owing to which a run-off factor of 25% will be applicable.

A run-off rate in association to 'other contingent funding obligations' is in the hands of the national supervisor's discretion. When seen in the context of Islamic banks, this is inclusive of guarantees, letters of credit and commitments that are unconditionally cancellable at any time without prior notice (IFSB, 2005a). A run-off rate of 100% is in all other contractual cash outflows. Examples can be taken of dividends and distributable profits to IAHs. The standard does not consider the outflows generated by operating costs.

14.4–2–2–2 Cash Inflows

Cash outflows are restricted to 75% so as to prevent banks from being completely reliant on future anticipated cash inflows. This implies that stocks of liquid assets must be held by banks which must be representative of a minimum of 25% of cash outflows. According to the framework of Basel III, inflows are categorised by counterparties. In this context, the recognition of inflows from retail and business customers is done at a 50% rate. On the flip side, the recognition of inflows from wholesale customers occurs at 100% for financial institution counterparties and 50% for the others (non-financial corporates, sovereigns, central banks, and public sector entities). In context of an Islamic bank holding *Sukuk* and arriving at maturity within the 30-day time horizon and if there are cash inflows from the realisation of the underlying asset, these inflows get treated similarly to those from financial institutions. As far as CMB and IMI are concerned, 100% of the recognition of inflows is done. Non-financial revenues are not considered in the calculation of net cash outflows. But as far as Islamic banks are concerned, certain particularities must be adhered to in the calculation of cash inflows. The profit generated from *Ijarah, Istisna, Murabaha* and *Salam* can be known in advance. Meanwhile, this is not applicable for the case of *Musharaka* and *Mudarabah* till the time that operations of these two investment instruments are completed prior to the calculation of the LCR, and the duration of transferring profits is within a 30-day time period. Except for these two conditions, cash inflows cannot be identified in advance for these two instruments. Therefore, for Islamic banks, inflows should be simultaneously categorised on the basis of financial instruments.

Irrespective of the limitations associated in implementing Basel standards subjected to Islamic banks, the IFSB's effort in developing develop standards or guidelines has to be acknowledged and appreciated. These guidelines attempt to address risk issues that are characteristically particular to Islamic financing. These standards have equally adapted elements from the Basel standards and made them more relevant to Islamic banks. In 2011, a risk management and capital adequacy guidance note was published by the IFSB for transactions corresponding to commodity *Murabaha*. This guidance note serves as a complementary contribution with reference to the previous work done by the IFSB in those particular areas (IFSB, 2011).

14.5 Conclusion

The ultimate goals are to stabilise banking systems nationally and globally and to prevent the extremes of crisis that switch from the financial sector into the real sector faster than one could anticipate. In order to achieve these goals, many countries have adopted and implemented the Basel I, II and III standards of capital adequacy and risk management in their authentic forms or modified them as per their respective requirements. The growing presence and importance of Islamic banking and financial systems demands more attention of the professional public corresponding to the business aspects of these financial institutions. An important dimension of Islamic banking and financial business is efficiency in maintaining the adequate capital level and risk management. Considering the exclusive nature of Islamic financial intermediation and businesses conducted by Islamic financial institutions, concerns have been raised regarding the possibilities and implications of applying the Basel regulations and practices of conventional banks in capital and risk management in context of the Islamic banks. This chapter has put forth the analysis of the possibilities of in applying the Basel standards to Islamic financial institutions without having to compromise the fundamental principles of *Shari'ah* during the course of structuring their capital, monitoring their capital adequacy ratios and reporting on their success in capital and risk management.

Review Questions

1. What are the Basel standards? Explain them in brief.
2. To what extent do Islamic banks really need Basel Accords? Are they likely to absorb Basel standards without being burdensome?
3. Briefly describe the capital adequacy standard of the Islamic Financial Service Board (IFSB) issued for Islamic banks in 2005 in light of the Basel standards, addressing the risk profile of Islamic banking and finance.

References

Basel Committee on Banking Supervision (2010a, December), *Basel III: A Global Regulatory Framework for More Resilient Banks and Banking Systems*, retrieved from www.bis.org/publ/bcbs189.pdf (Access date July 21, 2012)

Basel Committee on Banking Supervision (2010b, December), *Basel III: International Framework for Liquidity Risk Measurement, Standards and Monitoring*, retrieved from www.bis.org/publ/bcbs188.pdf (Access date July 21, 2012)

Basel Committee on Bank Supervision (2011, June), *Basel III*, revised version of capital framework, Basel: BCBS

BIS (2017), *Basel III: Financing Post Crisis Reform, Bank of International Settlements*, retrieved from www.bis.org/bcbs/publ/d424.pdf (Access date May 20, 2019)

Islamic Financial Services Board (2005a, December), *Capital Adequacy Standard for Institutions (Other Than Insurance Institutions) Offering Only Islamic Financial Services*, retrieved from www.ifsb.org/standard/ifsb2.pdf (Access date June 10, 2012)

Islamic Financial Services Board (2005b, December), *Guiding Principles of Risk Management for Institutions (Other Than Insurance Institutions) Offering Only Islamic Financial Services*, retrieved from www.ifsb.org/standard/ifsb1.pdf (Access date June 10, 2012)

Islamic Financial Services Board (2008, March), *Technical Note on Issues in Strengthening Liquidity Management of Institutions Offering Islamic Financial Services: The Development of Islamic Money Markets*, retrieved from www.ifsb.org/docs/mar2008_liquidity.pdf

Islamic Financial Services Board (2011, March), *Guidance Note in Connection with the IFSB Capital Adequacy Standard: The Determination of Alpha in the Capital Adequacy Ratio for Institutions (Other Than Insurance Institutions) Offering Only Islamic Financial Services*, retrieved from www.ifsb.org/standard/eng%20GN-4_IFSB%20CASAlpha% 20in%20Capital%20 Adequacy%20Ratio%20(Mar_2011).pdf (Access date June 10, 2012)

Muljawan, M, Dar, H and Hall, M (2004), A Capital Adequacy Framework for Islamic Banks: The Need to Reconcile Depositor's Risk Aversion with Managers' Risk Taking, *Applied Financial Economics*, 14, 429–441

Sundarajan, V (2008), Issues in Managing Profit Equalization Reserves and Investment Risk Reserves in Islamic Banks, *Journal of Islamic Economics, Banking and Finance*, 4(1), 1–11

15

CRYPTOCURRENCY

Shari'ah-Compliant Digital Currency

Learning Objectives

On completing this chapter, learners will be able to:

- Explain cryptocurrencies and blockchain technologies
- Describe Bitcoin and other cryptocurrencies
- Understand the viewpoints of various *Shari'ah* scholars on cryptocurrency
- Analyse the role cryptocurrency plays in blockchain
- Develop simple blockchains and distribute applications
- Know the risks involved in trading cryptocurrency
- Understand the hindrances to be encountered for cryptocurrency to become a state currency
- Scrutinise the Islamic legal status of commodity and money.

15.1 Introduction

The simplest way to define what cryptocurrency is that it is a digital currency. The transactional exchange takes place between people who have virtual wallets on decentralised computer networks. All the virtual currencies referred to as 'altcoins' act as tough contenders for Bitcoin. The period 2007–2008 witnessed global crashes, and after that, in 2009, Bitcoin came into existence as a cryptocurrency, the very first of its kind. As a digital currency, Bitcoins facilitates day-to-day transactions between individuals. Nakamoto (2008) is considered the founder of Bitcoin. When banks come into the picture of financial transactions as the go-between body, they become entitled to the identities of both the buyer and the seller, eventually leading to issues subjected to protection of personal data. This why cryptocurrencies, particularly Bitcoins prove more beneficial as there is no

DOI: 10.4324/9780429321207-15

intermediate monetary body involved. Based on a peer-to-peer (P2P) transaction model, there arises no need to reveal one's identity for a transaction to happen. The platform that Bitcoin offers has undeniably made the trading and transaction of cryptocurrency much easier and more independent without having to compromise on personal information and private details. Some people choose this method not only for making independent transactions but also for remaining anonymous.

With computers participating across a network within a transaction log, Bitcoins is considered to be the first digital coin in the world using the blockchain platform (Böhme et al., 2015). Equipped with one of the highest security systems, this blockchain does not allow fraudsters to use the currency more than once. The blockchain protocol relies on proof of work where it ensures miners converge to this structure. 'Hashing', a term used in this context, refers to computational operation. Therefore, hashing power denotes the computational power of mining the currencies (Kiayias and Panagiotakos, 2015).

In recent times, using cryptocurrencies for transactions like that of Bitcoin has been quite a topic of discussion under Islamic law, because Muslims worry that Bitcoin investments might be *haram* (unlawful). As per the latest scholarly interpretations (e.g. AbuBakar, 2018), Islam permits the use of Bitcoins for basic general purposes. However, at the same time, trading with cryptocurrencies in activities like gambling, lending and so forth is strictly forbidden.

15.2 Economic Significance of Cryptocurrency

The use of cryptocurrency is not limited to it being used as money only. Transactions made using cryptocurrencies simultaneously increase global economic participation as well as protection against excessive government reach.

15.2-1 Importance of Cryptocurrency

In the global context, an estimate of people not having bank accounts probably easily crosses two billion. The reasons might vary from their sheer lack of money to open a bank account or just the inability to maintain one. On the other hand, cryptocurrencies considered to be of equal value to that of a bank account do not specify minimum account requirements. To add to this benefit, cryptocurrencies also come with low adoption costs and are divisible into small fractions, meaning anyone with a telephone or an internet connection can trade using cryptocurrencies and in the process actively participate in the global economy.

15.2-2 The Value of Cryptocurrency

The ultimate idea behind a type of currency being valuable is its acceptance as a store of value. The value of the money is directly proportional to its acceptance among people. With growing acceptance, the stability associated with the value of the money equally increases. The issue of double coincidence of wants is ideally solved through cryptocurrencies as well as fiat money.

Cryptocurrencies operate using blockchain technology. As a comparatively new and ingenious technological concept, cryptocurrencies increase the security of the currency. Verification of transactions in the currency is simultaneously allowed.

The most distinguishable characteristic of cryptocurrency is its indefinite divisibility. In regard to this statement subjected to US dollars, the smallest amount one can receive is a cent, or particularly \$0.01. In contrast, depending on the need, users can receive as little as 0.00000000000001 Bitcoin.

15.2-3 Cryptocurrency Wallets

Software (apps) or hardware (thumb drive or card) are the two major forms of cryptocurrency wallets. As smaller versions of 'miners', these wallets help in recording and verifying transactions. The value of the coins is stored in these wallets and users know the total number of coins they have. On customers depositing Bitcoins into their respective wallets, verification is made of that transaction against the mining network's ledgers. This ensures that the network becomes aware of the fact that the coins have now become part of the wallet.

Both the software and hardware wallets have addresses that look like hash codes, or simply put, a long string of letters and numbers. When a customer deposits coins into their respective wallet, this address is used. This is how the network comes to know where to send the coins, and meanwhile, where to particularly store them.

15.3 Blockchain and the Operational Method

A blockchain can be understood as a digital ledger of transactions which is duplicated and distributed across the overall network of computer systems on the blockchain. Every block in the chain consists of a number of transactions. The record of every new transaction is added to every participant's ledger. Multiple participants are responsible for managing the decentralised database, which is why it is known as distributed ledger technology (DLT). Blockchain can thus be defined as a type of DLT which uses an immutable cryptographic signature called a hash in order to record transactions (Figure 15.1).

This would evidently showcase the tampering caused if any block in any chain was changed. If the intent is to corrupt a blockchain system, hackers would need to change every block in the chain across all of the distributed versions of the chain.

The constant and continuous growth of blockchain such as Bitcoin and Ethereum are a result of new blocks being added to the chain. This consistent growth happens to subsequently elevate the security of the ledger. A blockchain's distributive pattern is illustrated in Figure 15.1.

The contemporary world is built around entities that facilitate trust between parties and that maintain collective information. Examples can be taken from records of credits and debits, signatures on contracts, and the enforcement of contracts.

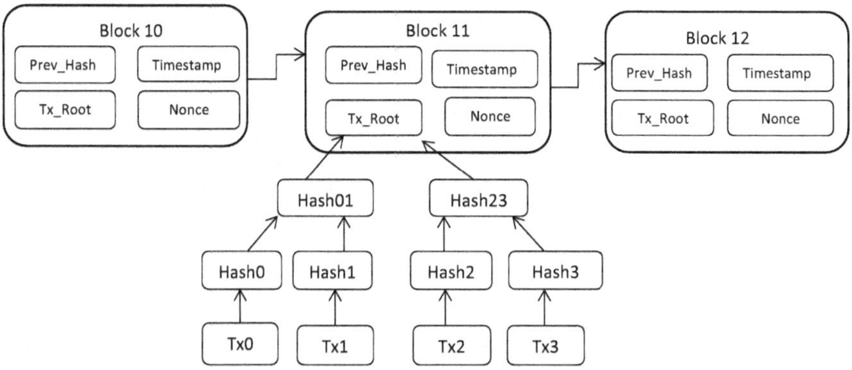

FIGURE 15.1 A blockchain's distributed ledger.

These gatekeepers can be found across all industries including finance, law, media, communications, insurance, and government. Blockchains represent a different architecture. Since collective information is maintained by default, central entities that maintain information become redundant. Cryptocurrencies have shown that this can be true for money; other industries are in earlier stages of disruption. At their heart, blockchains are powerful because they are the continuation of the 'story of the internet' and the march towards digitisation: the internet is unparalleled in its ability to connect computers globally in real time. Until the advent of the Bitcoin blockchain in 2009, the internet lacked the ability to exchange value natively between computers. Now, the design space has been blown wide open. Figure 15.2 shows how blockchain works.

Theoretically, blockchains are an amalgamation of mathematics, computer science, game theory, and cryptography. Several components are collectively responsible in determining whether blockchains will uptick or downtick.

1. Hash function: The cryptographic hash function is the crux of blockchain technology. Primarily used to 'chain-link' blocks, this component has two crucial features that ensure maintaining the security of blockchain:
    a. Hash functions are either asymmetric or one-way. An input or message of any length is compressed to generate an output of a predetermined length, which is referred to as the hash value. The input's hash value can be easily calculated, but decoding the input from the hash value is not a practical option.
    b. Hash functions are deterministic in their nature. This implies that there can be only one particular hash outcome as a result of a specific input. Any change in any character in that input would immediately change the hash value. The same input would undoubtedly produce the same output.

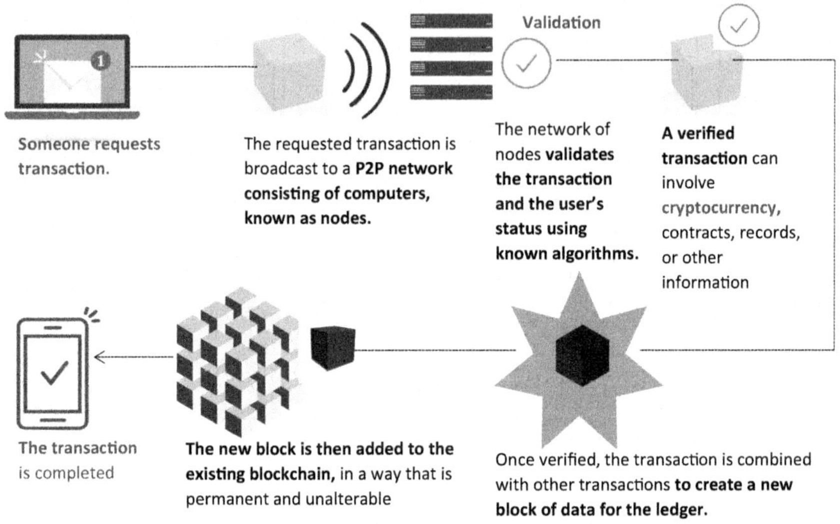

FIGURE 15.2 How blockchain works.

2. Public key cryptography: Transactions subjected to spending are generated using private and public keys within cryptocurrency networks, and so is the verification of their validity. A private key involves the digital wallet randomly curating a value that serves the purpose of an authorisation code or, simply, a unique password. A public key, on the other hand, is the equivalent of an account number which gets generated along with the private key and happens to be linked to it mathematically. It must be notably mentioned that the entire network is aware of the public key and the hash value associated to it.

   When a transaction is being conducted, the user's wallet cryptographically signs for it via the private key. Acting as fingerprints, these digital signatures would connect the transaction with the holder of the private key through a cryptographic method. Both the public key and the digital signature act as key parameters for individually verifying each and every transaction. On being considered in sync with each other, the transaction's approval is made by the network thereafter, leading it to get added to the blockchain. The public key cryptography is responsible for ensuring that only the person who has the private key is allowed to spend funds from and within their corresponding digital wallet.
3. Mining: The validation of blocks on a network takes place using a consensus mechanism in terms of proof of work (PoW). This can be summed up as the process of mining. On these networks, participants earn cryptocurrencies as incentives by helping to include transactions through mining. In mining, for a difficult mathematical problem to be solved through trial and error, time and

computing power form important requirements. Verification of the output of mining is comparatively easier. However, those who seek to cause tampering of legitimate transactions incur steep costs imposed on them.

15.4 Electronic Cash and Digital Payment

Some of the electronic currencies used in the different countries are briefly explained below.

15.4-1 Bitcoin

Bitcoin was the first widespread application of blockchain technology. Bitcoin was conceived as peer-to-peer (P2P) electronic cash for the internet, meaning that people can exchange it without the need for a bank, a government, or another intermediary. Transactions on the Bitcoin ledger are permanent, auditable, encrypted, and distributed. Importantly, the Bitcoin blockchain has never been hacked. Since its inception, the supply of Bitcoin has been limited by design, and only 21 million Bitcoins are issued. An increase in Bitcoin's value will not affect its supply. Bitcoin has emerged as one of the only verifiably scarce, immutable and capped-supply assets in the world, and it is attracting investment as a 'store of value' asset, which is why some call it 'digital gold'. Like gold, Bitcoin is a potential safeguard against macroeconomic trends and sovereign currency fluctuations. But unlike gold, Bitcoin lives on the internet: it can be transferred more quickly, it is easier to store and it is more easily divisible. Bitcoin also has more growth potential than gold; its market cap stands around US$200 billion, while gold represents a US$12 trillion market.

As on 15 September 2021:

- Price: US$4,799
- Market cap: US$907 billion

(*Source*: CoinMarketCap.com)

15.4-2 Ethereum (ETH)

These assets are primarily meant to support the emerging decentralised internet known as Web 3.0. After Bitcoin, the second-most popular cryptocurrency is Ethereum (ETH), the digital currency of the Ethereum blockchain. Ethereum is known to have provided the first of its kind platform, where 'smart contracts' were used to build decentralised applications. Smart contracts are self-executing code that automatically implements the terms of agreements between parties. These contracts have the potential to streamline processes across the business world. Developers have built hundreds of decentralised applications on the Ethereum platform in areas including finance, commerce, and social networks. ETH miners provide the computing power for the execution of smart contracts. The demand for these

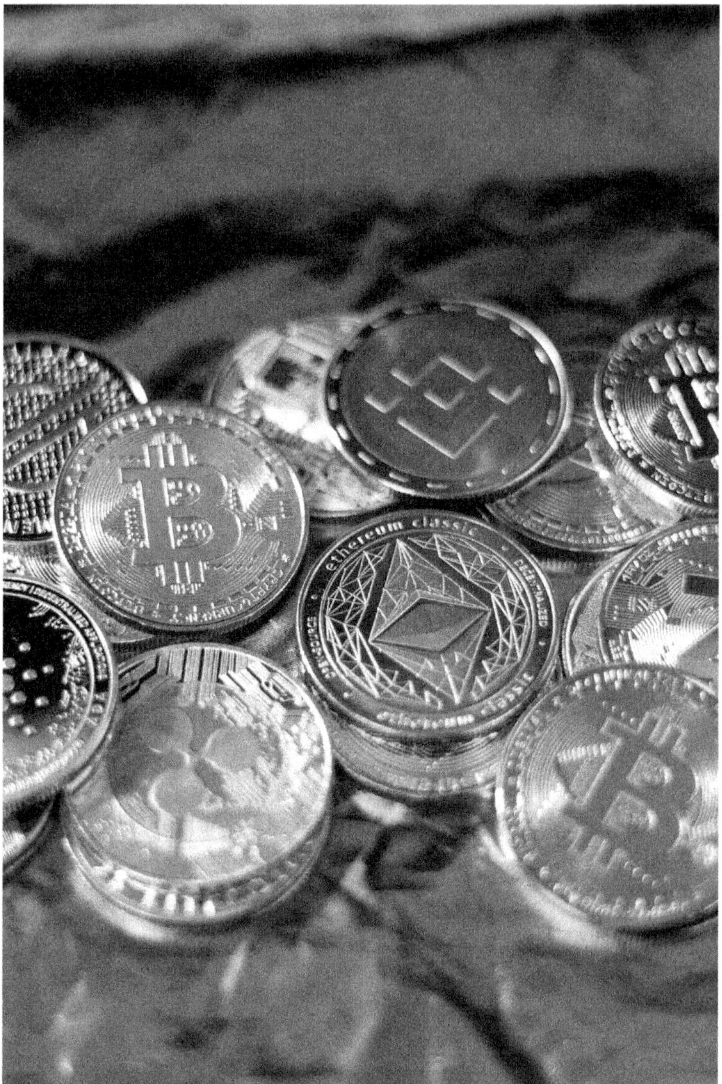

FIGURE 15.3 Several cryptocurrencies.

Source: https://unsplash.com/s/photos/cryptocurrency.

applications indirectly drives demand for ETH. Smart-contract blockchains such as Ethereum may become foundational for the decentralised internet.

As on 15 September 2021:

- Price: US$3,538
- Market cap: US$415 billion

(*Source*: CoinMarketCap.com)

15.4-3 Litecoin

Released under the MIT/X11 license, Litecoin is a cryptocurrency founded as an open source software project and is based on a P2P model. Initiated in the year 2011, Litecoin is addressed as an early Bitcoin spinoff or altcoin. The fact that Litecoin has been consistently ranked in the top 15 cryptocurrencies by market caps makes it relatively stable in comparison to other altcoins which were more or less created around the same time.

As on 15 September 2021:

- Price: US$172.15
- Market cap: US$11.825 billion

15.4-4 Cardano (ADA)

Cardano was created by the co-founder of Ethereum. Identity management is enabled in Cardano via smart contracts. The currency ADA is based on the cryptocurrency platform of Cardano.

As on 15 September 2021:

- Price: US$2.52
- Market cap: US$81 billion

(Source: *CoinMarketCap.com*)

15.4-5 Binance Coin (BNB)

In the global context, Binance is referred to as one of the largest crypto exchanges, and the cryptocurrency issued by them is known as the Binance coin. The original idea behind creating this digital coin was to use it in terms of a token for discounted trades. However, the Binance coin in the present day is conveniently used both for making payments and purchasing various goods and services.

As on 15 September 2021:

- Price: US$430
- Market cap: US$73 billion

(Source: *CoinMarketCap.com*)

15.4-6 Tether (USDT)

The fact that Tether is considered as a stablecoin has made its price being anchored at US$1 per coin. When the value of a digital coin is attached to the value of a specific asset, the digital coin can be referred to as stablecoin. In the context of the Tether, the value is associated with the US dollar. Tether is most likely to serve as a medium when traders switch from one cryptocurrency to another. Instead of moving back to dollars, traders would rather use Tether. However, a concern associated with using Tether among some people is the fear that this digital currency relies on using a short-term form of unsecured debt and isn't safely backed by dollars held in reserve.

As on 15 September 2021:

- Price: US$1.00
- Market cap: US$68 billion

(Source: *CoinMarketCap.com*)

15.4–7 XRP (XRP)

XRP was founded in the year 2012. Initially known as Ripple, an individual using this digital currency is entitled to offers that allow them to pay in several currencies of the real world. XRP uses a mechanism to facilitate payments which can be quite useful for cross-border transactions.

As on 15 September 2021:

- Price: US$1.12
- Market cap: US$52 billion

(Source: *CoinMarketCap.com*)

15.4–8 Solana (SOL)

Solana is one of the latest cryptocurrencies launched in March 2020. The robust 'web-scale' platform that it comes with allows it to tout its speed on completing transactions. The currency issued under it is called SOL and is capped at 480 million coins.

As on 15 September 2021:

- Price: US$160.64
- Market cap: US$48 billion

(Source: *CoinMarketCap.com*)

15.4–9 Polkadot (DOT)

Considerably one of the latest cryptocurrencies, Polkadot was launched in May 2020. It is a digital currency which connects diverse blockchains from many different cryptocurrencies. A co-founder of Ethereum is said to be one of the inventors of Polkadot, which many industrial watchers see as a possible hint of Ethereum getting dethroned by Polkadot in the future.

As on 15 September 2021:

- Price: US$36.56
- Market cap: US$37 billion

(Source: *CoinMarketCap.com*)

15.4–10 Dogecoin (DOGE)

As a digital currency, Dogecoin is mostly used for making payments or sending money. In contrast to most digital currencies that limit the number of existing coins, the issuance that Dogecoin approves of digital currencies is unlimited. Interestingly, Dogecoin came into existence as a result of a joke after the run-up in Bitcoin. The term 'Dogecoin' was adopted from an internet meme featuring a Shiba Inu dog.

As on 15 September 2021:

- Price: US$0.24
- Market cap: US$32 billion

(Source: *CoinMarketCap.com*)

15.4–11 USD Coin (USDC)

Very similar to that of Tether, USD Coin is a stablecoin, the value of which is tied to the dollar, implying that its value must not fluctuate. According to the founders of the currency, USD Coins are backed by fully reserved assets or ones with 'equivalent fair value'. The founders also claim that these assets are responsibly held in accounts with regulated US institutions.

As on 15 September 2021:

- Price: US$1.00
- Market cap: US$29 billion

(Source: *CoinMarketCap.com*)

15.4–12 Uniswap (UNI)

Contrary to centralised exchanges like that of Coinbase and Binance, Uniswap acts as an exchange for other coins. This digital currency was launched in November 2018. A decentralised form of network running on the Ethereum blockchain is what the Uniswap actually is.

As on 15 September 2021:

- Price: US$25.91
- Market cap: US$16 billion

(Source: *CoinMarketCap.com*)

15.4–13 Terra (LUNA)

On the basis of real currencies like that of a dollar or an euro, Terra acts as a platform which helps backstop a variety of stablecoins. Terra uses its currency LUNA and ensures in stabilising the price of stablecoins. In doing so, multiple technicalities are used by Terra. This platform equally supports smart contracts.

As on 15 September 2021:

- Price: US$36.73
- Market cap: US$15 billion

(Source: *CoinMarketCap.com*)

15.4–14 Libra

The cryptocurrency Libra was created by Facebook. The foundation of this digital currency was intended to be a simple, low-fee exchange medium for global usage. The stability ensured by Libra is because of the basket of assets it is backed by, comprising major currencies and government debt securities. The Libra association, formed as an independent not-for-profit association, is responsible for handling and managing the cryptocurrency and its related reserve. In September 2019, Facebook announced that the reserve basket would comprise 50% US dollars, 18% euro, 14% Japanese yen, 11% British pounds and 7% Singapore dollars (Bartz, 2019; Wagner and Kharif, 2020).

As on 15 September 2021:

- Price: US$0.0388
- Market cap: US$2 billion

15.5 Digital Payments

The race for digital payments broadly splits into two categories: central bank digital currencies (CBDCs) and 'stablecoins' on public blockchains. Bitcoin forced central banks to recognise that cryptographic payment rails are more efficient than legacy payment rails. The announcement of Facebook's Libra further underscored that point. In the global context, more than 80% of central banks at present are either studying or developing their own CBDC, according to the Bank for International Settlements (BIS). CBDCs are blockchain inspired but do not need to live on blockchains. According to a European Union task force, CBDCs stand to provide state-of-the-art payment services which increase choice, competition and accessibility and reduce overall costs and ecological footprint of the monetary and payment systems. On the other hand, stablecoins – dollar-pegged cryptocurrencies like USD Coin, Tether, Dai, Celo, and Libra – live on public open-source blockchains like Ethereum and have grown to more than $20 billion in market size, up 213% from $6.7 billion on 1 January 2020 (Andolfatto, 2021). Stablecoins are cryptocurrencies with reduced price volatility, making them more suitable for exchange. Celo, a promising start-up out of San Francisco, built a blockchain specifically tailored to mobile-first transactions and aims to serve 1.1 billion users who have smartphones but lack access to banking services.

15.6 Do Cryptocurrencies Signify Real Money?

The ultimate question that revolves around Bitcoin since its inception is about its authenticity: should these cryptocurrencies be considered real money?

To understand the authenticity associated with cryptocurrencies, one must first understand money. According to Ali et al. (2014), certain criteria act as determining factors as to what can be considered as money:

1. A store of value: This entitles users with a purchasing power which they can manipulate according to their needs and wants for purchasing goods in the present or in future.
2. A medium of exchange: This constitutes of the ability for making payments.
3. A unit of account: For a good to be sold, it needs to be measured so that an estimate of value can be made.

In theory, money must adhere to all of these criteria. However, the same does not always apply when in practice.

Considering the criteria as mentioned above as prerequisites for any commodity to be given the stature of money, cryptocurrencies need to be accepted on the basis of their usage and application. Radford (1945) reported that during World War II, prisoners in war camps used cigarettes to make transactions, as cigarettes as a commodity qualified all the parameters. History also shows how cooking salt was once regarded as having value during the kingdom of Roman empire, where the wages of the troops were paid in salt. Cryptocurrency can be conveniently regarded as money to users who are computer and internet enabled. This is where the problem lies, as we know that the fraction of people having access to the internet devices is trivial in comparison to the global population. In all these examples, it is evident that only a specific group gains access to the commodity of value. In World War II, it was the prisoners. In the Roman Empire, it was the troops. Today, it is the ones having access to the internet. A report by Ali et al., (2014) depicted how out of approximately 20,000 Bitcoin holders in the United Kingdom, the number of transactions made per day roughly add up to only 300. Developing nations would have to witness even a smaller number than this owing to its people lacking access to the internet.

15.7 Legal Status of Cryptocurrency

Bitcoin and cryptocurrencies alike have mostly been on the border of finance and payments. Some countries are still giving a serious thought of granting cryptocurrencies or crypto-assets legal tender status and are even considering making these digital currencies a second (or potentially only) national currency. If the legal tender status is being granted to cryptocurrency or crypto-assets, creditors will then have to acknowledge and accept digital payments subjecting to all monetary obligations, including taxes. The role will be similar to notes and coins (currency) issued by the central bank. In this regard, countries might even go ahead by bringing in laws and putting them into effect for encouraging the use of cryptocurrency as a national currency. This will then shape into the official monetary unit and become the only mandate to be used in all kinds of payments for everyday purchases (Adrian and Weeks-Brown, 2021).

Countries characterised by the presence of credible institutions and countries experiencing stable inflation and exchange rates are hardly going to be influenced by cryptocurrencies. If in a parallel world, cryptocurrencies (e.g. Bitcoin) were given legal tender or currency status, households and businesses would have very little incentive to price or save. This is chiefly because of their value being highly volatile and not related to the real economy. A considerably less stable economy would be tempted to opt a globally recognised reserve currency (e.g. dollar, euro) than adopting a cryptocurrency. Despite that, a cryptocurrency might very well serve as a means for unbanked people to make payments. However, its acceptance as a store of value is not most familiar. A receipt would assure the immediate exchange of cryptocurrency into real currency. But at the same time, one must note that real currency might not always be conveniently available or easily transferable. In some countries, legal provisions ban or disapprove of payments in other forms of money. This can eventually encourage widespread use of cryptocurrency (Adrian and Weeks-Brown, 2021).

15.8 Risk Involved in Trading Cryptocurrencies

The volatile nature of cryptocurrencies is considered to be the root cause of risks associated with trading cryptocurrencies. There are certain high-end risks and certain speculative risks that investors are most likely to face while trading crypto-assets:

1. Cryptocurrencies are volatile: Because of this volatility, any unexpected change in market sentiment might lead to sharp and sudden changes in the prices of cryptocurrencies. It is even likely for the value of cryptocurrencies to go through a severe downfall, to an extent of hundreds of dollars.
2. Cryptocurrencies are unregulated: As a decentralised form of exchange, cryptocurrency markets are unregulated by both governments and central banks. The idea behind developing cryptocurrencies was to let them remain free from any kind of governmental influences. An internet protocol based on the P2P method is rather used for monitoring.
3. Cryptocurrencies are subject to error and hacking: Cryptocurrencies are a form of digital currency, and a slightest technical glitch, human error or a hack might result in sensitive alterations.
4. Cryptocurrency trading carries additional risks: When a radical change is encountered and impacts the price volatility of cryptocurrencies, trade is most likely to be suspended owing to the cryptocurrencies not having reliable prices from the underlying market. The additional risks associated with trading cryptocurrencies include fast divides or discontinuation.

15.9 Islamic Legal Criteria on Money and Commodity

The concept of money under Islamic law pertains to everything which is widely accepted as a medium of exchange and store of value. The nature and form of that thing do not act as the deciding factors (Turki, 1988). Anything that might be used as a medium of exchange can be addressed as a money. This includes gold, silver, flower petals, skin, paper, and so forth; the only parameter is its large-scale acceptance.

Usmani (2005) states that there are three prominent attributes, intrinsic to money:

1. It can be used as a medium of exchange.
2. It serves as a unit of account.
3. It acts as a store of value.

These definitions of scholars are synonymous with the ideologies of modern economists subjecting to the definition of money. Economists define money as 'something generally accepted as a medium of exchange, a measure of value, or a means of payment'. On the basis of the definition as accepted by economists, an expanded definition of money is inclusive of all the following attributes: (1) medium of exchange, (2) widely accepted as a means of payment, and (3) a measure of value.

15.10 Unit of Account Differences Between Money and Commodities

According to *Shari'ah* law, money does not signify an equivalent to a commodity. It must be carefully understood that *Shari'ah* puts an emphasis on treating money just for the primary purposes, particularly as a medium of exchange and measure of value. The basic differences between money and commodities are further explained below.

Ibn Taymiyyah is of the opinion that dirhams and dinar (gold and silver coins) have been created to be used as a medium of exchange only. No such intrinsic use or purpose is associated with them (Blossomfinance, 2018). Another explanation of money carrying a similar undertone has been put forth by Ibn Qayyim, who says that money isn't desired for itself but its creation is associated with facilitating the trade of goods (Blossomfinance, 2018). Thus, the idea of classifying money into either a good or bad commodity would ultimately ruin the Islamic ethical perspective. In the simplest of words, money must serve as a medium of exchange only.

Three fundamental differences between money and commodities, as observed by Usmani (2005), are as follows:

1. There is no intrinsic value associated with money. The direct needs of human beings such as eating, drinking, clothing and shelter can be fulfilled using money. On the other hand, commodities do offer an intrinsic value, and they

are characterised by direct utilisation, which means that they need not be exchanged with something else.

2. Commodities are characterised by varied qualities and attributes. In the context of money, the attributes are restricted to it being used as a medium of exchange and measure of value only. This is why all the units of the same denomination of money are equal to each other and possess the same value. In theory, an old US$100 bill and a new US$100 bill are equivalent to each other in terms of value.
3. Transactions for sale and purchase are applicable to a particular item or a commodity. An example can be used to understand this better. In a transaction of selling a car, the seller has to give the same car to the buyer of which the money has been paid. A similar car cannot be substituted by the seller in place of the particular car he has been paid money of. Unlike money, commodities aren't fixed in an exchange transaction. Here, it wouldn't matter if someone offering to pay US$100 by shows a particular bill and then ends up paying with a different US$100 bill.

The rules mentioned above help in possibly evaluating cryptocurrency and further discuss whether it fulfils the ethical criteria of currency in Islam. The most familiar cryptocurrency, as we all know, is Bitcoin. Thus, Islamic financial literature and particularly, *fatwa* (experts' legal opinions) are generally concerned with Bitcoin. AbuBakar (2018), an Islamic scholar based in Indonesia, has used certain principles and arguments to scrutinise and conclude that most of the cryptocurrencies created are almost the same, especially those which have been created to serve the purpose of currency and act as a medium of exchange. Therefore, the existing Islamic literature associated with Bitcoin is largely inclusive of benefits with regard to cryptocurrency. Scholars and *Shari'ah* experts have two distinctively different opinions. The first group of scholars believes that cryptocurrency is *haram*, meaning that *Shari'ah* does not absolutely approve of it. The other group holds the idea that cryptocurrency pertains to the principle of *halal*, referring to being allowed.

15.11 Are Cryptocurrencies *Shari'ah* Compliant?

Islamic finance has remained quite confused regarding blockchains and cryptocurrencies while investors and financial institutions all around are getting increasingly involved in speculating and exploring the potential possibilities of the same products. The Indonesian scholar and head of *Shari'ah* compliance at Indonesian FinTech start-up Blossom Finance, Mufti Muhammad Abu Bakar, conducted a case study to make a decision on whether digital currencies should be considered *halal* (permissible) or *haram* (forbidden). The results of the case study were published on 10 April 2018.

AbuBakar (2018) says, 'Bitcoin is permissible in principal, as it is treated as valuable by market price on global exchanges and it is accepted for payment at a wide variety of merchants'. However, he clearly mentioned that his paper must not be considered as a final '*fatwa* or *Shari'ah* verdict' (Blossomfinance, 2018). The report of his case study gathered global attention irrespective of the fact that not much was known about either Bakar or Blossom Finance. Commentators were of the opinion that the potential value of cryptocurrency-investment markets could possibly open up to the 1.6 billion Muslims worldwide. The price of Bitcoin escalated by US$1,000, reaching up to almost US$8,000 on the very day the report had been published. Bitcoin's price gain is often considered to be an outcome of Abu Bakar's *fatwa* (Blossomfinance, 2018).

The founder of Coinfluencers, Jamal Aezaz proposed an identification parameter of analysing whether Bitcoin's use is intended for *haram* or not. The idea is to simply consider if fiat currencies, used for similar purposes, would also be declared impermissible. Aezaz talks about the prevailing misconception where if anything is associated with Bitcoin, it gets automatically considered as *haram*. The birth of this misconception has taken place owing to Bitcoin being a cryptocurrency instead of being a regular tangible currency issued by a central bank. It must be carefully noted that similar to that of fiat currencies, holding Bitcoin as a means of payment and store of value would be definitely considered *halal*. Apart from this, using Bitcoin for any purpose that is being considered *haram* with fiat currency would equally be considered *haram* (Philips, 2021).

15.12 Conclusion

Cryptocurrencies, specifically Bitcoin, serve more like a platform for payment instead of just a currency because of it being convertible into conventional currency of fixed value in real time. What distinguishes it from other assets is through all of its analyses of portfolio, risk management and sentiment. Cryptocurrency and the understanding of its mining, tradability, security and systematic impact has been under a consistent evolving process. Hence, *Shari'ah* opinions on cryptocurrencies must be influenced under proper information. The blockchain not only acts as a platform for Bitcoin and other cryptocurrencies; it equally serves as a decentralised digital ledger technology to record anything of value in the form of currency or assets. In the context of transparency and disclosure that *Shari'ah* laws require, blockchains might be considered a blessing. Simultaneously, blockchains can conveniently enhance trust factors for transactional exchanges and transfers. For exchange of currency and commodities, blockchains might even serve as the principle of cash transactions. With regard to the current *Shari'ah* status of Bitcoin, a majority of Islamic scholars are of the opinion that Bitcoin is permissible in principle since it is treated in terms of its value. This is reflected by its prevailing market price on global exchanges and its acceptance for payment transactions across different merchants ranging from bakeries and restaurants to e-commerce retailers.

All in all, the cryptocurrency market is best addressed as a Wild Nest. It is thus advisable for the speculators of this digital asset not to put in more money than they can afford to lose. Crypto-assets can witness significant fluctuations owing to intense volatility within a single day. The presence of highly sophisticated players amidst this digital asset can make the trading experience for an individual beginner quite rocky, nerve-racking and overwhelming.

Review Questions

1. How does cryptocurrency work?
2. What is Bitcoin?
3. What are the major differences between money and commodity in the light of Usmani's viewpoints?
4. Under what criteria is money qualified in Islam?
5. Explain how blockchains work.
6. Are cryptocurrencies *Shari'ah* compliant?
7. Describe the risks involved in trading cryptocurrencies.
8. Can a cryptocurrency become a state currency?

References

AbuBakar, M (2018), *Shari'ah Analysis of Bitcoin, Cryptocurrency, & Blockchain*, Blossom Labs, Inc. retrieved from https://blossomfinance.com/bitcoin-working-paper

Adrian, T and Weeks-Brown, R (2021, July 26), *Cryptoassets as National Currencies? A Step too Far*, IMF Blog, retrieved from https://blogs.imf.org/2021/07/26/cryptoassets-as-national-currency-a-step-too-far/ (Access date August 2, 2021)

Ali, R, Barrdear, J, Clews, R and Southgate, J (2014), Innovations in Payment Technologies and the Emergence of Digital Currencies, *Bank of England Quarterly Bulletin 2014 Q3*, retrieved from SSRN: https://ssrn.com/abstract=2499397 (Access date August 2, 2021)

Andolfatto, D (2021, February), Assessing the Impact of Central Bank Digital Currency on Private Banks, *The Economic Journal*, 131, 525–540

Bartz, T (2019), Absicherung von Kryptogeld: Facebook verzichtet bei Libra auf chinesische Währung, *Spiegel Online*, Archived from the original on October 3, 2019 (Access date September 30, 2010)

Blossomfinance (2018), Is Bitcoin *Halal* or *Haram*: A *Shari'ah* Analysis, *News & PR*, retrieved from https://blossomfinance.com/posts/is-bitcoin-halal-or-haram-a-Shari'ah-analysis (Access date January 2, 2020)

Böhme, R, Christin, N, Edelman, B and Moore, T (2015), Bitcoin: Economics, Technology, and Governance, *The Journal of Economic Perspectives*, 29(2), 213–238

Kiayias, A and Panagiotakos, G (2015), Speed-Security Tradeoffs in Blockchain Protocols, *IACR Cryptology*, ePrint Archive 1019, retrieved from https://eprint.iacr.org/2015/1019 (Access date October 12, 2020)

Nakamoto, S and Bitcoin, A (2008), A Peer-to-Peer Electronic Cash System, *Bitcoin*, retrieved from https://bitcoin.org/bitcoin.pdf (Access date December 10, 2019)

Philips, D (2021, January 22), *Is Bitcoin Halal, Decrypt*, retrieved from https://decrypt.co/37286/is bitcoin-halal (Access date June 2, 2021)

Radford, RA (1945), The Economic Organisation of a P.O.W. Camp, *Economica*, 12(48), 189–201

Turki, AK (1988), *Al-Siayasa Al-Naqdiyya Wal Masrifiyya*, Beirut: Muhassah al-risalah

Usmani, MT (2005), *The Historic Judgement on Interest: Delivered in the Supreme Court of Pakistan*, Karachi: Idaratul-Ma'Arif

Wagner, K and Kharif, O (2020), Facebook-Backed Libra Plans Multiple Single-Currency Coins, *Fortune, Bloomberg News*, Archived from the original on May 28, 2021 (Access date April 17, 2020)

16

FINANCIAL TECHNOLOGIES IN ISLAMIC FINANCE

Learning Objectives

On completing this chapter, learners will be able to:

- Understand a wide range of knowledge and information on the FinTech ecosystem and its main participants based on practical cases and world experiences, reflecting the Islamic financial market
- Explain the categories of Islamic FinTech and the platforms associated with it
- Clarify concepts of Islamic FinTech application through relevant case studies
- Appreciate the social dimensions of the use of technology in Islamic financial markets
- Identify the risks and potential mitigation in Islamic FinTech.

16.1 Introduction

In simple words, FinTech can be best described as financial technology which broadly translates into the concept of finance plus technology. Its design comprises technological innovation for improving the delivery of financial services and products. The automation of the same is simultaneously ensured. FinTech is largely driven by data growing at a rapid pace subjecting to the quantity, types, sources, quality and technological advances that ultimately help in capturing and extracting information from it. Analysis of large datasets, analytical tools, automated trading, automated advice, and financial record keeping are some particular areas that FinTech development caters to, in the context of the investment industry.

Traditional banking, insurance, and investment products have paved the way for innovative products that are massively dependent on the internet and cloud-based solutions. For example, one can conveniently open a savings account in a bank or

DOI: 10.4324/9780429321207-16

apply for a loan without having to leave the comfort of one's living room. In the context of insurance, policyholders are generally rewarded for their healthier lifestyle by health insurers based on data gathered through wearables. The application of FinTech makes these innovative practices possible.

16.2 Islamic FinTech

Islamic FinTech can be defined as a segment of financial technology which follows the principles of *Shari'ah* or Islamic law. The law prohibits any profit earned from debt or interest payments and equally disapproves any kind of investments made in businesses related to certain sectors such as alcohol, tobacco, and gambling. The Global Islamic FinTech Report, produced by DinarStandard and Elipses in 2021 depicts that the volume of transactions in the Islamic FinTech sector within Organisation of Islamic Cooperation (OIC) countries is expected to grow at an annual compounding growth rate of 21% to reach up to $128 billion by 2025 (CARG). The CARG in conventional FinTechs subjected to the same time period is expected to grow by only 15%. The report illustrates that the volume of Islamic FinTech transactions within OIC countries was reported to be $49 billion in 2020, which is representative of only 0.7% of the global figure (Table 16.1).

16.2-1 Key Areas for Islamic FinTech

Technological growth is undoubtedly the driving force for the rise of Islamic FinTech and is equally suggestive of the fact that Islamic FinTech tends to operate in extremely high-growth markets with young populations. Saudi Arabia, Iran, United Arab Emirates, Malaysia, and Indonesia are the leading countries in terms of Islamic FinTech transaction volumes within the OIC countries, as per the Global Islamic FinTech Report 2021 (Table 16.2). Table 16.2 illustrates relevant examples in respect of Islamic FinTech.

TABLE 16.1 Top Five Islamic FinTech Market Sizes Within OIC Countries, 2020

	Country	*Estimated Islamic FinTech Market Size 2020 (Billion US$)*	*Proportion of OIC FinTech Market Size 2020*
1	Saudi Arabia	18	37%
2	Iran	9	19%
3	United Arab Emirates	4	8%
4	Malaysia	3	6%
5	Indonesia	3	6%
6	Rest of OIC countries	12	25%

Source: Global Islamic FinTech Report (2021).

TABLE 16.2 Islamic FinTech Examples in Terms of the Type of Financial Services

Financial Services	*Islamic Financial Services*	*Islamic FinTech Examples*
Funding	• Custody-based deposits (can also be based on *Qard*) • Investment accounts • *Shari'ah*-compliant payment, collection, and liquidity management	• PayHalal (Souqa FinTech Sdn Bhd, Malaysia) • AmalPay (Malaysia) • Investment Account Platform (IAP – Malaysia)
Trade finance	• *Murabaha* working capital • *Murabaha Wakala/Mudaraba/* Letter of Credit	• Waqfe – Bahrain (Digital banking platform provider)
Financing	• *Murabaha/Mudaraba/Musharaka/ Salam/Istisna/Ijara* Financing • Islamic Microfinance	• Ethis Crowd – Singapore, Indonesia, Malaysia, Australia • Blossom Finance
Capital market	• Islamic Bank Treasury • *Sukuk* (Islamic Bonds)	• Adab Solution (Crypto exchange)
Wealth management	• *Shari'ah*-compliant wealth management for retail and HNWIs	• Wahed – US (Robo advisory investment platform) • HelloGold (blockchain-based gold investment)
Insurance	• *Takaful* • Re-*Takaful*	• Uplift Mutuals • Insure Halal

Source: World Bank (2020).

The Global Islamic FinTech Report (GIFR) 2021 makes a revelation about the Islamic FinTech landscape being at a young and patchy stage. The data is representative of the fact that the majority of Islamic FinTechs are applied in fields related to raising funds, deposits and lending, wealth management, payments, and alternative finance. Islamic FinTech are referred to as FinTech technologies which are capable of either exponentially enhancing or causing disruptions in 21st-century Islamic financial services, operations, business models, and customer engagement. Six financial services are used as categories for specifying the possibilities of innovation or disruption.

Lending is an important aspect for Islamic FinTech firms. The growth of wealth management is associated with *Shari'ah* components, and there are multiple finer elements to it. Digital banking has grown equally familiar post the launch of neobanks, which are virtual financial technology firms that offer internet-only financial services. These neobanks do not have physical branches and are most appealing to tech-savvy consumers who opt for mobile applications in managing a huge chunk or all of their money. The Global Islamic FinTech Report 2021 mentions areas of insurance, digital assets, capital markets, operations and social finance as other active areas of Islamic FinTech.

The significance of social finance is paramount in Islamic FinTech. A World Bank report on Islamic FinTech states that Islamic FinTech can utilise the opportunity of galvanising the multibillion-dollar Islamic social finance pool from *Zakah* (obligatory charity or alms), *Sadaqah* (voluntary charity), and *Waqf* (Islamic endowments). *Zakah* corresponds to the practice of a Muslim giving 2.5% of his wealth to a certain charity. According to the UN Development Programme, this practice has the potential to pitch in a contribution ranging between US$200 billion and US$1 trillion and can thus help in alleviating poverty (World Bank, 2020, p. 12). Practices like *Zakah, Sadaqah,* and *Waqf* undoubtedly bring a positive impact by working on the welfare of the poor and can, therefore, help in achieving the targets of UN Sustainable Development Goals 1 (concerned with eradicating poverty) and 2 (concerned with eradicating hunger).

16.2–2 Islamic Finance Vis-à-Vis FinTech

Islamic financial institutions get the opportunity to adopt the risk sharing model and apply them through small scale innovative start-ups wanting to contribute towards the Islamic finance industry. This has been possible because of the development of Islamic FinTech. Neobanking, or what we understand as virtual banks can be taken as the perfect example for this. With the Islamic neobanking model, financers and investors are able to get hold of opportunities that ensure true Islamic risk sharing, interest-free products and services which are generally not offered by already existing Islamic banks. The operational structure of Islamic FinTech must completely be in sync with the asset-backed, interest-free, risk sharing, under-leveraged real sector model of the ideal Islamic economy (Oseni and Ali, 2019).

New digital channels can be used for the democratisation and delivery of Islamic financial services. This is exactly where Islamic FinTech has a key role to play in articulating the same by ensuring the elimination of any asymmetric information, fraud, no confidence and distrust between counterparties irrespective of them being financial institutions, regulators, family offices, or the customers. Any kind of ambiguity in transactions or deceptive trading subjected to financial operations or business models gets reduced. This is not only limited to counterparty transactions. It simultaneously creates positive ripple effects throughout the entire supply chain within the entire Islamic economic ecosystem. An example can be taken that of monitoring through a public distributed ledger (blockchain) in the application of smart contracts. Islamic FinTech can undoubtedly make the operations more efficient and transparent. On a similar note, submission and processing of insurance claims can move ahead in a swifter way by using internet of things (IoT) devices in *Takaful*. IoT devices can be understood as pieces of hardware, such as sensors, actuators, gadgets, appliances or machines, being programmed for certain applications that can help in transmitting data over the internet or other networks. They can be simultaneously incorporated into other mobile devices, industrial equipment, environmental sensors, medical devices, and so forth.

In *waqf* management, the cash *waqf* model on blockchain can be considered as giant leap forward. Islamic FinTech promises to ensure the social and ethical impacts of the financial services that it provides. An example can be used here to understand the assurance of ethical mandate. More often not, it is not possible to finance a welfare project without traditional banking and financial institutions. However, at present, crowdfunding can work wonders. Likes of Launch-Good and Skola Fund make it possible for not only individuals but also small businesses of any sector to get access to funding subject to their social impact schemes.

Newer technology and innovative solutions are being increasingly adopted in leading jurisdictions offering Islamic financial services owing to current the application of FinTech in the Islamic capital market. One can consider the example of Malaysia in this regard. Here, the Investment Account Platform (IAP) was introduced as a cross border multi-currency platform so that regional and global financing opportunities for emerging business ventures could be well facilitated. The IAP is based on the alliance of several Islamic banks. These serve as financial intermediaries for channelling the funds to business ventures that are deserving. At the same time, other innovative solutions have been designed in Malaysia for liquidity management such as the Bursa Suq Al-Sila (BSAS). This online platform manages commodity *murabaha* transactions (Oseni and Ali, 2019). It simultaneously provides a *Shari'ah*-compliant trading mechanism that makes the *tawarruq* (monetisation) and *murabaha* transactions possible online. Thus, the entire transactional process becomes fast and seamless. Introduced way before in 2009, this platform has since then won global attention because of it being increasingly used across borders (Oseni and Ali, 2019). The growing acceptance of this platform from participants across borders is from different jurisdictions, especially from the regions of the Middle East, North Africa and Asia.

In 2013, in UAE, the Dubai Multi Commodities Centre (DMCC)'s Commodity Murabaha Trading Platform (CMTP) stood to be absolutely functional. The transfer of ownership and possession using the online platform is being enabled through the tradable warrants model adopted by the CMTP. Just like the BSAS, the CMTP is also a fully electronic platform for commodity *murabaha* transactions and is in compliance with *Shari'ah*. In the midst of addressing concerns subjected to *Shari'ah*, the platform provides the means to make sure the underlying commodities exist and that the relevant parties get to inspect the transaction before the documentation is finally executed or/and trade is concluded. It equally ensures the underlying warrants are verified so as to have faith in the documents as being legally recognised. It also ensures a retrievable document trail with standard audit capabilities for both conventional and *Shari'ah* audit functions (Nazir, 2013). The Nasdaq Dubai *Murabaha* Platform can be equally considered as another innovative solution in Islamic financing through *Wakalah* (agency) investments in the form of underlying assets. The online platform makes the process seamless, easy, and fast for Islamic banks offering finance to customers.

Apart from FinTech's application in the Islamic capital market, crowdfunding platforms are being increasingly used for financing of *Shari'ah*-compliant projects. This applies especially for small and medium-sized enterprises (SME), housing, and agricultural financing.

16.3 Islamic FinTech Landscape

Islamic FinTech can be classified on the basis of three types: financial services, technology and geography (DinarStandard, 2018).

- Classification by financial services: Involves 65% of financing, 15% of wealth management, and 5% of other parameters.
- Classification by technology: Involves 65% of P2P finance, 14% of distributed ledger technique, and 14% of other parameters.
- Classification by demography: The reach of FinTech in different countries can be observed as 31% in Indonesia, 12% in the United States, 11% in UAE, 10% in the United Kingdom, 7% in Malaysia, and 22% in different countries.

DinarStandard (2018) claims that at present, 93 Islamic FinTech companies are predominant in financing services, followed by wealth management and funding. Sixty-five companies provide P2P finance. Fourteen companies provide distributed ledger tech. P2P platforms are popularly used as Islamic FinTech platforms because of its ability to hold the essence of Islamic finance in absolute integrity as it directly connects the capital provider with the users of capital through technology (World Bank, 2020).

Indonesia is on the lead with most of its companies offering Islamic FinTech (31 companies). This is followed by the United States, UAE (driven by the Dubai International Financial Centre [DIFC]), United Kingdom, and Malaysia with 12 companies or fewer (Table 16.3).

To be proficient in the development of Islamic FinTech, a sound technological base is required along with a hunger for innovation. Proficiency cannot be achieved in the form of having expertise in Islamic finance. This idea holds true since two out of the top five jurisdictions for Islamic FinTech do not fall under the major jurisdictions for Islamic finance. The growth of Islamic FinTech is being driven by increasing government and regulatory support, younger, technology-minded customers, innovation attractiveness, and the availability of start-up incubators and accelerators, being mostly state-sponsored (World Bank, 2020).

Table 16.3 shows how governments are coming to this realisation that Islamic FinTech can potentially benefit in the long run and are thereby actively supporting its development. Countries are building centres and providing early-stage funds for start-ups to interact and collaborate. FinTech companies are being connected to investors. All of this is being done under the influence of a hospitable regulatory and policy environment.

The support coming from accelerators and incubators is helping contenders to quickly adopt to the preferences of youthful customers. Islamic FinTech start-ups are consistently embracing the preferences of the younger generation corresponding to innovation and easy accessibility. The incubators for early-stage start-ups and accelerators that connect start-ups with investors have become an imperative

TABLE 16.3 Governments Facilitating Islamic FinTech in OIC Countries

Organisation	*Country*	*Facility provided*
National Islamic Finance Committee (KNKS)	Indonesia	The National *Shari'ah* Finance Committee (KNKS) is institutionally a federal government entity. It acts as a catalyst in not only developing Islamic finance but also the Islamic economy at large, particularly at a national as well as international scale. The ultimate goal of establishing this body was to execute the Indonesian *Shari'ah* economic master plan, the issuance of which had been done in May 2019.
Bank Negara	Malaysia	Bank Negara established the Investment Account Platform (IAP). It is considered to be the first Islamic P2P initiative to have been established by a central bank.
Malaysia Digital Economy Corporation	Malaysia	A network of investors got connected with halal business owners. Halal certifications had been provided. The Malaysian government owns this entity.
Dubai International Financial Center	UAE	Acceleration of the financial technology sector in Middle East, Africa and South Asia (MEASA) region through the DIFC FinTech Hive programme that supports FinTech, regtech, insurtech, and Islamic FinTech start-ups. Access to a $100 million fund and network of financial institutions has been provided.
Bahrain FinTech Bay	Bahrain	FinTech companies are offered opportunities to co-operate and develop their technologies. IFIs operating in Bahrain and throughout the GCC are partners with the Bahrain FinTech Bay.
Other	UK, Turkey, Abu Dhabi	UK Islamic FinTech panel to promote Islamic FinTech sector. UK, Turkey Islamic FinTech Working Group to consider opportunities in Islamic FinTech sector. Abu Dhabi General Market's New FinTech Ecosystem.

Source: World Bank (2020).

part of it. Both incubators and accelerators enable start-ups in the development of their technologies and business models while simultaneously enabling these companies in identifying potential equity partners. Several organisations such as the Islamic FinTech Alliance in Singapore as part of Asia Pacific, DIFC FinTech Hive in UAE, AlBaraka Bank in Turkey, and Affinis Labs in the United States are crucial in anchoring the international networks.

16.3–1 Islamic FinTech Categories and Platforms

FinTech has been becoming an increasingly active segment of the Islamic financial market. The latest Islamic FinTech platforms are leveraging on social media data and analysing them for practical purposes, like in the case of targeted marketing or estimating user behaviour. On the basis of their services and underlying technologies, the global landscape of the Islamic FinTech platforms have been divided into different categories:

- Islamic crowdfunding platforms
- Islamic FinTech deploying blockchain
- Robo advisors
- Those who collect the user behavioural data to activate machine learning.

16.3-1-1 Islamic Crowdfunding Platforms

16.3–1–1–1 Beehive

Beehive constitutes to be UAE's initial online Dubai-based marketplace for P2P finance. With this platform, the access and processing of SME loans for business purposes is quickly facilitated. Individual investors get the opportunity to generate returns higher than savings rates in an environment which also facilitates risk-sharing. It also works with Islamic legal advisors and Islamic financial services experts in establishing structures which ensure approval of investments that are in complete adherence with *Shari'ah*. *Shari'ah* scholars keep a check on the sites of businesses who campaign so as to ensure that the business activities and the utilisation funds are in harmony with the *Shari'ah* principles. Any kind of business which does not sync with *Shari'ah* principles will be considered as a conventional investment and will be processed in the conventional way.

A platform called the Commodity *Murabaha*Trading Platform (CMTP) has been launched by Beehive. This has been done in cooperation of the Dubai Multi Commodities Centre (DMCC). With the CMTP, the online transfer is easily facilitated. At the same time, through warrants that are tradable, the CMTP also facilitates the exchange of the ownership and possession. Solutions are provided to the Islamic finance industry at large. Accessibility to locally stored *Shari'ah*-compliant commodities to be able to execute commodity *murabaha* transactions is also a facility that can be used here. This platform is characterised by electronic transfers of ownership and possession. Besides DMCC, CMTP Dubai has also collaborated with Emirates Islamic Financial Brokerage (EIFB) to be able to offer the Islamic financing digital platform called the Nasdaq Dubai *Murabaha* Platform. In Beehive, modes of commodity *murabaha* are applied for purchasing and reselling of the commodities traded on the DMCC at fixed prices.

Beehive does not directly deal with loans, even though they have received 250 funding applications from start-ups from around the world. Six thousand investors are registered on Beehive, the majority of them belonging to UAE. As of 2018, a total worth of US$40 million is reported to have been channelised by Beehive among their customers. Its formal and official working license was received in March 2017 after the issuance of P2P regulations from the Dubai Financial Services Authority

DFSA. These regulations are indicative of the willingness of the regulators towards embracing FinTech owing to their aim of eventually becoming the FinTech hub. In December, 2017, Beehive began its first venture round and was led by Riyad Taqnia. Interestingly, it was able to secure US$5 million in its first venture itself owing to a proper P2P regulatory framework in place.

16.3–1–1–2 Ethis Crowd

The first Islamic crowdfunding platform which is based on the real state is Ethis Crowd. With it, funds are facilitated for real estate projects. There are 17,000 investors on board on this platform. These investors particularly invest in Asia's real estate projects. In Singapore, the headquarters of Ethis Crowd are located. Regional offices can be found in Jakarta, Kuala Lumpur, Dubai, and South Africa. One of its major achievements is how in the first 20 months of its campaign itself, it was able to accomplish a housing project in Indonesia valued at US$2.2 million. The platform provides opportunities, manifold, to its users who seem to be interested in businesses and start-ups and have the capacity to fund them from a minimum of $800 in the initial process. In this platform, an investor is matched with a start-up depending on the background and preferences of the individual. It is fully compliant with *Shari'ah* law and thus, dealings associated with alcohol, pork, gambling, speculation, or loan and interest-based finance are not a part of this platform. This clause of being fully *Shari'ah* compliant is largely responsible for attracting a variety of audiences and investors, particularly from Southeast Asia, and the Middle East (Ali et al., 2019).

There are multiple collaborations which Ethis has been able to build with different communities and organisations. Some of these collaborations include TanganDiAtas.com, one of the largest SME/entrepreneur groups in Indonesia, and Kapital Boost, based in Singapore, which provides hybrid Islamic crowdfunding. It is also focused on SMEs with LOKAmotion Malaysia which is a retail start-up incubator and is being talked about quite a lot (Ethis Crowd, 2016).

16.3–1–1–3 Ethos

The largest *Shari'ah*-compliant, FinTech-focused private equity fund in the world is the British asset manager, Ethos Invest. It has been created by raising a massive amount of £1 billion (US$1.37 billion). However, it is not focused on being the biggest of its kind but is rather concerned about being able to create momentum in the sector. This platform wants to catalyse capital investments and work on the advancement of the market which has remained largely underserved in the past. Its considerable size marks its space as important. The large space is equally indicative of growth opportunities for investors and how more companies can be equally encouraged to get involved into it. As per S&P Global Ratings, it is reported to be a US$2.4 trillion *Shari'ah*-compliant finance industry and completely prohibits interest payments and pure monetary speculation. It is expected to grow at a rate of

10%–12% annually. The industry grew by 10.6% in the year 2018 on the back of higher-than-expected *Sukuk* issuance with growth of 17.3% in 2019. The partners at Ethos Invest observed an increasing appetite for Islamic finance during the pandemic as the world grappled with the economic hit from COVID-19.

16.3–1–1–4 Easi Up

Founded in Paris, in 2014, Easi Up has been designed as a platform focusing on charitable educational projects. It provides scope for European residents to make their projects and campaigns visible to the investors. This in turn gives them an opportunity to receive investments and funding which could possibly help them convert their dreams into reality. However, the lack of proper *Shari'ah*-compliant funding in educational projects restricts the number of activities that could otherwise be put into action. This platform acts as an opportunity for youth entrepreneurs and students to get access to funds for promoting ethically binding and *Shari'ah*-compliant projects through Islamic morale (Ali et al., 2019).

16.3–1–1–5 Mambu and Ta3meed

Contributing to the ecosystem in Saudi Arabia, Mambu is a pure software-as-a-service (SaaS) banking platform while Ta3meed is one of the leading Islamic FinTechs in trade finance. Both of these platforms have been founded in Saudi Arabia and are crucial contributors to the financial ecosystem in Saudi Arabia. They have entered into a strategic partnership agreement for delivering innovative digital Islamic financing for SMEs and investors. The automated purchase order (PO) financing platform of Ta3meed integrates the active core banking technology of Mambu. The combined solutions give shape to the ultimate goal of accelerating the digital transformation of financial institutions combined with financing and investment solutions in Saudi Arabia. These solutions are necessarily *Shari'ah*-compliant. The partnership between Mambu and Ta3meed makes it a point to highlight the financial inclusion and accessibility of working capital finance to small and medium-sized enterprises. SMEs are considered to be crucial contributors to Saudi Arabia's economic development. However, at present, they account for only 8.3% of banks and financing companies' total credit facilities.

16.3–1–1–6 Eureeca

Launched in 2013, Eureeca constitutes to be one of the earliest equity crowdfunding platforms. Its member-investors can be casual or angel investors and institutional firms. This platform provides an opportunity for its member-investors to purchase shares in growth-oriented businesses. In 2015, the platform received a license from the UK Financial Conduct Authority and Securities Commission Malaysia. Its offices are located in several countries, such as London, Dubai, and Kuala Lumpur. According to its website (Eureeca.com), Eureeca offers potential investment opportunities to a wide network of investors from the Middle East, Europe, and Southeast Asia. The provision of equity finance through this platform makes it more aligned with the principle spirit of Islamic finance, particularly that of risk-sharing through *mudaraba* and *musharaka* models.

16.3–1–1–7 Kapital Boost

Founded in July 2015, Kapital Boost was conceptualised to focus and tackle the issues of lack of opportunities in the field of *Shari'ah*-compliant retail services. The primary focus of this platform is based on micro-small and medium enterprises (MSMEs) to enable the growth and development of less privileged communities. A hybrid crowdfunding model was adopted by this Singapore-based platform. This model includes an option of reward- and donation-based crowdfunding. This opens up the scope for investors to be able to invest in MSMEs or partake in a donation campaign. The *Murabaha* crowdfunding structure of this platform made it receive a *Shari'ah* pronouncement from the Financial Shari'ah Advisory and Consultancy (FSAC). It took several months for the completion of the total pronouncement process. As a part of its review, FSAC's Shari'ah Committee was presented with the business model, processes, legal structure, and documentation relating to Kapital Boost's crowdfunding.

The capital requirements of MSMEs are met through asset purchase and invoice financing, provided by Kapital Boost. The working process of this platform can be understood through the figures discussed here. MSMEs are matched with the investors who pool funds to collectively purchase goods or equipment. Later, they sell the same to the SMEs at a mark-up. Kapital Boost generates competitive annual returns of about 15%–24% for its investors. The platform is the only platform in Singapore where no investor fee is charged. Starting from its launch in July 2015, Kapital Boost has been able to raise more than US$1.3 million for 26 MSME campaigns, with an annualised average return of 22%. Reports say that 12 of its campaigns have paid off their funding as of 27 October 2016.

16.3–1–1–8 Funding Lab

A non-profit Scottish charitable incorporated organisation, Funding Lab as a crowdfunding platform provides finances for empowering underprivileged students and young entrepreneurs. The crowdfunding model of this platform is reward based. The platform wholly abides by *Shari'ah* principles. Its network of investors is primarily from Pakistan, Palestine, and Bangladesh. They want to develop this crowdfunding model to enable more people, particularly young entrepreneurs, students and fresh graduates who are willing to start their businesses but have very little or zero capital. The intent of this platform is to ignite the spirit of doing business among the young Muslim population for which it has also initiated collaborations with different platforms and academic institutions in Southeast Asia and the Middle East.

16.3–1–1–9 Launch Good

Launched in October 2013, Launch Good stands as one of the most active crowdfunding platforms in the present day and time. It is simultaneously the largest Islamic crowdfunding platform with its primary focus on the Muslim community across the world. The date of maturity and a minimum funding goal are selected by the project creators. This platform also has a provision of rewards to give to contributors at various levels. Amany Killawi, the co-founder and chief operating officer of this platform, considers it to be different from other platforms owing to its empathetic approach. According to him, this platform is designed to help people raise funds with the help of a complementary campaign coach to provide support and feedback on every step of the way. Thus, this makes the platform unique and distinguishable from its other counterparts. According to her claim, Launch Good campaigns is likely to have a double success rate when compared to other campaigns solely because the team is deeply invested in all the campaigns. The success of the campaigns marks the success for the Muslim community as a whole. Other factors which contribute to its success are it having the lowest fees in the industry and the access to a community that cares and believes in your cause.

At present, a wide range of crowdfunded projects have been launched by the platform through their site (LaunchGood.com). These projects are not limited to helping Muslim communities only. Projects have been launched for repairing Jewish cemeteries, rebuilding torched churches and so forth. They have not only raised millions of dollars but simultaneously, raised their profile in the course of the process. Thousands of users and donors in almost 75 countries are active on this platform. This attribute is symbolic of their truly inclusive Islamic spirit.

16.3–1–1–10 Narwi

Launched in June 2015, Narwi was founded as an online non-profit Islamic crowdfunding platform by Silatech in Qatar. One of the world's largest online microlending platforms, Kiva.org supports this platform. Narwi funds projects which are financed through *Shari'ah*-compliant products. The platform provides services in Palestine, Yemen, Iraq, Jordan, Egypt, Lebanon, and Somalia. It intends to expand into Morocco and Tunisia as well. As a platform, Narwi allows donors to support very small and micro enterprises. The micro-entrepreneurs can establish Narwi-Waqf, or what can be understood as endowment, with as little as US$25. This helped in creating a significant number of jobs in the Middle East and North Africa.

16.3–1–1–11 Shekra

Seven people from very diverse backgrounds (like aviation, technology, investment, and banking) came together and founded the platform, which went 'live' in Cairo in November 2016. The founders pooled their resources to form the platform,

Shekra in order to be able to support Egyptian start-ups. The opportunities existing in the MENA market and the platform's core features were defined through a framework, established by Shekra. The platform is dependent on a closed network of investors because of the regulatory restrictions in the MENA region (Marzban et al., 2014).

16.3–1–1–12 Zoomal

Launched in 2013, Zoomal claimed itself to be on the lead in the equity crowdfunding region. Two hundred crowdfunding projects have been covered by this platform. Most of these projects were associated to Egypt, Jordan, Morocco, Algeria, and Lebanon. The platform provides financing alternative to the regulated institutions (e.g. banks) and thus, assists individuals by leveraging the internet and social media (Oddone, 2015).

16.3–1–1–13 Skolafund

As a web platform, Skolafund has been founded for needy students who find it difficult to pay their school fees. Having no alternative option, they have to be dependent on crowdfunding for fulfilling their goals of higher education. The inception of Skolafund happened in April 2015. In the beginning, it happened to be just an alpha version website which remained active till August 2015. During this course of the first four months, the platform raised an approximate amount of RM25,000 from 125 members of the community and was thus, able to fund six students. After this initial success, the team decided to increase their online presence and have since then, crowdfunded more than 42 scholarships and counting. They aim to ensure accessible and affordable higher education for those who qualify but do not possess the means or resources to pursue. They strongly believe in not letting anyone get deprived of an education just because one cannot afford it.

16.3–1–1–14 Wahed Invest

With its headquarters in the United States, Wahed is an online investment platform for those focused on Halal and *Shari'ah*-compliant investment opportunities. As a robo advisor, this platform provides advice to investors, thereby, assisting them to make educated investment decisions which undoubtedly have to be aligned with the *Shari'ah* norms and guidelines.

It is one of the world's leading Islamic FinTech start-ups. Wahedna, the present CEO of Wahed Invest, has raised a total of US$19.8 million and already claims to have generated a revenue of US$3.5 million. The platform has even expanded into the UK market in 2018 after being launched in the United States in 2015. The stats of the platform show that 84% of its users are either new to or somewhat familiar with investing. The residents of more than 130 countries get to have access to

Islamic value based investing through this platform. The major markets are spread over Nigeria, India, Pakistan, and the MENA region (FINTECH, 2020).

16.4 Islamic FinTech Application in Blockchain

16.4-1 Goldmoney Inc

As a Canadian FinTech company, Goldmoney Inc has been certified as *Shari'ah* compliant for its gold-based financial products. In order to be able to provide *Shari'ah*-compliant financial products, the firm has deployed blockchain technology. The firm claims their financial products to be absolutely backed by gold reserves and that they use the immutability of the blockchain ledgers to collect money or investments from the investors and the disbursement of funds and returns (Vizcaino, 2018). Goldmoney's certification of being *Shari'ah*-compliant has been provided by the Bahrain-based Accounting and Auditing Organization for Islamic Financial Institutions (AAOIFI) and simultaneously ensures that Halal gold standards by AAOIFI are implemented (Maierbrugger, 2017). A company statement claims of it having more than 1.3 million users across 150 countries and manages US$1.7 billion in client assets. They believe that the company's adherence to *Shari'ah* law will help in elevating their profile in the market. This will, in turn, increase their demand from the Muslim-majority countries across the world.

16.4-2 Blossom Finance

Initially established as a start-up in San Francisco, Blossom Finance eventually was relocated to Jakarta, Indonesia; the primary intent being able to emphasise on the microfinance in Indonesia. Blossom did not publicly reveal the details of its first investment in a microfinance institution in Indonesia until May 2015. Blossom is based on the ethical rule that it gives money to the particular microfinance institutions, the operational structure of which is based on the principle of sharing profits and losses and not subjected to risk transfer of interest-based systems.

It must be carefully noted that Blossom does not handle loans directly but rather works with *Shari'ah*-compliant microfinance institutions. They work in the form of partnerships built with institutions. Blockchain technology is used for collecting and disbursement of funds. The blockchain technology is deployed for transferring money from investors to microfinance institutions. This helps in cost reduction and equally cuts down on time consumption, particularly for cross-border money transfers. Blossom ensures the implementation and adherence to *Shari'ah* rules throughout the whole process for moving money within a short period of time at low cost, all of which ensures total transparency. The beneficiaries receive money in the local currency (Indonesian rupiah) and the investors can invest and cash out their returns in their local currencies like euros, British pounds, and US dollars (Freischlad, 2016).

16.4-3 Finterra

Finterra serves as a *waqf* (Islamic charitable trust) chain platform and the overarching technology used here is blockchain. The head offices of Finterra are found in five countries including Singapore, Malaysia, Hong Kong and United Arab Emirates. There are 700,000 subscribers on board having subscribed to Finterra's digital wallet. For public trading, they are offering 1 billion digital tokens. In addition to all of these, Finterra also provides consultancy, solutions, and software subjected to the application of blockchain. Finterra is aiming to grow and expand their platform in more countries (Finterra, 2018).

16.5 Islamic Robo Advisors

16.5-1 Wahed Robo Advisor

The first automated Islamic investment platform in the world is in the form of a robo advisor and is named as Wahed Invest. A financial advisory company based out of New York launched Wahed Invest Inc as a platform on 26 September 2016. As an automated platform, the robo advisor possesses the ability to analyse thousands of Islamic (*halal*) securities globally for allocating assets that have greater growth potential for their customers. The primary objective of this platform is to give easy accessibility to *Shari'ah*-compliant asset management for the two billion Muslims living all across the world and simultaneously, for non-Muslims who are willing to invest as per the ethical code of the Islamic law. The minimum investment amount offered by Wahed Invest is fixed around US$7,500 to be able to start (Maierbrugger, 2017). The regulatory body, the Securities and Exchange Commission (SEC), provides the license. At the same time, the Board of Ethical Review supervises and monitors them.

16.5-2 Algebra

The first robo advisor in Asia to have offered financial advice to its clients subjected to *Shari'ah*-compliant investment options, as well as the *Shari'ah* non-compliant ones, is Algebra. Interestingly, the platform offers fee financial advice. Algebra's headquarters is located in Malaysia. It constitutes to be a part of Farringdon Group Ltd. The platform is being regulated by the Labuan Financial Service Authority. Since the company's establishment in 2007, it has never received a regulatory complaint against the firm. The subsidiaries and associate offices of Farringdon Group are located in five countries including Singapore and Seychelles with global assets, worth over US$500 million under its management and advice. The primary target of this platform is the Asian market. This platform provides a variety of tools like that of education planning offering different investment solutions for clients opting for *Shari'ah*-compliant or other forms of ethical investment. As a platform which is solely digital, Algebra provides its customers with a series of goals, takes them through these goals and indicates them on monetary levels so as to aware them about how much they need to invest for successfully reaching their goals. This plan then gets automatically integrated in a risk-weighted portfolio being managed over time for the customers to help them to achieve their desired financial goals. Investors from any jurisdiction can avail and utilise this platform in exchange of a monthly fee of minimum US$200 (Abdullah and Rizal, 2018).

16.5-3 Aghaz Investments

The FinTech start-up, Aghaz Investments, was founded in January 2020 and is currently launched with a private group of testers on an invite-only basis. The robo advisor already has more than 200 investors on its platform. Aghaz launched its mobile app on Google and Apple iOS. The minimum investment amount is kept at US$1,000 with an annual fee structure kept at 0.49% and a monthly subscription fee of US$2. The firm enters the market facing competition with Wahed, a New-York based Sharia-compliant digital investment platform that had raised US$25 million and also expanded the business into the Middle East and North Africa.

Aghaz excludes all companies whose core businesses involve or serve interest-based products, health or mind-altering products, betting and gambling operations, pork and non-*halal* foods, human genetic manipulation and any other non-*Shari'ah*-compliant businesses. It raised US$400,000 in pre-seed funding. While the initial launch was targeted for the Muslim investors, the FinTech will produce a custom values product for non-Muslim investors as well.

16.5-4 Others

16.5-4-1 Investment Account Platform (IAP)

It holds undeniably true that Malaysia is considered to be one of the major jurisdictions of Islamic finance, where the Islamic financial services industry has not only introduced new standards but also brought in innovative Islamic financial products. The Investment Account Platform (IAP) is very similar in that context. In the form of a multibank platform, this new initiative helps in providing channels to the cross border multicurrency by linking it to the regional and global economies. Funds get channelled faster from institutional investors to be able to finance large-scale viable ventures. Investors will eventually gain the access to a wide range of investment opportunities, Islamic banks and new sources of funds through the IAP. The platform is owned and developed by a wholly owned unit of Raeed Holdings, IAP Integrated Sdn Bhd, supported by a consortium of Islamic banks comprised of Bank Muamalat Malaysia, Maybank Islamic, Affin Islamic Bank, Bank Islam Malaysia, Bank Kerjasama Rakyat Malaysia, and Bank Simpanan Nasional. More banks are expected to join the platform and simultaneously, the number of companies listed is anticipated to go double in the near future (MIFC, 2016).

16.5-4-2 Bursa Suq Al Sila (BSAS)

Launched in Malaysia, Bursa Suq Al Sila (BSAS) is an online platform developed by Bursa Malaysia Bhd for commodity *murabaha* transactions. In the form of a digital trading platform, it facilitates *murabaha* and *tawarruq* transactions. In the years between 2009 and 2014, the platform experienced an exponential annual growth rate of 178%. The growth rate is symbolic of the huge demand and wide acceptance of its *Shari'ah*-compliant products, particularly from the customers of the MENA and Asian regions (MIFC, 2016).

16.5-4-3 ETHIXS International Turnkey Solutions (ITS)

Launched in Turkey, this FinTech platform, called the ETHIXS International Turnkey Solutions (ITS). Apart from other banking services, this platform offers innovative solutions for Islamic banks subjected to core banking, trade finance, delivery channels, online banking, branch automation and reports. The working mechanism of ITS ETHIXS is in complete synchronicity with the International Accounting Standards (IAS) and Accounting and Auditing Organization for Islamic Financial Institutions (AAOIFI). An integrated system is being offered for financial institutions and banks to deliver *Shari'ah*-compliant products. With the usage of this platform, Islamic banks are empowered to improve their operational efficiency by cutting down on costs in multiple banking areas. As a standalone module, it can be easily integrated and it offers complete support through its back-end accounting functionalities with straight-through processing (STP) built on a service-oriented architecture (SOA) platform and web services–based model. All in all, ETHIXS offers software based services and *Shari'ah*-compliant IT solutions for Islamic financial institutions.

16.5-4-4 Dubai International Financial Centre (DIFC)

DIFC has been making large scale investments into FinTech for fuelling the growth of the Islamic finance industry of United Arab Emirates. UAE is being acknowledged of having secured the position of the fourth-largest Islamic FinTech hub in the world, primarily because of the contribution by the continuously growing FinTech ecosystem of the centre. Among the 450 applications listed for DIFC's 2019 FinTech Hive programme, multiple Islamic start-up ideas were seen to emerge out of which four Islamic finance start-ups were finally selected to join the elite group of participants.

Based out of Malaysia, HelloGold is making an attempt to develop the first *Shari'ah*-compliant gold mobile application in the world. An innovative start-up, called IslamiChain is leveraging blockchain technology for enabling philanthropic services and compassionate giving. Hakbah, another Islamic FinTech start-up specialises in cooperative savings. The FinTech platform, called Wethaq, focuses on the structuring and distribution of securities in *Sukuk* capital markets.

The DIFC serves as the chief networking hub for 46 Islamic finance institutions to get involved with innovative start-ups. The FinTech Hive accelerator equally partners with specialist organisations. This includes the Dubai Islamic Economy Development Centre, Emirates Islamic Bank, Dubai Islamic Bank and Abu Dhabi Islamic Bank. The representatives of leading banks, financial institutions, as well as public and private companies Market have been collectively brought into the first Dubai Sustainable Finance Working Group launched in 2019 by the DIFC. To encourage using green financial instruments and responsible investing, the initiatives of Dubai's finance sector are being combined by the group in order to be able to create a sustainable financial hub in the region which syncs with the UN Sustainable Development Goals 2030. The synergies between environment, social and governance (ESG) goals essential throw light upon how Islamic finance can serve as the primary driving force for ethical financial solutions (Amiri, 2021).

16.6 Case Studies

Described underneath are crucial case studies of a market-leading Islamic FinTech company. The briefs of these platforms as stated below cover their founding principles, value proposition, traction to date and roadmap for the future.

16.6-1 Founding Principles

HelloGold is an award-winning wealth management Islamic FinTech. Brought into effect in 2017, HelloGold was the first mobile application to provide its users the opportunity to buy gold in a *Shari'ah*-compliant manner. HelloGold has earned numerous awards, such as Best Islamic Wealth Management FinTech Company by World Islamic FinTech Awards 2018 in Bahrain, and Prominent in Wealth, Asset and Investment Management of the Year by Malaysia FinTech Awards 2018. This application is backed by physical quantities of gold which happen to be stored in Dubai or Singapore, while any fractional trading is considered as part of the gold bullion.

16.6-2 Value Proposition

Amanie Advisors has certified HelloGold as a *Shari'ah*-compliant asset-backed investment. The target customer base is 60% of Malaysians who are practicing Muslims. The customer base also extends to Malaysian households that have a minimum RM76 of savings from disposable income (low income). While 98% of Malaysians were using smartphones in 2018, the availability of a *Shari'ah*-compliant investment via smartphone, with a trivial amount of investment (i.e. RM158 has been quite beneficial.

16.6-3 Traction to Date

Since its inception, there have been more than 150,000 downloads and about 80,000 customers. The transaction value is estimated to be RM6.5 million. It has simultaneously launched in Thailand.

16.6–4 Roadmap for the Future

The product is anticipated to be launched in Indonesia and Middle East in 2019. A partnership with Baobab in Africa has been finalised which will help in expanding the same to a further nine African countries. The ultimate aim is to be not restricted to the gold investment business, but to eventually become a virtual bank, regulations permitting (World Bank, 2020).

16.7 Risks of Islamic FinTech and Potential Mitigations

Irrespective of varied reasons which have been acting against the customer's ability to open a bank account, *Shari'ah*-compliant P2P financing can largely come into play in this context and enable financial inclusion by accessing unbanked population. However, the easier accessibility of these funds can possibly encourage people to borrow more than required thereby, leading to an accumulation of excess debt. Instead of financing micro or small businesses, the final outcome can take the shape of increased consumerism fuelled by debt. P2P finance is convenient where credit approvals can be granted within minutes based upon personal data and telephone numbers. However, higher fees are charged in P2P financing when compared with Islamic investing in a project. In cases of default, financiers might apply aggressive measures to coerce repayment.

According to World Bank (2020) report, certain other potential risks associated with Islamic FinTech are as follows:

- Data analytics could end up potentially advising IFIs to only provide services to the most profitable customers, excluding all others.
- The functionality of risk management of Islamic banks could possibly end up being obsolete. This would require upgrading to avoid mis-selling and customer exploitation.
- Scarcity of Islamic scholars who can issue pronouncements (*fatawah*) on complex products. The scarcity is likely to be caused because of a knowledge gap subjected to technology.

Some methods that can help in mitigating risks are as follows (World Bank, 2020):

- Islamic FinTech must be in absolute adherence to the spirit of *Shari'ah*-compliant finance by prohibiting products that are likely to accumulate debt by providing easy credit. An example can be taken of Islamic microfinance co-operatives in Indonesia which provide financing, only to genuine micro and small businesses.
- The spirit of *Shari'ah* should not be just exhibited for the sake of it but deeply ingrained and incorporated in the products and services. Financing provided using *Qard-ul-Hasan* should not be have considerably high processing fees that increase transaction costs for the customer.

- To manage the widely spread FinTech start-ups, robust risk management policies and procedures are imperative. It is only through technology that companies gain access to sizeable segments of underserved consumers. This should be effectively used for the creation of holistic KYC, AML, and risk management frameworks and controls. This includes generating digital identities for unbanked populations.

16.8 Conclusion

Islamic FinTech serves as an opportunity for the Islamic financial industry in general and for the entrepreneurs. In the present day, the world is primarily driven via digital transformations thereby changing the dynamics of customer behaviour with every advent of latest technology in the market. In the similar context, their expectations from the service providers are equally escalating. Islamic finance industry has to initiatively develop strategies in the field of digital transformation in such a way so as to utilise the full power and potential of FinTech.

Notably, the banking and financial industry is facing disruptions from the new entrants on one hand and from the customers on the other. This situation can result in the conceptualisation of robust strategic decisions. The banking industry has been able to recognise these facts. It has anticipated that the industry's growth will come into real stagnation as an outcome of utilising innovative technologies and with the introduction of the latest and disruptive business models. Financial institutions are competing and striving to meet the expectations of customers by offering convenient and simple services through their digital channels. Another key challenge involves the tech companies are entering into the financial industry by launching payment applications, peer to peer lending platforms, and robo advisors. In addition to these, the regulatory strictness and harder liquidity criteria from the regulators are acting as hurdles for banks. This has led to a reduction of their leverage on balance sheets.

FinTech and the blockchain are potentially capable of creating a mechanism for financial transactions and activities which can be claimed as unduly transparent and trustworthy within the existing global economy. The blockchain will remove the need of an intermediary thereby, bringing a trust mechanism in banking operations in both impersonal and personal exchanges.

The role of governments and regulators play is imperative in fostering a holistic and healthy FinTech ecosystem. A majority proportion of FinTech players are introducing the latest solutions in the market, the regulators cannot be stuck at keeping the same pace but have to remain one step ahead to be able to efficiently advise the companies. The lean and responsive nature of start-ups enables them to move fast, and regulators who behave similarly will benefit from developing a healthy and leading ecosystem. The formula that they seem to follow is having the right amount of red tape to protect the user and balancing it with clear policies and processes for allowing start-ups to go to market effectively.

The need of the hour is to have solid risk management systems and policies especially subjected to FinTech start-ups because of their wide reach. RegTech can be used to assist authorities in not only monitoring and regulating industry participants but also in identifying when exactly to do so. The truly transformative potential of RegTech lies in its capacity to enable the real-time monitoring of financial markets. This would, in turn help in reconceptualise financial regulation. Markets have been evolving to grow more data reliant. The institution with the most data on borrowers will be best placed to assess their credit risk and extend them credit, and those institutions increasingly are more likely to be large tech companies (e.g. Google, Alibaba, Apple) or retail giants operating customer loyalty schemes, rather than traditional financial institutions.

Review Questions

- Is FinTech developed for a social cause or intended for profit games?
- What kind of technology does FinTech employ in investments?
- What are your opinions on the collaboration of FinTech and banks?
- Are they disturbed by negative market sentiments?
- Do you think customisation and enhanced data tools reduce the requirements for the wealth advisor's skill set?
- What is Islamic FinTech? Describe its key areas and platforms.
- Discuss the employment of blockchain technology in Islamic social finance.
- What are the risks of Islamic FinTech in investment and their potential mitigations?

References

Abdullah, A and Rizal, MN (2018), A Framework for the Development of a National Crypto-Currency, *International Journal of Economics and Finance*, 10, 14–25

Ali, H, Mohamed, H, Hashmi, H and Abbas, M (2019), Global Landscape of Islamic Fintech: Opportunities, Challenges and Future Ahead, *COMSTAT Journal of Islamic Finance*, 4(2), 29–53

Amiri, A (2021), *FinTech Can Help Islamic Finance to Innovate and Grow, Business*, retrieved from www.thenationalnews.com/business/fintech-can-help-the-islamic-finance-sector-to-innovate-and-grow-1.1046089?gclid=CjwKCAjwk6-LBhBZEiwAOUUDp3zAdZILlgJ85-Q1OFh0Jn-_E2UjoQEAPl1GFeKHiiEY5c9E_EWrMhoChH8QAvD_BwE (Access date March 3, 2021)

DinarStandard (2018), *Islamic Fintech Report 2018 Current Landscape*, New York: DinarStandard

Ethis *Crowd* (2016), *Ethis Islamic Crowdfunding Report*, retrieved from https://ethis.co/id/ (Access date March 3, 2020)

FINTECH (2020), *A Report on Technological Innovations in the Financial Services Industry*, CFA Society, Pakistan

Finterra (2018), Social Solution for Blockchain: Finterra The Financial Frontier, retrieved from https://finterra.org/ (Access date March 26, 2020)

Freischlad N (2016), *Blossom Offers Islamic Micro-Financing in Indonesia Using Bitcoin*, retrieved from https://www.techinasia.com/blossom-offers-islamic-microfinancing-indonesia-bitcoin (Access date March 10, 2020)

Global Islamic Fintech Report (2021), *DinarStandard and Elipses*, retrieved from https://www.salaamgateway.com/specialcoverage/islamic-fintech-2021 (Access date March 3, 2021)

Maierbrugger, A (2017), Philippines Planning Islamic Finance Scheme to Rebuild Southern City, *Gulf Times*, retrieved from https://www.gulf-times.com/story/557077/Philippines-planning-Islamic-finance-scheme-to-reb (Access date March 3, 2020)

Marzban, S, Asutay, M and Boseli, A (2014), *Shari'ah Framework for Entrepreneurship Development in Islamic Countries*, Eleventh Harvard International Islamic Finance Forum, Boston, April.

MIFC (2016), *Islamic Finance Technology and Innovation*, Malaysia International Islamic Finance Centre, retrieved from https://islamicmarkets.com/publications/technology-and-innovation-in-islamic-banking (Access date March 10, 2020)

Nazir, M (2013), UAE's DMCC Commodity Murabaha Trading Platform, *International Financial Law Review*, retrieved from www.iflr.com/Article/3248060/UAEs-DMCC commodity-Murabaha-trading-platform.html?ArticleId=3248060 (Access date May 11, 2020)

Oddone, K (2015), The Top Technologies Every Librarian Needs to Know – A LITA Guide, *Australian Academic & Research Libraries*, 46(4), 317–317

Oseni, U and Ali, S (2019), *FinTech in Islamic Finance Theory and Practice*, Oxon: Routledge

Vizcaino, B (2018), *After Downturn, Islamic Finance Eyes Profits*, Fintech: Survey, Reuters, retrieved from https://www.reuters.com/article/us-islamic-finance-strategy-idUSKBN1I30KV (Access date March 3, 2020)

World Bank (2020), *Leveraging Islamic Fintech to Improve Financial Inclusion*, Kuala Lumpur: World Bank, retrieved from https://openknowledge.worldbank.org/handle/10986/34520 License: CC BY 3.0 IGO (Access date May 1, 2021)

17

INTERNATIONAL ISLAMIC ACCOUNTING STANDARD-SETTING BODY (AAOIFI)

Learning Objectives

On completing this chapter, learners will be able to:

- Describe the factors in determining the conformity with AAOIFI financial and governance standards set by IFIs, and describe the extent of compliance
- Comprehend the influential role that AAOIFI accounting standards play in reporting IFIs.

17.1 Understanding the AAOIFI

The foundation of the Accounting and Auditing Organization for Islamic Financial Institutions (AAOIFI) took place in Bahrain in 1991. As an Islamic international entity, the AAOIFI is involved in the development and preparation of services related to accounts, audits, governance, ethics and *Shari'ah* standards for guiding Islamic financial institutions (IFIs) and the Islamic financial services industry. It was not until 1993 that the AAOIFI started developing and setting up these standards and has been doing so ever since then.

The practices of conventional accounting are not applicable to be utilised for Islamic financial transactions. The AAOIFI in conformity with *Shari'ah* norms consists of the following policies and objectives:

1. Policies and procedures

    - The IFIs have adopted certain policies and procedures. The AAOIFI must work for the harmonisation of the same by preparing, issuing and interpreting the accounting standards for the IFIs.

DOI: 10.4324/9780429321207-17

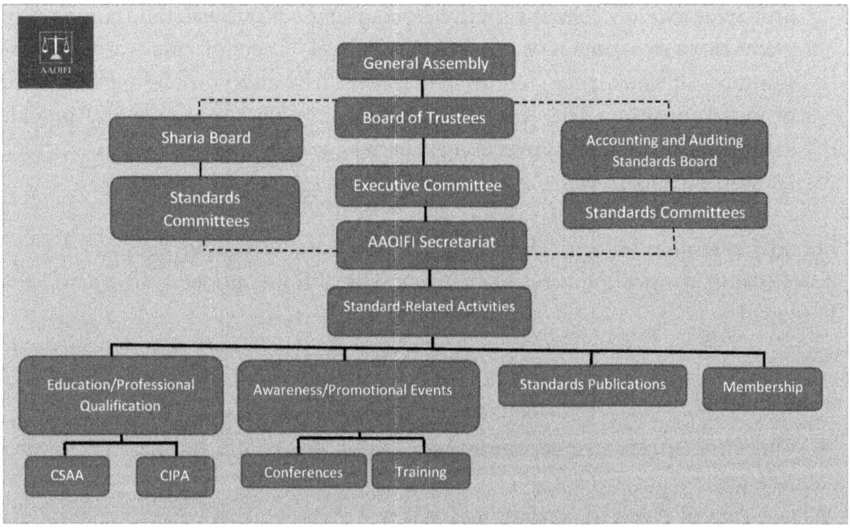

FIGURE 17.1 Structure of the Accounting and Auditing Organization for Islamic Financial Institutions.

CSAA: Certified Shari'a Adviser and Auditor
CIPA: Certified Islamic Professional Accountant

- The AAOIFI must look into improving the quality as well as uniformity of auditing and governance practices subjecting to IFIs. Similar to that of accounting standards, this is simultaneously done by developing, issuing, and interpreting the auditing and governance standards for IFIs.
- The AAOIFI should be inculcating and promoting ethical practices corresponding to IFIs. This is done by preparing and issuing ethical codes of conduct that are supposed to be followed by these institutions.

2. The AAOIFI must develop the standards in such a way that the *Shari'ah* supervisory boards of IFIs accept the conceptual appeal of these standards as well as their applicability. This will help in overcoming contradictory views and inconsistent procedures that might arise between the *fatwas* (rules prescribed by *Shari'ah* scholars) and the applications by these institutions. The idea is to effectively bring into action, the role of the *Shari'ah* supervisory boards of IFIs as well as central banks by developing, issuing and interpreting standards and rules in adherence to *Shari'ah* for investment, financing and insurance purposes.
3. The AAOIFI has to approach institutions offering Islamic financial services in order for their developed standards to be implemented and followed in accordance with their published guidelines. The institutions which can be approached include concerned regulatory bodies, IFIs, accounting and auditing firms and so on.
4. The AAOIFI must take steps in promoting and spreading knowledge across the verticals of accounting, auditing, ethical conduct, governance, *Shari'ah*

principles and any relevant topic by organising educational and training programs that can be inclusive of professional development programs as well. Distribution of knowledge and awareness will help in accomplishing the spirit of professionalism. The AAOIFI is likely to conduct, examine and provide certifications for these programmes, either by itself or by coordinating with relevant organisations.

The major responsibility of AAOIFI is developing and issuing standards for the global Islamic finance industry. The current standards mentioned below have been developed.

Accounting Standards

1. Objective of financial accounting for Islamic banks and financial institutions (IFIs)
2. Concept of financial accounting for IFIs
3. General presentation and disclosure in the financial statements of IFIs
4. *Murabaha* to the institution/body that has purchased the order
5. *Mudaraba* financing
6. *Musharaka* financing
7. Disclosure of bases for allocating profit between equity of owners and the holders of investment accounts
8. Equity of investment account holders and their equivalent
9. *Salam* and parallel *Salam*
10. *Ijarah* and *Ijarah Muntahia Bittamleek*
11. *Zakah*
12. *Istisna* and parallel *Istisna*
13. Provisions and reserves
14. General presentation and disclosure in the financial statements of Islamic insurance companies
15. Disclosure of bases for the determination and allocation of surplus or deficit in Islamic insurance companies
16. Investment funds
17. Provisions and reserves in Islamic insurance companies
18. Foreign currency transactions and foreign operations
19. Investments
20. Islamic financial services offered by conventional financial institutions
21. Contributions in Islamic insurance companies
22. Deferred payment sale
23. Disclosure on transfer of assets
24. Segment reporting
25. Consolidation
26. Investment in associates.

Auditing Standards

1. Objective and principles of auditing
2. The auditor's report
3. Terms of audit engagement
4. Testing by an external auditor so as to check whether the compliance to *Shari'ah* principles is maintained
5. The auditor has the responsibility to keep in check any fraud and error when auditing financial statements.

Governance Standards

1. Sharia supervisory board: appointment, composition and report
2. *Shari'ah* review
3. Internal *Shari'ah* review
4. Audit and governance committee for IFIs
5. Independence of Sharia supervisory board
6. Statement on governance principles for IFIs
7. Corporate social responsibility.

Ethical Standards

1. Ethical code of conduct for accountants and auditors of IFIs
2. Ethical code of conduct for employees of IFIs.

Shari'ah Standards

1. Trading in currencies
2. Debit card, charge card and credit card
3. Default in payment by a debtor
4. Settlement of debt by set-off
5. Guarantees
6. Conversion of a conventional bank to an Islamic bank
7. *Hawala*
8. *Murabaha* to the institution/body purchasing the order
9. *Ijarah* and *Ijarah Muntahia Bittamleek*
10. *Salam* and parallel *Salam*
11. *Istisna* and parallel *Istisna*
12. *Sharika (Musharaka)* and modern corporations
13. *Mudaraba*
14. Documentary credit
15. *Jua'la*
16. Commercial papers

17. Investment *Sukuk*
18. Possession (*Qabd*)
19. Loan (*Qard*)
20. Commodities in organised markets
21. Financial papers (shares and bonds)
22. Concession contracts
23. Agency
24. Syndicated financing
25. Combination of contracts
26. Islamic insurance
27. Indices
28. Banking services
29. Ethics and stipulations for *Fatwa*
30. Monetisation (*Tawarruq*)
31. *Gharar* stipulations in financial transactions
32. Arbitration
33. *Waqf*
34. *Ijarah* on labour (Individuals)
35. *Zakah*
36. Impact of contingent incidents on commitments
37. Credit agreement
38. Online financial dealings
39. Mortgage and its contemporary applications
40. Distribution of profit in *Mudarabah*-based investment accounts
41. Islamic reinsurance
42. Financial rights and the disposal management of the same
43. Liquidity and the instruments associated with it
44. Bankruptcy
45. Protection of capital and investments.

17.2 Conclusion

Islamic banking has exhibited a hike in its popularity across the world, particularly in the GCC countries. The standards developed by AAOIFI have been put into action in order to address and fill the existing loopholes. The accounting standards help in analysing the primary requirements of the Islamic financial institutions (IFIs). According to AAOIFI, Islamic banks in Bahrain and Qatar have witnessed considerably higher degrees of compliance with disclosure of the AAOIFI *Murabaha, Mudaraba* and *Musharaka* financial accounting standards. It must be noted that the Islamic banks in both of these countries were not fully complied every standard as developed by AAOIFI. This is an implication of gaps subjected to compliance with certain requirements and the necessity of following up by the Islamic banks and central banks in the member countries of AAOIFI. Moreover, compliance with disclosure standards has to be strictly followed to maintain the reputation of

IFIs internationally. As per the data of AAOIFI (2018), the highest compliance of disclosure was found to be of *Murabaha* financing financial standard in comparison to the *Mudarabah* and *Musharaka* financing financial standards. The compliance of disclosure to *Musharaka* standards ranged from moderate to high, while that of the *Mudarabah* standards depicted a lower compliance level which exposed the complexity of and problematic mandates involved in *Mudarabah* contracts.

Review Questions

1. Why is there a need to have separate Islamic accounting standards when we already have International Financial Reporting Standards (IFRS) existing worldwide?
2. How many standards have been developed by AAOIFI until now?
3. Is there any collaboration of AAOIFI with the International Accounting Standard Board (IASB)?

Reference

AAOIFI (2018), *Objectives, Vision and Mission*, Bahrain: AAOIFI, retrieved from http://aaoifi.com/?lang=en (Access date February 21, 2018)

18

INTERNATIONAL ISLAMIC FINANCIAL SERVICES BOARD (IFSB)

Learning Objectives

On completing this chapter, learners will be able to:

- Comprehend certain verticals of IFSB including effective supervision, regulation, risk management, and disclosure criteria
- Realise the different standards developed by IFSB and their purposes.

18.1 Introduction

The Islamic Financial Services Board (IFSB) became officially operational on 10 March 2003. Kuala Lumpur is the base location of IFSB. As the host country, Malaysia has legally established the Islamic Financial Services Board Act 2002 providing IFSB with certain immunities, facilities and privileges which are otherwise approved for international organisations and diplomatic missions. IFSB has the following specific objectives (IFSB, 2021):

1. To initiate prudence and transparency while developing the Islamic financial services industry. This objective can be achieved by bringing in the latest or adapting to the existing international standards that are in sync with *Shari'ah* principles and at the same time recommending the same to be integrated with the industry.
2. To offer guidelines on how the supervision and regulation of institutions offering Islamic financial products can be done in an effective manner. The role also entails developing several parameters for the Islamic financial services industry subjected to the identification, measurement, management and disclosure

DOI: 10.4324/9780429321207-18

of risks in consideration to international standards for valuation, income and expense calculation, and disclosure.

3. To establish and build liaison and cooperation with relevant organisations of member countries who are involved in designing standards for establishing stable and robust international monetary and financial systems.
4. To establish facilitation and coordination of initiatives for developing instruments and procedures to be able to efficiently handle risk and manage operations.
5. To ensure and boost cooperation among member countries with the aim of developing the Islamic financial services industry.
6. To ensure facilitation of training and personnel development of skills in the fields that can effectively regulate the Islamic financial services industry and markets associated with it.

18.2 Constituent Members

Until December 2017, the IFSB's total membership summed up to 185, out of which 75 members were regulatory and supervisory authorities, eight were international inter-governmental organisations, and 102 were market players (financial institutions, professional firms, industry associations, and stock exchanges). The overall membership spreads across 57 jurisdictions.

The IFSB can be viewed as an international body, comprising regulatory and supervisory agencies, which helps in designing and developing standards to be able to build a stable and robust Islamic financial services industry that integrates multiple services starting from banking and capital market to insurance. To be able to take this mission ahead, the IFSB promotes transparency in the Islamic financial services industry through the incorporation of the latest or by adapting to existing international standards that are in conformity with *Shari'ah* principles. IFSB simultaneously recommends the same for adoption. Until up now, IFSB's working vertical acts as a complementary aid to that of the working verticals of the Basel Committee on Banking Supervision, International Organisation of Securities Commissions, and the International Association of Insurance Supervisors.

18.3 Adoption of Standards

From the very beginning, a total of 27 standards, guiding principles and technical notes have been successfully issued by the IFSB for the Islamic financial services industry. The documents that have been published so far cover the following topics (IFSB, 2018):

1. Risk management (IFSB-1)
2. Capital adequacy (IFSB-2)
3. Corporate governance (IFSB-3)

4. Transparency and market discipline (IFSB-4)
5. Supervisory review process (IFSB-5)
6. Governance for collective investment schemes (IFSB-6)
7. Special issues in capital adequacy (IFSB-7)
8. Guiding principles on governance for Islamic insurance (*Takāful*) operations (IFSB-8)
9. Conduct of business for institutions offering Islamic financial services (IIFS) (IFSB-9)
10. Guiding principles on *Shari'ah* governance system (IFSB-10)
11. Standard on solvency requirements for *Takāful* (Islamic insurance) undertakings (IFSB-11)
12. Guiding principles on liquidity risk management (IFSB-12)
13. Guiding principles on stress testing (IFSB-13)
14. Standard on risk management for *Takāful* (Islamic insurance) undertakings (IFSB-14)
15. Revised capital adequacy standard (IFSB-15)
16. Revised guidance on key elements in the supervisory review process (IFSB-16)
17. Core principles for Islamic finance regulations (IFSB-17)
18. Guiding principles for *Re-takāful* (Islamic reinsurance) (IFSB-18)
19. Recognition of ratings on *Shari'ah*-compliant financial instruments (GN-1)
20. Guidance note in connection with the risk management and capital adequacy standards: commodity *Murabaha* transactions (GN-2)
21. Guidance note on the practice of smoothing the profits payout to investment account holders (GN-3)
22. Guidance note in connection with the IFSB capital adequacy standard: the determination of alpha in the capital adequacy ratio (GN-4)
23. Guidance note on the recognition of ratings by external credit assessment institutions (ECAIS) on *Takāful* and *Re-takāful* undertakings (GN-5)
24. Quantitative measures for liquidity risk management (GN-6)
25. Development of Islamic money markets (TN-1)
26. Stress testing (TN-2)
27. Guiding principles on disclosure requirements for Islamic capital market products (IFSB 19).

18.4 Conclusion

All in all, Islamic Financial Service Board (IFSB) can be defined as an international body which includes regulatory and supervisory agencies involved in developing standards across various verticals for the Islamic financial industry with the aim of keeping it sound and stable. The verticals include the following segments: banking, capital market, and *Takāful*. Standards developed by IFSB serve as a benchmark for the promotion of consistent practices that are regulatory as well as supervisory. At the same time, the standards help in the identification of hindrances and challenges through numerous means such as surveys, quantitative impact studies, and so on.

The functional framework developed by IFSB is designed to support the sustainable growth of IFIs worldwide. A range of cross sectoral standards has been brought into effect by IFSB with the intent of being able to offer a prudential framework, both consistent and robust so that it can withstand comparison with international standards, the issuance of which is being done by global comparators. Most of the programmes of IFSB have been developed to bring Islamic finance in alignment with the latest global regulatory architecture.

Review Questions

1. What is IFSB?
2. What roles have been played by IFSB so far?
3. Discuss in brief the important standards developed by IFSB?
4. Examine the liquidity and capital adequacy standards to Islamic banks.
5. Briefly describe *Shari'ah* governance standard developed by IFSB.

References

IFSB (2018), *IFSB's Background, Mission, Core Values, Objectives and Governing Documents*, retrieved from www.ifsb.org/maindoc.php (Access date January 3, 2018)

IFSB (2021), *Islamic Financial Service Stability Report*, retrieved from file:///C:/Users/abulh/Downloads/Islamic%20Financial%20Services%20Industry%20Stability%20Report%202021_En%20(1).pdf (Access date September 3, 2021)

19

ISLAMIC INTERNATIONAL RATING AGENCY (IIRA)

Learning Objectives

On completing this chapter, learners will be able to:

- Know that the ratings given by IIRA will act as a standard reference for financial market regulations
- Understand the types of ratings offered by IIRA
- Realise why IIRA is required for Islamic financial institutions (IFIs).

19.1 Introduction

The Islamic International Rating Agency (IIRA) was founded in Bahrain and became operational in July 2005. In the beginning, IIRA was designated to act as an infrastructure institution for supporting Islamic finance as devised by the Islamic Development Bank (IDB), which places it on the same platform as that of other system supporting entities like the Accounting and Auditing Organization for Islamic Financial Institutions (AAOIFI) and Islamic Financial Services Board (IFSB). The IDB continues to remain a prominent shareholder. It supervises through its nominee, as chairman of the board of directors. The structural design of IIRA is purposely aimed to not take away from its independence. The IDB consists of a board of directors and a rating committee which is entirely independent in its decisions. It also includes a *Shari'ah* supervisory board (SSB), where multiple field experts have been taken on board.

In 2000, the establishment of IIRA took place in Manama in terms of a shareholding company subjecting to authorised capital of US$10 million at the invitation of the IDB. The bank owns 42% of the total capital of the agency. The remaining capital belongs to institutions in varying portions as detailed below:

DOI: 10.4324/9780429321207-19

- 11% of the capital is owned collectively by Bahrain Islamic, Kuwait Finance House, Abu Dhabi Islamic Bank, and Takaful Malaysia
- 5% of the capital is owned by Al Baraka Islamic Group
- 5.3% of the total capital belongs to GCI, a company owned by a Pakistani business group
- 2% of the total capital is owned by the Cyrus Capital of Antwerp
- The remaining capital is distributed among several companies, financial institutions, and rating agencies.

The establishment of IIRA has been aimed at the following:

- Classify between public and private entities
- Conduct evaluations that are independent to be able to put forth opinions on probable losses of the categorised entity to be faced in future
- Make independent evaluations without compromising on the entity's or financial instrument's conformity with *Shari'ah* principles
- Transmit data and information so that the Islamic capital market can be boosted and developed
- Effectively work as a tool for developing standards that can attain a higher degree of disclosure and transparency
- Make a contribution to promoting the international Islamic capital market and Islamic financial instruments
- Strengthen the infrastructural capabilities of the Islamic financial market so that the work of IFIs can be conducted in a transparent way which will eventually help them in assessing the extent of the risks they might face
- Develop Islamic banking in a way that its products and services gain a wider acceptance across the world.

19.2 Type of Ratings Offered by IIRA

Broadly, two different types of ratings are offered by the International Islamic Rating Agency (IIRA):

1. Credit technical rating: This rating type intends to provide demonstrations on the financial strength and solvency of the Islamic bank and the products, it offers.
2. *Shari'ah* rating: The rating intends to be able to gauge the extent of compliance that Islamic banks or their products have put into effect in conformity with the norms of *Shari'ah* or the directive principles as prescribed by the *Shari'ah* Supervisory Board (SSB).

Apart from the major two types of ratings discussed above, the IIRA simultaneously offers sovereign ratings and corporate governance ratings. Sovereign and credit ratings are designed for assessing the probability of an entity in repaying its debt obligations within the prescribed time frame. *Shari'ah* quality ratings have been developed in evaluating the Islamic bank's degree of compliance with the regulations of *Shari'ah*. The corporate governance ratings are designed for assessing the demarcation of the rights and responsibilities of the stakeholders by analysing the practices of an entity. The compliance with the existing decision that framed the rules and procedures is also assessed.

To understand things in a better way, the next section discusses the possible categories of IIRA sovereign *Sukuk* (Islamic bonds) ratings. There are six categories that the IIRA primarily uses for the analysis of sovereign *Sukuk* and the possibility of any default on debt obligations at maturity:

- Politics and policy continuity
- The economy – structure and growth prospects
- Budgetary and fiscal policy
- Monetary policy and flexibility
- External accounts
- Internal and external debt.

19.2-1 Sovereign Ratings

- Here, an opinion is given by a reliable third party. The opinion seeks to address the viewpoint on whether the repayment of the issuer or an issue of its financial obligations is feasible within the time frame in record.
- Initially, the general rating of countries in the form of sovereign entities is conducted before rating a particular issue or institution.

Methodology

- A combination of qualitative and quantitative factors is used.
- Assessment regarding the probability of default on debt obligations for sovereign *Sukuk* is conducted.

19.2-2 Issuer Ratings

- The *Sukuk* issuers are being rated, the focus being on their ability to meet the financial obligations.
- Non-financial organs such as the corporate and *Shari'ah* governance of the entity from the *Sukuk* ratings.

Methodology (in rating the Issuer):

- Non-financial organs being prescribed with particular ratings on the basis of their credit value and continued ability to meet stakeholders' debt obligations.
- The issuer's entire financial and institution credit value acts as a determinant.

19.2-3 **Sukuk** *Ratings*

- *Sukuk* ratings in financial markets are crucial for investors and issuers alike.
- Investors look to get dividends on time after their *Sukuk* subscriptions.

Methodology

- The documented agreements based on the issuance of *Sukuk* are evaluated to be able to measure the associated risk and probable returns.
- Subscriptions are likely to soar higher if *Sukuk* in the secondary market goes on to become more viable.

19.2-3-2 Insurer Financial Strength Ratings

- The *Sukuk* insurer's financial strength is most likely to help in risk mitigation.
- The *Sukuk* insurer must possess the corporate ability and considerable financial capability to fulfil the contractual obligations.
- One can rely on IIRA in terms of information and ratings, thereby making it a strong factor in the amplification of the insurance industry that is also financially strong.
- Prudent management of insurance companies is a specific area that IIRA focuses on. It works in encouraging and caters to the improvement of the industry's strengths to benefit the stakeholders.

19.2-4 **Shari'ah** *Quality Ratings*

This category of ratings is an attempt to analyse the degree of *Shari'ah* compliance of Islamic financial institutions, corporate entities or conventional financial institutions that offer Islamic financial services or products. One such instance is *Sukuk*. The purpose of the *Shari'ah* quality rating is to offer the investing public, information, and knowledge subjected to how compliant the corporate entities are in adherence to *Shari'ah* norms.

19.2-4-1 Methodology

Assessment is done on the compliance levels of financial institutions and corporate entities with the principles and regulations of *Shari'ah* (IIRA, 2018):

- An analysis of whether products and services are authentic
- Prevents the funds from getting commingled, especially in the case of an Islamic window or branch of a conventional financial institution
- Ethical code of conduct is being adopted by the institution
- Sharing of profit or loss is based on the calculations as devised by respective policies.

19.2-5 Corporate Governance Ratings

Prior to making investments, the ratings of corporate governance/corporate entities are being thoroughly considered by prospective investors. The methodology of corporate governance ratings are as follows.

19.2-5-1 Methodology

The best practices adopted from the findings of corporate governance rating of corporate entities are used as references and parameters for assessing instead of using standards developed in a specific country/jurisdiction. The evaluation process of these ratings are fair and transparent. The process of evaluation is responsibly done and ensures full accountability.

19.3 Conclusion

The IIRA is aimed at assisting Islamic banks in developing their business. When IIRA gives the Islamic bank a rating, particularly an international one corresponding to that of foreign banks, it is able to put up its bonds on the international market. At the same time, IIR makes sure to provide transparency to the work of IFIs and helps enable them to analyse the level of risks they are likely to encounter.

To give international accreditation to the agency's rating, the International Islamic Rating Agency looks forward to recruiting global rating agencies such as Standard & Poor's or Moody's and imparts a crucial role to them in the agency, either in the form of shareholders or as advisors. In this way, their support is acquired on one hand as well as benefits are obtained from their familiarity with international rating agencies.

The IIRA's recognition as a rating agency comes from the fact that it had been officially recognised by Bahrain's Central Bank as the External Credit Assessment Institution. This agency also happens to be listed with other rating agencies approved by the Islamic Development Bank.

The foundation of the International Islamic Rating Agency has stemmed from the aim of establishing rating agencies such as Moody's and Standard & Poor's, both of which have specialisations in providing consultancy and services to Islamic financial institutions and products. The IIRA is anticipated to be the final benchmark for the credit rating in conformity to *Shari'ah* principles.

Review Questions

1. Why is a separate rating agency like IIRA required for IFIs?
2. Describe *Shari'ah* quality rating and its methodology.
3. Briefly discuss corporate governance rating and its methodology.
4. Define sovereign rating and state its methodology.

5. Why does a low credit rating or relegation of a country from a high rating to a low rating discourage investors from purchasing the country's Islamic bonds or *Sukuk*?

Reference

IIRA (2018), *Corporate Profile of Islamic International Rating Agency*, retrieved from http://iirating.com/corprofile.aspx (Access date February 7, 2018)

20

INTERNATIONAL ISLAMIC LIQUIDITY MANAGEMENT CORPORATION (IILM)

Learning Objectives

On completing this chapter, learners will be able to:

- Know the importance and purpose associated with establishing IILM
- Discuss liquidity management tools
- Realise the features of the IILM *Sukuk*.

20.1 Introduction

The establishment of the International Islamic Liquidity Management Corporation (IILM) has been done on 25 October 2010 for strengthening the capacity of the Islamic Financial Institutions (IFIs) in liquidity management. The foundation of the IILM includes 14 major stakeholders, out of which 12 are central banks from the following countries: Indonesia, Iran, Kuwait, Luxembourg, Malaysia, Mauritius, Nigeria, Qatar, Saudi Arabia, Sudan, Turkey, and UAE. The remaining two stakeholders are the Islamic Development Bank and the Islamic Corporation for the Development of the Private Sector, both of which are multinational institutions. The headquarters of IILM is in Kuala Lumpur. Following are some of the key objectives that IILM is designed to cater to IILM (2018, 2020):

- The facilitation of cross-border liquidity management for and among the IFIS. The IILM is supposed to ensure the availability of different *Shari'ah*-compliant instruments possible from a commercial perspective so that different liquidity requirements of the IFIS can be fulfilled.
- The cultivation and integration of regional and international co-operation to design the liquidity management infrastructure at national, regional, and international levels in a more robust way.

DOI: 10.4324/9780429321207-20

20.2 Diverse Membership and International Recognition

The IILM consists of stakeholders from multiple regions. The diversity in its founding members is not only limited to central banks of numerous countries but also multinational institutions. Individual and collective inputs through diversified membership helps the IILM in effectively designing collaborative, cross-border solutions to overcome familiar cross-border concerns. The role of IILM also revolves around giving strong accessibility options to IFIs so that they can get hold of highly rated liquidity instruments.

The beginning of issuing money market instruments was initiated with *Sukuk* issuance. High expectations have been put forth about IILM *Sukuk* to act as counterparts for the intermediate and long-term *Sukuk* available in the existing market. On 26 August 2013, the IILM was able to secure a breakthrough achievement with the issuance of the first US dollar–denominated, highly rated, short-term, tradable Sukuk (The Banker, 2013). The IILM inaugural *Sukuk* was worth US$490 million. The Standard & Poor's Rating Services has rated this *Sukuk* as A-1. The issuance was done within 3 months. Most interestingly, subscriptions were full.

On 20 October 2017, an auction has been conducted by the International Islamic Liquidity Management Corporation (IILM) subjecting to a 3-month *Sukuk*, the valuation of it being US$550 million. The issuance of the *Sukuk* was elevated from US$2.45 billion to US$3 billion so as to keep the pricing of the *Sukuk* at a profit rate of 1.67742%.

20.3 Islamic Liquidity Management Tool

Islamic liquidity management tools are characterised by the following:

- The programme being scalable because it is based on asset-backed commercial paper (ABCP)
- Denominations corresponding to US dollars
- Short-term *Sukuk* with regard to the term being lower than 12 months
- Lower risk, because:
  - S&P has rated this programme with an investment grade short term A-1
  - The underlying asset pool of sovereign, sovereign-linked, and supranational *Sukuk* is of superior quality
  - Jurisdictions are offered proper regulatory treatment.
- Conducive infrastructure for tradability, because:
  - The tradability of this *Shari'ah*-compliant liquidity instrument has been accepted by one and all
  - Multiple terms ranging 2-week to 7-month are being issued frequently
  - A large scale network of primary dealers helps in creating diversity that in turn supports primary market and eventually helps in the facilitation of the secondary market.

20.4 Conclusion

For the policy mandate of the IILM to be put into action, the establishment of a *Shari'ah*-compliant short-term certificate programme was done in 2013 for issuing *Shari'ah*-compliant instruments that could be used in trading and supporting the multi-dimensional requirements of institutions offering Islamic financial services (IIFS). Since the inception of issuing a 3-month *Sukuk* worth US$490 million in August 2013, there has been a consistent growth in the IILM program. At present, the IILM *Sukuk* outstanding is at US$3.51 billion. Issuance has been done by the IILM across a variety of terms to be able to provide IIFS with many varied options for their liquidity management needs to be met and solved in a better way.

Review Questions

1. What is ILLM? Why was it established?
2. What is an Islamic liquidity management tool?
3. Briefly talk about the characteristics and features of IILM *Sukuk*.

References

The Banker (2013), International Islamic Liquidity Management Centre, Islamic Financial Institutions Special Issue 2013, *The Banker Magazine*

IILM (2018), *International Islamic Liquidity Management Corporation*, retrieved from www.iilm.com/about-us/ (Access date January 11, 2018)

IILM (2020), *Home/About IILM*, retrieved from https://iilm.com/the-issuance-programme/ (Access date January 2, 2021)

21

CONCLUSION

Future of Islamic Financial Markets

Learning Objectives

On completing this chapter, learners will be able to:

- Understand the growth of the Islamic financial markets
- Know about the shares of the Islamic finance market, particularly in the GCC
- Realise that the COVID-19 provided an opportunity for the growth and transformation of the Islamic financial market by integrating a higher level of standardisation and a focused approach on the social role of Islamic finance
- Realise that COVID-19 also paved the way for large scale adoption of FinTech which led to the advancement of Islamic finance
- Understand how different stakeholders coordinate in the Islamic financial industry
- Comprehend how these multiple stakeholders leverage the opportunities available for sustainable growth of the Islamic financial industry
- Understand how sustainable green *Sukuk* is an area with a significant growth perspective.

21.1 Introduction

To be able to determine how well Islamic financial institutions and Islamic capital markets have been developing, one has to essentially observe and analyse all the possible sub-sectors of the industry and review their dimensions subjecting to size as well as performance. As a concluding chapter, the attempt made here is not only limited to discuss the financial growth, depth and performance of the entire Islamic financial industry but also to put forth a compact investigation with reference to its several sub-sectors that are actively operating across different regions. The chapter

DOI: 10.4324/9780429321207-21

is an analytic attempt at the major trends and opportunities occurring across its primary sectors: Islamic banking, other Islamic financial institutions, *Sukuk*, and Islamic funds.

Due to COVID-19, the governments faced unknown reasons that very quickly transitioned into managing risks that could potentially spiral to more substantially cripple physical operations and supply chains. As countries closed their borders and imposed physical lockdowns to try to limit the spread of the virus, it became familiar with the terms 'essential services' and 'frontline workers' that were critical for day-to-day living, and indeed for many people across countries, for survival. As many social and economic activities moved online, people encountered other risks, including technological and data disruptions that could equally be caused by nefarious agents as well as companies' own limited capabilities and capacities. These piled on the challenges that also included operational risks from remote working for a lot of employees and shifting customer behaviours that are still impacting financial institutions. The global crisis also fuelled oil price volatility and exerted pressures on the real estate sector in some Islamic financial markets. In response to these staggering situations, regulators designed and introduced support measures that have helped financial institutions mitigate the unprecedented challenges.

The concerns as stated above are only a trivial section of the uncountable number of debates happening subjected to Islamic finance. These debates are likely to put forth multiple opinions. However, these opinions cannot take away from the factual evidence of the statement that Islamic finance is the most prominent faith-based finance globally. A more apt description would be 'finance that is consistent with Islamic teachings'. Islamic finance should avoid 'sin'. This implies avoiding prohibited businesses. At the very same time, it must not cater to *riba* and excessive *gharar*, both of which are also forbidden. *Riba* corresponds to the practice of lending money at interest, while *gharar* involves uncertainty. Let us consider an example to understand the application of the prohibited segments of Islamic finance. Financing cannot be made for a brewery because the underlying activity (i.e. consumption of alcohol) is forbidden by Islam. In similar contexts, the money cannot be used for lending money at interest (as is the case in a conventional bond) or sale of risk (as in conventional derivatives and proprietary insurance) owing to the prohibitions of *riba* (interest) and excessive *gharar* (uncertainty). Islamic finance believes in the idea that the financiers and those being financed need to make an assumption of the risk associated with business outcomes or ownership of an asset so that the corresponding risk can be well managed through insurance or through agreements which involve sharing of risks mutually.

21.2 Growth Outlook

As per the Islamic finance development report of 2021, on one hand, irrespective of the scale of the challenges, the Islamic finance industry posted double-digit growth for the second year in a row, albeit by a slower 14% compared to 15% in 2019, to reach US$3.4 trillion by the end of 2020 (IFDI, 2021). On the other hand, according to the statistics provided by Standard & Poor's Global Ratings (2020), despite the COVID-19 pandemic, the Islamic financial market sectors are performing well with more than 14% growth during 2019–2020 as an improved economic environment, a rise in the number of large projects and an increased focus on environmental, social and governance (ESG) factors combine to drive demand. According to global rating agency Standard & Poor's (S&P), notwithstanding the twin challenges of COVID-19 and the rise and fall in global oil prices, the segment's assets grew by 10.6% in the year 2020. Although this was down on the 17.3% growth rate recorded in 2019. It was nevertheless a strong performance in light of the global recession, with many suggesting that the Islamic market segment's positive growth was a sign of its strong future potential.

S&P Global Ratings (2020) forecasted that the global Islamic finance industry will grow by 10%–12% annually in the coming years, and they expect that the industry will reach US$140–155 billion in the year 2021, up from US$139.8 billion in 2020.

21.3 Islamic Finance Increases Market Share

21.3-1 Growth of Mergers and Acquisitions

Expansion in Islamic finance asset value and market share has naturally led many conventional financial institutions to turn their attention to Islamic finance. Corresponding with a broader trend of mergers and acquisitions (M&A) in the GCC several conventional institutions have sought to buy out or merge with Islamic banks in recent years. For example, in 2019 the Abu Dhabi–headquartered Islamic finance institution Al Hilal Bank joined forces with the Abu Dhabi Commercial Bank and the Union National Bank in what is the region's largest tie-up to date. The merged body became the UAE's third-largest bank, with an estimated US$114.4 billion in assets.

In the year 2019–2020, M&A sustained with the National Bank of Bahrain (NBB) acquiring an 78.8% stake in the Manama-based commercial lender Bahrain Islamic Bank (BIB) in January 2020, while at the same time Qatar's Masraf Al Rayan finalised a merger with Al Khaliji Commercial Bank, creating Qatar's second-largest lender and one of the region's largest *Shari'ah*-compliant groups. Meanwhile, in July 2020, Oman Arab Bank completed the takeover of fellow Omani institution Alizz Islamic Bank.

While moving into lucrative Islamic financial markets is often a motivation for conventional banks, there is also a series of benefits that M&A can bring to Islamic lenders, which tend to be smaller than their conventional counterparts.

21.3-2 Islamic Funds

The global Islamic funds market grew by 22% to US$178 billion in assets under management in 2020. Islamic funds based in India, the United States, and the United Kingdom collectively accounted for 15% of global Islamic funds rose by double digits. In larger markets, Malaysia had a growth of 8.9% while the sector in Saudi Arabia grew by 33.2%. These markets account for 48% of global Islamic funds in 2020. The growth of the sector was also supported by the launch of 95 Islamic funds in 2020 that added US$1.5 billion in assets under management. Most of these are based in Malaysia, Indonesia, Pakistan, and Saudi Arabia. By asset type, equity Islamic funds performed relatively well, with an average cumulative performance of 6.8%. Around half of the Islamic equity funds enjoyed double-digit growth while 19% posted negative growth. Commodity and *Sukuk* funds both performed positively, registering average cumulative performance of 5.7% and 3.5%, respectively with many countries gradually re-opening.

21.3–3 Islamic Real Estate

Real estate Islamic funds suffered a setback because of the economic slowdown caused by the pandemic. The sector dropped by 3.2% during 2020 as 85% of funds – whether they were managed by real estate investment trusts or were mutual funds by asset managers – plunged into negative growth. These funds are mainly found in Malaysia and Saudi Arabia. In the UAE, Emirates REIT was negatively impacted by the pandemic that led to an oversupply of office spaces, business closures, and departure of workers. The company attempted to restructure its debt in mid-2021 but failed to win investor support. Sabana, Singapore's Islamic REIT and one of the largest in the world, also performed negatively in 2020 (Oxford Business Group, 2021). *Shari'ah*-compliant REITs avoid earning rental income from tenants or subtenants engaging in non-Islamic business activities. During 2020, the gradual full reopening of some key Islamic finance jurisdictions in 2021, such as Saudi Arabia and the UAE, is expected to clear the way for rental income for these funds. In July 2021, the country's first Islamic REIT in Pakistan was launched by Arif Habib Dolmen REIT Management, under its revamped regulatory framework that was previously dormant. This followed initiatives and incentives put in place by the Pakistan government to make REITs more attractive. The company will launch the first developmental REIT in Pakistan that will acquire land to develop commercial and other types of real estate. Arif Habib Dolmen expects to launch four more REITs in the near future (Arif Habib Dolmen, 2021).

21.3–4 Sukuk

The volume of outstanding *Sukuk* grew by 16% in 2020. There was a record level of demand in the first half of 2021 when *Sukuk* issuances crossed the US$100 billion thresholds, compared to US$88.7 billion for the same period in 2020. Forecasts point to US$180 billion by the end of 2021 (S&P Global Ratings, 2020). Higher issuances from the GCC and Turkey drove this strong start, as well as continued sizeable issuances from Southeast Asia (Malaysia, Indonesia, and Brunei). Saudi Arabia nearly doubled its domestic issuances during the second quarter of 2021. In 2020, governments in the GCC and Southeast Asia collectively accounted for US$588 billion in *Sukuk* outstanding, making up 93% of the supply of sovereign *Sukuk*. However, while governments in Southeast Asia continued to tap the *Sukuk* markets in the fourth quarter of 2020 to fund their economic recoveries due to continuing internal movement and travel restrictions, the GCC region tapered off significantly over the same period. In the fourth quarter of 2020, Southeast Asia issued US$23.2 billion in *Sukuk*, an increase of 44% over the same period in 2019 (US$16.1 billion), while the GCC issued US$10.5 billion, a decrease of 42% from the same three months in the previous year (US$18.1 billion). This GCC drop was due to previous high borrowing and fiscal measures undertaken by the region's governments (Oxford Business Group, 2021).

Oversubscription rates for sovereign *Sukuk* indicate constant strong demand, which sovereigns are meeting with several jumbo issuances in 2020 and more recently in the year 2021. In 2020, 15 countries issued *Sukuk*, with Nigeria and Egypt being notable returnees to the market after their absence in 2019. The top five sovereigns – Malaysia, Saudi Arabia, Indonesia, Turkey, and Kuwait – collectively made up 86% of total *Sukuk* issuances in 2020. In the first half of 2021, 12 countries issued *Sukuk*, with notable returning issuer the United Kingdom and new sovereign the Maldives.

The United Kingdom issued a US$686.9 million *Sukuk*, its second ever after its debut issuance in 2014, to help bolster its domestic Islamic finance industry and its credentials as a choice conduit for Islamic finance in the West. The Maldives' US$200 million issuance in April 2021 was its debut sovereign issuance and raised an additional US$100 million after being reopened. Key drivers for this issuance included economic diversification away from China and channelling funds to address the challenges caused by the COVID-19 pandemic in the tourism-driven economy.

Although the 57 Muslim-majority countries in the Organisation of Islamic Cooperation (OIC) are at various stages of economic and social recovery from the COVID-19 pandemic, one thing is clear: *Sukuk* will be an integral part of different countries governments' fiscal plans and help drive high demand over the foreseeable future. Because of the confluence of several key drivers that support upward pressure on demand for *Sukuk*, including continued economic recoveries, and vaccination efforts that are picking up across the OIC countries, especially in the key regions of the GCC and Southeast Asia. Policy easing in both monetary and fiscal terms in key Islamic finance jurisdictions such as Saudi Arabia, Malaysia, and Indonesia, as seen by sustained low interest rates, increased liquidity supply, and sizeable stimulus packages, are also driving demand from investors seeking less volatile securities, as well as Islamic banks and *Takaful* (Islamic insurance) providers. Other factors are driving strong investor demand for *Sukuk* are the recovery in oil prices to US$72 a barrel at mid-year (the first time since 2019), and the global bond market sell-off in the first-quarter of 2021, as well as the strong demand for recent Islamic issuances in the first-half of the year 2021, such as the Malaysian and Oman sovereign *Sukuk* (both oversubscribed more than six times), and the Saudi Arabia's Aramco *Sukuk* which oversubscribed 10 times.

21.3-5 ESG in Islamic Finance

Looking forward, the turn towards environmental, social and corporate governance (ESG) in global finance is also expected to provide Islamic banking with substantial growth opportunities. In effect, there are many key parallels between ESG values and those of Islamic finance, which similarly address social, environmental and governance factors. For example, in its discouragement of interest, strong focuses on profit and loss sharing and trust that Islamic finance not to be financing activities that cause societal harm. Islamic finance has social factors deeply entrenched in its core principles. Some socially minded products include *Qard Hassan*, which refers to a loan primarily granted for welfare purposes. Furthermore, annual alms (*Zakah)* giving in order to distribution to the poor is somewhat similar to a tax levied on people who earn above a certain threshold, which is used for social welfare purposes and *Waqf* is a philanthropic deed or donation. Moreover, with the 'protection of life' principle, *Shari'ah*-compliant finance also aligns with the environmental aspect of ESG, as both look to avoid financing projects or developments that could be harmful to the environment or the well-being of people in general.

In fact, the growing awareness of ESG in global finance has also coincided with an increase in demand for green or socially responsible *Sukuk*. Following the first issuance of a green *Sukuk* by Malaysian company Tadau Energy to fund a 50-MW solar project in 2017, interest in the product has grown steadily. Although it still makes up a small part of the overall Islamic finance market, green and socially responsible *Sukuk* is expected to have significant growth potential, particularly in the Gulf.

21.3-6 Islamic FinTech

There is a high degree of geographical concentration in the Islamic FinTech sector. According to data from the Global Islamic FinTech Report 2021, the top markets for Islamic FinTech (by transaction volumes) in 2020 were Saudi Arabia, Iran, the UAE, Malaysia, and Indonesia, which collectively made up 75% of the market by transaction volume. The fastest growing markets by 2025 are projected to be Egypt, Tunisia, Oman, Senegal, and Kuwait, all with compound annual growth rates (CAGRs) of over 25% during the period 2020–2025, pointing to strong growth ahead for Islamic FinTechs, especially in the MENA region (DinarStandard, 2021). There were 257 Islamic FinTechs as of August 2021, an 80% increase from the previous year's total of 142 in July 2020. The sector is poised for rapid growth. The Islamic FinTech landscape is no longer an emerging market space, and it is on most major Islamic finance regulators' agendas.

As countries cautiously navigate their post-pandemic recoveries, Islamic FinTech are increasingly at the forefront of innovation in the Opalesque Islamic finance intelligence (OIFI) sector, providing tangible use cases of *Shari'ah*-compliant financing in traditionally underserved segments. These innovative use cases include *Shari'ah*-compliant SME financing via purchase order financing, such as Saudi-based Ta3meed (the first purchase order financial platform), which entered into a partnership with the well-known German cloud banking platform Mambu in January 2021, and inventory monetisation solutions, such as UK-based SYME (Supply@me Capital Plc Ord 0.002P is listed on the London Stock Exchange, trading with ticker code SYME). Other powerful use cases that are gaining traction include wealth managers such as Sarwa (Middle East–based online investment platform), and Bahrain-based Cocoa raised US$15 million in a Series B funding round in August 2021. It is also used to develop its *Shari'ah*-compliant lending services to SMEs in Saudi Arabia (DinarStandard, 2021).

21.3-7 Shari'ah *Governance*

More governments are paying attention to the different aspects of *Shari'ah* compliance when it comes to regulating their local Islamic financial systems. In 2020, 19 Muslim countries had centralised *Shari'ah* boards to oversee their local Islamic banks, and 35 countries had any kind of *Shari'ah* governance framework. Among the latest countries to introduce a centralised *Shari'ah* board is Kuwait, which formed its Higher Committee of *Shari'ah* Supervision in October 2020. Among its tasks is the approval of *Shari'ah* board candidates for local banks. The Committee also provides guidelines for products and services offered. With Kuwait's move, the only GCC nations without centralised *Shari'ah* boards are Qatar and Saudi Arabia. Qatar previously announced its intention to set one up (Oxford Business Group, 2021). Other authorities that plan to establish a centralised *Shari'ah* committee is Bangladesh's Securities Exchange and Commission. Saudi Arabia strengthened *Shari'ah* governance in February 2020 with its *Shari'ah* Governance Framework for Local Banks Operating in Saudi Arabia. The framework defines the tasks of different stakeholders, such as the *Shari'ah* committee, in relation to this framework. In Turkey, the Banking Regulation and Supervision Agency created a legal infrastructure in October 2020 requiring participation banks to set up their own *Shari'ah* board to ensure alignment with *Shari'ah* standards. Members of the board must either have a postgraduate degree in Islamic finance or receive certified training in Islamic finance. Similarly, Pakistan amended its *Shari'ah* governance framework in February 2021, stressing the avoidance of conflicts of interest by limiting the number of *Shari'ah* boards of Islamic banks one scholar can sit on up to three IFIs.

According to S&P Global Ratings (2020), as of December 2020, there were 1,235 *Shari'ah* scholars representing IFIs. The number continues to increase with the addition of new scholars, especially those that represent single institutions. *Shari'ah* scholars and boards were called upon in 2020 as part of COVID-19 mitigation efforts. For instance, the Higher Shari'ah Authority of the UAE had to approve a set of *Shari'ah* parameters to mitigate the fallouts from the pandemic, which included a payment moratorium and how to deal with it based on the type of transactions and *Shari'ah* contracts. This was also addressed by the industry's standards-setting organisations such as the Islamic Financial Services Board (IFSB) which also looked at *Shari'ah*-compliant government guarantees, profit-sharing investment accounts, and expected credit loss accounting to ensure that they do not conflict with *Shari'ah* principles.

21.4 Challenges Faced by Islamic Finance

In the process of growing and expanding, the Islamic finance sector has to face certain challenges. The first challenge Islamic finance faces in respect of tax neutrality in the context of tax regulations on financial products relates to providing the same treatment to products where the economic substance, effects and implications are the same. The horizontal equity principle demands that businesses with similar revenue and cost structures (from a finance view) must be treated similarly. Islamic banks are not granted an approval for lending money for the sake of earning compound interest. They offer asset-backed financing, which is why they have to responsibly take ownership of real assets. After they are able to attain ownership and possession of assets, they can sell these assets at a profit or offer them on lease to earn rent. Thus, this unique form of participatory intermediation involves asset ownership and multiple asset transfers. However, Islamic finance transactions eventually result in the same outcome as compared to conventional finance transactions from the point of view of finance, cash flows and legal perspective. Therefore, Islamic banks shall not be treated in a way which makes them uncompetitive due to additional taxes that are levied on Islamic finance transactions.

No tax neutrality creates several tax issues, such as duplication of duties in assets transfer, registration and multiple sales for indirect taxes and in the tax treatment of income for direct tax purposes. Islamic banks or their customers have to pay double duties, since at least two sale contracts are usually involved in Islamic banking products (i.e. one between the bank and the vendor and subsequently, a sale transaction between the bank and the client). Double taxation in the form of GST, VAT, registration duties or stamp duties could create extra costs in the Islamic banking products. So, these products may become unattractive and uncompetitive for other customers and Islamic banks. In Europe, some legislation and accommodation has been made in legal rules to provide tax neutrality to Islamic banking, such as in the United Kingdom, Luxembourg, France and Ireland. In Southeast Asia as well, Malaysia and Singapore in particular have introduced legislation to provide tax neutrality to Islamic banking. But, in many other countries jurisdictions, Islamic banks do not have tax neutrality.

The second challenge encountered by Islamic finance is the absence of an Islamic interbank market and sometimes liquidity problems facing *Sukuk* in both short- and long-term maturities. Also there is a lack of a Islamic discount window at the central bank level for Islamic financial institutions. In liquidity management, banks often have surplus liquidity as well as a shortage of liquidity. The problem becomes more pressing as there are lesser alternatives for managing liquidity shortage for Islamic banks. An Islamic bank can take investments from any financial institution and invest them in *Shari'ah*-compliant financing assets. However, it cannot invest its surplus liquidity on an equity financing basis with conventional banks, since they are operating on the basis of interest-based loans.

The third challenge is the constraints in product design, pricing and efficiency. In Islamic finance, provision of making investments is made for buying an asset. This asset has to be initially owned by the bank prior to the execution of the second-leg sale. Upon the agreement made between the client and the bank subjected to the contract's financials (i.e. sale price), no further change can be done. In this context, issues relating to moral hazard and adverse selection turn out to be very significant. If a firm is looking for distress financing or working capital financing, Islamic finance has limited products. *Salam* and *Istisna* can be used in providing financing for non-asset based needs. However, *Salam* and *Istisna* cannot be used in every situation.

21.5 Future Opportunities for Growth

Data shows that in 2011, less than 20% of adults held accounts in 25 out of 48 OIC countries. In 2014, 17 out of 45 countries had less than 20% adult population holding bank accounts. In 2017, only 3 out of 46 countries had less than 20% population holding bank accounts (World Bank, 2020). Still, 32 out of 46 countries have less than half of the population holding bank accounts in OIC member countries (World Bank, 2020). The averages for middle income and high income countries on this indicator are 65% and 94%, respectively (World Bank, 2020). It is quite evident that interest-free banking in these Muslim majority regions is the current need. Owing to the fact that interest is forbidden, Muslims, in particular, need alternative financial solutions which are in harmony with *Shari'ah*.

According to World Bank (2020), in only 17 out of 51 OIC countries is the savings-investment gap positive. Two-thirds of the countries have a negative savings-investment gap. In almost half of the countries, the gross savings to GDP ratio is lower than 20%; whereas the average gross savings to GDP ratio in middle income countries is 30.8%. Moreover, the gross domestic savings to GDP ratio is below 20% in 32 out of 56 OIC countries probably due to poverty, but also due to aversion from *Riba*-based banking. Therefore, there is a need for financial inclusion which in the Muslim majority regions pivots growth and penetration in Islamic banking.

As public infrastructure financing, *Sukuk*, as an alternative investment vehicle in Islamic finance, can be utilised to obtain finance from a wide array of investors. The scarcity in financial availability has become a big hindrance for minimal use of renewable energy in developing countries. In this regard, Islamic banks can finance the government for the purchasing infrastructure to be utilised in development projects. Further, sovereign *Sukuk* issuances can enable the governments to fund public projects and also ensure liquidity in the financial markets which can allow Islamic banks to manage liquidity risk and remain competitive.

In Islamic finance contracts, the integration of technology can assist in the completion of multiple steps involved in a typical Islamic finance transaction at a faster pace with improved efficiency. Simultaneously, efficient monitoring gets done and documentary requirements get fulfilled. For the capitalisation on the benefits that come with using FinTech, standardisation in *Shari'ah* rules seems to be of vital importance. Standardised basic operating procedures can help in enhancing the scope of automation for bringing in FinTech in the contract mechanics and execution.

> How can you buy or sell the sky, the warmth of the land? If we do not own the freshness of the air and the sparkle of the water, how can you buy them?
>
> – *Suquamish Chief*

Review Questions

1. Briefly discuss the growth of Islamic financial markets.
2. What shares of the Islamic finance market are particularly in the GCC?
3. Do you think that COVID-19 offered an opportunity for a more integrated approach and helped in transforming growth with a stronger focus on the social role of Islamic finance and meaningful adoption of FinTech?
4. What is green *Sukuk*, and how is it significant?
5. What role can Islamic FinTech play in the further rapid development of Islamic financial markets?

References

Arif Habib Dolmen (2021), *Dolmen City REIT*, retrieved from www.arifhabibdolmenreit.com/ (Access date August 5, 2021)

DinarStandard (2021), *Global Islamic FinTech Report 2021*, retrieved from https://cdn.salaamgateway.com/reports/pdf/6127a0965afd7898a34f69dadc24b8d17ada0b1b.pdf (Access date August 21, 2021)

IFDI (2021), *ICD-Refinitive Islamic Finance Development Report 2021*, Refinitiv Eikon, retrieved from https://www.refinitiv.com/en

Oxford Business Group (2021), *What Does the Future Hold for Islamic Finance*, retrieved from www.arifhabibdolmenreit.com/ (Access date November 20, 2021)

S&P Global Ratings (2020), *Islamic Finance Outlook 2020*, retrieved from www.spglobal.com/_assets/documents/ratings/research/islamic_finance_2020_screen.pdf (Access date March 23, 2021)

World Bank (2020), *Leveraging Islamic FinTech to Improve Financial Inclusion*, Washington, DC: World Bank Group, retrieved from www.worldbank.org/en/country/malaysia/publication/leveraging-islamic-fintech-to-improve-financial-inclusion (Access date May 3, 2021)

INDEX

Printed in the United States
by Baker & Taylor Publisher Services